On and By Frank Lloyd Wright
A Primer of Architectural Principles

ROBERT MCCARTER, EDITOR

On and By Frank Lloyd Wright
A Primer of Architectural Principles

ROBERT MCCARTER, EDITOR

Phaidon Press Limited
Regent's Wharf
All Saints Street
London N1 9PA

Phaidon Press Inc.
180 Varick Street
New York, NY 10014

www.phaidon.com

First published 2005
© 2005 Phaidon Press Limited

ISBN 0 7148 4470 5

A CIP catalogue record of this book is
available from the British Library.

Designed by Kobi Benezri
Printed in China

To the memory of Bernhard Hoesli,
Werner Seligmann, and Colin Rowe.

On and By Frank Lloyd Wright
A Primer of Architectural Principles

Abstract Essence
Drawing Wright from the Obvious

BY ROBERT MCCARTER

"This is what it means to be an artist—to seize this essence brooding every-where in everything, just behind aspect."[1]—*Frank Lloyd Wright*

It is the shared premise of the following studies that the work of Frank Lloyd Wright is well known but rarely thought about. Being familiar, even being famous, has led not to a deeper understanding of his architecture but, rather, to its being obscured by the now-standard interpretations it has been given. The studies in this volume attempt to rediscover Wright's work, to give insight into what inspired it, and to reveal its underlying ideas and ordering principles.

Why reexamine the work of Frank Lloyd Wright today? When we review the seemingly innumerable publications that exist on Wright and his works, all the answers appear already to be known. But have all the fundamental questions been asked? How did Wright imagine, design, and construct the extraordinary buildings he left us? How can our studies of these buildings reveal and relate this complex process of conception and construction? What were the ordering principles that Wright utilized in designing these buildings? What meanings might these buildings contain, and how do we understand them through our experience? What is the significance of Wright's work for architecture today?

These questions are in fact rarely asked, much less answered, in most of the existing writings on Wright, which tend to fall into one of three cate-gories: biographical, devotional, or scholarly.

While many who study Wright believe that insights into his architecture may indeed be drawn from biographical studies of his life, the results to date in this line of inquiry have served only to distract us by focusing on events that, while certainly sensational, have proved irrelevant to any fundamental understanding of the mind and the process of creative thought. Even a cur-sory examination of the numerous buildings by Wright makes it clear he was obsessed as few have ever been with the construction of form and space—with the making of architecture—and that his daily life was determined almost exclusively by this creative activity. Yet the existing biographies con-tain only passing references to the endless hours Wright spent working on designs, and the authors of these studies approach any close examination of Wright's buildings only with evident trepidation. The result is that this essen-

tial part of Wright's life—his life as an architect—remains virtually unexplored. We await the biography that will give a more complete account of Wright's life: a life dedicated to working "in the cause of architecture."

Perhaps most disappointing to many of us who never knew Wright are the accounts given by his followers at the Taliesin Fellowship, which frequently read more like devotional tracts than like critical inquiries into the creative thinking that took place right in front of them as Wright sat at their drawing boards. While the apprentices' writings often relate intriguing anecdotes, the authors are in a strange way too close to Wright, whose personality seemed from their perspective overwhelming, his creative powers unfathomable. It has sometimes been maintained that Wright intentionally hid his design process from his associates and apprentices, yet statements made by many of them indicate that they were in fact fully versed in the design "system" and, indeed, were often expected to further develop and even finalize what Wright had started.

But while the early Oak Park studio was run almost as a cooperative, employing a shared "system" of design, with many of Wright's associates later going on to open their own individual practices, the later Fellowship at Taliesin was from the start set up as "the Master" and his much younger apprentices. Despite working with Wright every day, the Taliesin apprentices remained at a distance that could not be crossed, and their relationship to Wright inevitably became a kind of worship, which the ritualized lifestyle of the Taliesin compound did little to deter. The different distance—time— that now separates us from Wright may perhaps be something positive; we must seek him not "in person" but in his works.

And yet, according to one of his foremost scholarly interpreters, Wright has become a historical figure, separated from us by history itself.[2] What kind of "history" is it that separates us from the subject of our inquiry? Many scholarly studies, despite providing an overabundance of historical facts, do not bring us closer to understanding Wright. When we seek to comprehend the mind that could create and construct these astonishing buildings, architectural history too often offers us meticulously documented research oddly devoid of insight, rarely inquiring into how Wright was inspired, and inevitably concludes that Wright was "influenced" by a particular precedent or that he fits comfortably into a preconceived theory or stylistic category.

Yet the reliance on a one-to-one correspondence between the individual work and its historical "source" is based on a superficial visual "reading" of architecture—one conveniently accomplished within the confines of the university library. It is therefore not surprising that these studies seem strangely disengaged from the physical reality of the building and its experience. This is not to say that such interpretations are wrong but that they are largely incomplete and inadequate, oversimplifying the rich and complex process of design. The most telling characteristic of the majority of scholarly studies of Wright is their total lack of astonishment, of wonder: one is reminded of Martin Heidegger's comment "Few indeed understand the difference between an object of scholarship and a matter thought."[3]

Wright himself made great efforts to make known his own descriptions and explanations of his buildings, and, for designs ranging from the early

Ladies' Home Journal Prairie Houses to the late "Automatic" Usonian Houses, he tried to pass on to the public the discoveries he believed he had made. His articles on the Usonian Houses, appearing in national magazines at the time of their construction, presented clearly and concisely the fundamental ideas of functional definition, spatial articulation, and innovative construction in house design, distilled from his lifetime of work.

Wright's own writings, with their often aggressive, combative, and highly polemical manner, must be checked against the architecture itself, as they sometimes tell only part of the story; being a master at writing his own press, Wright always managed to portray himself in the most favorable light. Yet in the matter with which we are concerned—Wright's ordering principles, his process of design, and the buildings that resulted—his writings often provide illuminating glimpses of the mind at work. The generative potential of the writings themselves was consciously developed; Wright frequently stated that while the forms of his work were often imitated, the principles on which they were based were rarely understood.

One type of study consistently offers insight into the architecture of Wright and also hints at a more productive approach: the single building study.[4] While appearing to be of limited scope, as measured by the grand sweep of architectural history theories, these focused studies broaden our understanding of Wright as he engaged in the act of design and construction. Of course, the buildings are inevitably more complex, subtle, and deeply layered than any historical study or formal analysis can capture or convey.

Oak Park Studio
Oak Park, Illinois, 1895; view of drafting tables, with plaster model of Larkin Building at upper left

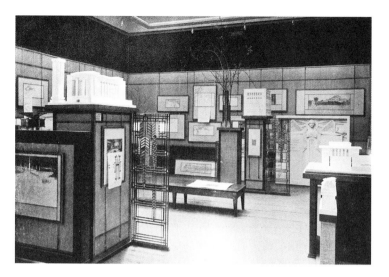

Bearing this fact in mind, the studies in this volume make no claim to "completeness," which would be seen as a closure. Rather, these studies may best be understood as attempts to open, to bring near, and to engage the works of Wright. As Ludwig Wittgenstein wrote, "Remember the impression one gets from good architecture, that it expresses a thought. It makes one want to respond with a gesture."[5] The essays that follow may be understood as such gestures, gestures of the hand and eye: multiple views, pointing to different approaches, sometimes overlapping and at other times contradicting one another, but collectively giving a glimpse of the incredibly complex and creative mind of Frank Lloyd Wright at work *in* his works.

Utilizing biographical facts and Wright's own writings as confirmation of insights first drawn directly from the buildings and projects themselves, these essays endeavor to invert the usual relationships wherein buildings are seen as the results of biographical events, historical "influences," and preconceived theories. Perhaps this could be characterized as the architect's approach as opposed to that of the historian, but this is also an attempt to find a method more appropriate to the matter being studied. Wright himself wrote, "Everyone engaged in creative work is subject to persecution by the odious comparison ... because the inferior mind learns only by comparisons ... But the superior mind learns by analysis."[6] While this is a typical example of Wright's pugnacious prose, it also points to *analysis* as a method, employing the work of architecture itself as the primary source.

Many scholarly studies of Wright "read into" or "read onto" his works, imposing preconceived theories or interpretations. Yet, in order to understand the architecture and the process by which it was created, it would seem more appropriate to "draw out of" or "draw from" his works themselves, searching for the ordering ideas and principles that generated them. To "abstract" means to "draw out"; the following essays attempt to abstract essence, to draw out what is essential in Wright's work. One of the primary motivations of most of these studies is the belief that for architects and students of architecture it is highly instructive simply to *draw* the plan of a building as a way of "knowing" it: this involves an experience of the hand that theoretical thought cannot replicate.[7] Analysis and composition are here understood to be reciprocal; subjecting Wright's designs to formal, spatial, constructional, and experiential analysis is in effect an attempt to find *the marks of their making.*

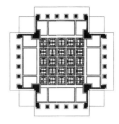

This approach finds support when one investigates the formative experiences of Wright's development as an architect. Of these, the earliest was the Froebel kindergarten training he undertook as a child under his mother's supervision and—far more significantly—that he later used in educating his own children during the late 1890s, just as his evolution of the Prairie House was reaching its critical stage. This kindergarten training consisted of philosophical and formal principles imparted to the child through rigorously organized play with a series of "gifts" or toys given in a predetermined sequence, increasing in complexity and subtlety as the child grew up.

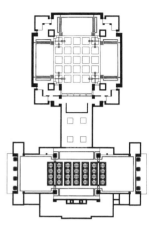

The parallels, both formal and philosophical, between Froebel training and Wright's designs and thought are too numerous to be coincidental, and the Froebel training must be given prominence of place in the development of Wright's mature system of design. Froebel emphasized learning from nature, which reinforced Wright's early experiences on his uncle's farm in Wisconsin, and it introduced Wright to the formative geometries that became the basis for his architecture. As Wright wrote, "I soon became susceptible to constructive pattern evolving in everything I saw. I learned to *see* this way and when I did, I did not care to draw casual incidentals of nature. I wanted to *design.*"[8]

The Froebel training was directed toward the development of analytical thinking. The child learned to see that geometric forms and patterns structured everything in nature and to see each thing as "a whole both in its organic unity and its component parts," as Froebel wrote. For the child who observed, took to pieces, and reassembled things the desire to create shape and form came naturally. Through the training, the child came to understand that there was an inner coherence in all things and that the material and spiritual worlds were one. Froebel declared of his training methods: "They begin by establishing spatial relationships" and operate through "inference from the general to the particular, from the whole to the part." This education was nonverbal and nonrepresentational and relied absolutely on the child's own analytically produced knowledge. As Froebel wrote, "It is not a question of communicating knowledge already acquired, but of calling forth new knowledge."[9]

When we examine the work of Wright, we repeatedly see evidence of his incisive analyses of natural form, historical form, and the forms of his own making. Yet the fundamental ordering geometries employed by Wright are in fact truly ancient in origin—indeed, the oldest things in human history—and thus we should be suspicious of claims to exclusivity of any single philosophical or formal influence on Wright's design abilities. But, at the very least, the case of Froebel training and Wright must be seen as the fortuitous meeting of an unusually comprehensive method and an astonishing natural talent. The result was a mind more interested in *designing* the world than in *representing* it: designing here understood as discerning the underlying structure of nature and building with it.

Unity Temple
reflected ceiling plans, showing leaded-glass patterns; redrawn under author's supervision

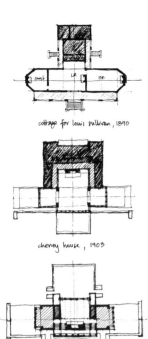

cottage for louis sullivan, 1890

cheney house, 1903

hardy house, 1905

Analytical Diagrams
Cottage for Louis Sullivan, 1890,
above, Edwin H. Cheney House,
1903, center, and Thomas Hardy
House, 1905, below; showing the
development of spatial types
through successive projects;
drawn by author

The philosophy underlying the Froebel kindergarten education found many parallels in the thinking of the American transcendentalists, and especially in the writings of Wright's lifelong inspiration, Ralph Waldo Emerson. This is indicated by Emerson's definition of analytical thinking: "The intellect pierces the form, overleaps the wall, detects intrinsic likeness between remote things, and reduces all things to a few principles."[10] Wright was an inheritor of and party to the vigorous transcendental culture of nineteenth-century America, exemplified by Emerson, Thoreau, Whitman, Melville, and Greenough.

In his mature architecture, Wright believed that he had given transcendental thought built form and, through his work, connected American transcendentalism to similar Oriental philosophies. In this regard, we should note the critical aspects of this transcendental culture and Wright's interpretation of it, opposed as it was to the attitude of dominating nature that characterized the emerging industrial age, seeking instead a harmony with nature. Wright displayed an enormous confidence, typical of the transcendental thinkers, that democracy in America could achieve a dynamic integration of individual man, collective culture, and the evolutionary forces of nature, to be played out across the enormous spaces of the continent.

Emerson believed that because mankind was a product of nature, we were eminently suited to intuit the principles of nature. Following from this, Wright believed that the true function of architecture was to tell mankind about our own nature, for, as Emerson wrote, "truth was in us before it was reflected to us from natural objects." Emerson perceived Nature to be characterized by the endless combination and repetition of a few fundamental laws and forms. Wright in turn analyzed nature and its underlying geometric structures, using their purity of form and clarity of purpose to critique historical and contemporary architecture. Emerson wrote, "we are always reasoning from the seen to the unseen," and this is a perfect summary of Froebel's intentions, all of which found expression in Wright's early habit of "seeing into" or "seeing from within," as he called it. Wright's design principles were always profoundly affected by materials and construction methods, reflecting his constant search for a comprehensive constructional and compositional order similar to that which he found in his analyses of natural forms.

The transcendentalists held that each physical thing was the consequence of, or had consequences for, spiritual thought. Therefore, all form had moral meaning. Emerson wrote, "Esteem nature a perpetual counselor, and her perfections the exact measure of our deviations." It is important to note that, for Wright, the philosophical ideas of integrity and natural order were not merely "means" of designing: they were visions of the world as it should be. Wright's principles are thus understood as having both formal and moral power. Emerson wrote, "All form is an effect of character," and Wright deeply believed this to be true, pointedly stating, "The sins of architects are permanent sins."[11] Wright also felt that character is an effect of form and that our character could be positively (or negatively) affected by form. In his works, Wright endeavored to make present in the contemporary world the ancient understanding of building as a sacred act, and buildings as sacred places.

Wright was profoundly affected by Emerson's belief that only the individual, through the discipline of principles learned from experience, could affect the integration of culture and nature. Emerson held that the individual's powers of perception and analysis were vastly superior to that of any larger society and that one should concentrate on one's own particular strengths and abilities: "Insist on yourself; never imitate. Your own gift you can present every moment with the cumulative force of a whole life's cultivation." The origins of Wright's combative stance in his dealings with the press and public can be found in Emerson, who wrote, "Whoever would be a man, must be a nonconformist. . . . Nothing is at last sacred but the integrity of your own mind. . . . To be great is to be misunderstood." Yet this emphasis on the validity of individual experience was essentially optimistic; it resulted in a mind that probed history for the fundamental principles of human existence, looking beyond the particular failings of contemporary society to find the essential and unchanging nature of mankind. As Thoreau wrote, "The improvements of the ages have but little influence on the essential laws of man's existence."[12]

Emerson himself was affected by the writings of Horatio Greenough, an American sculptor and writer who lived half his life in Rome, where he wrote extensively on modern mankind's relationship to historical form. Architecture was of particular interest to him, and his method for learning

Susan Lawrence Dana House
Springfield, Illinois, 1900; view
of dining room, with entry
hall beyond

from history was succinctly stated: "Let us learn principles, not copy shapes."[13] He first enunciated the principle "Form follows function," and held that "the edifices in whose construction the principles of architecture are developed may be classed as organic."[14] Paralleling Froebel, Greenough called for the close study of nature and the development of forms from an inner conception: "Instead of forcing the functions of every sort of building into one general form, adapting an outward shape for the sake of the eye or of association, without reference to the inner distribution, let us begin from the heart as the nucleus, and work outwards."[15]

Louis Sullivan, Wright's mentor, also inherited this transcendental philosophy, as his writings clearly indicate, and contributed to it by attempting to remedy Greenough's charge, "the mind of this country has never been seriously applied to the subject of building."[16] While Sullivan keenly felt the absence of a particularly American architecture, he warned against efforts to speed its arrival by "transplanting or grafting" historical styles onto the new continent.[17] He felt that any truly organic American architecture would develop on a regional basis, with variations dependent on climate, landscape, and local building methods rather than on arbitrary formal or theoretical preconceptions.[18] He was skeptical as to whether contemporary architectural education would encourage the development of forms that followed functions, observing that such schooling did not cultivate the "common sense" of analytical thinking but, rather, resulted in designs that were:

> dependent upon the verbal explanation and comment of its exponents. A knowledge of their vocabulary is often of assistance in disclosing softness and refinement in many primitive expedients, and revealing beauty in barren places. Familiarity with the current phraseology of the applied arts is also useful in assisting the student to a comprehension of many things apparently incomprehensible. Metaphor and simile are rampant in this connection, a well-chosen word often serving to justify an architectural absurdity.[19]

In his own work, Sullivan built from his belief that nature could give form to architecture through structure and ornament. Sullivan concentrated on clarifying the tectonic elements of the frame (expressive structure) rather than the plan (inhabited space), believing that the structural frame was fundamental to all architecture: "When a lintel is placed upon two piers, architecture springs into being."[20] In order to create a truly organic architecture, he believed, ornament must be *of* the surface and substance rather than *on* it. Sullivan's theory of ornament was in effect both a philosophy and method of formal evolution; it reintroduced Wright to a world of ancient forms and geometries that served as a beginning for all of Wright's subsequent designs. Wright's relationship to Sullivan was in many ways similar to a medieval guild apprenticeship, especially in its emphasis on how things are put together. Sullivan was the final, catalytic event in Wright's formation as an architect, bringing into focus the formal and philosophical principles learned in his youth and directing him toward the development of a new American architecture.

With Wright, architecture began again. Every element, every compositional and formal conception, every essence of reality "brooding just behind aspect" was questioned, rethought, and reinvented, not to deny inherited traditions, but, far more originally, to return to the fundamental beginnings of all architecture. As Emerson wrote, "I believe in eternity. I can find the genius and creative principle of each and all eras in my own mind."[21] Wright's formative experience emphasized analysis, and this opened the entire history of art, architecture, and natural form as the source of ordering principles.

Wright subjected his own works to similar analysis, always seeking to perfect them, to eliminate all but the essential. Wright's mature works were not derived directly from any particular historical or contemporary architecture: they were of unassignable origin. He handled forms in an analytical rather than imitative manner; "seeing into" them to discern their underlying spatial structure and ordering principles, understood as manifestations of mankind's spirit. Wright wrote, "We must believe architecture to be the living spirit that made buildings what they were. . . . It begins always at the beginning."[22] This return to beginnings would be one of numerous aspects of Wright's work that would be later taken up by Louis I. Kahn.

Wright's beginning holds particular fascination for architects. At this formative moment, before the system of design that produced the great Prairie-period buildings had been developed, Wright struggled to arrive at a

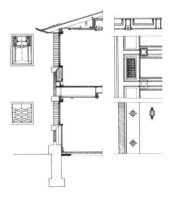

Frederick Robie House
section of living room, above, and playroom, below; leaded-glass windows to left, ceiling and carpet patterns to right; redrawn under author's supervision

fully integrated order in his designs. "I couldn't invent terms of my own overnight," Wright wrote in his autobiography,[23] and Wright studied contemporary and classical designs in an effort to give a different form to every project. Wright's "invention of terms" of his own came only with his realization that a few fundamental ordering ideas could be manipulated so as to produce a virtually infinite variety of forms and spaces. It was this principle that finally released Wright into the confident and profusely productive Prairie period.

Wright's early work was in every way exceptional. From the very start, in strong contrast to the work of his picturesque, shingle-style, neoclassically trained contemporaries, Wright utilized complete forms and ordered relationships composed with absolute rigor. It is interesting to contrast Wright's early work and that of contemporary architects trained in the Beaux-Arts system; whereas the other architects used an inherited system without much conviction, Wright was unquestionably more skillful and inventive, despite his lack of formal training in the traditional neoclassical methods. At age twenty-four, Wright had already reached an astonishing level of abstraction, as can be seen in the Charnley House, designed while he was still in Sullivan's employ.

Wright's mature Prairie period work, coming only ten years later, in 1901, achieved a level of formal and spatial resolution that is, even today, still difficult for many to fully appreciate and acknowledge. Equally remarkable is the fact that this unparalleled work was the result of a "design system," a method of design Wright endeavored to impart to his Oak Park associates. While in his work Wright abandoned the traditional forms of neoclassical architecture, he nevertheless understood from his Froebel training and his study of architectural history that the underlying order of symmetry and axial planning were fundamental to mankind and part of our very nature; as Wright wrote, "Principles are not invented, they are not evolved by one man or one age."[24]

In this way, Wright was closer to the Renaissance masters Leonardo and Michelangelo than to any of his contemporaries: not in style or form, but in the

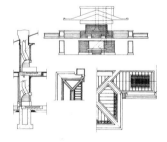

Avery Coonley House
Riverside, Illinois, 1907; view of living room

Avery Coonley House
detail of living-room fireplace and ceiling; redrawn under author's supervision

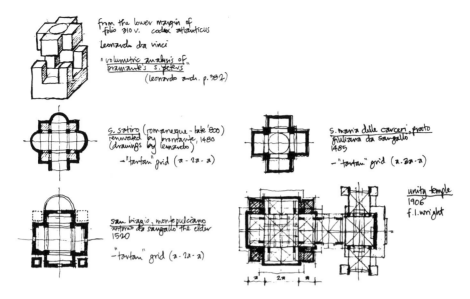

way he thought about architecture, in his analytical approach to space, and in his belief in the universal validity of ordering principles. In beginning the introduction to the first national publication of his work in 1908, Wright wrote:

> Radical though it may be, the work here illustrated is dedicated to a cause conservative in the best sense of the word. At no point does it involve denial of the elemental law and order inherent in great architecture. It is a declaration of love for the spirit of that law and order, a reverential recognition of the elements that made ancient letter of great architecture in its time vital and beautiful.[25]

Wright's understanding of the generative potential of ordering principles is clearly evident in his lifelong fascination with traditional Japanese art and architecture, which he analyzed extensively and to which he often referred as being influential on his work. Wright found in Japanese architecture the order and abstraction that he pursued in his own work; it seemed to him that many generations of Japanese culture had already achieved the "modern" forms and spaces that were just becoming clear in his own early work, shortly after the turn of the century. Japanese architecture's elemental approach to form and its ordering by a modular grid, its fundamental reliance on symmetry and axial planning in public buildings, its employment of asymmetry and diagonal planning in private buildings, its sensitivity to materials and efforts to harmonize with nature, taken together, were both an inspiration to and an affirmation of Wright's own emerging ideas of order.[26]

It is important to note that the idea of "progress" was not fundamental to Wright's understanding of history; his intentions were to create timeless, elemental forms and spaces and to find architecture's eternally valid principles. It was with satisfaction rather than disappointment that Wright found his own "discovery"—the room as the generating idea of architecture—first articulated hundreds of years ago by the Chinese philosopher Lao Tzu. Rather than hide this ancient source of inspiration, Wright had a paraphrase of Lao Tzu's words carved over his fireplace at Taliesin: "The reality of the

Analytical Diagrams
continuity of ordering principles in centralized church plans; drawn by author

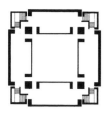

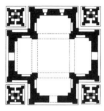

building does not consist in the four walls and the roof but in the space within to be lived in."

Wright developed his comprehensive architectural conception remarkably early, reaching an extraordinary level by his midthirties with the design and construction of his masterpiece, Unity Temple. This great building is ordered by the principles on which all of Wright's later work would be based—its design developed as a precisely articulated and adapted transformation of universal ordering principles; as Wright wrote, "The form is a consequence of the principle at work."[27] Taken altogether, Wright's works constitute as rich and comprehensive an architectural "system" of design for human inhabitation as any that had gone before—or that have evolved since.

Today, Unity Temple should act as a sharp reminder of what we have lost, and what we must regain if we are to project a significant architecture in our own time. Our contemporary architecture, for all its apparent energy and diversity, seems to be secretly driven by fear of its unacknowledged lack of principles and is desperately seeking escape in the diversionary adventures of form. The idea of architecture as a *discipline* is the only way out of this impasse. Frank Lloyd Wright, who worked "in the cause of architecture," found a unique combination of philosophical and formal principles that allowed him both *confidence* and *wonder*.

The studies in this volume form a comprehensive critical overview of Frank Lloyd Wright as a maker of architecture. A majority of the essays employ the newly available archives of Wright's drawings (which came about in no small part through the prompting of some of the authors); other essays mark defining moments of critical insight dating back to Wright's lifetime, written by those seeking to understand Wright's design system while he was still practicing; and all the essays endeavor to critically analyze Wright's work so as to reveal the underlying principles that act to order his architecture— something that has been common practice in academia for many years regarding the works of other modern architects but which has been rare in the case of Wright.

In the US, this type of analysis was initially applied to modern architecture at the University of Texas, where from 1952 to 1956, dean Harwell Hamilton Harris, disciple-at-a-distance of Wright, assembled a young faculty that included Bernhard Hoesli, Colin Rowe, Robert Slutzky, John Hejduk, and Werner Seligmann. These architect-teachers went on to evolve methods of spatial and morphological analyses that dominated and characterized

Plans of Centralized Plan Sanctuaries
Unity Temple, top, Antonio Sangallo il Vecchio, San Biagio, Montepulciano, Italy, 1520, center, and Giuliano da Sangallo, Santa Maria della Carceri, Prato, Italy, 1485, bottom; redrawn under author's supervision

Isometric Analysis
comparison of sketch of St. Peter's originally by Leonardo da Vinci for Bramante, left, and similar viewpoint of Wright's Unity Temple, right; redrawn under author's supervision

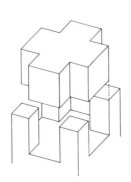

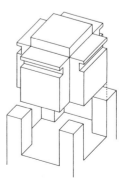

much of architectural education and criticism for the latter half of the twentiethth century. In many ways this book is an outgrowth of this school of analysis: not only are there essays by three of the principals of the school, Hoesli, Rowe, and Seligmann, but there are three essays by those of us who, as students, were influenced by these teachers—Jonathan Lipman, Patrick Pinnell, and myself.

Also beginning in the 1950s, an important strengthening of this analytical approach was achieved by the parallel British school of thought, all of whose members were trained as architects. By fusing formal and spatial aspects with equally critical constructional and experiential aspects, this group of British architects produced a more comprehensive mode of analysis; three essays exemplifying this approach are included in this book, by Kenneth Frampton, Richard MacCormac, and John Sergeant—the latter two having been students of Rowe at Cambridge University, where he taught after leaving the University of Texas.

As Lipman related in the postscript to the first edition of this book, at the founding of the journal *Oppositions* by the Institute for Architecture and Urban Studies (directed by Peter Eisenman, student of Rowe at Cambridge, and Frampton), the editorial board intended to produce an issue on Wright, along with ones on Le Corbusier and Kahn. Pinnell, as the initial editor, invited Neil Levine to write his first essay on Wright, which is included in this book. In 1981, Pinnell handed the editing task off to Lipman, and when *Oppositions* went out of business in 1984, the Wright issue was only two issues away from publication. In 1988, Lipman bowed out, because of pressures of his growing practice, and at Frampton's urging I assumed the editorship of what had now become a book, the first edition being published in 1991. This second, revised edition has been enlarged to include twice the number of studies, in addition to three essays by Frank Lloyd Wright. All the critical studies here published share the approach of analysis, employed to discover the underlying ordering principles that structured Wright's work.

This volume opens with Patrick Pinnell's study (1991) of Wright's early years as an architect, during which Wright initially endeavored to produce a different house plan for every different client, his great breakthrough to the Prairie House coming with his recognition of the generative potential of the plan-type. Werner Seligmann's essay (1991) documents Wright's evolution of the Prairie House and the manner in which Wright explored the limitless potential of a few ordering principles in the development of his archetypal plan and massing, culminating in the Darwin Martin House of 1904. This is followed by Colin Rowe's classic essay (1956) on Chicago steel-frame buildings and his penetrating analysis of Wright's work within the Chicago School, centered around Sullivan, and the fundamental differences in the approaches of these two founders of American modernism: Sullivan's emphasis on expressive structure and Wright's equally emphatic emphasis on inhabited space.

Gwendolyn Wright (1988) examines Wright's Prairie-period practice and the manner in which his work engaged a progressive social vision for everyday life and was intended to give order to the entire social realm, from private home to neighborhood to region, including an important aspect often

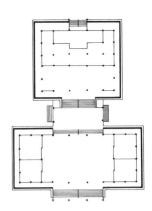

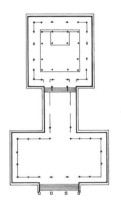

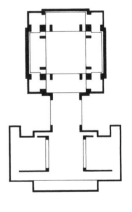

Plans of Temples
Tosho-gu temple, Nikko, Japan, top, Taiyu-in-byo temple, Nikko, Japan, center, and Wright's Unity Temple, bottom; Wright visited the temples at Nikko during his first trip to Japan which ended in May 1905, one month before he began the design of Unity Temple; redrawn under author's supervision

overlooked in Wright studies: his conception of the single-family house not as an object in the landscape, but, rather, as the essential element in the spatial construction of the collective neighborhood. In his essay on Wright's Oak Park Studio practice during this same Prairie period, David Van Zanten (1988) explores the development of Wright's "system" of design, its underlying ordering principles, and its employment of abstract geometries and modular assembly—emphasizing Wright's focus on how to put things together, an attribute he shared with the larger Chicago School.

Richard MacCormac's essay (1974), building directly on Grant Manson's "Wright in the Nursery" of 1953, was the first to fully present the numerous formal and philosophical connections between Wright's Prairie-period design system and the Froebel training method. Otto Antonia Graf's essay (2003) and accompanying diagrammatic analysis of the Steel Cathedral project explore the ancient system of formal order lying at the beginning of all human civilizations and the manner in which Wright brought this forward and engaged it in the architectural spaces and lived experiences of modern times.

Unity Temple
view looking up at sanctuary corner, with corner pier, hanging lights, and ceiling leaded-glass windows

Kenneth Frampton's essay (1991) explores Wright's career-long efforts to engage Gottfried Semper's concept of weaving as the foundation of construction—in particular the "woven wall," with its Celtic and Islamic connections—which Wright employed to bind together experiential space and tactile material through the manner in which architecture is constructed and the manner in which the building is woven into its site. John Sergeant's essay (1976) examines Wright's redeployment of the ordering principles, presented in MacCormac's earlier essay, in the Usonian Houses, indicating the manner in which Wright's later asymmetrical house plans allowed a more complete engagement of the experience of inhabitation within the landscape and nature. This direct connection, in terms of shared ordering concepts, between the early houses, from the Prairie period, and the later houses, exemplified by Fallingwater, is explored in Bernhard Hoesli's study (1980), and he emphasizes Wright's discovery and application of the "continuity of space" throughout his career and the strong contrast between Wright's fundamentally spatial and experiential works and our contemporary infatuation with superficial form.

In her essay, Kathryn Smith (1998) explores the critically important place of water in the development of the landscapes inhabited by Wright's architecture and the manner in which, throughout his career, Wright employs moving water, and our experience of it, to connect his buildings to nature. Neil Levine's essay (1982) examines the manner in which Wright employed diagonal planning—a timeless design principle—first to open corners, so as to connect adjacent rooms in his early houses, and later to project the space of his architecture so as to be fully integrated into his late conception of the inhabited landscape, and the disappearing city.

In his essay, Jonathan Lipman (1991) indicates how all of Wright's public buildings share a common ordering principle, consistently applied from 1895 until Wright's death in 1959: this involved a separation of the primary and secondary functions into two unequal volumes, symmetrical and asymmetrical, respectively; a spiraling entry sequence from dark and compressed to light and expansive; and flooding the primary space with light from above, in order to give it a sacred and ennobling character. Despite the great variety of expressions and forms employed by Wright throughout his seventy-two year career, he insisted that the ordering principles underlying his work were ever the same, as indicated in my essay (1991), where I examine Wright's ideal of integrity and analyze the complex interweaving of principle and place in Wright's method of design and in his works of architecture.

To present these principles in his own words, three of Wright's essays, dating from the beginning, middle, and end of his career, have been reprinted herein as a sort of "conclusion" to the critical studies in this volume. Taken together, these fourteen critical analyses of Wright's work indicate that, rather than being the creator of arbitrary form, as he is often portrayed, Wright was in fact the most principled architectural designer of our modern time, consistently employing a rigorous set of ordering principles that he believed to have both ethical and aesthetic meaning; principles that impart to Wright's architecture a sense of being both old and new, both universal and of its place, both inevitable and full of wonder.

Academic Tradition and the Individual Talent
Similarity and Difference in Wright's Formation

BY PATRICK PINNELL

"He in whom there is much to be developed will be later in acquiring true perceptions of himself and of the world."—*Johann Wolfgang von Goethe, Wilhelm Meister's Apprenticeship (1796), Translation by Thomas Carlyle*

Frank Lloyd Wright himself would have known the term for the tale that follows.[1] It is the story of a young artist's education and self-discovery, a variety of *Bildungsroman*, the German romantic term for a novel of youthful education. How did Frank Wright, green kid from Wisconsin, become Frank Lloyd Wright, architect? It is possible to retrace the projects and encounters of his earliest professional years and find an answer, or at least answers, to the question.

The hallmark of the *Bildungsroman* is a final revelation that the disconnected adventures along a picaresque journey turn out to have unsuspected links, a cumulative wholeness understood by the protagonist only in hindsight. However random or irrelevant individual episodes seem at the time of occurrence, or to other observers later on, all are found to have contributed to education and identity. The moment of seeing connection is the moment of completed apprenticeship, the coming-of-age. Such is Wright's story. To understand the mature artist, the Wright, say, who designed the Ward Willits House in early 1902, it is necessary to understand his peregrinations in the years before.

The design trail between the nineteen-year-old youth's arrival in Chicago, early in 1887, and the first buildings definitively designed in his own new idiom, fifteen years later, is picaresque indeed. There are works usually accounted first-rate, the Charnley and Winslow houses in particular, because they somehow adumbrate the modern, but then there is the rest of it. Wright in these years wanders the forests and fields of architectural style, from vernacular to pseudo-Tudor to straight academic classical, pursuing any number of adventures in design that seem to have little to do with finding the elements of a new way of building. If mentioned at all, these other performances are treated in the tone a *Bildungsroman* adopts when its young hero somehow persists on stumbling into brothels.

Once a long-standing editorial agenda, the one wanting to see in Wright's early career only that which anticipates what he and others would

do in the twentieth century, is removed, another thread of argument concerning his formation becomes visible. It is too easy to look at the late 1880s and the 1890s, for instance, merely in terms of elimination of traditional ornament and development of a different way of handling interior space. Arguments of that sort, in their emphasis on the *difference* between Wright's work and anything preceding or surrounding it, isolate Wright and by implication turn him into an architect distinct in kind, not just quality—a morally and historically doubtful procedure. They isolate as well the individual moments of his formation, rendering tenuous the connecting logic, thereby losing sight both of the forces driving change and growth and of the true richness of reference in the mature work.

Difference must be balanced by consciousness of *similarity.*

That act of judgment, wherein degrees of difference or similarity are discriminated, is in two ways the heart of the present essay. First, I intend to show how Wright, at certain moments, chose to make himself like, not different from, other architects, and thus in a small way redress an imbalance in historical writing. Second, I contend that the individual episodes of Wright's *Bildungsroman* form a larger shape, a parabola whose vertex is a revelation and reversal in which he finds his identity and understands the shape of his own arc by turning around the priorities given to similarity and difference in the way he designs. It will be seen in the end not paradoxical that Wright came to mature individuality only when he realized in what ways he should acknowledge similarity.

This period of Wright's architectural formation can be seen as a series of voluntary encounters with academic ideals and emulations of academic practice. The encounters ranged from contemporary American work to the great monuments of European architectural history and occurred in a variety of stylistic guises, from vernacular and medieval to, far and away most significantly, academic classical tradition. His maturation can be described as an ever-deepening and more subtle understanding of that inheritance.[2] It makes no difference that he later excoriated its more conventional practitioners. Struggle with the use and meaning of that tradition, especially the strictly classical aspect of it, is the *Leitmotiv* of Wright's *Bildung* (his education and self-discovery). His transcendence of literal academic styles, coinciding with his understanding and appropriation of basic academic *methods*, not only marks the moment of his maturity but makes it possible. Out of the seeming confusion of enthusiasms in his progress through the 1890s, Wright emerged equipped with fundamentally academic and classical habits of mind that shaped his work throughout his career.[3]

[I]

To cut ambiguity short: there never was exterior influence upon my work, either foreign or native, other than that of *Lieber Meister*, Dankmar Adler and John Roebling, Whitman and Emerson, and the great poets worldwide. My work is original not only in fact but in spiritual fiber. No practice by any European architect to this day has influenced mine in the least.
—*Frank Lloyd Wright, A Testament (1957)*

Frank Lloyd Wright was born June 8, 1867, in Richland Center, Wisconsin. He was the first of three children born to William Cary Wright, an itinerant musician-minister (sometimes Baptist, sometimes Unitarian), and Anna Lloyd-Jones Wright, one of a large, literate, intensely clannish family of Welsh immigrant farmers, preachers, and schoolteachers.[4] Wright's move out of his mother's territory back to his father's native New England is not often enough noted or given weight. Several years' worth of the future Prairie architect's upbringing occurred in Pawtucket, Rhode Island (1872–74), and Weymouth, Massachusetts (1874–78).[5]

The family's return to Wisconsin in 1878 was followed by steady deterioration of the parents' marriage. A divorce was granted William Wright on April 24, 1885, and shortly thereafter a listing appeared in the *Madison Directory* for "Frank Wright, Draughtsman." The two facts are likely not unconnected; even given all his mother's relatives close by, seventeen-year-old Wright was in some degree now the source of the family's income. Under such circumstances, working for an architect-builder named Allan D. Conover, Wright fell short of finishing high school.[6] During the winter months of early 1886, and then in the fall of the same year, Wright worked for Conover while taking courses at the nearby University of Wisconsin. Among his classes was a rigorous descriptive-geometry class from which a few drawings have survived.

In the summer between his only two terms of college, Wright worked on interior colors and ornament for a new country chapel. Unity Chapel was located west of Madison in the Helena Valley, "Valley of the God-Almighty Joneses," the extensive farmlands of his mother's family. The chapel's dedication that summer, on August 14 and 15, was a grand event, and the little building was later lyrically recalled by Wright.[7] His uncle Jenkin Lloyd-Jones, a prominent Unitarian minister with base of operations at All Souls Church in Chicago, presided over the dedication as he had over the little structure's design.[8]

At the moment Unity Chapel came into service, work would have just been finished on a much bigger project, a new building for All Souls itself, proposed in the spring of the year before.[9] Chapel and Church had the same architect, Joseph Lyman Silsbee, who had transplanted his office to Chicago from upstate New York in May 1882. Quickly, he had become a certain sort of success, obtaining speculative housing work for developers, large residences, and some institutional commissions. Silsbee was a Harvard-educated gentleman architect practicing mostly in the sophisticated new mode of the day, emanating from the East Coast, ultimately derived from the example of Henry Hobson Richardson, and since come to be called the shingle style.[10]

Chapel and Church are accomplished professional exercises. If considered as a pair of commissions done for a single client, the designs unexpectedly reverse conventions. Silsbee treated the larger, more complex, institutional building, sited in a city, like a house, giving it a domestic quota of turrets and dormers, but he endowed the smaller one, set in the countryside, with the grave simplicity of a monument. Despite its size and wooden construction, Unity Chapel is allied with much larger masonry structures. Silsbee could have consciously compressed into this small package the lesson on weight and permanence given not long before by Richardson in Austin Hall, at Harvard University (the alma mater of Silsbee, Richardson, and Charles Follen McKim). Two floors

R. A. Waller House
J. L. Silsbee, River Forest, Illinois,
1889

Hillside Home School
Spring Green, Wisconsin, 1887

of Austin Hall are transformed into one floor in the Chapel, windows and doors packed even more tightly into the zone of wall between a big hipped roof and a low foundation wall. A wood-shingle pyramid overhead and a stone base underfoot signal the *axis mundi* where Richard Lloyd-Jones, the family patriarch, had been buried a few months before.[11] Wright's drawing of Unity Chapel was his first published work.[12]

Richardson died on April 27, 1886, a little before Wright began work on the chapel's construction. The death left American architecture without a spiritual design-father (Richard Morris Hunt did not grow into that role, if he ever did, until 1893). Only the second American (after Hunt) to study at the École des Beaux-Arts, Richardson bestrode the fledgling American architectural profession the decade before his death, and his designs continued to be preeminently influential for more than a decade. Silsbee was hardly alone in looking closely at Richardson's work and, secondarily, at that of his only real rivals (Wright later called them "elite running competition"), McKim, Mead & White—New York architects trained in Richardson's office.

Wright's tale of surreptitiously leaving Madison for Chicago to slip anonymously into a job with Silsbee seems improbable, given his work on the chapel and the nature of some drawings done around the beginning of 1887. The drawings are of All Souls Church, already finished, and are essentially updates of Silsbee's own presentation sketches.[13] It seems most plausible that Wright did them either to show off his skills to Silsbee to get a position (in which case his access to drawings to copy would hint at his identity as the client's nephew) or as a task set by his new boss (Silsbee doing something nice for a repeat client by hiring his nephew to do a set of presentation drawings for his church). In any event, Wright seems to have got himself to Chicago and settled in by March 9, 1887, to judge from a letter from Aunt Nell Lloyd-Jones. "How is it with you in the great city?" she asks, and closes hoping he is "well, happy, and satisfying Mr. Silsbee."[14]

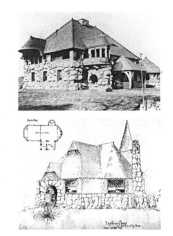

At Silsbee's, Wright worked on a variety of residential commissions—free-standing houses and urban row-house schemes. He also quickly began designing his own freelance projects at night. Aunt Nell's same letter urged him to send ideas for a building she and another aunt, Jane, were contemplating for their newly established Hillside Home School. Wright must have been both dutifully prompt and ambitious, since a drawing for the project, his name given as architect, was published by August. Some interplay of Wright's design with his employer's is immediately evident. Motif transfer between day- and nighttime projects is natural, perhaps almost unconscious, but similarity of whole buildings is another matter. Silsbee's Waller House and Wright's Hillside Home School share overall massing, round-arched front porch, and swept-up railing corners. Timing leaves the direction of influence open to question, as Silsbee's design is apparently dated two years later than his draftsman's.

In June of that first year in Chicago, Wright published his first independent design—another commission from a relative, his Uncle Jenkin. The Unitarian Chapel at Sioux City, Iowa, never built, is a reworking of the Unity Chapel of the previous summer. It is a young man's homage to his experience with Silsbee, but its designer also looked back to Richardson. Wright's drawing, considered in relation to Silsbee's Chapel design, shows an even more dominant roof and an exaggerated base of cyclopean masonry that expands upward into a chimney and entry arch. These are decidedly the features of a structural optimist, an ensemble of demonstrative motifs the suave Silsbee would never have permitted himself. Richardson's Ames Gate Lodge is the stoneworks source, almost certainly, because Wright looked to it as a source at least once more in this period. But Wright's picturesque masonry should not distract from the fact that the little building's plan is quite ordered; two asymmetrical image-giving pieces are added to a large, simple axial volume with bowed end walls. This strategy may also owe something to the example of Richardson.

In early 1888, after a year or so with Silsbee, Wright heard of an opening at Adler & Sullivan and mustered materials with which to interview. He seems to have included one sheet on which he subsequently wrote,"Drawing shown to Lieber Meister when applying for a job." (*Lieber Meister* was, of course, Louis Sullivan. One suspects Wright's tribute-name to have origi-

F. L. Ames Gate Lodge
Henry Hobson Richardson, Easton, Masschusetts, 1880

Unitarian Chapel
Sioux City, Iowa, 1887; drawing by Wright for J. L. Silsbee

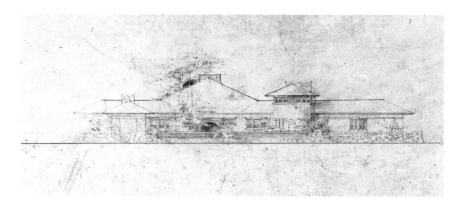

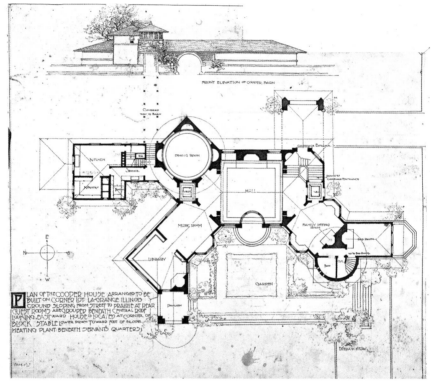

nated either in some affectionate irony by Adler or in recognition that Sullivan—like Goethe, with his ambition to establish a truly German form of drama in *Die Lehr und Wanderjahre des Wilhelm Meister*—saw himself having nationalist responsibilities within his field.) The sheet contains a single drawing, an elevation drawn with a luminous sort of dot-and-feather touch that testifies to high skill with a pencil. If Wright's recollection of the date is accurate, it is a remarkable technique for someone twenty years old.

The elevation matches closely the plan on another extant sheet, this one drawn in ink in a style characteristic of the mid- to late 1890s and labeled as being for a client named Cooper; Wright apparently thought enough of the design to attempt to develop it further later on. The second sheet also contains an elevation for a barn behind the main house. Even if this is a revision done several years later than the drawing Wright remembered showing

"Drawing Shown to Lieber Meister when Applying for a Job"
late 1886 or early 1887

Henry N. Cooper House
La Grange, Illinois, 1890;
perspective and plan

Sullivan, it is interesting to see its correspondences with the "Gate Lodge, North Easton" published in Mariana Griswold Van Rensselaer's memorial biography of Richardson.[15] The general organization in Richardson's sketch remains intact, if abstracted, including a tree thrown in for atmosphere; both buildings are conceived as hip roofs riding over arched openings in walls, pinned down by small entry towers. (This was also Richardson's way of composing his libraries.) By the time Wright's design was done, the gate house's muscular stonework no longer held much interest for him and did not transfer.

Richardson is not the only architectural ghost haunting Wright's design. The Cooper House plan draws on McKim, Mead & White's 1883–84 Julia Appleton House, published in the first volume of G. W. Sheldon's sumptuous *Artistic Country Seats* of 1887–88. (One convenient place in which Wright could have seen the book was Sullivan's library, where a copy is known to have been at the time of a forced sale in 1909.)[16]

From comparing the plans, three things indicate that Wright was designing with his eyes open. First, he certainly was looking directly at McKim's plan when he did his own plan and the corresponding elevation shown to Sullivan: the peculiar disposition of the wings is too close for coincidence. Second, by implication, he was considering the role of the Appleton House's delicate colonial classical detailing in the play of the whole scheme, and coming to the conclusion that other equally delicate but more vernacular details would do as well. The third and most interesting point is that Wright starts with the McKim plan but redoes it *more academically*, with far stricter attention to exactitude of order. Axes between rooms now line up, *poche* is employed, room hierarchies are more definitively identified than in the loose and easy plan of the earlier house. McKim, Mead & White knew very well how to do that sort of rigorous planning, but they reserved it for commissions more significant than private houses. A kind of impatient seeing of possibilities and a determination that no aspect of a design ought to be immune from formal order show through in Wright's design; his models may have been lax, but *he* would get it right. It may have been this attitude that let Wright so vociferously claim his career innocent of influence.[17]

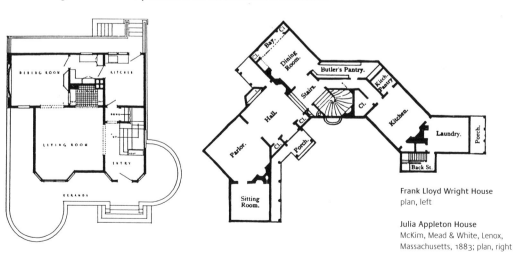

Frank Lloyd Wright House
plan, left

Julia Appleton House
McKim, Mead & White, Lenox, Massachusetts, 1883; plan, right

Wright's drawings got him the job at Adler & Sullivan. By the available evidence, Wright did not exaggerate the importance he soon gained there. Two and a half years later (June 7, 1890), a plan of the new Adler & Sullivan office in the Auditorium Building showed Wright with a room, shared with George Elmslie, next to Sullivan's own.

A little over a year after joining Adler & Sullivan, on June 1, 1889, Wright married Catherine Tobin, whom he had met at All Souls Church. In the fall, the couple built their small house in Oak Park, paying for construction with a loan from Adler & Sullivan. It was a version of an absolutely standard plan-type of the day, the most common builder-developer arrangement, called a "four-square" for obvious reasons: entry hall with stair to second-floor bed-rooms, living room, dining room immediately adjacent, and a kitchen/serv-ice area partitioned off from the rest made four basic spaces on the ground floor of the house. Wright, like Beethoven with the publisher Diabelli's "dumb little theme," saw the high potential of the seemingly banal and, later, turned the plan from a mere pragmatic scheme into a rich set of variations.

Wright always acknowledged that one condition of his employment, hence too for the house loan, was that he foreswear the then-common prac-tice of moonlighting on his own commissions. Circumstances did not bode well for strict adherence to that condition. There was the drain of his own dandyish habits and his wife's only-child self-indulgence; his mother and two sisters had come from Wisconsin to be supported in a white frame house next to his and Catherine's; and nine months after the wedding, in March 1890, came Frank Lloyd Wright Jr., first of the young and apparently ardent couple's six children.

In 1890, besides all his other work in the extremely busy Adler & Sullivan office, Wright had a hand in the design of two houses in Ocean Springs,

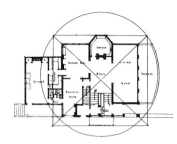

Mississippi. One was an increasingly needed retreat from Chicago for Louis Sullivan himself, who had bought the property for his house while on a long vacation, in January and February, after the official dedication of the Auditorium Building. The Sullivan House's original drawings rest in the Wright archives, indicating his strong role in the project, but it is probably too early to see in the house's extended wing prefiguration of Wright's maturity. Sullivan surely would have kept himself involved no matter how distasteful he typically regarded designing residential architecture.

In the winter of 1890–91, Chicago planned an event whose intentional side effect was to show itself off to the world. The federal government had awarded Chicago the rights to the official celebration of the five-hundredth anniversary of Columbus's discovery of America. The city rallied its forces, including a committee of architects to design the buildings, and designated the Chicago firm of Burnham and Root to take on the enormous task of coordination. The young campaign suffered an almost immediate setback when John Wellborn Root died on January 15, 1891, of pneumonia. Pressing onward, Burnham hired Charles Bowler Atwood as his designer on April 21. Atwood, a brilliant, stylish, cape-wearing Harvard man, was brought to his attention by Professor W. R. Ware of Columbia.[18]

Over the same winter, Wright's resolve to stay faithful to his contract must have given way. In July the commission for a house for Dr. Allison Harlan, a dentist, was announced in two Chicago journals. Listed as architect was Cecil S. Corwin, Wright's close friend from their time in Silsbee's office. Corwin was a plausible cover even for fairly radical designs. Not only had he recently left Silsbee's, he had done so to form a partnership with George W. Maher, then and later known for wanting to have "ideas" in his buildings. Since these announcements seem to have been made close to the onset of construction, and since a fifteen-thousand-dollar house was a good-sized one, the decision to take on the work must have been made early in the year, several months before.[19]

The Harlan House, the first of what Wright himself labeled the "bootleg" houses, is nevertheless worthy of notice. It is as though, losing his honesty, Wright resolved to make the loss worthwhile. Though Sullivanian in many details, the design adumbrates later work in at least one notable way. The square main body of the house sits below a perfectly square pyramidal roof whose vertical axis marks the center point for a low curved wall with which the house confronts the street—a thoroughly three-dimensional design idea.

The Harlan House is the sibling of two houses Wright worked on for Adler & Sullivan in the same year, 1891. The first was for Sullivan and his brother Albert's widowed mother, Andrienne Sullivan. The brothers found a lot in the Hyde Park/Kenwood neighborhood, territory familiar to Wright since his own mother- and father-in-law lived three blocks away.[20] The Sullivan House showed the now-typical Sullivanian contrast of delicate ornament with expansive plain background; its beautiful ornamented bay set against the flat stone facade is akin in concept to the second-floor loggia of the Harlan House. It also acknowledged its tight urban setting, even as it gained privacy from it, by raising the main level quite high off the street. Whether or not Wright was principally responsible for the design, he was

A. W. Harlan House
Chicago, Illinois, 1890; plan analysis; drawn by author

learning about the architectural tactics appropriate to different settings: rural in Ocean Springs, loose suburban in Oak Park, tighter and barely free-standing in Hyde Park, or densely urban in Chicago, where the house for James Charnley was built.

The Charnley House is a great work, an astonishing performance for any architect of the day, let alone one turning twenty-four. While determinedly urban in the way it occupies its corner of Astor and Schiller streets, the design is not much concerned with the specifics of its site. It is about more archetypal issues of form and bears witness to one of those moments in history when an architect of talent determines to get back to the basics of the field, and does so even while producing a design of great elegance. It could be compared to Claude-Nicolas Ledoux's attempts to purify the language of architecture of the conventional niceties of late-eighteenth-century design. Where the use of the entry from the "White Temple" on the Charlotte Dixon Wainwright Tomb, probably by Wright himself in his tenure at Adler & Sullivan, would be merely evocative of the convention of Egyptian motifs in funerary design, its presence here is more generally archaicizing; the lintel is more fundamental than the arch, and Wright here is undertaking basic research. The design was considered important enough that a drawing of it, not in Wright's hand, was nationally pubished early in 1892, probably before construction was started.[21]

Besides the Charnley House, Wright's office projects then included the Schiller Building and Sullivan's allocated share of the Columbian Exposition, the Transportation Building. Site work had already commenced for the Exposition, and the winter months of 1891–92 saw drawings of projected structures appearing in every issue of the architectural journals. Joseph Lyman Silsbee had received a number of commissions for smaller buildings scattered around the Exposition periphery, including the West Virginia Pavilion, published as early as November 1891.[22]

The timing of that publication is of interest because it means Wright would have had the opportunity to incorporate some of the pavilion's features in one of his next round of bootleg houses, the George Blossom House. The Blossom House and its Hyde Park/Kenwood neighbor the Warren McArthur House were announced in June 1892 and, like the Harlan House of the year before, named Cecil Corwin as their architect.[23] Henry-Russell Hitchcock long ago noted Blossom's kinship with McKim, Mead & White's H. A. C. Taylor House and pointed out that its colonial-revival massing and details would have been regarded as distinctly au courant at that date.[24] The Taylor House, like the Appleton Exposition design Wright had looked at four years before in preparing drawings for Sullivan's scrutiny, was in Sheldon's *Artistic Country Seats*. Both Silsbee's and McKim's designs would have come to Wright's attention, and both influenced the proposal to his client.

The Blossom House is enthusiastic in its use of informed and literal classicism; Serliana ("Palladian" windows) abound, and the porch features a sweep of Ionic columns done according to the Scamozzi model. The perfect-square pyramidal roof reappears from Harlan, now atop a ground plan even more in the classical tradition of geometric precision. It is a nine-square plan, as the type is known today, slightly expanded at the rear to accommo-

James Charnley House
Frank Lloyd Wright for Adler & Sullivan, Chicago, Illinois, 1892

Charlotte Dixon Wainwright Tomb
Adler & Sullivan, Saint Louis, Missouri, 1892

date service functions and a picturesque bay for the dining room. The four corner squares are slightly more dominant, their corners further defined by pilasters, than the remaining five. The Blossom House was clearly research work for Wright, a study of how, in the classical tradition, the pieces of a building go together. It is an exercise in precise edges and corners and how the literal elements of a received style relate to define a more abstract geometric pattern. The center bay recesses *exactly* the width of the corner pilaster; the Palladian windows rest *precisely* on the house's base; the upper windows refuse to encroach an inch on the entablature. Despite its affiliations with other architects' published projects, this is not a lazy exercise in style cribbing but a serious study.

One other aspect of the Blossom House draws attention. The house's plan can be looked at as an attempt to produce a new, contextually appropriate plan type by a strategy of hybridization. In the Blossom House, Wright puts the two towers of the urban Charnley House on the front of the suburban four-square plan of his own house. Hyde Park, looser than the former's situation yet still less spread out than the latter's, gets a building appropriately in-between in character. If that was the kind of reasoning going on, it is the first clear instance of the *typological* thinking so characteristic of Wright ten years later.

Blossom's nonidentical twin, the McArthur House next door, also seems to have a borrowed seed of inspiration. When considered without the porch Wright later added, McArthur bears considerable resemblance to John Calvin Stevens's Low House, just recently published in February 1890.[25] A gambrel upper floor in a tight volume, dominating a ground-floor base and resting exactly on the window heads, is a compositional motif common to the two houses, and the side entrance and disposition of ground-floor functions are identical. Wright, as usual, has corrected and generalized aspects of his model, this time taking Stevens's near-to-corner bays and testing them *on* the three non-service corners available to him, as if to see what happens when corners are blown out under the weight of all that roof.

Bootleg houses had a banner year in 1892. Besides Blossom and McArthur, there were the Robert Parker and Thomas Gale Houses in Oak Park and the Robert Emmond House in LaGrange. The last three are very similar in plan and elevation. They are simpler, less expensive houses than the two in Hyde Park/Kenwood and are slight elaborations of the straightforward four-square scheme Wright had built nearby for Catherine and himself three years before. Corner bays reiterate a McArthur theme, and a parlor/library is introduced between living and dining rooms, but otherwise the planning is the same.

Looked at another way, they seem to reveal a developing pattern in Wright's method. Though ever more sophisticated and constantly experimental, he seems at this stage of his development to need a model to start from, then correct. The Parker, Emmond, and Thomas Gale houses are instances. They are based on still another McKim, Mead & White item from *Artistic Country Seats*, the Charles T. Cook House of 1885. Wright edits away the model's site-specific porch, compresses the main volume's two roofs into one, and, as always, tightens the internal geometry of plan axes. The specifics of the colonial classical language, as well as the general volumetric strategy of

George Blossom House
Chicago, Illinois, 1891; period exterior photograph

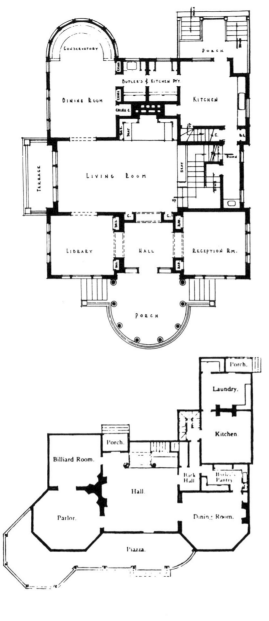

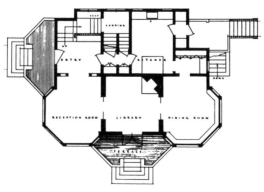

George Blossom House
plan

Charles T. Cook House
McKim, Mead & White, 1885;
plan

Robert Emmond House
La Grange, Illinois, 1892; plan

embedding twin octagonal towers in a simpler, larger volume, remain intact.

Louis and Albert Sullivan's mother never lived in the house designed for her. Andrienne Sullivan died on May 15, 1892, when it was in the final stages of construction. Instead, not long after, Louis Sullivan himself moved in. The now completed and quite distinctive Harlan House was less than three blocks away and, presumably, quite visible at the end of Morgan Place. Since Sullivan would have passed the Harlan House morning and evening if he commuted to the Loop from the Forty-third Street Station he had himself designed, there were probably some edgy moments for Wright. These would have multiplied on the move of Albert Sullivan, also in 1892, into a house on Kimbark Avenue almost directly across the block from the active construction of the Blossom and McArthur houses. Although the three houses had been announced to the world as the designs of Cecil Corwin, they would have been noted as quite distinctive by Sullivan's professionally sharp eye. It is more than a little puzzling that Sullivan did not find Wright out and, in effect, fire him until a good ten months after his move into the neighborhood. It seems probable that there is more to the tale than Wright's account in his autobiography.[26] What really happened between the two men is unlikely ever to be known, but it was certainly a matter of intense bitterness. Wright remembered Sullivan saying, "Wright, your conduct has been so perfidious there is nothing I care to hear you say." In any event, Wright was discovered, a confrontation ensued, and by spring of 1893 he was out the door and on his own.

[I I]

Consolation, if needed, came quickly. In early May, Wright won a competition to design a boathouse for Madison's Lake Mendota; the entry drawings likely had been done while still in Sullivan's employ.[27] The working drawings were stamped and dated on June 8, 1893, Wright's twenty-sixth birthday.

The Mendota Boathouse, long since destroyed, was a beautiful design. (In fact, it was to have had an even more astonishing sister boathouse on Madison's other principal lake, Monona. But this latter project, with its Boullee-like conical roof and Studio-prefiguring chain- hung upper level, fell victim to cost overruns.) Its plan was a hybrid, ingeniously grafting a back piece—a semicircular loggia with radial boat storage space beneath—onto a front of twin towers with a great segmental arch between them.

The scheme's origins are consistent with those of Wright's other work of the time. Logically enough, Wright chose as models two McKim, Mead & White buildings for general recreation situated next to water. One, for the back semicircle, was the Newport Casino loggia; the other, for the gatelike lakefront composition, was the Narragansett Casino. Again a kind of typological thinking is demonstrated, in this instance the variety that regards functional rather than formal organization as primary. Public buildings, of which the Mendota design is one, come out of public buildings; houses come only from houses. As an aside, it is worth noticing the sort of lighthearted tradition to which the boathouse affiliates itself; the bond with several English Palladian bridges is one of a spirit of deftly made classical forms at play with nature, rather than a direct debt.

The summer of 1893, Columbian Exposition summer in Chicago, could not have been a comfortable one for a newly independent architect with a family to feed. The country was entering a depression, in ironic contrast to the glamour and imperial power seemingly promised by the enormously popular "White City" of the Exposition. The place could be wandered in endlessly for the novelties it offered. The lessons, overt and implied, it held out for study to those who cared to study were astonishing. Not least among these was the United States of America announcing itself to the world as an economic, military, and, most surprisingly, cultural power. Hindsight makes it too easy to dismiss as kitsch such a central feature of the Exposition as Frederick MacMonnies's Columbian Fountain, which visitors encountered in the great basin immediately on entry; allegorically enthroned in a sort of *Santa María*–esque ceremonial gondola, the figure of America looks confidently ahead as Fame trumpets her glory from the bow, the nine elegant Muses labor at the oars, and Father Time steers the whole ensemble, significantly enough, eastward. The people who conceived the fountain and made the Exposition did so with high earnestness, a conviction of American mission, that deserves serious consideration today.

The single most admired building at the fair was the Fine Arts Building designed by Burnham's replacement for Root, Charles B. Atwood. Even more suave and knowing in its use of the classical tradition than McKim, Mead & White's Agriculture Building, it was the only exhibition structure rebuilt afterward in materials more permanent than the horsehair plaster ("staff") that was the standard surfacing for the steel and heavy timber skeletons that made the quick rise of the fair possible. Atwood showed here that he was an accomplished designer. For the Fine Arts Building, he utilized as his starting point an 1867 École des Beaux-Arts project for a "Palace for an Exhibition of Fine Arts" that had won its author, Émile Bénard, the Prix de Rome. Atwood's design calmed the precedent's jumpy gaiety by condensing multiple pediments into only a few, by broadening overall width, and by doing away with a lot of ins and outs in plan. Behind the neo-Grec portico he added a Pantheon-like dome and central room, a place where Americans could venerate the godlike great artists of the past and present. There is great ease and control in the whole design, a characteristic evident in many of Atwood's buildings.[28]

Frank Lloyd Wright understood both Atwood's intentions and the wider significance of American use of the classical language that the Fine Arts Building shared with most of the Exposition. In November of that year, Wright's was one of seventy-five entries to a competition for a library and museum for Milwaukee. Though he did not win the commission, he was proud enough of his design to show off its final inked elevation in the Chicago Architecture Club Exhibition and Catalogue the next spring.[29] Professor W. R. Ware of Columbia, who had sent Atwood to Burnham, was the professional adviser of the competition.

Wright's design is patently based on Atwood's. If anything it is even more confident and knowing in its handling of the conventions and precedents of the classical language. For example, he elides the Erechtheioid caryatid porches that Atwood had placed on either side of the central portico,

Lake Mendota Boathouse
Madison, Wisconsin, 1893;
period exterior photograph,
view from lake

Casino Narragansett
McKim, Mead & White,
Narragansett, Rhode Island 1886;
period exterior photograph

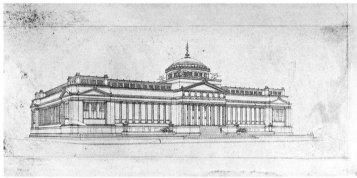

thus letting the rhythmic march of columns continue smoothly across the whole facade between terminal pavilions. Wright pushes toward even greater unity of effect and, toward that end, commits what for the contemporary canon of classicism was the deadly sin of running the same entablature across two different height column groupings. But this is just what the Erechtheion itself does. Wright omitted the part of Erechtheion quotation, the caryatid porch, that seemed to him inessential to Atwood's design but added into his project a more fundamental aspect of the Greek building's ordering system. Wright was looking back past contemporary practice to the monuments of the classical tradition.[30]

Another ancestor of Atwood's Fine Arts Building was the seventeenth-century East Front of the Louvre, attributed to Claude Perrault. In a preliminary drawing for the Milwaukee project,[31] Wright comes even closer to the Louvre facade than Atwood did, returning to its high base and low central entry. The continuous sweep of colonnade in Wright's final design is, of course, the most striking feature of Perrault's facade. In equating, by implication, the Milwaukee Library and Museum with the Louvre, he was proposing an enormously ambitious cultural agenda.

Wright's design continued by local means the national mission implicitly proposed by the Columbian Exposition. It is not insignificant that photographs of the Court of Honor at the Exposition resemble the frontispiece of Claude Perrault's 1673 translation of Vitruvius into French. That book's first plate was another arrangement of allegorical figures in the same tradition as the Columbian Fountain: Ceres, goddess of plenty, joins Geometry and

Fine Arts Building, World's
Columbian Exposition
Charles Atwood of Burnham &
Atwood, Chicago, Illinois, 1893;
period exterior aerial photograph

Milwaukee Public Library and
Museum Competition Entry
Milwuakee, Wisconsin, 1893;
perspective

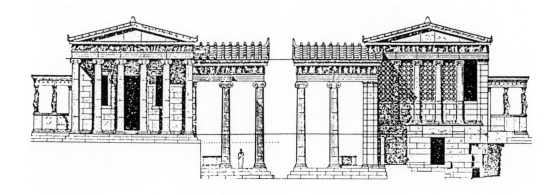

Arithmetic in presenting to La Belle France, with her imperial scepter and *fleur-de-lis* patriotic shield, the "Dix Livres d'Architecture de Vitruve." In the background, Perrault shows three of his own buildings (including the Louvre under construction), presumably because they were designed according to sound, authentically Vitruvian principles. Perrault, standing in for Louis XIV and his minister Colbert, is claiming that the legacy of Vitruvius and Rome now belongs to France. As of 1671 France had a Royal Academy of Architecture, and the claim was implicitly being made that the great classical mantle had passed from Italy to France as it had once gone from Greece to Italy.

At Chicago in 1893, Burnham, McKim, and company announced that the mantle had passed again, now to America, and Frank Lloyd Wright seems to have agreed with enthusiasm. That belief survived Wright's use of the literal forms of classical architecture to become a mainspring of the remainder of his career.

Despite the nationwide economic hard times, Wright managed to find commissions to carry him through the fall and winter. Certainly without the glory of the Milwaukee project, or even of the Mendota Boathouse, they had the virtue of being real, and at last they could be announced to the world under his own name. In two small houses for Francis Wooley and Peter Goan, he thriftily recycled some of his earlier efforts; the former is a variant on the two-tower Parker, Emmond, and Thomas Gale houses of the year before, while the latter revisits almost exactly the foursquare organization of his own 1889 home. For a third project, built for Walter Gale in Oak Park and blessed with a marginally larger budget, Wright tuned a foursquare plan up just a bit by turning to McKim, Mead & White's C. A. Whittier House.[32] The Walter Gale House features a side entry and a chunky round tower set in contrast to a tall, thin chimney and a tall, elegantly ornamented dormer. The whole composition is pulled together under a big roof with its ridge parallel to the street.

Two larger projects also came Wright's way late in 1893 or early 1894. The commissions were announced together in June 1894, with Wright named as architect, and were probably just then commencing construction. One of them was a commission for four row houses for Robert Roloson. It is not clear that the Roloson Houses owe anything to a source other than Wright's own talent. If they do, it is to an elegant formula for row-house facades being

Erechteion
Athens, 5th Century BC; entablature runs over two column sets of differing height, as indicated by horizontal lines

used at the time in the Philips and Lloyd Phoenix House by McKim, Mead & White.[32] Wright's central composition of windows with ornamental stone and terra-cotta, like the analogous feature of the Phoenix House, speaks of the non-load-bearing nature of the building's facade. Had a proposed revision been adopted, the moldings framing the upper windows, cutting across three party walls, would have announced that structural fact even more clearly.

The other large project, remembered in gratitude by Wright the rest of his days as his "first" house, was for William H. Winslow. So much has been written concerning the Winslow House that it is perhaps enough to note here that Wright was twenty-six when he designed it and that it is a world-class piece of architecture. Though certain aspects of its use of space will be revisited later, for the moment it will suffice to recognize it as "classic" in the widest sense of that term. For all its innovative aspects, Wright knew that in designing it he was operating in a particular tradition, one that he acknowledged in labeling it later not as "Haus" but as "Villa fur Herrn Winslow."[34] Wright might not have been looking at things like Palladio's Villa Zeno in the process of designing Winslow, for by this time the academic tradition, with its sense of absolute conviction, was in his fingertips. Still, there are some eye-catching similarities that might go beyond the general family likeness shared by geometrically disciplined ideal villas. For instance, the Winslow Stable has three-quarter columns at its corners, like Palladio's building.

Eighteen ninety-four also had its smaller buildings, and these are not without interest in understanding Wright's design sensibilities. Times still being thin, Wright designed a renovation and addition for Dr. H. W. Bassett; the refaced house culminated in yet another perfectly pyramidal roof. Like

Whittier House
McKim, Mead & White, 1881; elevation

Walter Gale House
Oak Park, Illinois, 1893; elevation

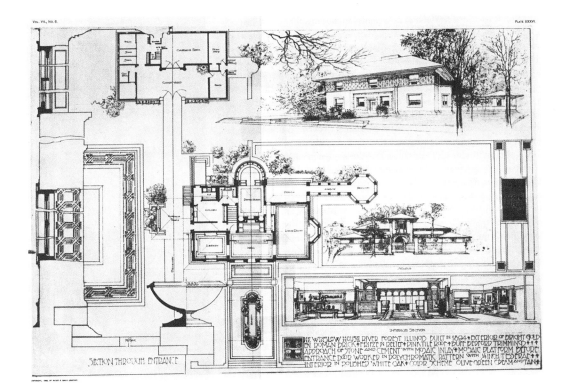

SECTION THROUGH ENTRANCE

THE WINSLOW HOUSE RIVER FOREST ILLINOIS BUILT IN 1894 EXTERIOR OF BRIGHT GOLD
ON ROMAN BRICK FRIEZE IN RELIEF DINA TILE ROOF BUFF BEDFORD TRIMMINGS
APPROACH OF STONE AND CEMENT WITH MOSAIC INLAY MOSAIC PLATFORM BEFORE
ENTRANCE DOOR WORKED IN POLYCHROMATIC PATTERN WITH 14 INCH TESSERAE
INTERIOR IN POLISHED WHITE OAK COLOR SCHEME OLIVE GREEN CREAM AND TAN

the Winslow House, the Bassett House pulled the facing material of the ground level up to the sill of the second-floor windows, effectively generalizing the old Richardsonian formula, learned under Silsbee at Unity Chapel, to encompass multilevel situations. The Peter Goan House had done a similar thing, but the Bassett renovation is more interesting because, with its two-story window bay and a little entry porch, it shows Wright beginning to experiment with the possibility of both defining volumes and overlapping them.

The other noteworthy project, announced in March, was the Frederick Bagley House. The construction documents do not show the semidetached octagonal library. The implication is that the space was added to the program sometime during the course of construction and that plugging the octagonal room into still another of his foursquare house plans caused Wright to have a critical realization that he later dated to 1894: on the ground floor of the typical American house, only four rooms were really necessary.[35]

Even if that recollection is accurately dated, two unbuilt projects show that at that moment it applied only to small houses, not to the bigger show-piece commissions. The plan for the Henry N. Cooper House in LaGrange resurrected the McKim, Mead & White–influenced design that helped get Wright his desk at Adler & Sullivan six years earlier. The surviving ink drawing discussed earlier, with its heavy black ornamental initial, is presented in a style datable to this time. The plan's sophistication and elaboration are notable, and it would be difficult to conclude that the layout demonstrated that only four rooms were requisite. To reiterate, Cooper is an exercise in manipulation of a "found" precedent, the Appleton House, pushing it in the direction of a *tour-de-force* multiaxial rigor that is only suggested by the origi-

William H. Winslow House
River Forest, Illinois, 1894;
analytique composite drawing
showing plans, section
perspective, perspectives,
and details

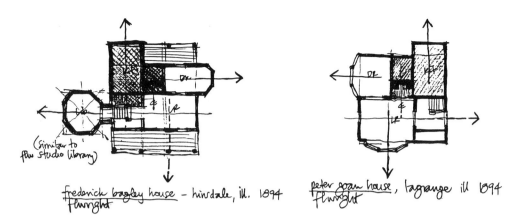

(similar to plan studio library)

frederick bagley house - hinsdale, ill. 1894
flwright

peter goan house, lagrange ill 1894
flwright

inal's loose diagonal planning. Not only are major and minor axes laid out and acknowledged in the *corps-de-logis*, but the wings are also disciplined by a clever system of axes in forty-five-degree angles that manage to tie into the fireplace and entry, using them as features terminating long diagonal vistas. Of Wright's early designs, the Cooper House best illustrates the developing tension between an interest in diagonal vistas and dynamic compositions, on the one hand, and frontal stability, on the other.

Though the Cooper House is an adept performance, its sister commission suggests Wright was clearly not always so good at managing his formal facility. The surviving drawing for the Orrin S. Goan House in La Grange, a perspective that includes a ground-floor plan in one corner, shows Cooper's stair tower and side chimney in the right background. The house is an elaboration of the Winslow House, and almost every bit of elaboration is for the worse, diminishing the ruthless clarity of its precursor. The *porte cochere* has been doubled, first-floor windows have donned shutters, and second-floor ones have become triply arched. Winslow's *axis mundi* (the chimney) is shouldered off center, seemingly for mere convenience. The visible corners of the house become narrow octagonal piers that, though elegant, weaken the solid expression of the masonry box. The plan, too, lacks the clear, central, Palladian order of Winslow. Wright's model in this instance was, for the first time in a larger commission, not McKim, Mead & White but Frank Lloyd Wright; as yet it was not a model from which he could draw with consistent success. The Orrin S. Goan House, though experimental in small ways, is a pastiche rather than a critique of Wright's earlier work.

Together, the 1894 Cooper and Orrin S. Goan houses illustrate a confusion one would not expect from the architect who had produced Winslow only months earlier. This confusion becomes increasingly evident over the next four to five years. Wright deploys enormous talents with as yet no clear idea of the end to which he is using them. Despite increasingly frequent publication in popular and professional journals, despite commissions generally growing in size and frequency, despite fairly frequent lectures, the independent Wright of 1895 through 1898 is harder and harder to regard as fulfilling the promise of the bootlegging Wright of earlier years. What occurred in those years to get him into such difficulties, and what got him out of them and into the "first golden age" of the Prairie Houses, beginning around 1900?

Analyses of Plans
Frederick Bagley House, 1894, left, and Peter Goan House, 1894, 1894, right; drawn by editor

The years in question were dominated by unbuilt office-building schemes and by a number of grand projects for waterside recreational complexes that were never constructed. These weekend "White City" visions were visited and revisited several times as the tides of developmental economics ebbed and flowed. At this moment, Wright must have thought that his practice was about to expand beyond the limits of suburban domestic work. Yet houses were the real mainstay of the office, and a series of large residential commissions presents the clearest evidence of Wright's line of development, his crisis, and its resolution that marked his full design maturity.

In the large-house category, 1895's job list included an unrealized commission, the Jesse Baldwin House, and two houses that were built, for Nathan Moore and Chauncey Williams. All three are peculiar exercises, almost never published because, one suspects, they seem hard to square with Wright's canonical mature work. Each has its interesting aspects. Some prefigure later Wrightian forms and methods, such as Moore's mechanically regular half-timbering, which anticipates later gridding of plans. Other forms, shortly abandoned, reveal the architect's preoccupations at the time. Principal among these is certainly Wright's developing fascination with octagonal forms.

The designs of both the Winslow and the Bagley houses include loosely attached octagonal pavilions: the former's a never-constructed gazebo, the latter's a library. These were managed, with no formal effort to speak of, simply by connecting them with necklike pieces to the main body of the house. But the octagonal corner piers on the Goan House and the Winslow Stable—manipulations on a smaller scale, at the level (to use contemporary academic terminology) of "elements of architecture" rather than "elements of composition"—were more difficult to handle. They introduce the problem of how to design their top and bottom in a way consistent with the rest of the formal language. Are they part of or separate from a division into a base, a high wall, and a narrow upper window band? These two pier experiments explored the fascinations of octagonal geometry at one scale; the Baldwin House design shows vividly the problem with trying to jump up in size and pull the semidetached octagonal pavilion back into the body of the house. To call the result unresolved is in fact kind.

The Heller House, extant in Hyde Park, was probably the next large residential commission. Preliminary drawings indicate the attempt to include both octagonal corner piers and two hemi-octagonal bays at the ends of living and dining rooms. The result is marginally better integrated than the Baldwin House but still fights itself. Continuous horizontals mark superimposed layers of volume, speaking a traditional language of base, wall, capping frieze, and roof, yet contradict this with octagonal corner piers indifferently lapping layers. One can argue such contradictions as being like those of the Milwaukee competition entry, but they do not work in the same way to produce a sweeping unity of effect. The house as built deals with some but by no means all of these problems, being both a horizontal and a vertical composition.

Two large houses for two brothers, George and Rollin Furbeck, dating from 1897 and 1898, show Wright at the nadir. The former revisits the

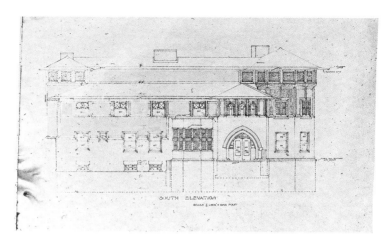

Charnley/Blossom paired-towers theme but now makes them octagonal. The towers are not simple tests of what happens when octagonal spaces overlap rectangular ones (as in the McArthur House) but are relentlessly inflected. Their corners turn outward in arrow-ended piers, diagonal detail piled on diagonal detail. It is the *legerdemain* of a smooth-pattering magician who knows dozens of small tricks to distract from the fact that he has no big one.

If possible, the Rollin Furbeck design is even more desperate. The street facade recycles a tower arrangement sketched, but not used, for the Heller House. Here Wright laid the tower on the front of a basic block like that of the Winslow House. All available corners were then equipped with gratuitous angled corner buttresses, and an entry porch, featuring star-shaped brick piers with no less than sixteen sides, was wheeled up and parked on one side. The culminating misplaced ingenuity occurs in back, where two long columns carry the load of a third-floor, overhanging mass down, apparently, to the first-floor roof. This, despite appearances, is not a rehab. We see here the work of an architect clearly unsure of his major direction.

[III]

What happened to get Wright out of this? The answer can begin to be understood by looking at a drawing that appeared in the first national publication of Wright's work in the *Architectural Review*, a Boston magazine, in June 1900.[36] It is for a house designed not long after the Rollin Furbeck House—the Joseph Husser House of 1899—and is a drawing that every moderately sophisticated architect of the day would have recognized as being of a particular, newly popular genre. It is an *analytique*.[37]

Beaux-Arts academic programs, beginning with the original in Paris, produced these compositions by the hundreds, usually as exercises by scales on a single page; details, plan, and elevational fragments were ordered in an attractive and informative way. But the intent of the drawing was more fundamental than to merely promote familiarity with received classical models and facility in watercolor technique. The assumption behind the whole exercise was *unity*; a good building can be represented adequately on one sheet of paper because it is one thing—an organism whose parts and whole, small scale to large, cohere completely. The *analytique* restates the academic clas-

Jesse Baldwin House
Oak Park, Illinois, 1895; elevation

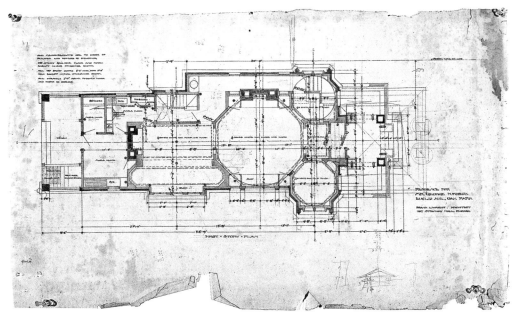

sical formulation that Beauty, the highest of the three fundamental qualities of architecture known as the Vitruvian Trilogy (Beauty, Durability, and Propriety) is, to quote Alberti, a "Harmony of all the Parts, in whatsoever Subject it appears, fitted together with such Proportion and Connection, that nothing could be added, diminished or altered, but for the Worse."[38] Wright had been in close association with graduates of Beaux-Arts-influenced architectural programs, especially MIT's, for years,[39] but it would not have taken that to make him aware of this underlying premise of the *analytique*, since it was one with which he was in sympathy his whole career.

The Husser House *analytique*, like those for the Winslow and Heller houses in the same publication, would have been regarded as unusual simply because it featured a private house. The genre was normally associated with grand public buildings or classical reconstructions—*monumental* projects (using the term in the exact sense) that are intended to contain activities of significance to the whole of the society that builds them. In this sense, the task of monuments is to admonish the viewer to call to memory (*ad monere*—toward memory) the social precepts embodied in the institutions they encompass.

Isidore Heller House
Chicago, Illinois, 1895;
preliminary design perspective

George Furbeck House
Oak Park, Illinois, 1897; plan

Wright's *analytique* was not just a misappropriation of a currently fashionable presentation mode; it reflected that his plan for Husser was the first one in several years to turn to another architect's work for an inspirational seed. Richardson's Winn Memorial Library in Woburn, Massachusetts, was likely mined out of the same 1886 Van Rensselaer biography that Wright had looked to early in his career when designing the Unitarian Chapel at Sioux City and the Cooper House Stable. While the Chicago house and the Massachusetts public building apparently have nothing to do with each other, if one looks at their stylistic language, they are so close in plan that it is highly unlikely their resemblance is coincidental. Wright's spatial vocabulary is much richer than Richardson's; the multitude of partial octagonal volumes now overlap, rather than merely abut, the rectangular prism of the main building. But the general disposition of shapes makes the derivation undeniable.

If the Husser plan borrows from Richardson, then it is different in one respect from all borrowings previously cited. Before this, the derivations remained *in type*: houses came only from other houses, museum buildings from museum buildings, recreation structures from recreation structures. Husser's plan, as well as its presentation technique, is that of monumental *public* construction. Taken together, the two affiliations indicate the presence of a state of mind that is fundamentally new to Wright's work. This requires some background to become clear.

Through the 1890s, Wright's houses fell into two groups. For small commissions he almost always employed a variation of the foursquare plan that was the ubiquitous developer standard of the day; his own 1889 house was the first instance. In these houses, individuality came not so much from the arrangement of the plan as from the elevation and roof treatments and the presence of certain detailing unique to the given project. For his larger-budget commissions, Wright left nothing undone in sorting out the plan; it seems that the client able to pay more got more ingenious and peculiar—more *individual*—overall spatial compositions. In these big commissions, his preoccupation with octagons became epidemic, each successive commission trying to enrich the house's internal spatial experience by plugging in polygons in ever-varying ways. In sum, for the small commissions, budget forced Wright to regard each project first and foremost in terms of its *similarity* to previous, economically constrained projects. For the larger jobs, the initial supposition was just the contrary. It was, instead, the *difference* between each new project and its predecessors that was paramount. "There should be as many kinds [styles] of houses," Wright wrote later, "as there are kinds [styles] of people and as many differentiations as there are different individuals."[40] The large, confused houses of the later 1890s reflect that sentiment; and that sentiment, Wright seems to have realized with the Husser House, was the root of his confusion in design. Husser has numerous progeny, both large and small. The house marks the beginning of Wright's treatment of almost all his plans as variants of a very small number of plan types; *similarity* henceforth dominates *difference*. What happened to trigger the change?

In presenting the Husser House as a monumental building, Wright was not just misappropriating languages of drawing and composition for his own

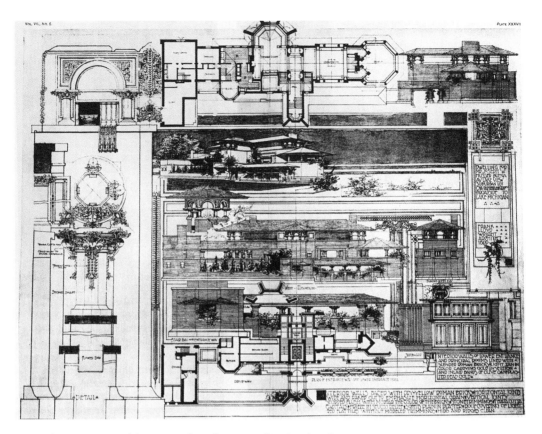

aggrandizement. Instead, he was implying his new realization that the most truly American monument was the freestanding, suburban, single-family house. The presence of such houses, large and small, many of them increasingly mechanized in their making as well as in their equipment, marked life in this country as distinct from that in any other. The house, signifying the dominant values of American culture, was the society's most characteristic and significant building type—by exact definition, a monument.[41]

This had been a widely held sentiment in the country for some time. An 1876 reviewer put the matter forcefully:

> The key-note of this age is the supremacy of the individual. Every man is now asserting himself. There is no strong feeling of nationality, none of clan, and but little of family. He has not yet achieved his independence, so as to learn to combine again, and to cooperate. Until he does, it is not to be expected that great monuments can or will be built, and we had better not attempt it. We shall and we do build great mills and railway stations, because the needs of the time demand them; and we may and do build excellent houses for the individual man. Here lies the path for architecture at this present time. What we need to keep in mind, however, in treating these temples of home, is simplicity, not ostentation; form first, decoration next; and more than that, we should not forget that for these temples great size is not demanded, while purity of ornamentation is.[42]

As a monument, the new American private home was completely worthy of all the traditional tools of design and presentation normally reserved for

Joseph Husser House
Chicago, Illinois, 1899; *analytique* composite drawing showing plans, elevations, perspective, and details

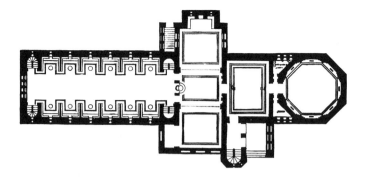

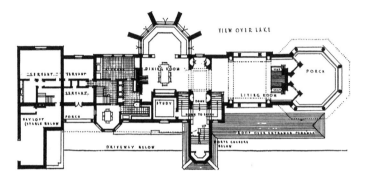

public buildings of collective significance—libraries, museums, and so on. Throughout the nineteenth century, the single most important design tool in the conception of monumental structures was the idea *of type*, which had to do with the fundamental likeness between a new structure of a given purpose and previously built things of similar purpose. (The bible of academic use of type was, of course, J.-N.-L. Durand's *Recueil et Parallele des Edifices de Tout Genre, Anciens et Modernes*, published in Paris in 1799–1800.) Understanding the house as a monument, Wright began to conceive of each new house first in terms of its similarity to previous designs, and second in terms of its difference from them. Not only his small houses but all his houses and, indeed, his whole body of work began to be produced on the premise of types. The galvanizing effect on Wright's work was immediate.

[IV]

Of many consequences, two deserve greatest attention. First, after the appearance of the Husser House in 1899, two plan types were quickly invented. Conceived very much as a logical pair, they embodied different, mutually complementary sets of characteristics. The two plans were then used as the tool of similarity, as it were, underlying all the apparent diversity in the work of the Prairie period. Second, for the first time Wright began consistently to underlay his plans with a regular square grid, a basic tool of some post-Durand academic practice.[43] Conceiving plans in this fashion implies perception of space as homogeneous and continuous, with no difference between inside and outside, and no need to regard wall making as the beginning act of building; certainly, Wright's use of the regular grid as a *concept*,

Winn Memorial Library
Henry Hobson Richardson, Woburn, Massachusetts, 1877; plan

Joseph Husser House
plan

not merely as a pragmatic or machine-sympathetic organizing device, was critical to his struggle to "break the box." Once Wright realized what he was doing—giving form to a monument—the whole traditional tool kit of academic monument making opened for him, and, when these tools were applied to the problem of the American house, they gave enormous new possibilities of expression and experiment to his natural talents. These two tools, the idea of type and the understanding of the grid, enabled Wright to pull the disconnected aspects of the pre–Husser House period together into a mature synthesis.

As indicated, the plan types came into being as a pair. One plan is basically centrifugal or dynamic, and developed from the out-spiraling, diagonal implications of Wright's 1889 foursquare house; the other is centripetal or static, and developed from the stable aspects—the in-line living and dining rooms, the central hearth, and the pyramidal front gable—of the same house. Having grasped that *all* houses could be susceptible to the procedures he had been using on his small commissions, he returned with renewed concentration to the house he had replicated most often through the 1890s, the house that he knew most intimately, his own. He unpacked its possibilities, transforming the two opposing sides of its character into two different sorts of plan. It is likely that he did this quite consciously, because the first realizations of the types were designed simultaneously for the Bradley and Hickox houses, built in Kankakee, Illinois, in the summer of 1900. Further indication that Wright's intention was conscious comes from national publication of the two plans in the *Ladies' Home Journal* the next year. "A Home in a Prairie Town," the stable plan type, appeared in February, while its mate, "A Small House with 'Lots of Room in It,'" was published in June.[44] In 1905, in another nationally published discussion of Wright's work, the Kankakee houses were placed in tandem again.[45]

Both plans can be extracted from Wright's own house by a quick series of formal operations (plan types I and II). Starting from the perception that besides "the entry and necessary work rooms there need be but three rooms on the ground floor of any house, living room, dining room, and kitchen"[46]— in other words, a straightforward foursquare plan—diagrams are easily derivable.

The "A Home in a Prairie Town" type comes about when the living and dining rooms are given extra space and the connection between them is widened, with the fireplace turned ninety degrees to face across the axis thus established (plan type IA1). Reflected, rotated, inverted, elaborated, puritanized—there are more than a half dozen versions of this scheme. It is worth pointing out that the plan is more fundamental than the material of the house; stucco, brick, even stone are used interchangeably to realize essentially the same scheme. Size, too, is a secondary concern, as the type comes in small incarnations like the Bradley House as well as large ones like the Martin House. The similarities among the successive projects take precedence over their differences.

When the living room/dining room has a fireplace that is not rotated from its original position in the 1889 house but, instead, is simply slid over to occupy the central axis, a house of modified but related character occurs (plan type IA2). (The Robie and Thomas Gale plans are here shown as mirror images of the way the houses were actually built.) Not only are they closely related to each other, despite the drastic differences in their sizes, but both of them are tied to the Martin House and, more loosely, to the type IA1 houses.

It is also possible to speculate about some of the more peculiar—one might even say notorious—aspects of Wright's work, for example, the legendary richness of the journey from front sidewalk to hidden front door in so many of his houses. The Robie House entry, tucked back behind the house, exemplifies Wright's procedure of thinking initially of overall disposition of the plan type on the site, then dealing with materiality, and finally inventing an ingenious assortment of design devices to patch together a path to a front door whose location has been set by considerations altogether separate from its visibility.

As Wright's wording indicates, the entry hall is a jump down in status from the living and dining rooms; by implication, it is more susceptible to variation. There exists a family of "A Home in a Prairie Town"–type variants that slide the entry around to the opposite side of the long living/dining space (plan types IB1 and IB2). Two subvariants on this theme come about when the other character in the interior drama, the fireplace, assumes two different locations.

As might be expected, the Husser House is the only big house of the 1890s to figure in a type series. It is the organizational precursor of Wright's other basic plan type, "A Small House with 'Lots of Room in It'" (plan type IIA). Starting again from the 1889 house but now emphasizing a different set of qualities, the type results from extending each of the four major ground-floor spaces out in a spiral, then sliding entry and dining room partially, but never completely, into alignment, and finally sliding living and service areas completely in line to give the whole composition a degree of stability around the never-moving fireplace. (It is as though in the type I plans that emphasize spatial stability, it was safe to move the chimney around, but in the spatially dynamic type II plans to do so would have threatened the coherence of the whole; space and chimney are counterweights to each other's actions.) As with type I plans, quite a number of variant type II incarnations can now be discerned, with plan type stable below all the vagaries of reflection, rotation, material, size, and degree of elaboration. Entry and dining room always exist with their axes slightly misaligned, while kitchen wing and living room axes invariably align.

Since its space is low in the hierarchy and therefore more mobile, the entry of one type II variant is slid around to occupy a position at the junction of the L made by living and dining rooms (plan type IIB). These houses tend to occur late in the Prairie period, possibly as a response to client demand for a more "formal" way of living, in the social sense of the term. Nationally, the foursquare plan was just then beginning to be superseded by the center-hall plan as the common stock of the residential developer, and such a type may have been Wright's parallel response.

To reiterate, it was in Wright's design of the Husser House, using Richardson's library as a starting point, that the critical elements came together to make all this variety-in-unity possible. The basis of the profusion

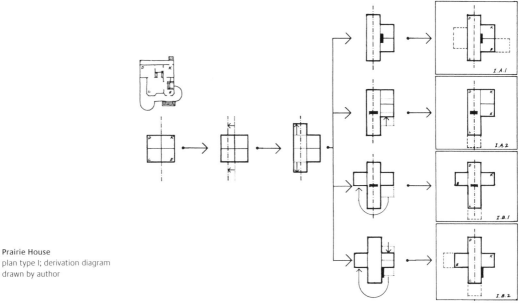

Prairie House
plan type I; derivation diagram
drawn by author

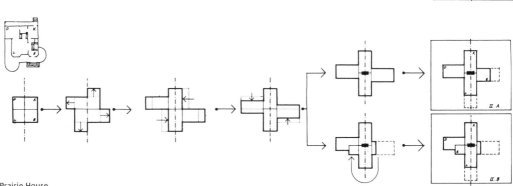

Prairie House
plan type II; derivation diagram
drawn by author

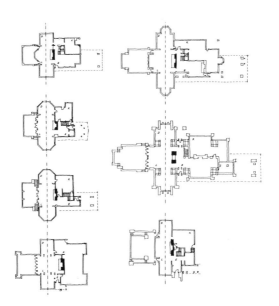

Prairie House
plan type IA1; drawn by author

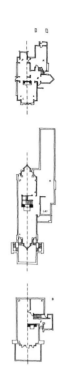

Prairie House
plan type IA2;
drawn by author

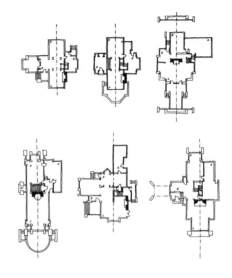

Prairie House
plan types IB1, IB2;
drawn by author

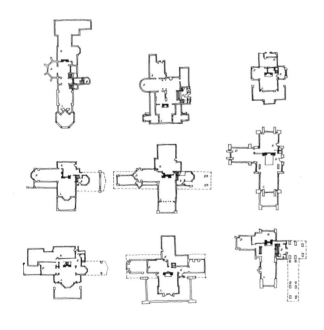

Prairie House
plan type IIA;
drawn by author

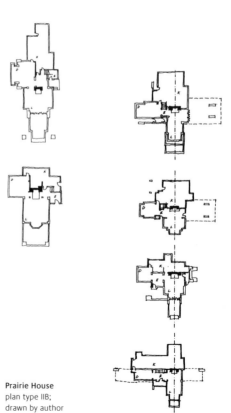

Prairie House
plan type IIB;
drawn by author

of experiment in the Prairie House period is the rhythmic repetition of a very few basic organizational motifs, and this pattern of creative action allies Wright with great artists in other fields. Wright would have cited Bach or Beethoven, but it can be argued that what he did was more closely allied with the *disegno* of the Renaissance.

> This is the characteristic of disegno: that it enhances the vitality of a form by our recognition of its completeness. The great draftsmen of this kind—Signorelli or Michelangelo—are not content to record a movement, as Tiepolo might do, but press round it, till it approaches some ideal pattern that lies at the back of the imagination: hence the continual hammering at the same motif, the tracings, copies, and replicas that so astonish the profane.[47]

Another point, and a speculation, can be made concerning the importance of Richardson and the Winn Memorial Library to Wright's maturation. Winn was one of several libraries, all clearly related in their organization, published in Van Rensselaer's 1886 book. It could have occurred to Wright that these buildings were conceived as a series—Richardson's demonstration of the idea of type he had learned in Paris.[48] But why should Wright choose to study and use the Winn Library over the others? The Winn Library was in construction from mid-1877 through October 1878, when the eleven-year-old Wright was living fairly close by in Weymouth.[49] It is therefore possible that Wright actually saw the building in person. If he did, it seems most likely to have been in the company of his father, William Wright, perhaps in the course of the standard ministerial journey to be visiting preacher in another town's pulpit. William Wright left his family in 1885, at the time Frank Lloyd Wright was acting on his vocation to become an architect; Henry Hobson Richardson died in early 1886, when Wright was working on his first building, which was greatly influenced by Richardson. At the very outset of his career, Wright lost both a personal and a professional role model within a year. Further, if the unverifiable speculation is correct that he visited the Winn Library with his father, they were interlinked role models. For Wright, that building could well have been something emotionally charged, not only an interesting point of departure. The Husser House, based on Winn, signals the moment of artistic adulthood when Wright realized his architectural mission and began to pursue it with conceptual tools acquired from the academic tradition. What Wright, as heir, received from Richardson, as representative of the tradition, was something much more important than a formal model; symbolically, he received his patrimony.

[V]

It is not necessary to maintain that Wright went through exactly these formal procedures to come up with his two basic plans; it is enough to accept that the plans relate closely to the 1889 house and, as formal systems, both complement each other and define a spectrum of possible character for the spaces of a house. It is also important to draw from this a lesson concerning Wright's design procedures. The plan types did not constrain but, quite the contrary, gave a sure base for his fecund inventiveness. The reinvention of the American house at the turn of the century, which many have credited to

Wright, was made possible by his use of a tool, the idea of type, borrowed from academic classical architecture. To repeat, Wright could not have appropriated the tool unless he had made the leap of understanding the house as the true American monument, the single problem most worth his attentions and talents.

Wright could not have come to this realization by any route other than the one he followed. What he borrowed from the classical tradition was much more than literal use of the orders and seed germs of plan and elevation garnered from McKim, Mead & White. It was even more than the feel for type and the use of abstract academic tools like a Durendesque grid, which he used throughout his career. It was the sense of having a mission. In 1893, Wright was one member of a group striving to achieve for America cultural respectability in the eyes of the world by claiming the mantle of classicism. In Wright's case, he claimed the Louvre, and all that it implied, as the appropriate precursor for his Milwaukee library entry. After difficulties, Wright came to have a sense of how to achieve that goal of cultural stature with the American house. In finding the mission he found himself. The *Bildungsroman* wanderings of the 1890s had come, surprisingly, back to where they had most promisingly begun, with all those picaresque episodes now understandable.

Wright needed to experience the influence of the Louvre and of Atwood's Fine Arts Building close under his eyes and hand in order to make the Ward Willits House, the work that signaled his reaching full architectural maturity. Atwood's building and Wright's house both attempt to be the American Monument. The *Wanderjahre* over, Wright, like Wilhelm Meister,

Ward Willits House
Highland Park, Illinois, 1901;
view from the street

Fine Arts Building, World's Columbian Exposition
entry portico

must have been more than a little sheepish about the period, and his later accounts of it greatly differ from those laid out here, particularly insofar as heroes and villains are cast.

But there remains at least one hint that he knew and acknowledged, if only to himself, the essential value of the wandering path he had traveled. The playroom Wright added in 1895 to his little, critically important foursquare house was intended to be more than a mere recreation room; Wright's mother and his wife taught the Wright children and neighbor children there, using Friedrich Froebel's kindergarten methods. The exercises were those Wright later claimed crucial to his own development.[50] As he photographed the room, it was furnished with exotic items like Japanese fishnet floats and an Arabian Nights mural depicting a fisherman and a genie. Opposite the mural, directly above the room's only entrance and exit, Wright placed a plaster figure. It was the Nike of Samothrace.

Wright chose this classical figure to watch over what was literally the path to education. (The picture, also above the door, is a reproduction of Alma-Tadema's "A Reading from Homer," exhibited in the Fine Arts Building of the 1893 Fair.) The Nike was the patron spirit of his children's daily journey to knowledge. He must have known where the original statue stood and stands still—at the top of the main public staircase of the Louvre, an emblem of entry to the level of Perrault's grand colonnade.[51] Was this Wright's acknowledgment of that building's emblematic importance, of the academic tradition summed up in the Nike and the West Front and what it had stood for in his own education? Consciously made or not, Wright's formative *Wanderjahre* find in this gesture an appropriate summation and ending.

Frank Lloyd Wright House
photograph of playroom taken
by Wright

Evolution of the Prairie House

BY WERNER SELIGMANN

A discussion of Frank Lloyd Wright's early work should begin with a reference to American domestic architecture of the latter quarter of the nineteenth century, known through Vincent Scully's writing as "the Shingle Style."[1] Wright's work in Chicago as apprentice to Lyman Silsbee, his earliest projects, and his own house of 1889 in Oak Park provide visual evidence of a connection to the shingle style. Scully speculates that the young Frank Lloyd Wright must have had considerable interest in the work of Bruce Price, most likely available to him through publications. Furthermore, Scully postulates that the plan of Price's Kent House of 1885–86 bears a strong kinship with Wright's first work in Chicago, his own house, and therefore probably served as the source of inspiration responsible for both the similarities in plan and in architectural expression. These assumptions have been promoted ever since, but I maintain that they are too superficial and presumptuous and that they obscure rather than enhance our understanding of the significance of Frank Lloyd Wright's contributions.

It is an unfortunate but customary practice in architectural history to search for the evidence of an uninterrupted lineage from one generation of architects to another, and to be suspicious of any major individual breakthrough or creative moment. Historical investigations operate with the underlying assumption that the work of any major artist must be directly linked to contributions and influences of others, especially those whose work was ultimately overshadowed and who, through fate, were denied appropriate credit and recognition. While it is certainly true that no architect lives in a vacuum and that creative impulses are primarily based on strong reactions to existing work and ideas, it is quite unlikely that there exists, for the truly creative mind, a single, predominant inspirational source. For a true architect, the mind constitutes an unfathomable storehouse of information and impressions that, in the process of creating, lose their identity and are converted into something new. To assume the influence of shingle-style residential work on the creative development of the young Frank Lloyd Wright, it is important, for a critical discussion, to identify that work's essential characteristics.

Beginning with the siting propositions, shingle-style houses generally stand isolated as single picturesque masses in the landscape. Their gardens

are seldom more than decorated landscape surfaces and bear little relationship to the plans of the houses. The site planning is unsophisticated and lacks any distinction between front and back. The houses are elaborate in their composition and prolific in their contours. In both plan and massing, they are conglomerations of formal fragments, solids with protrusions of balconies, bay windows, verandas, and pavilions. Elaborate sets of porches are attached to, or cut into, the mass of the house. Symmetry is avoided as much as possible. Such a dissolution of the massing of the houses would be intolerable if it were not for the unifying power of their extraordinary mono-material quality and the visual presence of superimposed, horizontal divisions into a series of organizing layers.

Essentially all exterior surfaces are covered by the same material, wood shingles, in a great variety of patterns but with a similarity in scale. Walls, roofs, floors, and soffits become one. Even the windows are divided into small panes, producing the effect of similar, though shinier, textures to those of the shingles. Brick chimneys are elaborately patterned and carefully blend in scale and texture with the other surfaces of the house. It is a simple compositional strategy: The mono-material quality and similarity in scale of all the surfaces unify the complicated interlocking and intersecting volumes of the building. In addition, horizontal layering constitutes one of the most potent architectural compositional devices in organizing such a profusion of different masses, where a single volume is rarely allowed to exist as a complete shape without interference of other volumes and where the total volume has no recognizable gestalt. The elements of the house are woven together by continuous horizontal bands, gathering eaves, ridges, windows, gables, fronts, and balconies.

Two houses by McKim, Mead & White, the Robert Goelet and Isaac Bell houses in Newport, Rhode Island, serve as a demonstration. Viewed from the seaside, the Goelet House ground floor consists primarily of a deep veranda that establishes the principal, most expressive layer, enhanced by the deep shade behind the columns. The zone, or layer, of the veranda extends around the entire house. Continuing upward, one layer after another gathers different parts of the house—roof ridges and cornices, heads and sins of windows, soffits and bay windows, balcony floors and railings.

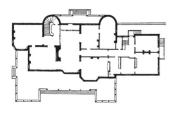

Robert Goelet House
McKim, Mead & White, Newport, Rhode Island, 1882; period exterior photograph

Robert Goelet House
plan

Bands of different shingle patterns, uninterrupted moldings, and a smooth surface of siding complete the stratification.

It would be too much to expect that such a compositional massing strategy would produce well-ordered plans. The casual nature of the plans and resultant spatial and formal problems in the interior spaces required elaborate jointing details in paneling, moldings, and decorative objects, as well as the dependence on interior decoration. It is therefore hardly surprising that the shingle style is not noted for memorable plans.

The plan of the Goelet House is typical of this. An entrance portico, symmetrically disposed between two round, towerlike protrusions and a central stair, suggests a correspondingly arranged set of rooms to follow. Instead one finds that the entrance door has been shifted to one side and that an entrance hall and reception area split the space announced by the facade. The entrance hall bears no relationship to the porch and its columnation, nor does it conform to the major features of the house: the seaside veranda and its essential symmetrical colonnade. The plan slips and slides awkwardly between the openings to the drawing room and the dining room, the fireplace and opening of the reception room, and the staircase and sitting room. For no particular reason, a servants' hallway coincides axially with the fireplace, the center feature of the house. One can only assume a deliberate casualness by the architect; the architecture remains decidedly not polemical, the result of a sleight-of-hand attitude. American pragmatism was finding its artistic expression.

The plan of the Isaac Bell House reveals the same attitude, though with greater resolution in some areas such as the dining room, the drawing room, and the reception room. The extraordinary openness of the ground-floor plan allows one to perceive the entire space, including the extensive porches; the view is interrupted only by a series of wall elements. Sliding doors, an important practical device introduced in Greek Revival houses, become a significant element in the spatial quality of shingle-style houses, particularly in the Bell House. The veranda visually extends the interior space beyond its enclosure and provides a spatial foreground layer between

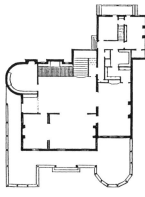

Isaac Bell House
McKim, Mead & White, Newport, Rhode Island, 1881; period exterior photograph

Isaac Bell House
plan

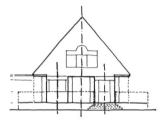

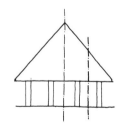

Chandler House
Bruce Price, Tuxedo Park, New York, 1885; period exterior photograph

Frank Lloyd Wright House
Oak Park, Illinois, 1889; analysis of elevations; drawn by author

inside and the uninterrupted visual expanse of the sea. Although the Bell House appears to lack correspondence in the relationship between interior spaces and the veranda, and between the window openings and the spacing of the porch columns, it is, compared with the Goelet House and other shingle-style houses, much more carefully resolved. The veranda relates more to the general distribution and structure of the plan than to the drawing and reception rooms. The square-ended projection of the veranda corresponds to the study and the vestibule, while the curved bay corresponds to the dining room. The porch is clearly an extension of the dining room, a reading that is further reinforced by the interior details. The plan of the Isaac Bell House is prophetic in terms of spatial and formal ideas. Did Frank Lloyd Wright see the plan or even consider it worth attention? This is no more supportable than the proposition that the ideas for Wright's early work derived from the houses by Bruce Price.

Frank Lloyd Wright was twenty-two years old and was working for Adler & Sullivan when he designed and built his own house in Oak Park. Although it is not an extraordinary house, we may assume that, since it was built for himself, it was intended as a statement of his ideas and architectural intentions. Since the house was clad with shingles, it might be classified as an example of the shingle style.

The house is dominated by an oversize gable projecting above a recessed ground floor with symmetrical bay windows, one of which contains the entrance door, and two projecting garden terraces at right angles to each other. The effect of the gable is one of a memorable singularity and assertiveness of will. It is clearly intended as an architectural statement. The proportions of the gable are not easy; they are the squashed and heavy proportions that appear again and again in Wright's work. The contrast to the Chandler House by Bruce Price is most informative. In the Wright House, the volume of the gable is forcefully articulated from the ground floor. The surface of the gable is tough and undifferentiated, uncompromising and of a single texture. Moldings around edges are kept to a minimum to prevent distraction

Affix stamp here

PHAIDON PRESS INC.
180 Varick Street
New York
NY 10014

Return address for USA and Canada only

PHAIDON PRESS LIMITED
Regent's Wharf
All Saints Street
London N1 9PA

Return address for UK and countries outside the USA and Canada only

Dear Reader, Books by Phaidon are recognised world-wide for their beauty, scholarship and elegance. We invite you to return this card with your name and e-mail address so that we can keep you informed of our new publications, special offers and events. Alternatively, visit us at **www.phaidon.com** to see our entire list of books, videos and stationery. Register on-line to be included on our regular e-newsletters.

Subjects in which I have a special interest

☐ Art   ☐ Contemporary Art   ☐ Architecture   ☐ Design   ☐ Photography

☐ Music   ☐ Art Videos   ☐ Fashion   ☐ Decorative Arts   ☐ *Please send me a complimentary catalogue*

	Mr/Miss/Ms	Initial	Surname
Name			
No./Street			
City			
Post code/Zip code		Country	
E-mail			

This is not an order form. To order please contact Customer Services at the appropriate address overleaf.

from the expressive power of the form. The tripartite window is a pronounced figural event in the gable. In the Chandler House the gable is
steeper and subdivided into two zones, the lower sheathed in half-timber
framing and the upper sheathed in shingles, destroying the architectural
impact of the gable. Furthermore, the feature Serlian window is reduced to
insignificance.

The two window bays at the ground floor of the Wright House produce a
highly plastic modulation of the surface underneath the prominent soffit.
The front surfaces of the bay windows are aligned with the front of the gable
and are articulated by a smooth, flat separating band that also functions perceptually as an architrave over door and windows. At the two outer corners
of the gable, Wright introduced a smooth board replacing a single row of
shingles. This is a common but effective device that allows the eave to continue to the front surface and to tie together the bay windows and gable.
Compared with the composition of the Chandler House, that of the Wright
House is marked by a much higher degree of sophistication in the articulation and differentiation of horizontal to vertical elements, of base walls to
soffit and roof.

If any similarity exists between plans of the shingle-style houses and
Wright's own house, it must be a shared openness. (In making such a comparison it should be kept in mind that this is a house by someone twenty-two
years old being compared with the work of mature architects in the prime of
their careers.) Yet aside from the overall spaciousness, there is a very different attitude pervading Wright's plan. It is imbued with a sense of order and
discipline very different even from the plan of the Bell House.

The entrance elevation of the Wright House suggests a tripartite scheme
that logically would require an entrance in the center. Shifting the entry to
the right side of the plan causes an inevitable reconfiguration. The dislocation of the entry can be compared to a force being applied to the corner of an
object, causing it to rotate. Wright accepts this as the inherent logic of the
composition and reinforces the implicit characteristics by locating a fireplace alcove at the hub, or axle, of the rotation. The pinwheeling garden
walls and the rear porch and steps join in a conceptual dance around the
core. The apparent conflict between the pronounced symmetry and tripartite division of the front of the house and the asymmetry of the entrance, the
stability of the one element and the movement of the other, is clearly deliberate. (The plan under discussion is the main-floor plan, since the plan of the
second floor is symmetrical.) The coexistence of the two aspects of the plan is
possible only through the pronounced separation of the volume of the gable
and the base. This base is a unique zone, the only part of the formal organization capable of accepting the deformations.

The plan of the house is carefully orchestrated. The entrance door is centered on the entrance hall and the treads of the stair. The opening between
the entry and living room corresponds to the stair on one side and the main
wall of the living room on the other. The bay window of the living room
aligns with the opening from the living room to the dining room, while the
inglenook responds to the solid section of the front wall and the symmetrically organized dining room.

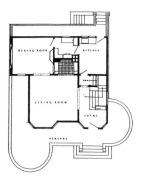

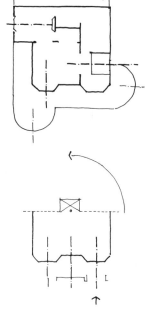

Frank Lloyd Wright House
analysis of plan; drawn by author

The interior of the house stood in contrast to other houses of the time. The interior, with simple plaster walls and straight-line, carefully positioned trim, must have appeared rather stark in comparison. There is no decoration in the house that is not inherent to its fabric. Like the exterior, the interior is emphatically striated. A continuous wainscot organizes cabinets, fireplace, and stair railing. The room openings are organized by a continuous molding and a flat, unadorned plaster band like an architrave. Beamlike projections, separated from the architrave by a continuous crenellated molding, divide the ceiling into a tartan grid.

It is apparent that the large, architrave-like band above the interior openings corresponds to the exterior blank surface above the bay window and that the crenelated molding takes the place of the molding directly beneath the soffit. The grid of ceiling beams in the living room is expressed by the smooth boards at the corner of the gable. Such direct relationship between inside and outside is rarely found in houses of the shingle style.

A comparison of two outwardly similar plans, those of the 1885 Wave Crest House in Far Rockaway, Long Island, by McKim, Mead & White, and Wright's Cooper House in LaGrange, Illinois, of 1887 or 1890, illustrates the difference in attitude between the proponents of the shingle style and Frank Lloyd Wright. It is impossible to ascertain if Wright ever knew the Wave Crest House (or the Appleton House in Lenox, Massachusetts, by the same architects); nevertheless, in comparing the two plans, one is struck by the formal rigor of the Wright plan. Noting its obvious difficulties in resolution, we may presume that the extraordinary complexity of the program presented problems beyond the skill of the young architect.

In the Cooper House, the entry, a half level below the ground floor, is entered from the *porte cochere*. After climbing a short flight of stairs, one arrives at a small square vestibule that is on axis with a large square hall with two ends serving as points of distribution. Each room in the plan retains its formal integrity. The square central hall is extended by two arms of principal rooms embracing small garden spaces. The entire plan, with the exception of the kitchen, appears to be a composition in which each room is a product of a simple basic geometric shape, relating to an overall geometric structure that includes the relationship of house to site. One only needs to compare the dining room, hall, and parlor relationship to that of the McKim, Mead & White house to understand the difference; the latter pales by comparison.

The Charnley House was built in 1891 and is officially on record as a project by Adler & Sullivan. Though it was probably designed by Frank Lloyd Wright, one must suspect, as for any office involving two strong design personalities, that the design was not without input from Sullivan. The Charnley House is a small *palazzo* composed of a simple rectangular block and, following the traditional classical prescription, is vertically divided into a base, a center section, and a top or attic. The principal facade on Astor Street consists of a tripartite division with special emphasis on the center section. The facade corresponds to an equally simple description in plan, yet beyond this apparent simplicity and orderliness lies an astounding sophistication.

The body of the house rests on a stone base of smooth ashlar. The base is raised in the center of the tripartite composition to provide a frame for the doorway. The base and the panel surrounding the doorway form an inverted T-shaped element in the facade. The center of the base is surrounded by the principal volume of the house, an inverted U-shaped mass of brick masonry that rests on the base. The mass not only interlocks with the center portion of the base but recedes at the second floor to receive an elaborate loggia with Sullivanesque ornamentation.

All the parts are interdependent and interlock like Japanese joinery. The base fits into the brick mass of the house, and in turn both secure the loggia in position, generating a powerful compositional play of visual forces, a contrast of solids and voids, of opposing direction and proportions. The forward-projecting volume of the loggia presents an opposing direction to the cavity of the brick mass; the upward direction of the base provides a counterforce to the downward direction of the door; the horizontal shape of the loggia contrasts the vertical brick flanks; and so on.

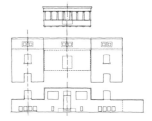

The slightly projecting base is very smooth and without detail. A delicate molding articulates the brick mass of the house from the base. The brick volumes are, typically for Wright, of Roman brick, set as smoothly as possible. The window openings, except for the attic, have no surrounding details and appear as if cut out of the wall by a sharp knife. A stone course separating the attic from the main body of the house appears as if it had been ground flush with the brick masonry. The lack of any projections and details in the two wings and the base heightens the effect of the finely detailed, figural center of the loggia. Compositionally, Wright ties base, brick walls, and openings together by placing the main-floor windows of the living room and dining room directly onto the base. The linkage between the brick wall and the base is further explained by interrupting and deleting part of the molding at the top of the base, leaving the base's flat, frontal surface to form the windowsill. The effect is an intentional, ambivalent condition of the windows appearing to belong to the base rather than to the brick mass, of an element of the base invading the upper portion of the house. This interpretation is reinforced by the neighboring windows of equal height that are set in the base panels adjacent to the entrance door. There can be no question that these moves are deliberate; for confirmation one need only examine other aspects of the house.

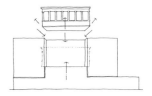

The entrance panel, the T-shaped part of the base, continues upward as one smooth surface without any articulation until it meets the loggia. Two disproportionately large and disturbingly horizontal windows flank what appears, by comparison, to be a diminutive door. The window openings are unquestionably oversized to light only the relatively small wardrobe areas and are therefore not a functional requirement. The head of the entrance door is placed lower than the windows and appears as if it had slipped out of position, producing a sensation of compositional discomfort. It has already been said that the downward motion of the door counteracts the upward direction of the panel itself. In the same way, the horizontal windows distinguish themselves from the vertical windows in the brick mass, though they are of the same height. Even the stonework in the panel surrounding the windows and the door participates in the composition by increasing the size of its vertical coursing relative to the rest of the base. The same sophistica-

James Charnley House
Frank Lloyd Wright for Adler & Sullivan, Chicago, Illinois, 1892; analysis of elevation; drawn by author

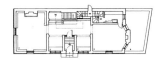

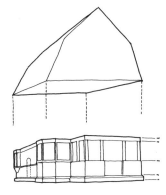

tion can be observed in the two flanking brick-masonry wings. The openings in the wall produce their own figure, reminiscent of the arrangement of openings in facades by Henry Hobson Richardson. Four vertical windows in the base and vertical single windows on the first and second floor are terminated by two horizontal windows with moldings in the attic. How does one explain these special windows? Are they meant to belong to the loggia, or to the horizontal windows, or to the base?

As already observed in his own house, the composition and proportions bear a distinct personality. They are not the proportions used by ordinary architects, nor is their composition without emotional intent. There is nothing commonplace about the rigor of the composition, the proportions, or the command of architectural expression that produces the extraordinary lyricism of the house.

Corresponding to the composition of the facade, the plan of the Charnley House is a simple three-part division with a central stair hall, a living room to one side, and a dining room to the other side. What appears at first glance to be a rather ordinary plan arrangement is made complex by a difference in direction of the two main rooms, the living room and the dining room. As in Wright's own house, there is an aspect of rotation, which will be discussed later in more detail.

Three houses from 1892, the McArthur, Blossom, and Harlan houses, illustrate Wright's continuing search for a coherent architectural language. The McArthur House is a variation of Wright's own house. The front surface of the gambrel roof is a simple uniform surface, but, unlike those of the Wright House, the openings in the composition are disconcertingly disruptive. Again Wright achieves a thoroughly articulated zone below the roof, between soffit and base, with two large bay windows embracing a projecting, roofed porch. Though it is possible to see similarities between the porch of the McArthur House and the loggia of the Charnley House, the porch is an awkward, disturbing addition. The zone between base and soffit is divided into a series of horizontal layers. Again Wright introduced an architrave-like band below the soffit and above the bay windows. The band articulates the vertical surface from the overhanging soffit and forms the heads of all the openings, including the openings of the porch. The base is a simple stone water table on which sits a sill-high brick wall. These divisions and articulations enable Wright to reinterpret the relationship between window and wall. The architrave and the sill gather the openings of the bay windows and the porch and generate a series of simple rectangular panels. Windows and wall panels join each other as a continuous band.

The McArthur House begins a series of designs for houses on narrow Chicago sites. These houses have the inherent difficulty of entry from the side, which presents an embarrassing condition in the McArthur House. Considering the street facade, one would expect the house to be entered in the center, through the attached porch. The center opening of the porch, however, is partially closed by a brick wall, giving the appearance of having been filled with brick at a later time. Despite all the obvious difficulties, the McArthur House is charming, perhaps because of its awkwardness. The plan of the house is not very distinguished, though it is possible to discover in it the presence of a pinwheel-like rotation. In its characteristics, however, it remains more like a shingle-style plan than any of Wright's other houses.

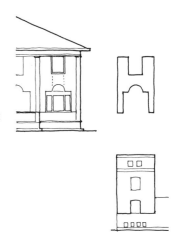

The Blossom House, adjacent to the McArthur House, occupies a corner site. Of its two most important facades, the principal facade faces Kenwood Avenue. Despite its stylistic overtones, referred to by Henry-Russell Hitchcock as "eastern traditionalist,"[2] the house is of considerably greater importance in the evolution of Wright's work than it is generally given credit for. The basic house is a simple two-story square block with a low-hipped roof. The facades again are based on a simple tripartite division and in many aspects are similar to the Charnley House. As in the Charnley House, the center section of the tripartite division is recessed (though it is rather shallow by comparison) and equipped with an apsidal portico of Ionic columns. The indentation in the facade is counteracted by the forward thrust of the porch. House and porch are interlocked so that, like the loggia of the Charnley House, the porch is no longer simply an attachment. Though the entry to the house is through the porch, Wright provides an additional narrow, rectangular zone for the stairs behind the semicircle of columns. This directs the entry into the house from the side, avoiding the conceptual difficulty of entering the convex form frontally.

A large, overhanging, relatively low-hipped roof caps the house. The tripartite facade consists of clearly articulated wall panels that are clamped between a pronounced brick base and a projecting soffit. The individual panels are framed at the corners by pilasters that are two stories high, at the top by a deep architrave, and at the base by a spandrel or sill panel surrounding a field of horizontal clapboards. A Serlian window at the lower floor and a window (of corresponding dimensions to the center section) at the bedroom level are attached to the surrounding frame and become part of a complex tracery. The windows, thematically similar to the windows in the flanking masses of the Charnley House, appear to invade the field of clapboards, one from below, another from above, producing an intentionally ambiguous situation in which windows are equally elements of the clapboard panel and parts of the surrounding frame. This deliberate assignment and compositional interdependence of the windows, pilasters, and frame suggest Wright's continuing search for an integration of the primary architectural elements of base, roof, wall, openings, and edges.

The plan of the Blossom House is much more disciplined than that of the McArthur House. It is a curiously neoclassical nine-square grid, though despite the rigidity of the grid divisions, Wright introduces a sense of rotation in the relationship of living room to dining room.

The Harlan House, also of 1892, is, as Grant Carpenter Manson calls it, "the most radical of the group in elevation and in plan."[3] Hitchcock refers to it as "Wright's best house of the early nineties, remarkable for its premonitions of his mature Prairie house a decade later."[4] Without a doubt, the house presents a surprising and significant development in the architect's work. Even in the 1950s, without the vertical members of its balcony, and in a naked, dilapidated state, the house retained an unusual sense of presence and dignity.

George Blossom House
Chicago, Illinois, 1892;
comparison of Blossom House and Charnley House elevations; drawn by author

George Blossom House
analysis of plan; drawn by author

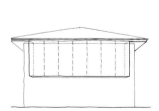

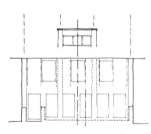

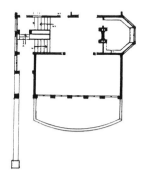

Allison Harlan House
Chicago, Illinois, 1892; period
exterior photograph

Allison Harlan House
analysis of plan and elevation;
drawn by author

Like the McArthur House, the Harlan House presents a solution to the narrow urban lot. The initial impression of the house is one of an unremarkable, simple volume with a very low-hipped roof penetrated by a large, rectangular dormer. A decorative balcony, reminiscent of the Charnley House, is attached to the house and to the roof. In front of the house is a slightly bowed brick garden wall screening a terrace. The entrance to the house is to the left between the bowed garden wall and a straight brick wall. The garden walls are the only visible brick surfaces, as the rest of the house is sheathed in wood.

The most pronounced element, and the focus of the facade, is clearly the balcony. Though the Harlan House was built only a year later than the Charnley House, its balcony is significantly different from the loggia of its predecessor. The Charnley House loggia rests on and cantilevers from a supporting base, while the Harlan House balcony appears to be suspended from the front edge of the low-hipped roof and is lightly attached to the body of the house. The openings in the balcony are decidedly square, and the decorated panels of double squares provide a composition of simple, easily read divisions. The vertical elements of the balcony make it appear as if a veil or screen had been hung before the actual facade of the house. The balcony is not simply attached but joins the front surface of the eaves. It becomes the mediating element between the frontal plane of the house and the soffit of the roof, or of the roof itself. It is equally possible to read the balcony as attached to the roof after having been dropped over the volume of the house. Whatever the interpretation may be, the result is no longer that of a box with a lid (the roof) on it.

The balcony spans two large pilasters that express the sidewalls and suggest that they support the roof. On the lower floor the area between the pilasters is divided into six equal openings. The wall surfaces between the openings have been reduced to piers so that the ground floor appears almost completely glazed. The division of openings into an even number centered on a solid, rather than void, would be very strange were it not that one of the openings serves as the entrance. The remaining five openings are, therefore, centered on the symmetrical living room. At the second floor, alternating openings in the seven divisions of the balcony correspond to three windows in the wall surface behind, with an unmistakable emphasis on the center. (The casement doors at the second floor are identical to those on the ground floor.) The dormer, composed of a row of squat windows clamped between two uprights similar to the pilasters framing the balcony below, continues the front surface to the roof. The decorations above the windows restate the decorative motif of the top of the balcony. If one traces the two piers of the dormer into the facade below, it becomes apparent that they represent a continuation of two of the piers between the windows of the ground floor. Even their details are the same. It is hardly "eccentric or capricious in design."[5] This orchestration of the facade is not an accident. A similar distribution in the number of openings occurs in the Charnley House and can be found in many of Wright's early houses.

The balcony and eaves create a transparent frontal surface. The second layer consists of the solid volume of the house. Since the balcony does not cover the entire width of the facade, a perceptible void results at the corner between the soffit, the side of the balcony, and the remaining piece of wall of the house. The result is a reentrant corner and a transition from front to side, forming a relationship much like that produced by the balcony between the front wall and the roof. The reentrant corner solution became a major theme in the development of the Prairie House.

The exterior development of the Harlan House supports the theory of Wright's deliberate search for formal, compositional systems for the integration of disparate architectural elements. Undoubtedly much in the search was intuitive, but first and foremost it was the product of a discriminating mind and the eyes of an artist.

One year later, in 1893, Wright received the commission for the Winslow House and Stable. This was the first significant commission after the establishment of his own office. It is a house of the size and stature of the Charnley House, and to this day it has been maintained in all its original splendor. Though it is only of moderate size, it has an extraordinarily majestic and serene presence. Henry-Russell Hitchcock refers to this quality as "classical,"[6] a spirit underlying the house that is undoubtedly the result of the careful distribution of the parts and refinement of proportions.

The obvious characteristics of the Winslow House are the simple rectangular volume capped by a broad overhanging hipped roof and the symmetrical, tripartite division of the front facade. The front of the house is more subtle and less articulated than those of either the Charnley or Blossom houses. Vertically, the facade is divided into a projecting stone base, a one-and one-half-story-zone of brick that extends to the sills of the second-floor windows, and, above it, a highly textured terra-cotta frieze that articulates the roof, with its broad overhang, from the mass suggested by the brick walls. The profuse texture of the ornamental frieze appears, like a pile of leaves, to be completely unstructural and promotes the perception of a physical separation of the horizontal surface of the soffit from the vertical surface of the brick mass below.

The ground-floor walls of Roman brick rest on a projecting base, or water table, and end in a molding at the bottom of the terra-cotta frieze, which simultaneously becomes the sill of the second-floor windows. The ornamen-

Allison Harlan House
analysis of elevations and reentrant corner; drawn by author

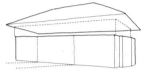

William Winslow House
River Forest, Illinois, 1893; view
from street

William Winslow House
analysis of roof and walls; drawn
by author

tal frieze is confined to a band between this molding and an elaborate profile of the soffit. In a similar manner to the McArthur House, the second-floor
windows are disposed symmetrically, resulting in a division of the frieze into
simple, rectangular panels of ornamentation. To further integrate the ornamental panels and the second-floor windows, a narrow, flat band surrounds
both panel and windows and becomes the sill as well as part of the profile of
the soffit. Window and panel have been made almost interchangeable.

The side panels of the tripartite facade are only suggested and are
marked by what appear to be two identical windows, one above the other.
The lower window is surrounded by a heavy molding, like that of a picture
frame, inserted into the flat brick surface; the upper window is produced by
the already discussed gap in the frieze. In a deliberate juxtaposition, the
upper window, an element of the frieze, is diminished in its role as an opening, while an identical window surrounded by a decorated frame is positioned, like a significant emblem, in the totally neutral brick surface of the
ground floor.

The center of the facade is expressed by a projection in the brick zone of
two shallow layers in a variation of the entrance panel of the Charnley
House. Unlike the Charnley House, the Winslow House has a projecting
molded base or water table. As part of the plastic profile of the base, Wright
introduces at its upper edge a narrow, flat stone course, flush with the surface of the brick. This course continues like a ribbon around the whole
entrance panel, effecting the base, together with the entrance panel, to
invade the corpus of the house. Furthermore, by projecting a large area of
stone pavement, like a special carpet, in front of the house, Wright extends
the stone surface of the entrance panel. The pavement is of the same width,
bordered by the same material and similar detail as the entry panel. The
pavement is almost indistinguishable from the wall.

Though similar in intention to the door panel in the Charnley House, the
Winslow entrance is even more involved. As already described, the panel is
surrounded by a band that is part of the profile of the base. The stone panel is

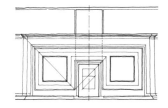

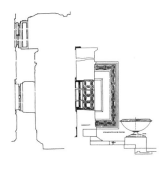

extremely compressed, low, and of extended horizontal proportions. Again, like that of the Charnley House, this entrance door is flanked by two disturbingly large windows cut severely into the panel as if excised by a sharp instrument. The opening is provided with the narrowest of moldings, in contrast to the door frame that is surrounded by the same decorative stone trim as the rest of the panel. The head of the door is considerably lower than the window openings, and one even has the impression that the area of the opening of the door is smaller than that of the adjacent windows. The Sullivanesque ornamental ribbon surrounding the door sets it off from the panel. The door may be perceived as an insertion into the panel in the same way that the panel itself may be perceived as an insertion into the mass of the house. The Winslow House door is considerably wider and proportionally more squat than that of the Charnley House, where the windows are horizontal and the door slender. The windows in the Winslow House panel are decidedly square in clear distinction to the horizontal windows in the brick wall. By surrounding the windows in the brick wall with a special stone frame, similar to but smaller in profile than the border of the entrance panel, and by locating them in proximity to the stone base, they clearly identify themselves as belonging to the entrance panel. Their low position within the brick wall and their details are visually as agitating as the large windows flanking the door. This is certainly deliberate. The Winslow House entrance is a work of exceptional compositional power.

Proportion remains a subject of much misunderstanding, though much has been written about it. Proportions are commonly considered a matter of precise mathematical relationships, equating mathematical ratios with qualities of beauty. If such assumptions were true, then anyone using numerical ratios or regulating lines would automatically design objects and buildings of beautiful proportions. Obviously this is not the case or there would be many more beautiful buildings today. I have seen many buildings that were based on the *modular* or some other proportional system, and if I had not been informed that such a system had been used by the author, I would never have guessed it. It is a matter that is very subjective, yet we are reluctant to accept proportions as a matter of the architect's personality and of the trained eye. It is particularly revealing to me that both Le Corbusier's and Frank Lloyd Wright's works, more than that of any other recent architect's, are unmistakable because of their unique sense of proportion.

Wright and Le Corbusier share a similar preference for squat, horizontal proportions—that is, the preference for slightly oblong, horizontal, almost square rectangles of a ratio of approximately 5:6 or 7:8. It is this preference for slight distortions that raises much of their work out of the ordinary. When Wright used a square, it was always for special, decidedly significant situations, such as the windows in the Winslow House entrance. A similar use of a square may be seen in the top-floor windows of Le Corbusier's Villa La Roche. The windows' proportions reveal what is personal for the artist, an intuitive sense specific to each designer. The sense of proportion of an architect is outside the production of something pleasing and may, quite possibly, result in relationships disturbing to a viewer. What I am describing is that particular inclination in proportion that goes beyond rationalization. It is

William Winslow House
analysis of proportional relations of entry facade, top, analysis of section and detail at entry, bottom; drawn by author

also closely tied to that unique quality of the personality that reveals itself in the shapes an artist produces. As the story about Amannati and the design of the Ponte Santa Trinita is told, he had asked his friend Michelangelo to assist him in the shaping of the curves. To many knowledgeable observers, these shapes are unmistakably Michelangelo's; they remain, even today in their reconstructed version, some of the most passionately felt shapes in existence, the shapes of a great artistic personality.

Mathematical proportions are without doubt important in assuring the consistency of a work. Underlying most of Frank Lloyd Wright's work is a system of dimensional grids, which he refers to as a "unit system":

> The only sure way to hold all to scale is to adopt a unit system, unit lines crossing the paper both ways, spaced as pre determined, say four feet on centers, or two feet, eight inches or whatever seems to yield the proper scale for the proposed purpose. Divisions in spacing are thus brought into a certain texture in the result; ordered scale in detail is certain to follow. A certain standardization is established here at the beginning, like the warp in the oriental rug. . . . Trained imagination is necessary to differentiate or syncopate or emphasize, to weave or play upon it consistently. Scale is really proportion. . . . Who can teach proportion? Without a sense of proportion, no one should attempt to build. This gift of sense must be the diploma nature gave to the architect.[7]

Much has been written about the rear of the Winslow House, suggesting that its complexity of intersecting planes and volumes foreshadows Wright's later work. Henry-Russell Hitchcock writes, "The fine composition of the rear of the house with its bold conjunctions of horizontal and vertical elements, its contrast of solid and void and of rectangular and polygonal forms was hardly understood by early imitators."[8] With the best of intentions, I can only consider it architecturally awkward, unresolved, and even embarrassing. The design of the rear of Wright's house is the result of purely pragmatic, not compositional, concerns. This situation remains, even in the later houses. One need only examine the back of the Willits or Martin House to find the same condition.

The Winslow House plan offers few surprises. The interiors are delightful. The width of the entrance approach extends to the interior hallway, where one confronts a slightly raised platform containing an inglenook screened by a slender row of columns and arches. The details are touching but are most unfortunately out of scale and inappropriate in the sequence of the preceding events, considering the power of the entrance facade. Such is not the case, however, in the dining area, where a set of Richardsonian columns of considerable presence articulate a pavilion-like conservatory.

The organization of the tripartite plan, rather similar to the Charnley House plan, has been overlaid with an aspect of rotation introduced by the directional changes of the library, dining room, and living room. The inglenook, unlike that in Wright's own house, does not participate in the rotation and remains statically part of the three-part division. The interior surfaces of the living room are organized by a set of continuous moldings, similar to the ornamental ribbon decorations in the entrance panel, engaging the window openings. The design intention is the same, that of

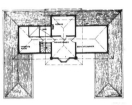

William Winslow House Stables perspective, above, and upper-level plan, below

interlocking and weaving disparate compositional elements into one homogeneous fabric.

On the north side of the house is the arched *porte cochere* (a distinct throwback to Wright's Sullivan days), which appears strangely out of context with the rest of the house. The Winslow Stable is reached through this *porte cochere*. In contrast to the main house, the forms of the stable are extremely complex. One can imagine that Wright, with the opportunity to design the stable, felt much freer to experiment. The *porte cochere* is on axis with the stable, and its arch appears to be answered by the arch over the entrance to the stable. The massing of the stable is symmetrical and pyramidal. Though the building forms a U shape enclosing a forecourt, the principal volumes are arranged in a T-shaped plan. The center volume is the tallest and carries an articulated, hipped roof. This vertical central volume appears to be penetrated by a perpendicular lower mass with its own hipped roof; its ridge adjoins the eaves of the central volume. The two wings embracing the carriage yard have their own hipped roof at another, lower level. The enclosing walls are composed of a stone base with brick walls above, topped by a band of stucco separating the brick wall from the soffit of the roof. This stucco band, similar to the terra-cotta frieze of the main house, incorporates the windows. These articulations of wall, soffit, and roof become, from this point on, important elements of Wright's architectural language. A small sketch (ca. 1904) by one of Wright's apprentices, Charles E. White, demonstrates the architectural motif of the Winslow Stable. As in the shingle-style buildings, each layer in the composition appears to be a continuous band organizing various parts of the building.

The significance of the stable lies in the diverse compositional possibilities of its apparent systematic interpenetration of volumes. It uses a device, derived from the shingle style, of continuous horizontal layers to organize the building. The barn of the Cooper House of 1887 suggested this compositional possibility, though it remained confined to the realm of shingle-style gatehouses. The Winslow Stable has a special place in the experiments of the evolutionary series of Wright's work. Almost prophetically, the stable suggests the compositional possibilities of a puzzlelike interlock of narrow, elongated volumes of a single room in width, with an exposure on three sides. This planning strategy clearly distinguishes it from any previous plans.

The stable includes other significant inventions. The central court focuses on the main entrance consisting of two large, octagonal, engaged pilasters with Sullivanesque capitals placed on patterned brick pedestals at the height of the wainscotlike band of the brick zone of the building. These pilasters support a large, widely overhanging hipped roof. At the ground level, clamped between the pilasters and pedestals, there originally was an arched decorative panel of the barn door, which has, unfortunately, been replaced by an overhead garage door.

A stucco panel with a bay window bridges the pilasters above the barn door. The face of the bay window aligns with the edge profile of the soffit and, like the Harlan House balcony, reads as if suspended from the roof between the vertical supports. In the composition of the central mass of the Winslow Stable, and earlier in the Harlan House, Wright suggested an archi-

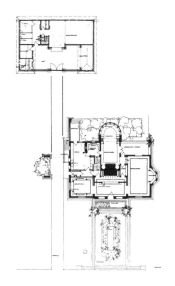

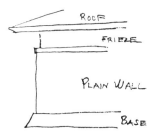

William Winslow House
ground plans of main house, right center, and stables, left above

William Winslow House Stables
sketch by Charles E. White of basic composition of wall and roof, top, and perspective analysis of central bay, bottom; drawn by author

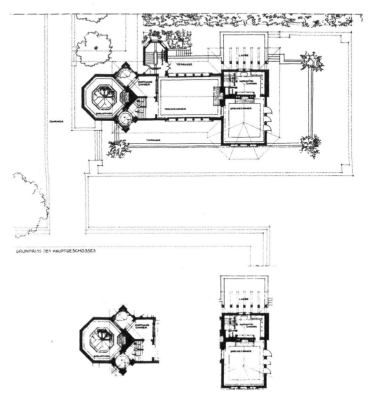

GRUNDRISS DES HAUPTGESCHOSSES

tectural language composed of a series of clearly articulated elements—vertical supports, hipped roof, and bay window.

The Winslow House was succeeded by other projects that searched for a method of integrating the building fabric. In a continuous process, with an astonishing rigor and critique of his own inventions, Wright established a repertoire of compositional devices, editing his work systematically and ridding it of inconsistencies and any vestiges of the shingle style, other than the horizontal ordering.

In this series of experiments, the McAfee House of 1894 presents the next significant stage. The plan seems to be a collection of various parts of the Cooper and Winslow houses and Wright's own house. Not surprisingly, however, each space in the house is a complete simple geometric figure carefully composed and related to the next. "In all these plans there is a rigid adherence to simple axial lines. Each principal room is managed in plan for symmetry and for a thoroughly coherent scheme of architectural treatment."[9]

A. C. McAfee House
Kenilworth, Illinois, 1894;
perspective

A. C. McAfee House
plan

A. C. McAfee House
analysis of plan elements,
bottom, drawn by author

The plan is composed of two clusters of rooms (one containing the library and entry, the other, the dining room and kitchen) that are joined by what appears on cursory view to be a loggia or breezeway—the living room. The two clusters are in a ninety-degree relationship to one another, which produces a strong rotational effect on the plan. Much like those of the Cooper House and many shingle-style houses, the living room of the McAfee House is devoted almost entirely to circulation between the two clusters—a program that remains an inevitable condition of the pinwheel plan.

The apparent openness of the living room is disappointing when one views the exterior. The windows are less integrated into the fabric than those in any of the earlier houses and remain simply a row of holes in the wall that even a border of Sullivanesque detail does not improve. The perspective drawing reveals the typical water-table base, the horizontal banding of the enclosing walls, and the broadly overhanging hipped roof. The projecting base of the Winslow House has expanded into a large platform with different-height garden walls and an elaborate arbor, resulting in a series of distinct terraces. The garden walls and the front wall of the dining room occupy the same plane and are unified by a common projecting water table, which is also the edge of the platform. The garden walls to the side of the dining room are further integrated compositionally through the interlocking motif of the triple window of the dining room. These walls have a projecting coping, which is introduced into the front surface of the dining room. The coping of the lower wall is the sill of a decorative panel, while the coping of the higher wall is the sill of the actual window openings.

The windows of the dining room are precise, severe cutouts of the masonry. The remaining wall surface between the windows has been reduced to a set of piers. The lintels are flush with the brick surface in contrast to the moldings and ornamental panels below the windows. The vertical surfaces are banded much like those of the Winslow House, though the overall form and detailing are considerably more complex. The primary zone of the house, belonging essentially to the ground floor, is increasingly more active and displays a new degree of independence from the frieze above.

Surprisingly, the octagonal library has no formal, compositional expression of its own. Its walls are part of the masonry zone of the ground floor and extend, like the terrace walls, beyond the main body of the house. A terracotta frieze at the top of the library walls appears to be out of place and does not establish any apparent relationship with anything else. In contrast, the frieze below the soffit is plain and without the decorative terracotta details of the Winslow House. It also does not include any interspersed windows. The design appears to return to the details and ideas of the McArthur House rather than to those of the Winslow House.

A. C. McAfee House
perspective analysis of base, with interlocking motif at dining-room window; drawn by author

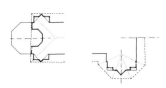

A. C. McAfee House
perspectival relationship of window to soffit, above, and planar relationship of window to soffit, below; drawn by author

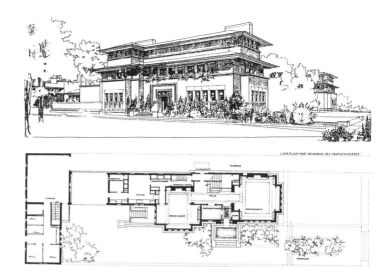

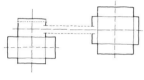

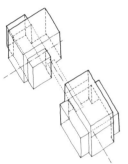

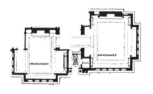

Isadore Heller House
Chicago, Illinois, 1896;
perspective

Isadore Heller House
plan

Isadore Heller House
plan analysis of two primary
rooms, top, space diagram,
axonometric analysis of two
primary rooms, center, plan
analyses of two primary rooms,
below; drawn by author

The McAfee House demonstrates another variation in the relationship of the window to soffit. The exterior treatment of the dining room wing is a thematic reversal of the condition at the library. Wright juxtaposes the rectangular soffit with the octagonal library and its almost towerlike anterooms, in contrast to an octagonal roof soffit over the rectangular dining room. At the library end, the sharp edge of the forty-five-degree volume of the anteroom joins the front edge of the soffit, while the bay windows align orthogonally with the eaves of the roof. Then, in a reversal at the dining room, the bay windows meet the roof edge at forty-five degrees, and the walls remain on the orthogonal. The juxtaposition of the two ends of the house is recapitulated in the positioning of the two massive chimneys, a confirmation of the rotational condition of the plan.

In summary, like the Winslow Stable, the McAfee House is composed of masses that are essentially a single room in width. Each wing ends at the second floor in an almost continuous zone of windows. The garden wall, the walls belonging to the ground floor, and the frieze establish an ever-greater degree of autonomy within the formal structure. In a remarkable process of articulating the various elements of his houses, Wright constantly invents new means of weaving together compositionally the various parts in richer and more sophisticated ways.

The Heller House of 1896 follows a series of projects, beginning with the Harlan and McArthur houses, for narrow and deep lots. In the drawings published in Robert C. Spencer Jr.'s *The Work of Frank Lloyd Wright* of 1900, and later in the Wasmuth edition of 1910, Wright showed the house next to another identical one, which should establish his conception of the house as a prototypal solution for the Chicago suburbs. The plan of the house is long and narrow, organized in the direction of the lot, and, as most of his other houses, is entered from the left side, thereby promoting a circular path toward the right into the front living room. The sequence begins with a small vestibule leading into a comparatively long, rather tall and narrow hallway, perpendicular to the entry. The opening of the vestibule corresponds to the landing of the stairs, which is seen behind a wooden screen through which light filters into the hall. The sequence ends in the cross-shaped living room.

The axis of the hall leads to a large opening into the living room, a high volume with four windows facing the street. This center space is flanked by two adjacent lower bays or niches. One of the niches contains the fireplace flanked by windows, while the other has bookshelves below a band of five windows. The drawing of the plan shows the pattern of the carpet, which serves an important spatial function but obscures the actual reading of the space. The living room of the Heller House is considerably more complex than that of the Winslow House. The Winslow House living room is a simple rectangular space with an attached bay window. Other than through its symmetrical disposition, the bay window does not affect the space. The short walls are punctured by equally positioned, identical windows, which are effectively integrated into the other openings of the room by a complex set of moldings. The reading of the space, however, remains that of a single, unambiguous volume. The Heller House living room is not simply a room with a bay window attached. The relatively tall, strongly directional center of the living room is spatially interwoven with the contrasting, lower, squat fireplace and bookshelf niches. The lateral direction of the lower spaces arrests and balances the forward-directional thrust of the center space.

The Heller House can be interpreted as a variation of the McAfee House. The living room of the McAfee House has been narrowed into a central hall-way, and the library has become the living room. In the Heller House, the long, narrow entrance hall connects the living room with the dining room. The dining room is a similar cross-shaped figure, placed at ninety degrees to the living room. It is again a tall space flanked by two lower niches that are, however, deeper than those of the living room. Perhaps because of their depth and their relatively narrow width in respect to the central volume, they do not alter the space as much as the niches of the living room do. While the living-room space is bilaterally symmetrical, the dining room is symmetrical only in one direction. The space is divided into three distinct zones, one belonging to the hall and the central figure, another to the two adjoining niches, and a third to the bay window. The division of the room makes it possible to read the fireplace zone of the dining room together with the living room as a primary, axial figure of the plan. This becomes even more apparent if one envisions the dining room in closer proximity to the living room. The opposing modes of rotational and stable plan figures are a constantly recurring theme, but they are never equivocal. One or the other aspect predominates, as is evident when comparing the plans of the Winslow and McAfee houses.

It is not unreasonable to consider the exterior of the Heller House as a more mature version of the Harlan House. The main low horizontal volume of the house is capped with a widely overhanging low-hipped roof that is penetrated by a narrow, vertical volume, crowned by its own hipped roof. In contrast to the Harlan House, where the relationship of the vertical divisions of the body of the house to those of the dormer were only latently legible, the readings in the Heller House are very explicit. The volumetric interpenetra-tions correspond to the internal spatial divisions of the living room and din-

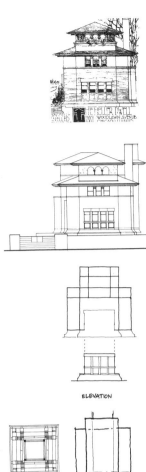

ELEVATION

WINDOW

PLAN

Isadore Heller House
analysis of elevations related to window and plan; drawn by author

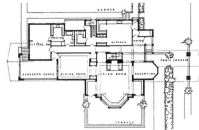

ing room. Like that of the McAfee House, the exterior form of the Heller House expresses the pinwheel structure of its plan. Living room and dining room have similar exteriors, creating two "front" elevations.

As in the Winslow and McAfee Houses, the vertical surfaces are placed on a water-table base and stratified into major horizontal zones, the ground level and the levels of the articulating friezes that collect the window and porch openings below the soffits of the two hipped roofs. The frieze of the lower volume is identified by a sill-like division and a change in the pattern of the brick surface (though Wright shows it in his drawings as stuccoed), while the frieze of the upper level has elaborate, delicately detailed reliefs by the sculptor Richard Bock. This sculptural frieze makes the central volume much lighter in appearance, and its perceived lack of structural substance, like that of the Winslow House, heightens the articulation of the roof from the solids below.

The Heller House presents another Wright experiment in the integration of the various elements of the house. The central volume of the living room extends to the front end of the soffit, creating a void between the lower brick mass and the roof. The effect produced by this trapped zone of space is that of a three-dimensional articulation through a void, rather than of the addition of architectural elements.

The front elevation of the Heller House is a further development of the dining-room fenestration of the McAfee House, with four instead of three windows. However, unlike the windows of the McAfee House, those of the Heller House are held together by a single continuous lintel of the same stone as the base. The brick piers between the openings connect lintel to base. The elaborate profile of the stone table ends at the top in a narrow continuous surface, flush with the masonry and in the same plane as the lintel. The window openings are severe and precise cutouts. While the McAfee sills respond separately to each opening, the Heller House sill is continuous across the four openings and projects beyond the front plane of the brick wall. This extension creates the visual perception that the vertical elements, the piers, penetrate the horizontal layer of the sill. The panels between the piers clearly belong to the base and the sill. As in the Winslow House, an element belonging to the base invades the corpus of the house. Here the result is very different. The elements are no longer decorative but now integrate the entire fabric. Window openings are not just holes in a wall but parts of a comprehensive compositional strategy. The visual formal interpretation of the elements of the window panels restates, at a detailed level, the relationship of the volumes expressed in the facade.

Warren Hickox House
Kankakee, Illinois, 1900; plan, left

B. Harley Bradley House
Kankakee, Illinois,1900; plan, right

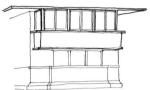

A similar perceptual and compositional relationship exists at the upper part of the house between the roof monitor and the frieze below the soffit of the lower volume. Wright intentionally distinguished the upper part of the house by reducing the openings in the friezes to three windows. The center interpenetrating volume of the window bay of the living room and the monitor is recognized in the frieze by a slight forward projection. This surface shares the same plane with the monitor above. Both are linked by the surface pattern of alternating layers of different-color bricks. The devices serve both to articulate—that is to separate—and to integrate. It should be noted that the openings in the lower frieze, contrary to Wright's published drawings, are not of equal dimensions: the center opening is narrower, rather than wider. Also, the piers between the windows are provided with Sullivanesque pedestals and capitals that make them appear as inserts and, since the shafts are brick, as elements of the wall. The monitor has a loggia of three identical arched openings with two sets of spindly double columns. The opening is peculiar since there are no engaged columns or pilasters at the edges of the frieze panels to receive the arch, making the center void appear larger than the flanking ones. The molding of the curve of the arch continues without interruption along the opening. As a result, the two double columns, like the piers below, are read alternatingly as special inserts into an opening of the frieze and as elements of the frieze.

The front elevation of the Heller House allows for multiple interpretations, as indicated in the diagrams. The facade diagrams are analogous to the multiple interpretations and readings of the plan. This formal interlocking of spaces and shapes constitutes the overall fabric of the building and reverberates thematically in the design of even the smallest details, such as the leaded-glass windows.

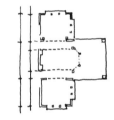

Following the Heller House, two distinct plan types emerged, the pinwheel and the tripartite or cruciform. Both were repeated in numerous variations. Two houses of 1900 in Kankakee, Illinois—the Hickox and Bradley houses—present the two types. In the following year, for the February and July issues of the *Ladies' Home Journal*, Wright presented designs for two model houses, "A Home in a Prairie Town" and "A Small House with 'Lots of Room in It.'" These houses, unlike the Kankakee houses, are obviously not subject to client pressures and idiosyncrasies, so it must be assumed that they were, for the architect, a set of ideal solutions for the small house. These houses represent the two plan types; "A Home in a Prairie Town," the tripartite, and "A Small House with 'Lots of Room in It,'" the pinwheel plan. The presentation of the two should give credence to the argument that Wright

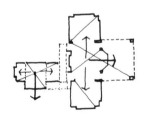

"A Home in a Prairie Town"
1900; perspective from *Ladies' Home Journal* (published 1901)

"A Home in a Prairie Town"
perspective analysis of bedroom/library corner; drawn by author

"A Home in a Prairie Town"
plan

"A Home in a Prairie Town"
analysis of plan; drawn by author

saw them as archetypal plan organizations, each embodying distinct spatial properties.

It is surprising that the first house presented was a solution based on the tripartite plan. Except for the Hickox House, which was almost synchronous with the *Ladies' Home Journal* publication, the tripartite plan is an almost entirely new plan type for Wright. It is a traditional plan type consisting of a significant center supported by adjoining spaces. It is typical of Greek Revival houses, where the house was often entered through a columned portico into a center hall, usually a stair hall, from which the circulation was distributed to either the living room to one side or the drawing or dining room to the other.

A generic problem of such a plan is that the most important space is relegated to circulation. In the plan of "A Home in a Prairie Town," Wright moves the entrance to the side, thereby approaching the main space of the house from the rear. This makes the center space the single most important space, adjoined by the secondary spaces of the dining room and the library. By maximizing the openings between the rooms, the three spaces become essentially one, producing an extraordinary sense of spaciousness. This is further heightened by the conversion of the traditional portico into a large deck or porch, which rivals the living room itself in size. A large bay window, acting like a screen between inside and outside, invades the porch and extends the living-room space perceptually by interlocking the two spaces and allowing them to be read as one.

Instead of entering the living room in the center, in accordance with the dictates of the plan, Wright occupies the center with a large fireplace, displacing the circulation to the side. The correspondence of the fireplace to the bay window produces a defined spatial zone within the living room. The plan shows a screen of columns in front of the fireplace, but it is deleted in the section. (Since its existence is an unfortunate interruption of the space, it is being deleted from this discussion.) The entrance into the living room aligns with a glazed casement door leading to the porch, creating an interstitial space between the occupiable spaces of the living room, dining room, and library. The windows in the library and dining room are similar to the windows in the Heller House and align with the openings to the living room, establishing a counteracting lateral spatial reading. Throughout, the house exhibits a careful orchestration of the various spaces within the public sequence, while, typically, the kitchen and pantry appear to be afterthoughts. The primary spatial, formal composition of the plan is stated by the living room/dining room/library configuration, though it is overlaid by the typical rotational properties produced by the off-center entry and the

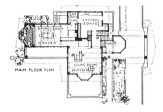

"A Small House with 'Lots of Room in It'"
1900; perspective from *Ladies' Home Journal* (published 1901)

"A Small House with 'Lots of Room in It'"
plan

subsequent relationship of the hall to the living room and the central fireplace. The relationship of the *porte cochere* to the porch reinforces this rotational reading.

The most significant achievement of this house is the quality of its spaces. The plan, with all its similarities to earlier houses, has become increasingly open. Each space and subspace is clearly defined. The spatial interfacing has become more complex and at the same time more explicit. The stair hall, the living room, and the porch are counteracted by the lateral group of spaces produced by the dining room, living room, and library. In addition, each spatial subzone is clearly defined and legible. For example, it is possible to read the dining room/living room/library relationship as *b-a-b* and also as *a-b-a-b-a*. Rooms are no longer compartmentalized as in the Winslow or Heller houses but present a new quality of space in which the viewer is presented with the simultaneous presence and experience of several spaces, a visual extension in different directions.

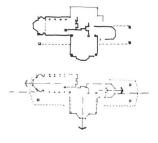

The front elevation of the house continues the experiments and investigations of the earlier houses and the Winslow Stable. The perspective view taken from the street presents the entry and the end wall of the library wing. The formal interpretation of the library wing derives unmistakably from the Harlan House. The Harlan House balcony has now been reinterpreted as a balcony with a ribbon of continuous casement windows. In the drawing, Wright shows the corner casement windows open, which must be interpreted as his desire to want to reduce even further the solidity of the flanking walls. Like the stanchions of the Harlan House balcony, the windows are aligned with the front edge of the eaves. The bay windows of the bedrooms projecting from the walls of the library produce the effect of a reentrant corner, allowing the corners of the library volume to rise uninterruptedly from base to soffit.

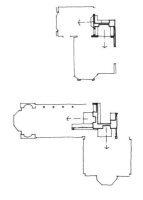

The same interlocking of volumes occurs at the library window. At the point of the introduction of the windows into the wall, the sill layer projects forward to create a flower box in front of the windows. The window opening is the result of the void between the corners of the room, the volume of the flower box, and the soffit of the bedroom bay windows. Therefore it is not just a hole in the wall but a screenlike infill of the voids, created by the joining of solids. Viewing the entire first-floor zone of the house, the only hole in the wall is reserved for the entry, whose arched opening appears to be an anachronism and pronounced inconsistency. The *porte cochere* and the living-room porch are formed by an extension of the lower roof, and each is supported by two simple solids. The garden walls, the walls surrounding the portico, and the walls at the *porte cochere* are a continuation of the sill walls below the window, an architectural solution that had its origin in the bay windows and porch of the McArthur House.

The second project published by *Ladies' Home Journal*, "A Small House with 'Lots of Room in It,'" is a reinterpretation, an advanced version, of Wright's own house of 1889. Here the pinwheel organization of the plan has become more explicit through an organizational idea that was already present in the Winslow Stable and the McAfee House, whereby each wing of the pinwheel constitutes a volume of a single room. Living room, dining room,

"A Small House with
'Lots of Room in It'"
development from Wright House;
drawn by author

"A Small House with
'Lots of Room in It'"
analysis of relation of dining and
living rooms to central fireplace;
drawn by author

and stair hall rotate around the large central fireplace mass; the inglenook of Wright's own house has now become a set of two fireplaces perpendicular to each other. The pinwheel configuration of the fireplace core and its wooden screens recapitulates the theme of the plan. The bay-window entrance condition of Wright's own house has been turned ninety degrees and forms its own articulated wing. Each wing is symmetrically organized and enriched by the addition of bay windows at the end, reinforcing the directional quality of each space.

The plan of the dining room has a great similarity to the living room of the McAfee House. However, in contrast to the McAfee House, where the windows of the living room remained essentially holes in the wall, these windows are a constituent part of the organizational fabric. The fenestration is a row of continuous-leaded casement windows that occupy the zone between the sill of the wainscot-type wall and the soffit, the same zone that was initially introduced in the 1892 McArthur House. The sectional view of the dining room published with the project gives a strong sense of the spatial effect. Assuming from the exterior perspective that the other side of the space is similar, it represents less a conventional room than an enclosed veranda. The dining room is a clarification of Wright's efforts in the evolution of a more open spatial language. By contrast, the living room of "A Small House with 'Lots of Room in It'" is only a slightly advanced version of the Winslow House. A large bay window with adjacent glazed doors opening onto a walled in terrace corresponds axially to the fireplace, but, unlike the living room of the earlier scheme for "A Home in a Prairie Town," the room remains essentially a simple, boxlike space.

The designs of the *Ladies' Home Journal* houses were published at a time when Wright was building a large number of commissions. However, none of them provide the kind of architectural clarification given by the Ward Willits House of 1902. The Willits House is the first true Prairie House. While its plan is a development of the plan for "A Small House with 'Lots of Room in It,'" the latter's stacked, folded roof planes have been abandoned in favor of the formal resolution of "A Home in a Prairie Town." The plan of the Willits House is undoubtedly of the pinwheel type, superimposed with a secondary symmetrical tripartite compositional structure.

The house develops the compositional ideas of the Winslow Stable. The form of the building consists of the primary, central, comparatively solid, vertical volume of the living room. A low extended horizontal volume intersects this volume perpendicularly. In the Willits House plan, the dining-room area, the porch, the entry, and the porte cochere are elongated considerably. The wings of the Willits House are clearly differentiated by their architectural treatment of the densely enclosed living room and the pavilionized dining room, so that the differences almost begin to conflict and affect the unity of the house. The living room, though carefully orchestrated, remains primarily a boxlike space. Even the large openings on the terrace side do not alter the perception. The windows of the sidewalls are relatively small and placed high in the wall. In contrast, the dining room dissolves into a continuous screenlike wall of glazed doors and windows. The solidity of the ending of the dining room of "A Small House with 'Lots of Room

in It'" has been converted into a constellation of different-sized piers. The last vestiges of enclosing walls have disappeared, and the residual voids between the piers have been screened with a filigree of stained-glass windows. The windows are divided into delicate patterns that not only break down the scale but also abstract the formal organization of the plan and elevations.

It is not unreasonable to suggest that the dining room of the Willits House presents a significant change in the making and shaping of architectural space. One only has to compare the space of the dining room with that of "A Small House with 'Lots of Room in It'" of the year before. There, the space ends in what appears to be a winter garden, with a bay window clamped between two exedral wall pieces. The line of doors and windows to either side of the room is held between solids. In the Willits House, the two exedral solids have been converted into four identical piers, and, though perhaps not so eloquently as in the more developed later houses, the screenlike windows continue the closure along the end of the room. The bay windows are no longer attachments but constituent parts of the enclosing system.

Almost ten years of continuous search and experimentation stand between the designs of the Winslow Stable and the Harlan House and that of

Ward Willits House
view into living room from entry foyer

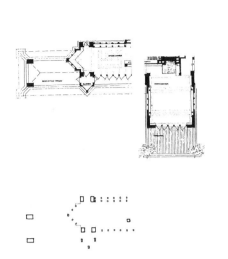

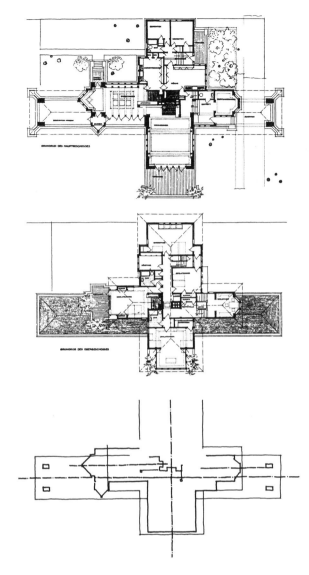

Ward Willits House
analysis of dining room and living
room, above left, and pier
formation of dining room, below;
drawn by author

Ward Willits House
plan of ground floor, top right,
and second floor, below

Ward Willits House
analysis of secondary plan
organization, bottom right;
drawn by author

the Willits House. Just as the dining room marks the conclusion of a long development, the architectural composition of the exterior, especially of the living-room wing, advances the compositional ideas of the earlier houses. The roof has been flattened further and the overhang has become larger than in any of the previous houses. The overhang extends well beyond the actual enclosed volumes. The roof is articulated from the lower solid body of the house by a continuous band of windows, producing the effect of a glazed-in porch. The bay of windows is five units wide, and its depth, which in all previous houses was merely one window deep, has now become three units deep. The overall effect is significantly different from that of any previous house, with a degree of articulation suggesting that the entire roof is floating above a series of glazed walls. Again, the window wall adjoins the edge of the eaves.

However, these windows are made part of a frontal panel of an extensive grid of glazed and white infilled panels connecting roof to base. The front elevation is a composition of rectangular surfaces and a linear grid. The white surfaces are seen as a single composition—the horizontal rectangle of the front surface of the terrace, the vertical surfaces at the corners, the square fields in the window grid, and the small white rectangles in the stained glass windows. The linear elements—the uprights between the windows together with the edge of the soffit, the copings and sills combined with the delicate lines of the divisions in the stained-glass windows—hold together, like a linear net, the various parts of the composition.

The articulation of the roof and of the resulting reentrant corner (which first appeared in the Harlan House) now creates a condition in which the walls no longer appear to support or even connect to the roof. The solid corners in the frieze of the Heller House have disappeared. The articulation of the Willits House roof is greatly exaggerated in the published photographs since the posts that support the roof at the corners are not visible.

The pinwheel condition of the plan deserves further comment. The entry, living room, and dining room are organized in a pinwheel relationship around the central fireplace core. This arrangement is overlaid by a secondary plan organization identified by the roof configuration, the piers of both the porch and the *porte cochere*, and the symmetrical disposition of the living room and terrace. The center lines of this plan figure are clearly noted in Wright's drawings. This overlay is further announced by the frontal aspect of the house, with the symmetrical condition of the living-room wing and the continuity of the front edge of the lower wing. It is therefore not surprising that Wright published photographs of the house seen frontally. This same compositional phenomenon of a stable symmetrical condition superimposed on a rotational one was already presented in the plan of his own house in 1889.

At the same time he was working on the Willits House, Wright received a commission to build a new school near Spring Green, Wisconsin—the Hillside Home School—which became part of the Taliesin drafting-room complex in 1933. Since the clients were his aunts who already had supported his career, it may be assumed that Wright had complete control of the architectural solution of the project. While almost any part of the project could serve as a demonstration of his work of that time, none of his buildings could more eloquently state his compositional ideas than the design of the assembly hall or, as one might also consider it, the living room of the school community. Following the sequence of development of his earlier projects, the solution appears almost inevitable. The assembly hall is a large pavilion sited on a gentle grassy slope. A series of sandstone piers rises out of the ground without any visual preparation. The earlier base or water table has disappeared, since, unlike his wood houses, the stone building is able to withstand direct contact with the ground. The stone piers rise to different heights and are connected to one another by thin, weblike stone walls. The largest piers, actually L-shaped walls, rise to the soffit, while sets of smaller piers step away into the site.

The large piers appear to support a widely overhanging, pyramidal red-tile roof whose edges and soffit are integrated with the masonry elements through the addition of a screen of windows. The windows are leaded-glass

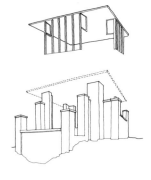

membranes without any horizontal divisions to interrupt their verticality. The tall, vertical, wooden divisions between the windows act like a series of slender piers. The trim of the eaves and the vertical mullions join and become one. Turning the corner, a small window connects the front face to the soffit and the large L-shaped pier. Roof and window can be seen as a distinct, lighter system of architectural elements invading and interlocking with heavy elements rising from the ground, an idea that was already suggested by the Harlan House and the Winslow Stable. There cannot be any question that the mullions are discrete individual architectural elements, smaller piers, since, even as the windows reach the stone wall, the mullions remain in one piece and uncompromised (a condition that must have presented considerable difficulties in detailing, to make the windows weathertight). The design of the Hillside Home School is a decisive moment in the evolution of the Prairie House, and it appears that Wright intended to use this building to summarize his inventions for the formal language of architectural space.

It is difficult to believe that only two years separate the Willits House and the Darwin Martin House. The Martin House is a unique event in architectural history in which a mature work emerged suddenly. Nothing of Wright's previous work quite prepares one for the Martin House. The plan is a more elaborate version of the *Ladies' Home Journal* house "A Home in a Prairie Town." It reads like a painting, like a delicate composition of bars and dots of different sizes arranged in a most intricate pattern; very few walls separate service areas from the primary spaces of the house. The piers follow a clear hierarchy in their assigned dimensions. The largest, the fireplace, rises the highest; the smallest are the enclosures of the heating pipes. Each element has a height allocated according to its size in plan and in accordance with Wright's own prescription. The thematic continuity observed in the Willits House pervades the Martin House from the details of the fireplace to the pigeon coop at the conservatory. Like those of the Hillside Home School assembly hall, the windows are a complete system of delicate screens filling the voids between the solids of the piers. Even the vertical members between windows at the bedroom floor are part of the system of pierlike elements articulated by delicate stained-glass windows an inch and one-half wide. The horizontal striations of the McArthur House have now become a series of continuous horizontal bands connecting and interweaving with the vertical piers, extending, as in the McAfee House, into the landscape, integrating the conservatory and the garage with the house.

The Martin House is an astounding clarification and elaboration of earlier ideas. The plan of the house utilizes the essentially static tripartite plan counteracted by an implicit aspect of rotation. The thematic ideas of the work leading to the Martin House continued to form the basis of the finest work of Frank Lloyd Wright to come, including the later Prairie Houses, the St. Mark's Tower, the Usonian Houses, and, in particular, Fallingwater. In one of his last houses, the Hagan House of 1954, near Bear Run, Wright exhibits once more the formal principles and ideas of the architectural language created in the first fifteen years of his practice.

Hillside Home School
Spring Green, Wisconsin, 1902;
period exterior photograph

Hillside Home School
analysis of roof and walls;
drawing by author

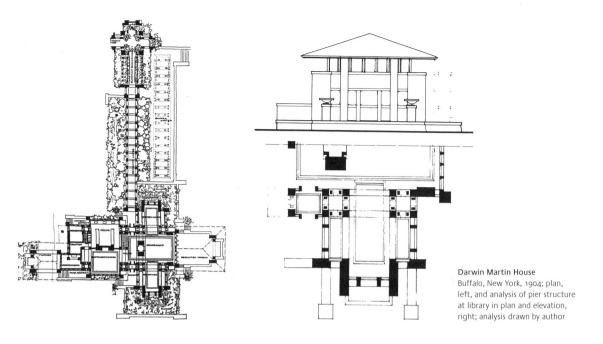

Darwin Martin House
Buffalo, New York, 1904; plan, left, and analysis of pier structure at library in plan and elevation, right; analysis drawn by author

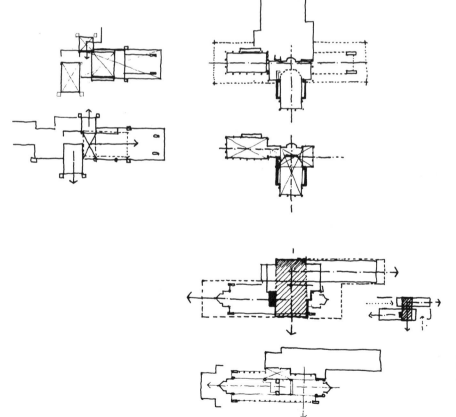

Analysis of Prairie House Plans
William Heath House, 1903, above left, Isabel Roberts House, 1908, above right, and Frederick Robie House, 1907, below; drawn by author

Chicago Frame

BY COLIN ROWE

The skeleton of the steel or concrete frame is almost certainly the most recurrent motif in contemporary architecture and is surely among the most ubiquitous of what Siegfried Giedion would have designated its *constituent elements*. Perhaps the role of the frame is most aptly summarized in the drawing by which Le Corbusier illustrated the structural system of his experimental Domino House; but, while its primary function is evident, apart from this practical value, the frame has obviously acquired a significance that is less recognized.

Apparently the neutral grid of space that is enclosed by the skeleton structure supplies us with some particularly cogent and convincing symbol, and for this reason the frame has established relationships, defined a discipline, and generated form. The frame has been the catalyst of an architecture, but one might notice that the frame has also become architecture, that contemporary architecture is almost inconceivable in its absence. Thus, one recalls innumerable buildings where the frame puts in an appearance even when not structurally necessary; one has seen buildings where the frame appears to be present when it is not; and, since the frame seems to have acquired a value quite beyond itself, one is often prepared to accept these aberrations. For, without stretching the analogy too far, it might be fair to say that the frame has come to possess a value for contemporary architecture equivalent to that of the column for classical antiquity and the Renaissance. Like the column, the frame establishes throughout the building a common ratio to which all the parts are related; and, like the vaulting bay in the Gothic cathedral, it prescribes a system to which all parts are subordinate.

It is the universality of the frame and the ease with which it has apparently directed our plastic judgment that has led to the focusing of so much attention on the Chicago commercial architecture of the 1880s and early 1890s. In Chicago, seemingly, our own interests were so directly anticipated that if, as we apparently sometimes conceive it to be, the frame structure is the essence of modern architecture, then we can only assume a relationship between ourselves and Chicago comparable to that between the High Renaissance architects and Florence, or the High Gothic architects and the Île-de-France. For, although the steel frame did make occasional undisguised appearances else-

National Life Insurance
Company Building
Chicago, Illinois, 1924; perspective
view from street

where, it was in Chicago that its formal results were most rapidly elucidated.

For some ten years, the architects of Chicago devoted themselves to the solution of typical problems of the frame; and, before the end of this time, they had achieved results that are still today unsurpassed for their elegance and economy. But, admiring these results and acknowledging this great achievement, one is still disposed to ask of these Chicago buildings whether they are indeed representatives of a "modern" architecture. Certainly the process of their design was as rational and as direct as that of any modern building is supposed to be. Certainly these buildings are lacking in both rhetoric and sentimental excess; but, also, there is about them a quality of rudimentary magnificence, a flavor at once more heroic and more brutal than is to be found in any building of the present day. These structures make no compromise with the observer; they are neither capricious nor urbane, and they display an authenticity so complete that we are disposed to accept them as facts of nature, as geological manifestations rather than as architectural achievements. "In Chicago," says Louis Sullivan, "the tall building would seem to have arisen spontaneously in response to favourable physical conditions. . . . The Future looked bright. The flag was in the breeze."[1] In Chicago we are led to believe that the slate was at last wiped clean, the break with "the styles" was made, and the route of future development defined.

The alleged debacle that overwhelmed these Chicago architects of the 1880s is common knowledge. The World Columbian Exhibition cut short their development; public taste no longer endorsed their decisions; and, although for some few their principles remained luminous, it was not until comparatively recently that their figures reemerged, sanctified and established in the pantheon of architectural progress.

Still, the disaster was never quite so complete as our sense of myth requires that it should have been; and, as we know, pockets of resistance survived which eclecticism could not obliterate, so that it was again in Chicago that a second and equally decisive contribution to present-day architecture

Fair Store
William LeBaron Jenney, Chicago, Illinois, 1889; perspective drawing of building in construction, showing steel structural frame

was made. Montgomery Schuyler, one of the most devoted apologists of the Chicago school, writing of the city in the 1890s, noticed that its architectural expressions were twofold: "places of business and places of residence." The image of Chicago that remained in the mind he found to be "the sum of innumerable impressions made up exclusively of the skyscraper of the city and the dwellings of the suburbs. Not a church enters into it," he says, "Scarcely a public building enters into it. . . . Chicago has no more a Nouvel Opera than it has a Notre Dame."[2] It was a relatively uncomplicated situation which Schuyler recognized, a situation dominated by two building types—the commercial structures of the Loop and their suburban complement. With the 1890s, the spirit of experiment may be said simply to have transferred itself from one of these types to the other, so that it became in Oak Park that Frank Lloyd Wright was to conduct those researches into architectural form whose results now seem to have been preeminently superior to any other achievement of that day. The much-publicized contributions of van de Velde, of Horta, Olbrich, Hoffmann, Loos, Perret, Mackintosh, and Voysey can only appear as irresolute and undirected when compared with the astonishing finality of these early works of Wright's, which although less implacable than the office buildings of the Loop, are every bit as conclusive. These houses are the monuments of an unerringly consistent development, and to informed observers of the time it was apparent that here a plastic statement of the very highest relevance was in process of delivery, that here a definite answer had already been given to those questions that many of the most advanced buildings of the day seemed to exist merely to propose.

The international impact of this early phase of Wright's career is a matter of history; and, if the exact influence that the publication of his work exerted in Europe may remain a matter of dispute, it can scarcely be denied that in such a building as the Gale House of 1909 Wright had already defined principles of form that at least very closely parallel those enunciated ten years later by van Doesburg or Rietveld in *de Stijl's* major architectural mon-

Mrs. Thomas Gale House
Oak Park, Illinois, 1909; period exterior photograph

Luxfer Prism Skyscraper
Chicago, Illinois, 1895;
perspective view from street

Press Building
San Francisco, California, 1912;
perspective view from street

Abraham Lincoln Center
Chicago, Illinois 1900; elevation

ument, the Schroder House of 1924. In each case the vision of an architecture as a composition of sliding planes predominates; and Wright's anticipation of this idea seems to have been as complete as Chicago's earlier anticipation of the formal role that the frame structure was destined to play.

This priority of Chicago's contribution need not imply a dependence elsewhere on it. Obviously both van Doesburg and Rietveld could claim a legitimate descent from the innovations that Cubism had introduced; obviously too, Le Corbusier's preoccupation with problems of the frame structure derives not from the steel skeleton of Chicago but from the reinforced concrete frame of Auguste Perret. But neither of these observations can obscure the apparent evidence that Chicago did seem to experience a prevision of two of the major themes of twentieth-century architecture—the frame structure and the composition of intersecting planes.

This apparent insight of Chicago's is widely recognized; but its recognition has created certain acute critical problems. Wright's achievement was scarcely likely to pass into oblivion, but the renewed consciousness of Chicago's earlier contribution, which has been stimulated by the later work of Mies van der Rohe, is responsible for a conspicuous interpretative embarrassment. Thus, although we know it to be different in kind, we are apt to feel that Mies's campus of the Illinois Institute of Technology is the polished culmination of a rationalism identical with that displayed by Jenney in the second Leiter Building, but, equally, we are obliged to believe that at least a partial explanation of the intuitive certainty, which so early distinguished Wright's work, was provided by his own personal relationship with the older masters of the Chicago school. We can understand that his own audaciousness was reinforced by their daring, his own sense of order by theirs, his own precocity by those qualities which have led so many observers to see in the commercial buildings of Chicago the most complete adumbration of contemporary forms.

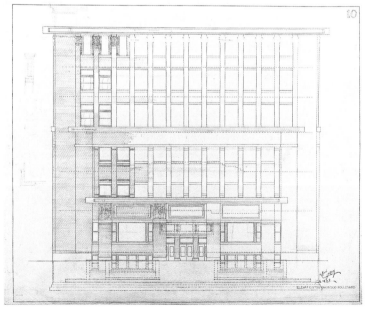

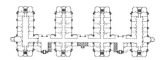

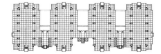

It is at this point that the judgment of the present day discovers its dilemma. We may assert that the architects of the office buildings in the Loop clarified a basic disposition of twentieth-century architecture, yet for the structural skeleton that their achievement exposed, it can only be said that Wright (who might be considered their most illustrious pupil) seems to have shown a most marked distaste.

With the exception of the Larkin Building in Buffalo and the S. C. Johnson Company's Administration Building at Racine, Wright has, of course, built no large office buildings; and it might therefore be claimed that he had no reason to employ the frame structure. Even in the Larkin Building, the cathedral-like internal space suggests a certain aversion to those conclusions of the Chicago School whose relevance is so enthusiastically acclaimed today, while in the Johnson Administration Building an entirely different conception of structure is entertained. Admittedly a number of early skyscraper projects, including the Luxfer Prism Skyscraper and the Abraham Lincoln Center, are for steel-frame buildings; and, in 1912, the Press Building for San Francisco shows a concrete frame. But in all of these designs, a Sullivanian influence is to be detected, and in none of them are we made aware of that inimitable world of Wrightian form which characterizes the domestic designs of the same years. We can believe that, in all these instances, Wright was struggling with a problem that he felt to be intractable and found to be unsympathetic. It is not until the National Life Insurance Company Skyscraper project of 1924 that this problem seems to become clarified and we find the sharp revelation of the differences in outlook that identify Wright's development as something apart from that of his predecessors in Chicago.

The classic Chicago office buildings, like the classic palaces of Renaissance Italy, were conceived as single volumes, or when situation did not permit the appearance of a volume, as single facades. Like Italian *palazzi* they overwhelm the observer by their economy of motif and consistency of theme, while, as architectural expression, they present no more than an unmodified surface exhibiting a rationally integrated and well-proportioned structure. But Wright's building is distinguished by the observance of quite contrary principles. Rather than a single structurally articulated block, it displays a highly developed composition of transparent volumes, while rather than the "static" structural solution of the frame, it presents the more "dynamic" motif of the cantilever, which had already been employed in the Imperial Hotel. Thus, while conceptually this building is radically distinct from Chicago's earlier contributions to skyscraper design whose architects had attempted neither such elaboration nor such openness, technically it is also distinct, since both its construction and its curtain wall constitute an innovation in the Chicago tradition.

According to Henry-Russell Hitchcock, "Wright has likened the special construction used in the [Imperial] Hotel to the balance of a tray on a waiter's fingers,"[3] and the structural members both in that building and in the 1924 project do seem to have been conceived in that way as a series of nuclei generating around themselves intelligible volumes of space. This preference, already presumed by Wright's old preoccupation with the central

National Life Insurance
Company Building
plans at upper floors, above, and
middle floors, below; redrawn
under editor's supervision

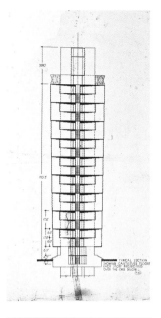

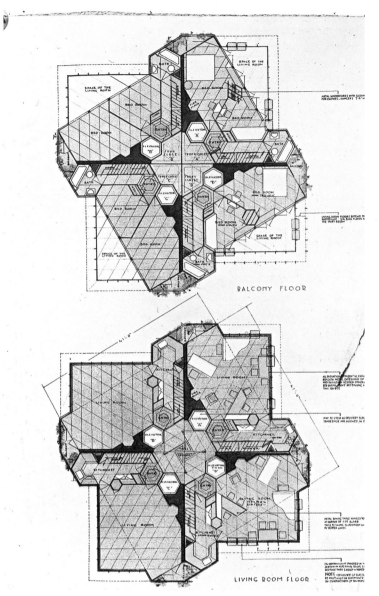

BALCONY FLOOR

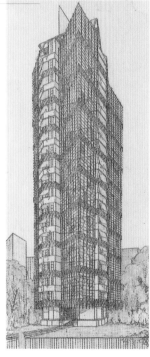

LIVING ROOM FLOOR

St. Mark's-in-the-Bouwerie
New York, New York, 1929;
section, top left

St. Mark's-in-the-Bouwerie
floor plans of two levels of typical
two-story apartment, right

St. Mark's-in-the-Bouwerie
perspective view of exterior,
bottom left

chimney stack, must explain some of his reluctance to use a regular skeletal frame, which scarcely permits such an interpretation of structure. But the indivisible fusion of structure and space, which Wright has designated "organic," is scarcely realized in either the Tokyo building or the National Life Insurance Company project, and it is not until the St. Mark's Tower scheme of 1929 that it first becomes explicit at a major scale.

The spaces created by the St. Mark's Tower are at last of an unmistakably Wrightian order, and, understandably, the tower has been the prototype for all the tall buildings by him that have followed. Aggregations of St. Mark's Towers are the basis for the 1930 apartment-house project and again for the Crystal Heights Hotel design of 1940, while the tower appears in condensed form as the laboratory building at Racine, Wisconsin, before being finally transcribed as the Price Office Building at Bartlesville, Oklahoma.

Conceptually all these structures present the nucleus of a gigantic mushroom column supporting a series of trays, which, as shown by the apartment-house and hotel projects, is implied to be systematically extensible by approaching column to column until the circumferences of their trays impinge or even overlap. Like the central core of the chimney and the real mushroom columns of the Johnson Administration Building, the idea of the St. Mark's Tower may seem to derive from the "organic" demand for the integration of space and structure; and, as fulfilling this demand, the building becomes a single, complete, and self-explanatory utterance.

As an extension of the domestic theme, the St. Mark's Tower is among Wright's most brilliant and ingenious achievements, and the virtuosity with which it is organized can only arouse the greatest admiration. Its vitality and coherence are undeniable, its plastic control little short of awe inspiring. Admitting the basic premises on which its inspiration depends, the tower is a superbly logical development, but for very many observers, both it and its derivatives can only stand as a series of enlarged question marks. Admiring it as an individual achievement, recognizing it as a highly suggestive exception, these observers are still disposed to ask whether after all it is not a most elaborate evasion of a normal and standard structural fact. The frame, by so many modern architects, has been received almost as a heaven-sent blessing. Why, one inquires, has it been so distinctly rejected on the part of Wright? Did he consider it a merely adventitious shortcut to unimportant solutions? Did he consider it too great a restriction of a "creative" freedom? Just why did he remain so very unbeguiled by Chicago's first great architectural discovery?

The question is so pressing that one may be justified in proceeding with speculation, and a number of immediate answers suggest themselves. The answer that Wright's career has been largely in the field of domestic architecture considers the problem only superficially. The use of the steel or concrete frame in domestic architecture may not be necessary, but many conspicuous monuments of the modern movement survive to prove it not abnormal. The answer that America had already discovered an alternative structure in the balloon frame is more convincing, but not completely so. Economy in America recommended the balloon frame, but in Europe economy equally recommended a brick or masonry structure, and by the more significant innovators economy's recommendations were frequently disregarded.

A partial answer has already been suggested in the notice of Wright's highly developed and individual demand for "organic" space, and here one of the most obvious differences between him and his predecessors in Chicago may be found. Louis Sullivan, for instance, was by no means typical of the Chicago school in general, but a major and unnoticed distinction between Wright and Sullivan, as also between Wright and his other Chicago predecessors, may be found in their feeling for the plan.

For Wright, as for Le Corbusier, the plan has always been a generator of form. If the plans of his earliest buildings are in no way remarkable, by the Blossom House of 1892 it is quite clear that a disciplined orchestration of spaces had become one of his primary interests, while almost any of his

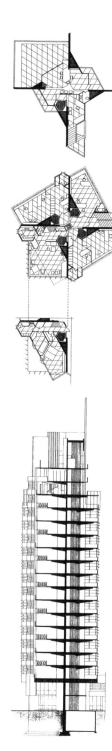

Harold C. Price Company Tower
Bartlesville, Oklahoma, 1952;
plans at three levels (lower two
plans are of typical two-story
apartments), top; and section,
bottom; both redrawn under
editor's supervision

Harold C. Price Company Tower
view from street

houses of the next thirty years will reveal how intensively this interest was sustained. Wright's *partis* (architectural schemes) develop without apparent effort. There are few lapses in his plans, few volumes where his basic rhythms are not experienced, and, in all this, he is very definitely to be distinguished from Sullivan, whose most ardent admirers have never claimed for him any highly developed interest in the formal possibilities of the plan. Sullivan's buildings may often be superb assertions of the primacy of structure, but one finds it hard to believe that for him the significance of their plans was other than a negative one. The plans of the Wainwright and Schiller buildings, for instance, are hardly those of a master, while such a plan as that of the National Farmer's Bank at Owatonna, Minnesota, will scarcely bear analysis.

Sullivan was not primarily a planner. Indeed, there was little in his practice that could prompt him to any sophisticated evaluation of the plan. Sullivan was primarily an architect of commercial buildings; and, of all buildings, the office block is obviously that without the need of any but the minimum of planning. It requires elementary circulations and a well-lit floor area; but apart from these, it neither can nor should present any spatial elaboration. Thus, the unobstructed evenly-lit floor and the indefinite number of floors that it permitted recommended the steel frame to the architects of Chicago as the answer to a practical dilemma; but also, by the nature of the context in which they explored it, they were necessarily inhibited in the exploration of its spatial possibilities.

With a lack of stylistic prejudice and with a discretion, which seem remarkable to us today, the Chicago architects projected onto their facades the neutral structure that they felt to be the reality of the frame behind. If, as was the case with Sullivan's Wainwright Building in Saint Louis and his Guaranty Building in Buffalo, it was considered aesthetically desirable that the frame should be modified, this process was rationalized in terms of the need for psychological expressiveness in the facade rather than in any need for internal spatial excitement.

With little occasion to use the frame for any other program than that of the office building, it is not surprising that the Chicago architects remained unaware of certain of its attributes, so that some explanation of Wright's unwillingness to employ it may possibly be found here. To repeat: Unlike Sullivan, who had approached architecture primarily with the object of realizing an expressive structure, Wright was, from the first, abnormally sensitive to the demands of an expressive space. These demands (one might surmise) he was compelled to satisfy, and it was only later (one might believe) that his Sullivanian training reasserted itself to demand a rationalization of this spatial achievement in terms of a generating structure. The monumental construction of the Hillside Home School suggests that a rationalization of this kind was already under way around 1902, and, by 1904, in the Martin House, this process had taken on unmistakable definition. By then, and supposing Wright to have wished a predominantly structural rationale, his space compositions were already of a richness that would scarcely permit their accommodation within any system so austere as that provided by the Chicago frame.

However, an answer along these lines, suggesting that a cause for Wright's rejection of the frame may be discovered exclusively in the nature of his formal will, can at best provide only a partial explanation of the problem, and a further reason must be offered that may, perhaps, be found to lie in the varieties of significance with which the frame has been endowed.

At the present day, Chicago's failure to arrive at any statement of the frame as a vehicle of spatial expression seems to be curious. We are now completely accustomed to regard the skeleton structure as a spatial instrument of some power, since it is, after all, some considerable time ago that a formula was evolved permitting the simultaneous appearance of both structural grid and considerable spatial complexity, and most of modern architecture, the so-called International Style, may be said to have been dependent on this formula.

In order to arrive at an equation of the demands of space and structure, Le Corbusier and Mies van der Rohe had been led to postulate their functional independence, for example, the independence of partitions from columns. In contrast, Wright's development, which may be said to proceed from a conviction as to the "organic" unity of space and structure, the International Style may be seen to issue from an assumption of the separate existence of both according to distinct laws. Wright's structure creates space or is created by it, but in the International Style an autonomous structure perforates a freely abstracted space, acting as its punctuation rather than its defining form. There is thus in the International Style no fusion of space and structure, but each in the end remains an identifiable component, and architecture is conceived not as their confluence but, rather, as their dialectical opposition, as a species of debate between them.

That a solution in these terms was possible for European innovators of the 1920s derives, among other reasons, from a particular concept of the frame which they entertained—that such a concept was neither possible, nor to be envisaged, in Chicago of the 1890s must be partly explained by a different significance which was there attributed to the skeleton structure. In Chicago it might be said that the frame was convincing as fact rather than as idea, whereas in considering the European innovators of the 1920s one cannot suppress the supposition that the frame to them was much more often an essential idea before it was an altogether reasonable fact.

In order to clarify these too-general observations, a classic Chicago building, Holabird and Roche's McClurg Building of 1899–1900, might be paralleled with an almost contemporary European building of 1897, Horta's Maison du Peuple in Brussels. Both of the projects, though different in function, are comparable as advanced buildings of their day. Both show preoccupation with problems of the frame, but it is the contrast between the rather quiet elegance of the first and the frenetic restlessness of the second which is immediately apparent. The McClurg Building is a subtle and uncomplicated statement. The Maison du Peuple is an oblique and a highly involved reference. In the McClurg Building it is possible to suppose that certain practical requirements have been accommodated; in the Maison du Peuple it is impossible not to deduce that certain theoretical desiderata have been stated. In the first, the steel frame presents itself as the solution of a specific problem, while in the second, a *cast-iron prevision of the steel frame* is exposed apparently as the manifesto of an architectural program. Holabird and Roche's structure is primarily a building; Horta's is predominantly a polemic.

There is little doubt that Horta's building cost the greater aesthetic effort, but there is almost complete certainty that Holabird and Roche's is more generally pleasing to the taste of the present day. Of Holabird and Roche's self consciousness, however, the McGlurg Building offers no assurance, while of Horta's sophistication the Maison du Peuple is indisputable evidence. In Horta's case one can guess at a hyperawareness of the response his building was likely to evoke. One can sense the anticipation of extended controversy, critical explanations, avant-garde delight, conservative horror. The Maison du Peuple is a building offered to a society, and whether society will accept or reject it, Horta still assumes its participation as an audience. That is, Horta invites reaction, and, accordingly, the Maison du Peuple exhibits a humanity that the McGlurg Building does not display. For there, rather than any subject for the discussion of a coterie, Holabird and Roche have attempted to provide no more than the rational envelope for the activities of their clients' tenants.

Indeed, if the methods followed by Holabird and Roche at this time were in any way typical of the Chicago school in general, it might safely be assumed that they were definitely not anxious that their building should involve them in any of the excitements of artistic notoriety. In the word of the French novelist Paul Bourget, whose appreciations of the Chicago school have been constantly quoted, the Chicago architects had "frankly accepted the conditions imposed by the speculator"[4]—they had limited themselves to producing buildings that should be no more than the logical instruments of investment. In other words, being in no position to make manifestos in the cause of rationalism, they were simply obliged—and within the strictest terms—to be as rational as they might.

This distinction between two styles of argument (it is really a question of the idea of mechanization versus the fact) would seem to crystallize the basic differences of approach signified by the two buildings, and it is a distinction that might be extended further. "I asked one of the successful architects of Chicago what would happen if the designer of a commercial building sacrificed the practical availableness of one of its floors to the assumed exigencies of architecture as has often been done in New York," writes Schuyler. "His answer," he continues, "[was] 'Why the word would be passed around and he would never get another one to do. No, we never try tricks on our businessmen, they are too wide awake.'"[5] The businessmen of Chicago, then, were not prepared to make sacrifices for the idea, did not require the overt architectural symbolism that was apparently necessary in New York, did not even require those fantasies on mechanistic themes that could be obtruded on the citizens of Brussels; but the Chicago architects (or some of them) were still quite aware that symbolic meaning had ever been among the necessary attributes of architecture; and if, as Schuyler infers, they were compelled to be utilitarian, they were not always unconscious of the social significance of their utilitarianism. John Root, for instance, required that the modern office building should by its "mass and proportion convey in some elemental sense an idea of the great, stable, conserving forces of modern civilization."[6]

But, even in this demand, one might continue to notice a difference between Chicago and Brussels. In Belgium, Siegfried Giedion tells us, it had been discovered that architectural *forms* were impure, that the atmosphere was "infected," and that, in consequence, architectural "progress" was there conceived as a kind of "moral revolt."[7] But the Chicago architects had been scarcely allowed to subject *forms* to so detached a scrutiny, and had they enjoyed the leisure to do so, if their conclusions had conflicted with the requirements of the speculator, it is to be doubted whether they would have been enabled to put them into practice. "The great, stable, conserving forces of modern civilization" (or, perhaps, the great, expanding forces of a *laissez-faire* economic system?) represented for Root a power which it was desirable to express. But for Horta? One must doubt if Horta recognized any such imperative. He, one suspects, had arrived at certain critical conclusions as to the nature of contemporary society and had come then to envisage his work as the architectural manifestation of these judgments.

In Belgium, it is evident, the *art nouveau* was one of those revolutionary movements essentially dependent on a highly developed program; but in Chicago, it should be clear that the structural revolution was largely without any such theoretical support.

"The Chicago activity in erecting high buildings (of solid masonry) finally attracted the attention of the local sales managers of Eastern rolling mills," Sullivan tells us, and it was *they*, he says, who conceived of the idea of a skeleton that would carry the entire weight of the building. From then on, he continues, the evolution of the steel frame "was a matter of vision in salesmanship based upon engineering imagination and technique," and, in this manner, as a *product for sale*, "the idea of the steel frame was tentatively presented to Chicago architects." Sullivan asserts:

> The passion to sell is the impelling power of American life.
> Manufacturing is subsidiary and adventitious. But selling must be based on a semblance of service—the satisfaction of a need. The need was there, the capacity to satisfy was there, but contact was not there. Then there came the flash of imagination which saw the single thing. The trick was turned and there swiftly came into being something new under the sun.[8]

The Chicago structural revolution therefore was the result of a certain combination of ruthless open-mindedness and imaginative salesmanship. On Sullivan's admission, the architects of Chicago did not *demand* the frame; it was *presented* to them, and this simple fact may explain both the rapid and dispassionate manner in which they contrived to rationalize the frame structure and the way in which so many of them were able to abandon their method for another and different one. "The architects of Chicago," Sullivan adds, "welcomed the steel frame and did something with it. The architects of the East were appalled by it and could make no contribution to it." But from Schuyler we learn the opposite, that the architects of Chicago were not very different from architects elsewhere. "They are," he writes, "different on compulsion. . . . [They have] frankly accepted the conditions imposed by the speculator, because they really are imposed, and there is no getting away from them if one would win and keep the reputation of a 'practical' architect."[9]

Taken together, these two statements are confusing, but they are not perhaps as contradictory as at first they may appear. They describe a situation; they suggest a lack of theoretical awareness; they indicate a responsiveness to the new; and they illustrate a willingness to defer to the client. And the clients, Schuyler continues,

> the men who project and finance the utilitarian buildings [are not] the most private spirited [but] they are the most public spirited body of businessmen of any commercial city in the world. [They are] the same men who are ready to incur expenditures for public purposes with a generosity and a public spirit that are elsewhere unparalleled. They are willing to make the most generous sacrifices for their city to provide it with ornaments and trophies which shall make it more than a centre of pig sticking and grain handling. They are willing to play the part of Maecenas to the fine arts, only they insist that they will not play it during business hours.

The candor of these contemporary observations goes a long way to dispose of a critical scheme to which nowadays we pay our respects. It disposes of the dichotomy between the virtuous Chicago of the Loop and the depraved Chicago of the Fair. Magnificently undisguised, the office buildings of the Loop owe something of their authenticity to their being no more than the rationalization of business requirements, and although they are social documents of the highest importance, in spite of Root's endeavors they are scarcely, in any deliberate and overt sense, cultural symbols. They were conceived as the means to achievement, and for what was thought to be that achievement itself, it is necessary to look elsewhere, presumably both to the suburban residential development and to "the ornaments and trophies," the unparalleled expenditures, and "the generous sacrifices," of which those lavished on the World Columbian exhibition can only appear the most outstanding.

Thus, seen in terms of the admirable pragmatism that actually reared the buildings of the Loop, which was responsible for their directness and lack of gesture, both these and the structures of the Fair, like opposite sides of a coin, come to appear as complementary phenomena. Because business and culture were conceived of as distinct activities, because the commercial magnates of Chicago were not willing "to play the part of Maecenas to the fine arts . . . during business hours," it was possible for the architects of Chicago to proceed with the most audacious innovations; and, because in doing so they offended no expressed social or artistic preference, no check was offered to their remorseless evolution of a basic structural logic. As Schuyler tells us, this rationalization could not have been effected in New York. It could not, as we know, have been effected in Europe. It was possible in Chicago because there *business* was without inhibition; but unhappily, as the World Columbian Exhibition proves, *business* was not for this reason irresponsible.

Thus, what to us appears to have been Chicago's success and Chicago's failure were implicit in the same conditions. A primary architectural achievement was determined by the urgency of a physical need and by the lack of a specifically architectural program, and as a result an apparently complete architectural revolution was made possible.

But just this lack of program in the end made it not possible for this revolution to become decisive. The office buildings of the Loop were undoubtedly admired by contemporaries, but, however rational their structure and however immaculate their form, it is hard to represent them as the response to any very adequately acceptable notion of society. They invoked no completely receivable public standards; they stipulated only private gain; and for the taste of the time, which had not yet sufficiently expanded, or contracted, to be able to envisage the machine with a poetic bias, they were not so much architecture as they were equipment. Stimulating facts they might be, but they were scarcely to be received as facts of culture.

Distinctions such as these which go some way to clarify the other than technical and formal differences between a McGlurg Building and a Maison du Peuple, necessarily elicit questions of attitudes and mythologies. Such questions might possibly be brought into sharper focus by the brief analysis of a further pair of buildings that, in *Space, Time and Architecture*, Siegfried Giedion was led to compare: Daniel Burnham's Reliance Building of 1894 and Mies van der Rohe's Glass Tower project of 1921.

It is the similarity of these buildings with which Giedion is concerned; and, in terms of a Wölfflinian background such as his, which tends to ignore problems of content (implying that roughly identical forms suppose roughly approximate meaning), it is the common likeness of the American building and the German project which will command attention. But, if we have here, very obviously, two extensively glazed office towers, it is fundamentally not their similarity but their unlikeness which should most seriously involve us—and particularly so since to emphasize their unlikeness need not involve any great exercise of critical acuity.

Thus, we have a building and a would-be building—the concrete result of a particular problem and the abstract solution of a general one—a building that services an existing requirement and a proposal that relates to a possible future need. We have something that answers and something that anticipates. The Reliance Building rises above the streets of a commercial capital; the Glass Tower soars against a background of wooded hills and above an agglomeration of Gothic roofs, and if we can scarcely believe the Glass Tower to be a necessity in this toy city of an older Germany, then also we may know it to be not only the project for an office building but also the advertisement for a cause. For, if the Reliance Building, very largely, *is what it is*, the Glass Tower, like the Maison du Peuple, very patently, *is something which it does not profess to be—a highly charged symbolic statement*. While the Reliance Building is almost devoid of ideological overtones, the Glass Tower is not only a presumptive building but also an implicit social criticism.

From these differences of innuendo both building and project derive their weakness and their strength: if the one lacks poetry, the other lacks prose. Burnham, one might guess, is someone optimistic about the present, who accepts the prevailing ethos and who envisages the future as its continuance, while Mies, one could suppose, is someone not able to collaborate with the existing, who is constrained to reject the established and who insists only on the justifications of time. Which is, of course, grossly to simplify. But, if Burnham's complicity and Mies's protestation may be equally respectable, they do impose on their respective products a quite different significance; and, while the Reliance Building remains a direct answer to a technical and functional problem, the Glass Tower, by inferring an altruistic order of society, continues to be both much less and much more than this. For, unlike the Reliance Building, the Glass Tower engages both the moral and the aesthetic interests of our Utopian sentiment.

In Europe in the 1920s it might be said that the tall building such as Mies had here projected presented itself primarily as a symbol rather than as any object for use. It was a symbol of a technologically oriented future society and, to a lesser degree, a symbol of an America which seemed to anticipate that future development; and thus, by circumstances, the idea of the tall building in Europe became imbued with an ultimate persuasiveness that in America it could not possess. In Europe the idea of the tall building was apt to be the substance of a dream, but in America the idea become fact was prone to be little more than an aspect of a too-emphatic reality. "The American engineers," wrote Le Corbusier, "overwhelm with their calculations our expiring architecture." They are not, he asserts, "in pursuit of an architectural idea"; rather they are "simply guided by the results of calculation."[10] And although this may have been as true of the Chicago architects of the 1880s as Le Corbusier felt it to be of the engineers of a later date, it is only too obvious that the skyscrapers of the *Ville Radieuse* are not the results of any comparable calculation. Rather they betray a mind preoccupied with the ideal order of things. They exude what Dr. Johnson described as "the grandeur of generality." They are rational abstractions on the theme of the American skyscraper rather than what the American skyscraper itself was—a rational calculation (with trimmings if necessary) as to the worthwhile investment in a given speculation.

We are here at the place where different conceptions as to what is real, rational, and logical exist side-by-side and to stigmatize any as being radical or conservative, irrelevant or relevant, is not to be very useful. Simply, it is best to say that, while in Chicago certain things (the culmination of an unbridled empiricism?) were done, there was an incapacity and/or refusal to conceive of them in other than specific terms, that they were construed without any regard for their proper enormity, that one has to look to those European skyscrapers that existed only in the imagination to discover any even slightly plausible, public rationale for what Chicago had produced, and that, just as the European innovators of the 1920s related the skyscraper not simply to commerce but to a notion of society as a whole—even implying that the skyscraper might be an agent of social salvation—so these same innovators also ascribed an ideal, a general, and an abstract function to the structural frame. In America, the skeleton structure, conceived to be of utilitarian value, had been rationalized by the predominantly utilitarian tone of a Chicago business community, but in Europe, where simple issues of utility could not assume such prominence, it was given a logical form only by the sustained volition of an architectural intelligentsia. For these avowed protagonists of revolution the frame became something other than what it had been for Chicago: it became an answer not to the specific problem—office building—but to the universal problem—architecture.

Le Corbusier's drawing for the Domino House represents precisely such an evaluation and is perhaps the perfect illustration of the meaning of the frame for the International Style. What we have here is not so much a structure as an icon, an object of faith which is to act as a guarantee of authenticity, an outward sign of a new order, an assurance against lapse into private license, a discipline by means of which an invertebrate expressionism can be reduced to the appearance of reason.

Disposed to accept the frame as much for reasons of dogma as utility, the International Style was therefore led to envisage it as enforcing a system with which the architect was *obliged* to come to terms, and, for this reason, the exponents of the International Style felt themselves under the necessity of evolving an equation between the demands of space and the demands of the skeleton structure. In Chicago, a comparable obligation could not exist, and, therefore, no comparable equation could be reached. There, where the frame served as no more than empirical convenience, it was scarcely to be invested with ideal significance. It could predicate no city of tomorrow. Indeed, by the 1890s, it predicated a city of yesterday; its overtones were not so much prophetic as they were historical. Since it soon became increasingly possible to see the frame structure as the nakedly irresponsible agent of a too-ruthless commercialism, so it became—not around the office building conceived as paradigmatic and normative, but around the alternative program of the residence—that idealist and progressivist sentiment was able to effect a coherent expression.

It is by such inferences that Wright's continual unwillingness to use the frame may possibly be explained. He was too close to it to be able to invest it with the iconographic content that it later came to possess, too close to the Loop to feel other than its abrasiveness and constriction, and too undetached from Chicago to see the city as the idea that it so nearly is and that the reforming mind of the 1920s might have wished it to become.

To attribute an iconographic content to the frame was, for better or worse (and unknowingly), the prerogative of the International Style. If one can understand how for Mies, preoccupied with anonymity—again with the idea and not the fact—his own self-willed and classical anonymity could be equated with the empirical anonymousness of the Chicago school, one may also perceive how for other exponents and apologists of the International Style, unacquainted with the sociopolitical detail of the Loop, its technical and formal effects must often have been seen as derived from the same details as had comparable effects in Europe. That is, because structural renovation was unconsciously associated with the will to complete social reform, the Loop could be seen as some surreptitious adumbration of a *Ville Radieuse* and that therefore an intention could be ascribed to its architects that they did not possess.

But in the Loop, unlike the *Ville Radieuse*, the world was accepted as found, and while it remains ironic that, in terms of forms, this midwestern acceptance should be so comparable to the discoveries of European protest, it should not be curious that for Wright the forms conceivable as representing protest should have to be sought elsewhere.

Architectural Practice and Social Vision in Wright's Early Designs

BY GWENDOLYN WRIGHT

A familiar and self-avowed image portrays Frank Lloyd Wright as a resolute individualist, a man who believed that "democracy can live by genius alone. Its very soul is individuality."[1] Yet this individualism should not be read as an acknowledgment of the total independence of the self. Wright, like all people, existed in a society. Public and professional matrices significantly affected his development as an architect. The posture of the solitary genius—which he promoted and architectural historians have largely endorsed—cannot therefore be accepted without qualification. This artist, especially in the early decades of his career, engaged the world around him, and it, in turn, engaged him.

As we all know, Wright believed that place mattered. By this, he implied more than simply natural surroundings; he meant as well urban social life and the public exchange of ideas. For example, in a speech from 1918, at a time when Wright had in fact broken with former colleagues, he insisted that "in a great workshop like Chicago this creative power germinates."[2] He went on to praise that city's celebrated poets and playwrights, the educators and journalists of his generation, all men and women he admired. Each of these individuals, Wright declared, sought "to state his inspiration in terms of the character and need of his own time—of his own people; and his work is no less universal on that account."[3]

One can do for Wright himself what he called for in his appreciation of John Dewey, Jane Addams, Carl Sandburg, and others; that is, to locate his highly personal and innovative achievements in the larger context of the culture where he lived and worked. Wright's idiomatic statements, his buildings, and his public involvements disclose definite patterns of relation to urban cultural life. The task goes well beyond appraising the individual man, for the premonitions and echoes of his ideas in both the popular culture and the prevailing architectural canon of the time also deserve attention. This approach relies on recent methods of cultural history, in addition to established architectural studies, in an effort to analyze and situate Wright in the public sphere.[4] As Wright asserted in his 1918 speech, this makes the individual artist no less impressive and sometimes even more so.

In his autobiography, Wright declared that "the real book is between the lines. It is true of any serious book concerned with culture."[5] One way to read between the lines is to examine Wright's designs in relation to his specific points of contact with the architectural profession and with the general cul-

Oak Park Studio
Oak Park, Illinois, 1895; view of
Wright's private office

ture of the cities where he worked. Looking somewhat obliquely at the first major stage of his career, a period that focused primarily on the Chicago area between 1893 and his departure for Japan and California in 1916, one can, in fact, discern an articulate, highly engaged public persona.

The public dimensions of Wright's work that concern me here cluster in three distinct but interrelated realms. The first is Wright's relations with the larger cultural milieu of Chicago and the progressive Midwest during his early career. What did he learn from the various groups and organizations concerned with cities, and especially with homes, that thrived there? Why, in turn, did he seek to educate these groups about his own ideas on architectural criticism, pedagogical theories, and political philosophy?

The second realm is Wright's relations with his profession (a topic David Van Zanten insightfully analyzes at length in chapter 5 of this volume). This was a critical time, when Illinois architects debated the stylistic merits of Beaux-Arts civic centers, modern skyscrapers, and the vernacular house design espoused by local builders. In 1897, after seventeen years of lobbying, prominent practitioners persuaded the state legislature to enact the first American licensing law for architects, strengthening their hand over that of builders, engineers, contractors, and clients. Wright recognized the influence of innovators in his discipline first as a recipient, working with Louis Sullivan, then as a force himself, speaking and writing in several professional settings, sharing both Steinway Hall in Chicago and his Oak Park studio with other young architects of sympathetic bent.[6] Here, too, he is more than the ferocious individualist. But despite these positive contacts, Wright felt a profound distrust for the newly emerging profession of architecture, based on the conviction that neither architectural schools nor professional organizations would necessarily embody, or even uphold, the lofty goals he set for the ideal architect. "The architect is something yet to be classified," he told a group of fellow critics in 1900, "though he is tagged with a license in Illinois. So is the banana peddler and the chiropodist."[7]

Third, of course, are the designs Wright undertook during this time that belong to the "public realm," both executed work and projects. These include commissions for multiple dwellings; office buildings; clubs, resorts, and pleasure gardens; religious buildings; commercial structures; and, finally, several variations of neighborhood plans that grouped private and public structures together. While Wright's best-known work from this period is certainly his many single-family Prairie Houses, these other building types were by no means rare occurrences, nor were they insignificant. In them, Wright tried to formulate his principles about recreation and education, work and leisure, community and privacy.

In order to understand Wright's personal connections to public life in Chicago and his architectural prescriptions for the public world, one has to understand how he saw the public and private spheres in relation to each other. This involves analyzing both his life and his work. He did not yet want to separate himself as a private individual or as an artist from the public world, nor did he see the private house as a resolutely isolated, self-contained phenomenon. The design of such dwellings, and especially their possible siting in a residential community, had public connotations. Domestic

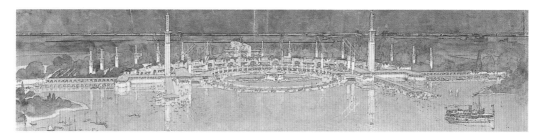

architecture—for him and for all of us—does not necessarily imply a denial of or alternative to public buildings or public spaces but, rather, a full vision of human experience that relates the two realms of public and private life.

Of course, in his own personal life Wright failed to reconcile the tension among individual freedom, family ties, and community mores, eventually fleeing his wife and children in 1909. He seemed sufficiently aware of the conflicts in his own life never to suggest that his own behavior represented a real solution for others. Even as he idealized home and family, Wright tried not to pose a radical split between the private and public world, realizing the difficulties this would present.

The commitment to what Wright later called "the sense of shelter"[8] did not represent an aversion to public life or a lack of interest in settings designed for public activities—even in primarily residential suburbs. Instead, Wright distinctly understood the close interrelation between the public and private, between inside and outside the home—a theme of great importance to the progressives who spoke of "domesticating politics," "urban house-keeping," and "democratic homes" in planned communities.[9]

To be sure, Wright also saw the Prairie House as a haven, even a sanctum, for familial intimacy. Architecturally, he represented this concept in the low sheltering roof, the central hearth, the protected front facade and entrance. These features figure prominently in all of Wright's single-family domestic designs from this period, not least of which is the Robie House. His efforts to give strong visual expression to the idea of family togetherness drew directly from nineteenth-century associationist theories, notably John Ruskin, and from popular American literature on what is now called the "cult of domesticity." However, in his perception of the home as a place for educating children or encouraging feminine values, Wright went beyond the insular focus of most Victorian writings. He did not, for instance, see the beauties and pleasures of home as a means to deter a child's interest in the world outside; quite the contrary, Wright wanted both the formal playroom and the myriad details throughout a house to enliven a child's sense of drama, ambition, and wonder—all of which would be carried into the public world outside the home, much like the Froebel kindergarten theories that seemingly so impressed him as a child. In fact, one can trace a progressive abstraction of conventional domestic imagery in the course of this first stage of Wright's career.

Moreover, a major element of Wright's work involves his consciousness of the changing status of women. In his joint translation of Ellen Key's 1912 feminist tract, *Love and Ethics*, undertaken with Mamah Bourthwick Cheney during their sojourn abroad, Wright extolled the modern woman's right to work and productivity outside the home so long as she did not

Waller Wolf Lake Amusement Park
Chicago, Illinois, 1895; aerial perspective view from lake

renege on her duties to those she loved. Much earlier, he had echoed the crusading modernist metaphors of the domestic scientists when he, too, spoke of the kitchen as "a chemist's laboratory" or "the working department."[10] Recognizing the work that went on in the home gave this space the worldly aura of a professional setting—although such alterations did not really address women's isolation in their homes. Still, for Wright, the private implied not the antithesis of the public world but, rather, a complement to it.

There are other ways in which Wright sought to harmonize the public and private spheres, even in commissions for single-family houses. He spoke, for instance, of an aesthetic diversity that would represent and enhance individuality; yet his definition of individuality specifically rejected the Victorian cult of the private dwelling, which had purported that the architecture of each home should reflect something of the owner's taste and personality. Essentially, when Wright endorsed the private home as a form of personal expression, he did not mean it to portray the personal quirks of the client but, rather, to show the architect's artistic ability to represent an idealized expression of a class of clients "with unspoiled instincts and untainted ideals."[11] The clients' existing home was important to study, "not so much for what it is as for what it may become."[12] Wright believed that the architect should "*characterize* men and women in enduring building materials for their betterment and the edification of their kind" and that it was crude commercialism to "give the client what he wants and let him go at that."[13] Here then was another ambiguous interplay of private individualism and public mission, in which the architect created what the clients could only imagine, designing a unique dwelling that would inspire its residents and idealize their role in the larger culture.

It is worth noting that many people in the 1890s recognized the paradoxes of Victorian domesticity: the isolation of women and children in the home now generated a demand for experience outside the domestic sphere that seemed, to some, a sign of the family's imminent demise; the hodgepodge of so many styles, so many flamboyant details, made residential streets seem frenzied, competitive battlefields for attention rather than peaceful communities. In addition to Wright, other Americans were also looking for a new resolution, both social and architectural, that would give "private architecture" a higher public meaning without destroying its rightful importance to the individual and the family. Journalist Herbert Croly, then editor of the *Architectural Record*, also favored a greater homogeneity in housing; he believed such architecture would be "characteristic of American democracy at its best," because it could strengthen a sense of commitment to the common good, to the public realm over the private.[14] Home economist Helen Campbell called on architects and housewives to discard Victorian norms for a simpler aesthetic, a less restrictive family life, and a greater participation in civic affairs, especially for women.[15] Both commentators praised Wright's work in particular, for they recognized his desire to assert the public presence of architecture, even—or perhaps especially—that of private architecture.[16]

Wright did not conceive homes only as individual, detached residences. He was more than willing to think of and design housing types that could be

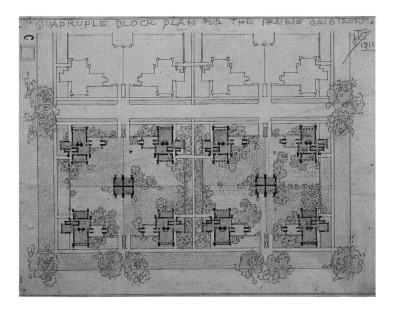

duplicated *en masse*, so that private residences (with distinct variations by socioeconomic class) would become a unified, collective whole and a context for, rather than an alternative to, public places for the community.

Moreover, several of his earliest independent designs involved multiple dwellings rather than single-family houses: the Roloson Apartments of 1894, Francisco Terrace, the Francis Apartments, and the Waller Apartments of 1895 each showed Wright's ability to balance ornamental details with an elegant, symmetrical massing that gave unity and dignity to the whole. Aesthetically and socially, the larger complexes of 1895 focused on various combinations of central public spaces—garden courts, hallways, and entrances—which shielded occupants from the street and dramatized the points where they came together. Wright's associate Robert C. Spencer Jr., describing Francisco Terrace in *The Brickbuilder*, specifically praised the "great courtyard which is treated as a small public garden and on which the majority of apartment entrances face."[17]

To be sure, these commissions came at a time when the city and the nation had entered a major economic depression, debilitating for the building industry and especially for a new architectural firm. The "flat fever" of the 1880s now sustained a weakened housing market, and permits for multiple units surpassed those for private residences in the Chicago area.[18] Yet the projects should not seem any less significant because of these conditions. The aesthetic Wright used was very much in keeping with the social and formal concerns, especially the desire for a simplified facade and harmonious urban design in residential neighborhoods, put forward by such local home economists and housing reformers as professors Marian Talbot, Sophonisba Breckinridge, and Charles Zueblin, all of the University of Chicago's Department of Sociology.[19] In an effort to promote greater efficiency, economy, and community life, they, too, advocated a more subdued and publicly oriented approach to residential design for both private dwellings and apartment buildings.

Quadruple Block Plan
1903; plan of four clustered houses, mirror-image configuration

Like these Chicago reformers, Wright did believe that residential areas needed to be kept separate from commercial and industrial districts. Hence, he designed specific building types for each kind of district or "zone." In the same vein, in 1911, the Chicago City Council, while actively promoting industrial and commercial growth, also limited the right to build or convert for nonresidential purposes in neighborhoods. When, at a more intimate scale, Wright spoke of "protecting" each house and household from its neighbors, the risk to him was the likelihood of an unsightly yard or a pretentious, ugly dwelling next door; he feared an assault on the public side of domestic architecture rather than the danger of public intrusions on private family life.[20] "Individuality is a national ideal," he told European admirers, yet the world of private rights had definite bounds, even in Wright's rarefied vision of American suburbs. The social and aesthetic risk of "petty individualism" required skillful residential planning to assure the public of good design.[21]

If Wright believed in insulating the family and protecting the Prairie House from irresponsible individualism, this did not imply isolation. He understood residential planning in the progressive context of providing all members of a family with access to a variety of public activities.[22] Consider, for example, his noncompetitive entry to the Chicago City Club's 1913 competition for a model suburb southwest of the city. Wright's plan featured a range of places for residents to congregate, informally and formally. Settings for outdoor sports were paramount, such as a children's park, playing fields, a gymnasium and natatorium, and lagoons for skating, swimming, and sailing. The scheme also contained modern commercial and cultural centers, including a "moving picture building" and a large structure to house the domestic-science group with its model kindergarten. The private by no means overshadowed or ostracized the public in Wright's plan. He was familiar with and responsive to these many kinds of public institutions.

Even the street pattern of Wright's community plan stressed a distinctly urban conception. The continuation of Chicago's grid underscored a connection to the larger city, and the groupings of apartment buildings and public places along the periphery created subordinate "business centers" for the 2,582 households living in the proposed new development.[23] While Wright did try to ensure privacy for the well-to-do in a spacious, single-family "Residence Park" (specifying a density there of four houses to the block), he also encouraged social mixing among classes by concentrating the generous public spaces. If domestic architecture was indisputably the central element in the scheme, it was cast in a light similar to that in the statement of Randolph Bourne, the brilliant young critic on literary and urban affairs for the *New Republic*, when he appraised the Chicago Club exhibit:

> Until architects and engineers, school children and the average citizen begin to think of the town or village not merely as a geographical expression or a business enterprise, but as a communal house to be made as well ordered and beautiful as the citizen would make his home, social effort will lack a focus and civic good-will and enterprise be shadowy and unreal.[24]

Lexington Terrace Apartments
Chicago, Illinois, 1901;
perspective of central courtyard

To be sure, the arrangement of structures and spaces in Wright's proposal involved formal choices, perhaps even more than social prerogatives. While he was unquestionably concerned about the allocation of public and private space and the development of specific building types for different users or kinds of users, Wright concentrated as much on pattern as on community planning in all his large-scale projects. This was true from the first Quadruple Block Plan of 1900 through the Como Orchards summer colony of 1910 and even Broadacre City of the 1930s. Yet the evident tendency to think in terms of formal configurations should not lead us to reduce all social implications to abstract patterns; the two should obviously coexist in good urban design. Wright's conception of urbanity at this time was, in truth, somewhat narrow and artificial, with little real understanding of the problems of poverty, ethnicity, or commercial growth. All the same, public life did imply the diversity and interchange of urban culture, even in an orderly suburb, if the planner wanted a true community. As Wright noted in pencil on an early sketch of the Quadruple Block Plan, "This plan is arranged on the assumption that the community interests are of greater value to the whole."[25]

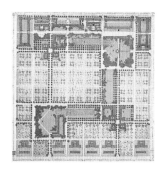

I would certainly not want to suggest by this that Wright trusted any aspect of the public realm without qualification. Both popular culture and public institutions, whether as large as the American Institute of Architects or as local as the Chicago Art Institute, came under his reproach. While the city indeed brought together creative people, he realized that its elite cultural institutions could overly formalize their ability to challenge the establishment, while more populist ones could easily dilute or pass over the most innovative ideas. This situation again suggests Wright's acute sense of the larger cultural issues of the time. Attacks on mass culture resounded with an awareness of what consumer capitalism was doing to vernacular conceptions of beauty and usefulness. "Blame the market if you will," he told the University Guild of Evanston as early as 1896, "but words fail to express proper contempt for the meaningless average household's stuff."[26]

Moreover, Wright grasped the fundamental tension between the liberal arena of public life at its best, with open access to new ideas, and the limited sphere of professional life, controlling access to important public responsibilities. Though he revered the "ideal" architect, he recognized the narrowly self-serving aspects of recent professionalization; it was not, in his definition, truly public.[27] Not only in architecture but also in law, medicine, social work, and education, those who sought to consolidate were openly motivated by a desire to restrict outside competition and control judicious experimentation.[28]

When he spoke to fellow practitioners, Wright stressed the need to break the narrow confines of professionalism, to go beyond petty concerns for commercial success and academic correctness. The architect, he implored, should listen to and learn from the public world around him, not only from individual clients and civic organizations, but also from sociological and industrial experts in other fields. Speaking to the Chicago chapter of the Architectural League, soon after he had taken part in founding this group of radical young designers, he insisted that an enterprising professional should work to acquire:

> a more intimate knowledge of conditions he is to be called upon to
> serve.... [The] problems of today, the problems of transportation, ware-

Model Quarter Section
1913; site plan for a model suburb outside Chicago; designed for Chicago City Club competition

housing, city building are his problems. Elevated railway systems and freight stations, manufactures, grain elevators and office buildings, the housing of highly organized industries . . . [the] housing of a people.[29]
These public issues, as much social as formal, represented his understanding of professional responsibilities.

Wright hoped that clients and critics would insist on such reform in the profession. He deplored, and thought they should too, the sorry state of the average contemporary architect, whose "duty to the public as professional man [is being] laid aside...and merely because the public was ignorant of its claim."[30] Acknowledging to a congress of the Central Art Association his own misgivings about "the untrained incompetence of the architectural sales-man of today," he called on the large crowd of listeners to place higher demands on architects, and on landlords, too.[31] The public needed an impe-tus to take the initiative, and Wright would provide it; together they would force architects to live up to human and artistic standards, rather than mere licensing standards.

In essence, both instances involved a personal dilemma as well as a social critique. Struggling to achieve his high ideals for cultural unity around "the finer forces," Wright denounced selfishness and commercialism wher-ever he saw it.[32] As a result, he often lambasted the popular and the profes-sional world around him for not living up to his standards. Whether he spoke of the majority of architects or the majority of homeowners, Wright condemned the tendency of allowing architecture to become what he called "a commodity—a thing."[33] His disdain expressed both a personal despair and a larger, quite perceptive analysis of a particular culture at a particular time. Household arts and general literature were indeed highly commercialized, and architects, like other professionals, were being transformed from "a cul-tured minority integrated with the whole of society to . . . a minority cul-ture."[34] Wright grasped the public significance of both changes.

Conversely, Wright's embittered claim that his own work was dispar-aged tended to evade reality. To the critics, he later wrote, it "was not only new, but destructive heresy—ridiculous eccentricity."[35] Even the title of his second *Ladies' Home Journal* model house of 1901, "A Small House with 'Lots of Room in It,'" suggests a preemptive strike at this perceived popular opin-ion, a sneer at the middle-class audience that seemed to challenge his aes-thetic with commonplace preoccupations. The text, moreover, blamed the "average homeowner" for this design, more conservative than his first house for the magazine, suggesting that he was having to pander to conventional taste. Personality inevitably came into play, as Wright projected counter-parts of his own exaggerated emotions—grandeur and scorn—onto an anonymous public. Yet what happened to the architectural profession, to the engaged Chicago public of the progressive years, and to Wright himself such that, by 1914, the popular democracy he had championed in his early speeches had become "the Gospel of Mediocrity," and he could look back on those years as a time when he had been "alone, absolutely alone?"[36]

In reality, both the popular and the professional worlds of Chicago responded, early and positively, though never unreservedly, to Wright's house designs. In his profession, Wright enjoyed a surprising amount of respect for a man so young and iconoclastic, as witnessed in the large section of the Chicago Architectural Club's 1902 exhibition devoted to his Oak Park studio, when Wright was only thirty-two years old, or his one-man show at the Chicago Art Institute in 1907, or the abundant coverage of his buildings and his ideas in the professional press after Robert Spencer's first article in 1900 in the *Architectural Review*. In 1897, just after its founding in Chicago, and again several years later, *House Beautiful* published laudatory articles on Wright's home and studio and even his aesthetics of flower arranging—somewhat before he came to the attention of architectural magazines.[37] A wide variety of organizations invited him to speak, especially women's groups interested in the arts or in community improvement, such as the Central Art Association, the College Endowment Association, and the Chicago Woman's Club. Even the local building workers, whom Wright so roundly criticized for their lack of standards, found photographs of his houses, accompanied by positive captions, in the Chicago-based *National Builder*, while *Construction News* reprinted his 1900 speech to the Architectural League of America.[38]

Wright, for all his early devotion to public education and good professional rapport, came to want nothing less than uncompromised authority and total devotion. This became evident in his anger at former associates, first manifested in 1914, when Wright decided that they had reduced his principles to a mere style: "piracy, lunacy, plunder, imitation, adulation, or what you will."[39] However, only a few years before, he had still spoken positively of Drummond, Griffin, Mahony, Perkins, Garden, and Spencer as his colleagues in a collective enterprise: "The New School of the Middle West."[40] Trusting other designers who espoused the same beliefs—and this could be taken as Wright's criterion for the title of "architect"—he had pleaded with popular audiences to "go, then, to an architect . . . and let this trained artist . . . work out your salvation in mortar, stone and bricks," to trust the "artist, brain of all brains."[41] Early in his career Wright seemed willing to conceive of his architecture in collective terms.

It could be said that when one is defining an artistic position, whether as an architect, a painter, or a writer, the surrounding world, both public and professional, seems indeed quite significant. Later, once the philosophy and the persona are formed, the larger world takes on less intellectual importance. In Wright's case, this resolution did not come until the later 1920s, when the magnificent geometry of his California houses and his rural vision of Broadacre utopia first took concrete shape. In a certain sense, Chicago itself seemed to fail him after 1910, as the locus of American intellectual life shifted more toward New York and Southern California. Wright, too, departed for these other regions, despite his plea in 1918 that the "independence of Chicago, her integrity, her destiny as the Capital of the American Spirit, is at stake!"[42] But Wright himself no longer believed that the public, even that of Chicago, could be trusted or motivated, except in the most abstract terms of "democracy" or "Usonia"—his new term for authoritarian collectivity.

In the early stage of his career, Wright had wanted to share ideas with the Chicago public and even to pick up cues from popular sources. His lectures sought to create a knowledgeable, critical clientele who would demand, good, modern, "American" work of any architect they might hire. Of course, they should use their knowledge, he contended, to choose the right architect and then give him total autonomy. All the same, Wright did see the exchange of ideas with popular audiences as an important step in creating the architecture he wanted. In 1898 he pledged to the Central Art Association, an organization promoting general education in the arts, that "the true place of the artist" is "with the people of average means with a genuine love for the beautiful without a pretense of critical ability, but an innate desire to learn."[43] In addition, he wanted "mutual education" among skilled factory workers, artists, and social scientists as the basis of Chicago's Arts and Crafts Society, founded at Hull House in 1897 with Wright as a charter member.[44] A belief in the possibility of creating in the city a new moral world, as well as a new physical setting, meant that he needed cohorts, and he sought them in many different milieus.

It would be naive to assume that Wright's engagement with public organizations was only for the purpose of mutual education. Certainly it served to promote himself and his practice. While the search for clients and admirers motivated much of his public speaking, I am willing to argue that Wright's principal goal was moral and artistic education. The architect, he told the Chicago Woman's Club, must "play the part of preacher."[45] At the height of his speaking career, addressing the fledgling Architectural League in Chicago, Wright castigated those who joined clubs or engaged in public speaking before wealthy potential clients in a vainglorious effort to "work the wires for the job."[46]

Instead of trying to woo clients with beguiling speeches and pleasant chat, Wright had a mission. He wanted to educate. Elected to the board of directors of the Central Art Association in 1898, he spoke on "Art in the Home" at their annual congress in Chicago that year. "A process of elimination is the necessity now," he explained; "to get rid of the load of meaningless things that choke the modern home; to get rid of them by teaching the teachable that many things considered necessities now are really not so."[47]

Wright then went on to elaborate, for the first time, the basic tenets of the Prairie House—even before he had carried them out fully in a design. "I should like to give you a set of golden rules for house building," he told his audience, and thereupon outlined the principles of organic design, simplicity, horizontality, the open plan, natural materials, and integral furnishings. That same year, this organization had commissioned Wright, as part of a committee with George Dean and Robert Spencer, to design a model house, "typical of American architecture," to be displayed at the Trans Mississippi Exposition.[48] While the design apparently did not materialize, the organization's recognition of Wright's significance—and of his potential appeal— closely parallels Edward Bok's decision, three years later, to commission the first of three model houses from Wright for the *Ladies' Home Journal*.[49] In these various instances, as Wright worked out the basic principles and the fundamental design elements of the Prairie House, he did so in conjunction with other architects and closely engaged with the general public.

Even in this context, Wright's goal was not yet self-promotion as a radical new seer, an Olympian individual, for he openly acknowledged that the points he made had become "well established principles" for popular audiences.[50] He knew and did not hide the fact that many aspects of his crusade paralleled the recent surge of general interest in reforming housing and house design: the suggestions of the domestic scientists, arts and crafts enthusiasts, public-health workers, and progressive reformers who dominated Chicago's schools, clubs, and political groups. One such example is Chicago's City Club, where Wright was a charter member of the City Planning Committee beginning 1908 (after the reform-minded businessmen voted to admit professionals). Here he attended lectures about European planning reforms, zoning, industrialization, overcrowding, and improved housing. Around 1911, when Taliesin I was under construction, Wright retired from active participation. As the organization itself was becoming increasingly oriented toward official intervention by experts rather than open-minded discussion of urban issues, Wright had less in common with its goals.[51]

Before this turn toward expertise, a general debate about urban problems, especially housing reform, infused many settings in Chicago. In the University of Chicago's Sociology Department and the Armour Institute of Technology, in the Commercial Club and the Woman's City Club, in numerous artistic and social groups around the city, a wide variety of men and women were talking about architectural change, and Wright had wanted to join in the debate. They strongly endorsed simpler, less obtrusive houses that would supposedly be more healthy and make a minimum demand on the housewife. On a larger urbanistic level, these groups called for lower densities, better use of modern industrial technology, and neighborhood facilities to encourage local civic improvements. Wright incorporated their environmental and aesthetic predilections; he shared their fascination with modern technology; he also responded to the more abstract desires for family stability, community life, the preservation of nature, and individuality in modern cities, reiterating the popular progressive belief that these qualities could be enhanced through good domestic architecture. Wright raised the architectural expression of such concerns to a remarkable, unquestionably innovative aesthetic level. But his principles were not as bizarre or disliked or out of pace as he sometimes implied.

While Wright did occasionally let fly savage attacks on both popular and professional taste, he wanted reform rather than a truly radical break. He was not, and did not consider himself, an isolated theorist. His goal was a general reorientation of the culture as much as an individual redefinition of architectural style. "You see," he told a meeting of Chicago businessmen as late as 1916 while promoting his partially prefabricated building system, "you in America have been led to believe that an artist is necessarily a queer fellow—one divorced from the life around him. The contrary is true."[52]

Both the means and the guiding philosophy for this reform involved a new synthesis of high culture and popular culture. As Henry-Russell Hitchcock (1944) and Neil Levine (1982) have shown, Wright drew many aspects of his horizontal formality from Beaux-Arts principles of design, while he abandoned the historical styles then so fashionable among the elite and their architects. Likewise, recognizing common chords in the popular appeals for domestic reform in the 1890s—the desire for economical and efficient layouts, space-saving built-in furnishings, modern technology, natural "organic" materials, and a new openness to the outdoors—he emphasized these aspects of his own work. Nonetheless, he made it clear that some facets of vernacular taste, notably the clumsy cult of "simplicity" in the Craftsman or Mission style and the fussy clutter of those who imitated the wealthy, deserved only contempt.[53] Wright's new idiom, as one would expect from a great cultural innovator, drew selectively from the prevailing themes in both popular and high culture, while denouncing others vehemently.

To a certain extent the desire to educate the public, giving their functional and social concerns a more refined architectural expression, sprang from Wright's conception of modern democracy. Sound ideas would flourish, he believed (or at least hoped), if they were freely exchanged, first in discussion and then in building design. Awareness and daring were essential qualities, yet to be effective they had to be unleashed among the larger population, not only among a privileged few. This belief in turn influenced Wright's aversion to an artistic fraternity. He spurned the idea of an academy that lionized an established, old-fashioned elite; nor would he accept the philosophy of "art for art's sake." He instead chastised innovative artists who saw no hope, or at least no potential, in popular American culture.[54]

For a time, Wright kept in step with other cultural progressives of the period. Correspondence schools, extension programs, and public lectures proliferated in the 1890s and early 1900s, especially since they could usually offer prominent speakers from a range of disciplines who wanted to reach a general audience with their ideas. John Dewey, for example, like Wright a frequent visitor to Hull House, attacked the sterility of formal education and its detachment from the issues of real life. At this stage, his philosophy of "experimental idealism" sought to strengthen democracy, by which he meant not mere governmental procedures but individuals involved in community education and community action. "I believe," Dewey declared, "that the individual who is to be educated is a social individual, and that society is an organic union of individuals."[55]

For Wright the key to innovation and social action was obviously formal and spatial. Yet he insisted on the critical role of discourse that could affirm and disseminate new ideas. In "The Art and Craft of the Machine," a lecture presented at Hull House in 1901 at the invitation of Jane Addams, he stressed the importance of spreading modern ideas about architecture as broadly as possible through the culture, making the most of the printing technology that had revolutionized all aspects of modern life. Wright described the demise, since the Renaissance, of architecture's ancient and noble primacy, due to the growing reliance on the printed text and lithograph, rather than the built form itself, to rally human sentiment. Now, he argued, it was time for the artist to accept these circumstances and to embrace the machine. By this he meant not only using new technology to erect skyscrapers and mass-produced houses but also creating a new interest in the more abstract problems and potentials of factory production, printed communication, and urban life.

Wright took up these same themes of discourse and education a year later in 1902 when lecturing to the Chicago Woman's Club. Founded in 1876, this organization had become the second-largest women's club in the country. Its members now promoted involvement in civic reform, especially where it regarded women, though they still revered art and literature as refined expressions of feminine culture. Adroitly, Wright sensed how to connect his Prairie House program with the audience's dual commitment to reform and uplift, on the one hand, and fine art and good books, on the other. Again stressing the theme of general education about house design and domestic life, he repeated his argument about the meaning of public discourse. Words, he said, as well as the designs they described, could teach everyone to demand a level of quality that had once been the province of the very rich. "*The power of types*," Wright declared emphatically, "*will have translated the beauty of the Cathedral to the homes of the people*; a broadening of the base on which the growing beauty of the world should now rest."[56] Once stated and freely discussed among popular audiences, this new domestic aesthetic could then be built, and built in quantity rather than isolated cases. The aesthetic would take hold in popular culture because the architect had demonstrated how closely it adhered to other progressive ideas being talked about at the same time; it resonated. Such was Wright's goal: "to translate the better thoughts of this time to the terms of environment that make the modern home."[57]

Wright specifically connected his positive, though cautious, image of the machine with his attitudes of the time about urbanity. If, in Wright's words, "the great city" was man's "first great machine . . . the greatest of machines," it was also, he contended, "at once his glory and menace."[58] Again he needed to use words—delivering lectures, writing articles, and listening to others—in order to find the right design solutions for the modern city. The goal was both specific and general: to delineate contemporary office buildings and economical dwellings and then to address the problems of overcrowded streets, inadequate parks, cacophony, and psychological stress. All of this was being done as part of the larger goal of managing, and thereby benefiting fully from, this "greatest of machines," the modern metropolis.

When Wright asserted the issues that preoccupied him at this time—high densities, sprawl, pollution, congestion, anomie—he wanted to tackle them directly in cities and their outlying suburbs. In 1913 he still advocated the familiar progressive tactics of public debate and the use of advanced technology in a decidedly urban setting (one that, typical of the time, included near suburbs as part of a complex metropolitan region), unlike his later schemes of Broadacre City, an isolated, agrarian retreat. This difference is not unrelated to his altered connection, both personal and professional, to the public. By the 1930s Wright saw public relations as a rather simplistic matter of dealing with adoring disciples and antagonistic critics. Earlier in his career the public had meant something quite different: he had indeed been a part of a shared world of mutual education, and he had profited from that complex exchange of ideas.

Schooling the Prairie School
Wright's Early Style as a
Communicable System

BY DAVID VAN ZANTEN

It is a truism that Frank Lloyd Wright's Prairie style is abstract, a vocabulary of simple geometric forms without historical or natural reference.[1] His Prairie designs are commonly described as compositions of planes or blocks placed in such loose juxtaposition that they seem to float in relation to each other and to the ground. "In his houses," Sigfried Giedion wrote, "Wright takes the traditional flat surfaces and dissects them in strips horizontally organized and in a juxtaposed play with solid volumes. . . . He dissects the wall and puts it together again with an unprecedented . . . keenness of imagination."[2]

This observation, in turn, introduced the temptation to link Wright's Prairie designs with cubist paintings, executed independently a few years afterward in Europe, and to the open, planar abstraction of the International Style, evolving after cubism in the 1920s. Thus Giedion concluded that Wright "is impelled unconsciously by the same forces that worked in Europe about ten years later."

This quality of abstraction in Wright's work is usually attributed to his childhood training with Froebel's modular kindergarten blocks.[3] This childhood experience may be historically dubious. When the anecdote was first set down by his friend Robert C. Spencer Jr. in his 1900 review of Wright's work, the story was specifically attributed to his teacher mother, as if Wright himself was doubtful of its validity.[4] Nonetheless, the influence of the kindergarten blocks has proved to be a tremendously resilient myth. The reason would seem to be that, while embracing the characterization of the Prairie work as abstract, it also evokes another, more rarely expressed Prairie-school quality: a sense of assembly, of being composed of modular units which that be arranged in many different patterns, reminiscent less of cubist paintings than of constructions made with children's blocks.

This second quality—modular assembly—is as important as the quality of abstraction. Because Wright has been cited as a precursor and justifier of abstraction in modern art generally, the quality of modular assembly in his work has been interpreted as traces of his effort to achieve geometric purity. Yet this may be putting the cart before the horse, especially when discussing the Chicago school, where the foremost issue was always how one put things together. In what follows, I would like to reverse this paradigm and examine the hypothesis that geometric purity was a means to expedite assembly, achieving a kind of mechanical self-generation in architectural composition.

Wright's Prairie style coincided with his Oak Park studio, the office and drafting room attached to his own house, which he organized cooperatively.[5] One of the draftsmen, Barry Byrne, later intimated that Wright had developed a system by which a design could be made to generate itself on the office's boards once Wright had set it in motion with a general layout:

> Endowed as he was with an unerring sense of the third dimension, Mr. Wright, in the period between 1902 and 1909 when I was in the studio, always arrived at his designs in plan and elevation, the last usually the determining one upon which perspectives were based. In the later years of my tutelage, and when projects were turned over to me to develop into working drawings, the original Wright-made studies would come into my hands with the plan established and the main theme of the exterior design clearly defined in elevation. The development of all implied but not delineated portions of the project then became the problem of the student draftsman, subject to the master's approval and often to his correction.[6]

More immediately and more tellingly, Byrne's contemporary in the studio Charles E. White wrote a friend in 1904:

> Wright's greatest contribution to architecture, I think, is his unit system of design. All his plans are composed of units grouped in a symmetrical or systematic way. The unit usually employed is the casement window unit of about these proportions. These units are varied in number and size to suit each particular case, and the unit decided upon, is consistently carried through every portion of the plan. His process of getting up a new design is the reverse of that usually employed. Most men outline the strictly utilitarian requirements, choose their style, and then mold the design along those lines, whereas Wright develops his unit first, then fits his design to the requirements as much as possible, or rather, fits the requirements to the design. I do not mean by this that he ignores the requirements, but rather that he approaches his work in a broad-minded, architectural way and never allows any of the petty wants of his client to interfere with the architectural expression of his design. The petty wishes are taken care of by a sort of absorption and suppression within the scope of the plan as a whole and are never allowed to interfere with the system, or skeleton of the house.[7]

Observing the results rather than the process, the Dutch architect J. J. P. Oud wrote of Wright's work, "Whereas it is a peculiarity of our day, that even the work of the cleverest nearly always betrays how it grew to be as it is, with Wright everything is, without being at all perceptible any mental exertion to produce."[8] Wright himself summarily confirms all this in the same issue of *Wendingen*:

> All the buildings I have built—large and small—are fabricated upon a unit system—as the pile of a rug is stitched into the warp. Thus each structure is an ordered fabric—rhythm and consistent scale of parts and economy of construction are greatly facilitated by this simple expedient—a mechanical one, absorbed in a final result to which it has given a more consistent texture, a more tenuous quality as a whole.[9]

In analyzing Wright's Prairie buildings themselves, Richard MacCormac in 1968 observed an irregular grid—a "tartan grid," to use his excellent term— implicit in Wright's Prairie plans into which the piers defining his spaces are fitted. The tartan grid itself is continuous and indeterminate: Wright can move his pier blocks around within it to define whatever configuration of spaces he wishes. It can be made to organize square, rectangular, T shaped, or whatever volume while maintaining unity and harmony. It can be filled in with just a few elements to generate a small house, like the Gale dwelling in Oak Park, or made to organize many elements to produce a large one, like the Darwin Martin mansion in Buffalo. It remains an elastic system with unifying limits and clearly defined axes of development so that compositions suggest their own elaboration. Once a design was "set moving" by Wright, all that his draftsmen had to do was carry it through to completion.

In this context Wright's often reiterated reference to Bach's fugues as his source of inspiration makes great sense. Music is a unit system, and these fugues were specific musical compositions that derived elaborate self-generating configurations from simple arithmetic progressions.

That quality that has been called abstraction in Wright's Prairie work was therefore the manifestation of a self-propelling system of design. As such, it was a posited solution to Sullivan's search for an organic, natural architecture which acknowledged that nature, in building, was necessarily transformed into blocks instead of curves. Wright depicted his own designing of ornament in Sullivan's office as geometricizing, whereas Sullivan's curled and interwove.[10] But we should take this even more broadly: Wright's whole enterprise was the accomplishment of Sullivan's general objectives by geometric means.

To explain this we must examine one of the most pivotal and at the same time most vaguely perceived incidents in the history of the Chicago school.[11] In 1900—when Wright simultaneously set up his Oak Park studio and "discovered" his unit system of design—he and Sullivan, as well as a group of young admirers and sympathizers, were engaged in the formulation and proclamation of an organic system of composition designated by the now-forgotten catchphrase "pure design." Their objective was to create not individual works of genius but a whole new school of American architecture, and for a moment they seemed to believe they would succeed.

The story begins in 1885 with the founding of the Chicago Architectural Club, composed of draftsmen not senior enough to be architects in their own right. It became increasingly active in the support of the Arts and Crafts movement during the 1890s, and its executive positions were slowly taken over by its younger members.[12] In 1897, club rooms were made available to them in the newly completed Art Institute building by the director, W. M. R. French. Originally a landscape architect himself, French had already founded an architecture program in 1889 at the Art Institute, headed at first by Sullivan's friend and collaborator Louis J. Millet. Toward the end of 1899, French hired a young architect from Detroit, Emil Lorch, as assistant director to manage architectural affairs at the Art Institute. Lorch, who soon became an officer of the club, joined the other young members of the Architectural Club in mounting an impressive exhibition of their work in 1900, including an Arts and Crafts room and a separate display of the work of Frank Lloyd Wright.[13] The newly emerged Prairie style was prominent in the next two annual exhibitions: the 1901 catalog included Wright's essay "The Art and Craft of the Machine," and the 1902 catalog devoted a separate section to Wright's designs.

At about this same time, in 1899, the club joined a number of other clubs of younger architects in founding the Architectural League of America at a convention in Cleveland.[14] It was a confederation of architectural clubs dedicated to the Arts and Crafts enterprise of creating an indigenous American architecture. "Progress before Precedent" was their motto, and archaeological revivalism was the object of their special wrath. Wright was one of the Chicago delegates to the first meeting of the league in 1899 (along with Max Dunning, George R. Dean, Dwight Perkins, Birch Burdette Long, and Peter B. Wight), and Sullivan sent a message that was the "event of the meeting."[15] In 1900, the league held its second meeting in Sullivan's Auditorium Building in Chicago, and Sullivan and Wright both gave addresses. During this same period, 1901–02, Sullivan wrote his "Kindergarten Chats" in the Cleveland-based *Interstate Architect*.

In spite of the fact that Sullivan forced Wright out of his office in 1893, they continued to work toward the same end, if not side by side. A group of admirers gathered around them, and all were broadcasting a message meant for a wider audience. What was it? Sullivan's addresses to the Architectural League in 1899 and 1900 and his "Kindergarten Chats" were obtuse, evoking the spirit of a natural, democratic architecture while avoiding specific details.[16] The same was true of Wright's 1900 address, "The Architect."[17] The other addresses to the Architectural League, however, focused on the more concrete problem of principles of architectural design. The Beaux-Arts and the Arts and Crafts points of view were presented.[18] Lorch tried to make a synthesis and coined the phrase "pure design." Basing his ideas on the writings of several contemporary art theorists, he attempted to formulate a purely abstract, geometric system of design. His ideas set the tone for the third convention of the Architectural League, held at the University of Pennsylvania in Philadelphia in 1901.[19]

Soon, however, this movement lost its impetus. After 1902, Wright and the Prairie architects were relegated to a more modest position in the Chicago Architectural Club exhibitions and catalogs. Subsequent conventions of the Architectural League were less exciting and fruitful. The league became merely an umbrella organization for architectural clubs, then it faded away. Lorch himself was let go from the Art Institute by French in the summer of 1901. He then went to Harvard to study "pure design" under one of its advocates, Denman Ross, before commencing, in 1906, his very distinguished career as head of the Department of Architecture at the University of Michigan.[20]

In 1908, the young Chicago Prairie school architect Thomas Tallmadge published an article in *Architectural Review* entitled "The 'Chicago School.'"[21] It was the first precise use of that now-familiar term, applied to the movement that Tallmadge viewed as initiated by Sullivan and carried on by Wright and the Prairie designers.[22] He wrote of the Chicagoans' rejection of historical precedent and of their combined efforts in the Architectural League:

> Some ten years ago much effort and ingenuity were expended in trying to prove this very thing [that the genius of the American people, the materials at their disposal, and the purposes of their buildings, do not justify the use in their architecture of *any* of the historic styles]. A great deal of time and energy was wasted in articles and speeches, in which the classic style, the Ecole des Beaux-Arts, Broadway, and pretty nearly everything else not in accord with the new dispensation, were attacked and derided. The slogan of "Progress before Precedent" was adopted—a motto as illogical as it was tactless, as it contained the assumption that progress and precedent could not journey together. Like Abbé Sieyes' epoch-making riddle, "What is the third estate?" so our Revolutionary tribunal had its great question, "What is pure design?" The answers filled the columns of the architectural papers for some little time, until it was pretty well demonstrated that nobody knew what it was, but that pretty near everybody was willing to produce a pet theory on the subject. In looking back at this period of agitation, the storm center of which was Chicago and its Architectural Club, it is not hard to see that all of the pleading was on one side. Very little interest and no concern was manifested by the East, and it is largely on this account that the Chicago men have arrived at their present entirely healthy and proper point of view and position. Divorcing themselves from the idea that they were the evangelists of a new dispensation and that their mission in life was to convert the architectural unregenerated and to fill the land with the glories of a new and an American style, they have devoted themselves to the task of justifying their principles by their works [*Tallmadge's emphasis*]."

Tallmadge ornamented the first page of his article with two photographs of Sullivan's Transportation Building at the Columbian Exposition. In 1927, he used the same image to start his chapter on Sullivan and Wright in his *Story of American Architecture*. Today we think of Sullivan as a skyscraper architect and start the story of his mature work with the Wainwright Building in Saint Louis, designed almost simultaneously with the Transportation Building. The Transportation Building was constructed of plaster and staff; it seems a digression to later European critics like Giedion, who perceive Sullivan's contribution to be the formulation of an architecture expressive of steel-cage construction. But Tallmadge is probably right in putting it first: it was in the buildings of the Columbian Exposition that the nation's architects sought to present a new, post-Richardsonian architectural system. In some quarters at the time, it seemed that Sullivan had prevailed. This was the demonstration building, the first proclamation of a new Chicago style, and the subsequent skyscrapers were only proof of the elasticity of the vocabulary.[23] There was another architectural system demonstrated at the Exposition as well, of course: the classical revival system of McKim and Burnham. As the lessons of the event sank in, lines were drawn between the progressives, led by Sullivan and an increasing group of adherents around Wright, and the revivalists. By 1900, the progressives thought they had a solution: the principles of the Arts and Crafts movement given architectural substance in "pure design," especially as it was justified by the new work of Wright. There followed a time of great enthusiasm, then, disappointment. The system didn't "gel"; it could not be widely applied. The movement in the end was what it had been at the beginning: Sullivan's and Wright's, with a crowd of imitations of either or both.

Depicted in this way, following MacCormac, Wright's unit system of design seems brilliant and self-sufficient. But it was, of course, only a method of composition—the structure of his architectural music but not its content. In 1966, Norris Kelly Smith published a study of the social ideals embodied in Wright's buildings.[24] Starting from the Prairie designs, Smith explored the suggestive symbolic content of Wright's spreading, enclosing roofs and his organization of interiors around embracing fireplaces. He examined Wright's profoundly ceremonial and basically conservative way of life and cited Wright's own numerous declarations about the traditional, symbolic qualities in house design. Neil Levine has been carrying this line of research further.[25]

Such emphasis on the social content of Wright's work makes one sensitive to an anomaly in the Prairie vocabulary. While these symbolic elements are palpable and solidly rendered—the roof casting its deep shadows; the fireplace with its arch or broad lintel and masonry—the unit system he uses to compose the space-enclosing walls seems light and ephemeral. The walls are always defined by a dark wooden grid, sometimes enclosing light plaster, sometimes glass openings, implying that the two are equivalent, mere membranes like the screens composing a Japanese interior. This grid is what is left of conventional moldings in a Wright design. They have been given a radically different form to accomplish a radically different function. Traditionally, the molding was where the mass and substance of architectural form was made palpable by excavation and elaboration. The moldings of American wooden houses were placed and shaped to extend this sense of rendered form to timber construction. But Wright's cross sections are all right-angled, making the moldings read as mere boards attached to the surface, while he plays with the deep shadows that result to make their planes seem to float in an indefinite relationship to one another. These moldings, which traditionally were essentially horizontal expressions of the thick masonry, laid-up wall, are set on end by Wright and linked together in a horizontal and vertical mesh moving through his spaces, measuring them and articulating the voids. The result is that the walls, the mere "prose" of Wright's architecture, "read out" and recede from attention, while the symbolic elements, his architecture's content and "poetry," "read in" and insist on attention.

Wright's Prairie system, then, was not just a manner of spinning out architectural music but also a way of producing an appropriate vessel for specific social content. This, too, brings us back to Sullivan. As in the case of Wright, Sullivan's fervent declarations about democracy have been interpreted in terms of the details of his facades, when in fact, as Joseph Siry has recently suggested, we should likewise accept his buildings as frames for modern social life and so look for the content in the voids within.[26]

It is illuminating in this context to examine the response of the draftsmen in Wright's Oak Park studio to his design system. Wright himself seems to have looked on this office as a kind of school where instruction in his unit system of design not only enabled the staff to be productive employees but also trained them for creative design in a sort of architectural kindergarten. Not surprisingly, most of the draftsmen copied his unit system in their subsequent work, but, sadly, they rarely used it with originality. Even after leaving Wright, they still elaborated his paradigms and imitated his motifs as if they were still in his office. There were two, however, who were especially close to Wright and who responded differently: the principal draftsman and renderer, Marion Mahony, and the office manager, Walter Burley Griffin.[27] Mahony seems to have been particularly close personally to Wright; Griffin appears to have been the man Wright discussed things with to get them made clear in his own mind. Griffin had gone out on his own in 1906. He and Mahony had collaborated in finishing up Wright's work after his abrupt departure for Europe in 1909, and they married in 1911. Wright later regarded the two with particular scorn, perhaps because they, unlike all of his other "students," tried to appropriate the symbolic language of his art as well as its neutral system of elaboration. Like the sorcerer's apprentice, Mahony and Griffin were not content with learning the master's lessons but had to discover his secrets as well.

Superficially, the work of Mahony and Griffin seems the most individual and experimental of all the studio draftsmen, but, in fact, behind most of their innovations lies a suggestion of Wright's that they merely blurt out. Their Frank Palma House of 1911 seems a strikingly original design, but actually it combines Wright's interest in Native American architecture with his use of raised, open rooms with panoramic views (like the Cheney, Tomek, and Robie houses) and is embodied as a somewhat flat concrete pueblo. Again, their Melson House of 1912, in Mason City, Iowa, is striking in the way it projects from a limestone cliff, but its masonry is clearly a derivative of Wright's recently completed (and very personal) Taliesin, which maintains a much subtler relationship to its natural surroundings. Finally, in the 1912 house they designed for themselves in Winnetka, Illinois, Griffin and Mahony adopted a baroque architectural unit system of their own that, in the end, is essentially decorative: the spaces remain closed and conventional.

This is a sad note, but we do not necessarily have to end on it. Mahony and Griffin produced one design that was their real claim to fame and the test of the Chicago school: their winning plan in the 1911–12 competition to design Canberra, the new capital city of Australia. If the essential contribution of Sullivan and Wright was to posit architecture's purpose as the enframement of modern life, here was a whole city laid out in the spirit of the Chicago school. The task posed a double challenge: first, to define the content—the functions—of a modern city; second, to find a unit system of design that would be an urbanistic equivalent of Wright's architectural system. Griffin, apparently, conceived the layout of the plan around a lucid diagram of functions. Mahony executed the exquisite plan and perspectives with their monumental Prairie-style ensembles. They met the first challenge by placing a lake surrounded with public gardens at the heart of the city, with museum and athletic facilities spread along one bank facing the government buildings terracing up the other. The government group culminates in an open memorial hall, a belvedere topping a low hill from which a star of avenues lead across the city. They met the second challenge by adopting a unit system, though one very different from Wright's. It consists of a series of hexagonal and octagonal cells in the city plan that generate a network of binding avenues along their diagonals while defining separate, humanly scaled quarters. Griffin's greatest power evidently was organizational, and here, with no direct precedent of Wright's to cramp his thinking, he laid out a democratic city with clarity and disarming frankness.

When Wright erected the studio wing of his Oak Park House in 1898, he placed his office in the center, with two separate geometric volumes to either side: the drafting room on the east, an octagonal "library" to the west. Libraries were the chief resort of historicizing revivalist architects, Wright's proclaimed enemies in his project to create a new, unprecedented American architecture. Why did he give a library such prominence in his studio complex?

The answer may be that this little space was, in fact, much more than a library. It contained very few bookshelves, the walls being mostly cabinets. There were no windows through which one might look out and rest one's eyes. A single table was in the center, its surface amply illuminated by an encircling clerestory around the top of the space. We know from old photographs and from Alfred Granger's description in *House Beautiful* that the room was filled with the beautiful objects Wright collected and displayed at the exhibitions of his early work: Japanese prints and ceramics, dried flowers, medieval and Renaissance bits of decorative art.[28] That is, this room was not a library but a museum-laboratory, a *Wunderkammer* of odd but intrinsically beautiful things. In the context of this essay, I would hypothesize that the room had two functions: First, it was a laboratory where Wright hoped to work out for himself the ideas about "pure design" that Sullivan had suggested to him and that Lorch had picked up from them both. Second, it was Wright's "kindergarten" for the studio draftsmen, the place where they, like the children in his wife's kindergarten at the other end of the house, could touch and examine all these beautiful things and thereby absorb spontaneously the abstract essentials of design.

Tallmadge observed that by 1908 the preaching side of the Chicago movement had faded, replaced by a more fruitful concentration on practical design. This is precisely what seems to have happened in Wright's case: as his Prairie vocabulary matured after 1900, he must have found the need for research in his *Wunderkammer* unnecessary and tedious. He also must have found his efforts to teach his draftsmen unrewarding, as they simply appropriated his style. In 1909, he abruptly abandoned his family and his studio—his six children in his wife's kindergarten and his dozen draftsmen in his own professional "kindergarten"—and retreated to Europe, then to Wisconsin, to think things through again.

Form and Philosophy
Froebel's Kindergarten Training and Wright's Early Work

BY RICHARD MACCORMAC

Frank Lloyd Wright's architecture has been thought to be idiosyncratic. His buildings pose such a complexity of subtle decisions that it is difficult not to see them as essentially personal, their conspicuous characteristics—interpenetrations, extended plans, cubic forms, and projecting eaves—as products of a subjective and impenetrable system of thought. Such a view of "great" architecture tends to emphasize the mystery of genius at the expense of communicable ideas. This view sustains the glib attitude toward style that has been encouraged by postmodernism and other recent developments: The art of architecture is so personal that it is unnecessary to discuss architecture as a formal language.

This study acknowledges Wright's special genius but concentrates on certain formal experiences. These experiences provided him with a motive for interpreting his role in the particular terms that he did. In addition, they offered the characteristics of a visual system that, as Robert C. Spencer pointed out, sharply distinguished his work from that of his contemporaries and predecessors.[1] The experience to be discussed is Wright's Froebel kindergarten training and the subsequent confirmation of its discipline in Louis Sullivan's ornament. In tracing the early development of Wright's work, it becomes apparent that this background was the source of some features that we regard as particularly "Wrightian."

Friedrich Wilhelm August Froebel's program of educational reform originated in his belief in the basic uniformity and unity of nature's laws, a possibility that he apprehended while studying rock crystals and while working as a forester shortly after leaving school. Unable to substantiate his intuition by becoming a natural scientist, he studied architecture for two years at Frankfurt am Main. It may have been this experience that suggested he could convey his ideas through the medium of building blocks. It would be interesting to know the curriculum at Frankfurt at that time. In the last quarter of the eighteenth century, Boullée and Ledoux initiated a revival of interest in primary solids, cubes, spheres, and pyramids. By 1795, Durand was teaching at L'École Polytechnique with an array of abstract room shapes that could be assembled on graph paper to form ideal symmetrical designs resembling those formed with the Froebel blocks.[2]

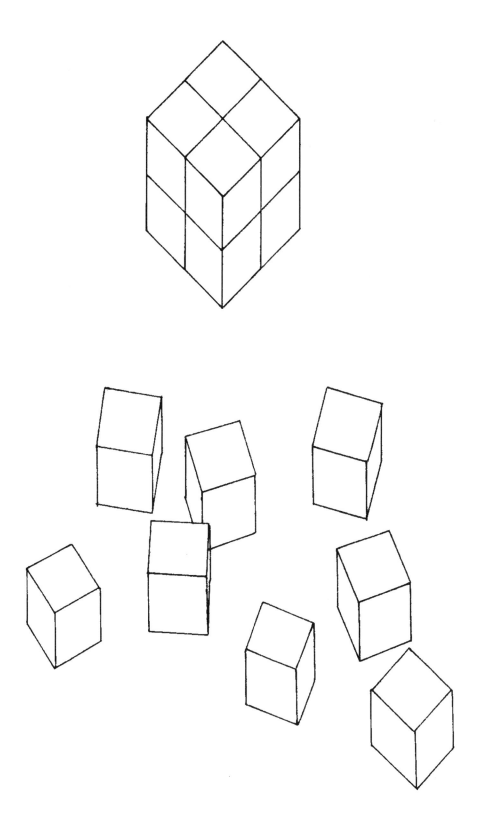

Froebel's teaching method was adapted from that of Johann Heinrich Pestalozzi, to whose school he was attached from 1807 to 1809. Like Pestalozzi, he believed in the principle of teaching through voluntary activity and accepted that children were most impressionable up to the age of seven. Ideally, during these years, they would be under the guidance and supervision of their mothers, to whose influence he attached special emphasis: "Lives which have attained true greatness will, in nearly every case, be found to have received their molding and impression under a mother's care." In Wright this theory found remarkable fulfillment.

Grant Manson has demonstrated the striking affinity between some of Wright's works and the Froebel patterns and models.[3] He also observed that these miniature exercises in building could have contributed to Wright's extraordinary confidence, "that he had the power to build anything he could ideate." Indeed, the handbook instructions remark, "The child may find employment for the power of will.... It becomes now architect, mason, carpenter, shipwright, or whatever its imagination suggests by means of this simple material."[4] Manson compares appearances and concludes that the resemblances are due to a common concern to give expression "to the nature of materials." He does not follow Wright's appreciation of form as something to be looked at or "into" as structure rather than something simply to be looked at and does not recognize the Froebel exercises as an essentially abstract organizational discipline (independent of materials) backed by a philosophical program that forms the basis of Wright's own intentions.

Wright may have gained his image of himself from the kindergarten experience. His mother was determined that he should become an architect. and, having obtained the Froebel manuals as part of her design, she gave him a thorough education in its method.[5] Her Unitarian beliefs would have disposed her to take seriously Froebel's claim that his teaching revealed "the original Unity" behind all natural appearances. This "Unity" would lead the child to "unity with itself ... God's works reflect the logic of His spirit and human education cannot do anything better than imitate the logic of nature."

The handbook encourages the child "to learn early and in a practical manner that 'order of Heaven's first law.'" The capricious and arbitrary child who does not fulfill the conditions of the exercises spurns what is implicitly a God-given revelation and lacks a basic development of character. Consequently, for Wright, aesthetic ideas could have acquired a moral urgency. As an architect, he assumed an almost messianic role on behalf of what he regarded as an unenlightened people:

> Would you worship life amid this confusion of today remember again the prophesy of the ideal Man, 'The Kingdom of God is within you.' By nature worship, by revelation of your own nature alone can your God be reached.... I saw the architect as Saviour of the culture of modern American Society ... Saviour now as for all civilizations heretofore.[6]

Furthermore, the identification of the Froebel patterns (from which, as we shall see, Wright derived the discipline of his own architecture) with natural law provided Wright with a background comparable to that of the Renaissance architects, who regarded their work as having the absolute value of an echo of universal harmony,[7] "given inherent vision, there is no source so fertile, so suggestive, so helpful aesthetically for the architect as a comprehension of natural law."[8]

THE FROEBEL GIFTS

The gifts are a series of exercises that gradually develop the child's mind and manual dexterity. The first two gifts—the worsted balls, and the sphere, cylinder, and cube suspended on strings—are intended to be regarded individually and to familiarize the child with the character of primary forms. The third, fourth, fifth, and sixth gifts—exercises with assemblies of wooden blocks—are most pertinent to the present study, while the seventh gift—composed of tablets, which combine into flat patterns, rather than of blocks—repeats the kinds of exercises performed with the earlier gifts but in a more abstract and less tangible medium. Wright himself suggests that it was the blocks and tablets which made most impression on him.[9] The eighth, ninth, and tenth gifts are composed of slats and sticks to make up frameworks, which do not yield the kind of formal discipline to be considered here. Of the later "occupations," which include embroidery, modeling, and exercises of a practical kind for the older child, only the mat-weaving exercises seem relevant to this study.

For each of the gifts to be discussed in this paper, the handbook describes three forms of combination: the forms of knowledge, the forms of life, and the forms of beauty. The first form teaches arithmetic visually, using the blocks as counters. The forms of life are models of familiar objects, generally buildings or furniture; the forms of beauty, or crystallization, are two-dimensionally organized patterns. These last two categories exhibit the qualities to be investigated.

The handbook instructions emphasize the importance of conveying to the child a sense of unity. Each gift is introduced as a set of blocks assembled as a cube in a wooden box, and the child's destructive tendency, which Froebel interprets as a "desire to know the inside," is channeled into systematic exercises that explore the qualities of the constituents in a series of renewed syntheses.

The general rules for the third gift, a cube composed of eight smaller cubes, state the rather strict conditions to which the child must submit in order to execute the exercises of this and the gifts that follow. These conditions, set out below, are followed by characteristic statements by Wright that indicate the profound impression that the kindergarten made on him.

The Kindergarten Guide: *The child is first taught to take the cube out of the box, undivided, in order to inculcate alike the sense of order and the idea of completeness.*[10]

Wright: *Any buildings should be complete, including all within itself. Instead of many things, one thing.*[11]

The Kindergarten Guide: *Care should be taken that the child is not allowed to develop a destructive tendency. . . . Lead the child to play methodically with the cubes. The law of intermediation and development should be inculcated and caprice of arbitrariness should never be permitted.*[12]

Wright: *Perfect correlation, integration is life. It is the first principle of any*

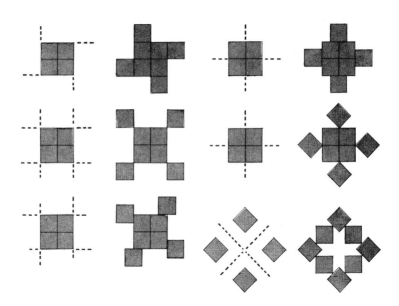

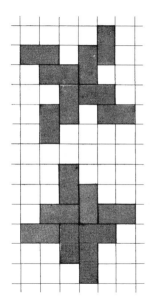

growth that the thing grown be no mere aggregation . . . and integration means that no part of any thing is of any great value except as it be integrate part of the harmonious whole.[13]

The Kindergarten Guide: *In life we find no isolation. One part of the cube, therefore, must never be left apart from or without relation to the whole. The child will thus become accustomed to treat all things in life as bearing a certain relation to one another.*[14]

Wright: *. . . the each in all and the all in each throughout.*[15]

To imbue the child with a sense of method, each pattern evolves from its predecessor by a symmetrical redistribution of parts. Each new form develops from the structural order of its predecessor. If we compare the blocks in these patterns with those arbitrarily scattered in the chapter opener, it is apparent that here they have to some extent surrendered their identity (in favor of fewer, larger wholes) to the structure to which they contribute. For Wright this is a fundamental recognition—parts added need not be sensed as additional but can become intrinsic.

The kindergartner provided the child with a "network table" ruled with a grid to guide the arrangement of the blocks. The disciplines of standardization and a modular grid, rather than be inhibiting, provide the requisite conditions for parts to correlate and imply larger wholes. Wright wrote, "In the logic of the plan what we call standardization is seen to be fundamental groundwork."[16] In some of these exercises, these disciplines lead to the effect of interweaving. The individual blocks and even the spaces between give the illusion of being plaited together. Again, Wright wrote: "The kindergarten training, as I have shown, proved an unforeseen asset . . . a properly proportional unit system all to scale . . . like a tapestry, a consistent fabric woven of interdependent, related units, however various."[17]

In the later mat-weaving "occupation" (already alluded to), the phenomenon is repeated, but in a condition that, in a sense, is reversed from the former exercises. The mats are plaited from continuous strips of black or white paper through a white or black background. The product appears as a checkerboard of isolated black and white squares but gives the illusion of actual continuity.

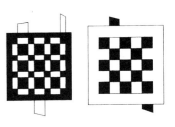

The coordinating effect of grids and standard parts sheds light on the importance that Wright attached to the use of T square and set-square, for along the edges of these instruments, components could be induced to align themselves. It is characteristic of Wright's sketch plans in their fluid state that they are matted with exploratory lines—a mesh to be gradually refined and tightened to correlate appropriate parts. Wright explains the origin of this technique as follows: "This principle of design was natural, inevitable for me . . . it is based on the straight line technique of the T square and the triangle. It was inherent in the Froebel system of kindergarten training given to me by my mother."[18]

Gestalt psychologists might have claimed that Froebel patterns attain a degree of simplicity in comparison with a disorganized aggregation of the blocks.[19] Yet the nature of this simplicity needs qualification. The engaging quality of these patterns is not simplicity in the obvious sense; otherwise the cube or sphere would be the ultimately pleasing forms. It seems that the perception of simplicity is more appealing than actual physical simplicity.[20]

In the patterns made with the third Froebel gift, a square composed of four smaller squares holds more attention than a single square of the same dimension. There is tension set up between what exists and what is implied. It is apparent that the incomplete form has attained positive properties. It has additional structural characteristics, without losing its squareness, so that it can readily accommodate additional parts. In the cruciform pattern the eight blocks have resolved themselves into two figures "which interpenetrate without optical destruction of one another."[21] Georg Kepes has called this "phenomenal transparency."[22]

In the Froebel patterns, symmetry is employed not only to effect balance but to realize interpenetration. The handbook states, "In making forms of beauty, which are simply symmetrical forms, we must bear in mind the rule: 'keep the opposites alike.'" As we shall see, the sense of interpenetration in Wright's interiors is often achieved by a symmetrical correlation of opposite components. External symmetry exposes internal organization.

It seems likely that Wright recognized in the exercises the principle that interior and exterior should have a common identity, for they are related as cause and effect. The handbook itself suggests that the gifts "enable the child to strive after the comprehension of both external appearances and inner conditions." Wright's distaste for what he considered the arbitrary sculpting of unrelated interiors and exteriors in classical building can be appreciated when one considers the essentially immutable blocks, which become pattern producing both interior and exterior effects.

It is impossible to consider the perimeter of the patterns of the fifth gift as independent of their intrinsic structure. It is not only the solids that affect this perimeter; the spaces defined within them also appear to break through to the outside.

Fourteenth Froebel Gift
paper mat weaving;
drawn by author

Third Froebel Gift
patterns; square, pinwheel, and
cruciform; drawn by author

Fifth Froebel Gift
patterns ; drawn by author

Sixth Froebel Gift
patterns; drawn by author

With the sixth gift, the theme of cruciform and square is elaborated into more complex plaiting, which is expressed in the jutting profiles of the patterns. During the development of Wright's Prairie period, such cruciform-in-square plan forms became a typical expression of the internal organization of the buildings.

Some of the "forms of knowledge" indicate how the intentions of these plans might be realized in three dimensions: a "bath" that can be built with the sixth gift is comprised of the intersecting square and cruciform considered in the forms of beauty. These are articulated by raising the four blocks of the square and relatively suppressing the cruciform. The release of these features from the ground plane enables a third figure, composed of four flat tablets, to take up coordinates of both square and cruciform and imply a podium interlocking with both.

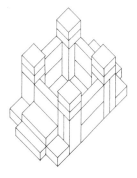

Unity Temple in Oak Park, Illinois, is basically an alternative three-dimensional projection of this type of plan, and Wright makes it clear that he saw the architectural relationship between plan and form: "I have endeavoured to establish a harmonious relationship between ground plan and elevation of these buildings considering the one as a solution and the other as an expression of the conditions of a problem of which the whole is a project."[23]

Wright's sympathy and admiration for Sullivan, whom he acknowledged as *Lieber Meister*, suggests that there might be a definable relationship between their work and ideas. The obviously different contexts of their architectural practices disqualifies comparison at this level, as Colin Rowe points out in his essay "Chicago Frame" (chapter 3),[24] and Sullivan's florid and sensuous ornament seems antithetical to Wright's straight-line aesthetic. With only Wright's verbal acknowledgments of inspiration,[25] the relationship seems, to quote Manson, "nebulous and over publicized."[26] Yet it was the quality of Sullivan's ornament that impressed Wright: "Yes, the significant implication of *Lieber Meister*'s gift to me was his practice 'of the thing—not on it' which I recognized and saw most clearly in his unique ornament."[27] Wright seems to have benefited from the organization rather than from the superficial art nouveau appearance. "This innate or organic property of all form, if not merely looked *at* but looked *into* as structure, absorbed me."

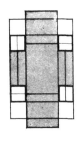

Sullivan's *A System of Architectural Ornament According with a Philosophy of Man's Powers*[28] is based on the nineteenth-century confusion between organic and inorganic growth. Goethe included the structures of living and nonliving forms under the term "morphology," or science of form. Sullivan and Wright inherited this view from the writing of Herbert Spencer, who, as late as 1898, "could still assert that the growth of crystals and organisms was 'an essentially similar process.'"[29] For Wright this was a confirmation of Froebel's precept that "forms of crystallization"—geometric disciplines—could be considered representative of natural law in general. This is one of the ways in which Wright's association with Sullivan (Sullivan gave him Spencer to read) resurrected the experience of the kindergarten. Thus we find that Wright's personal vocabulary combines meanings and words derived both from the manuals and from the biological terms used

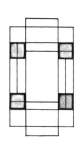

"Bath" made with the Sixth Froebel Gift
square and cruciform; drawn by author

by Sullivan: nature, organic, crystallization, integrating, efflorescence, structure, etc.

The theory that Sullivan proposes in the somewhat involved introduction to *A System of Architectural Ornament* analogizes natural growth to the creative process of the artist:

> Hence for the germ of the typical plant seed with its residual powers he may substitute, in thought, his own will as the seat of vital power in a figurative or imagined seed germ which shall be the utterly simple energy basis of a theory of efflorescence involving concordantly a theory of plastic control over the inorganic.[30]

Sullivan demonstrates the evolution of a "figurative or imagined seed germ" with several series of illustrations. Some of these are derived from stages of actual plant growth and are probably taken from Asa Gray's *School and Field Book of Botany*.[31] Others have a geometric basis of development and show an affinity to the disciplines considered in the Froebel exercises.

Sullivan sees the primary geometric figures—square, triangle, pentagon, etc.—as having a latent structure according to which they can grow. It is in this that they are analogous to a seed germ, their structure being the "residual power" that the imagination can bring "to the finality of its characteristic form—the expression of its identity [as] efflorescence."[32] In addition to the illustrations from Sullivan, consider the illustration showing the development of the third Froebel gift, in the context of Sullivan's description of the development of his own ornament from primary forms:

> The above forms, rigid in their quality, are to be considered in our philosophy as containers of radial energy, extensive and intensive; that is to say; extension of form along lines or axes radiating from the center and (or) intention of form along the same or other radial from the periphery toward the center. Here then occurs the will of man to cause the inorganic and rigid to become fluent through his powers. Note also that we assume energy to be resident in the periphery and that all lines are energy lines. This may be called plastic geometry.[33]

At the budding of his professional career it seems that Wright confirmed his childhood discovery:

> Perhaps because the "interior" character of his sense of efflorescence gibed [*sic*] with my own wrestle with nature circumstance out there on the farm. It was square with the Unitarianism of my old Welsh grandfather. The Froebel kindergartening my mother discovered at the Centennial, and herself gave to me, pointed that way. All this background came forward a step and began to "click."[34]

WRIGHT'S WORK

The buildings illustrated in this essay convey Wright's transposition of the Froebel disciplines into architecture. It should be emphasized that the analyses nowhere imply the original sequence of design, nor are they presumed to reveal the complete specification of Wright's aesthetic. They are intended to demonstrate, within the context of many decisions, a certain continuity of principle.

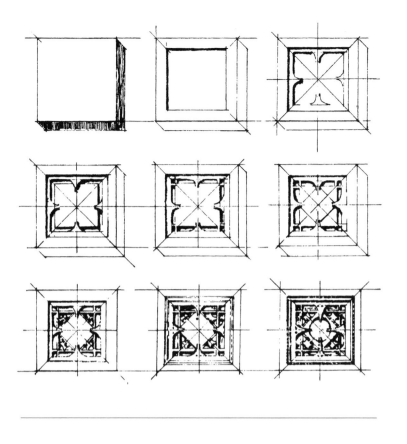

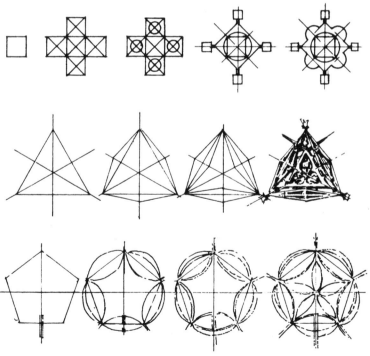

Development from a Square
Louis Sullivan, from *A System of Architectural Ornament*

Development from a Square, Triangle, and Pentagon
Louis Sullivan, from *A System of Architectural Ornament*

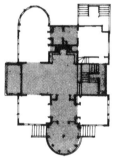

GEORGE BLOSSOM HOUSE

The plan of this house may have been derived from the Palladian parti of McKim, Mead & White's Taylor House.[35] But Wright's version is more consistent in its intentions: all the external parts are located by the internal structure (in a conceptual sense), and this structure is implicit in the recession or projection in each facade of the central bays, where the porches and balconies are located. The plan is a square interpenetrated by a cross—one of the prevailing figures in the Froebel manual.

WILLIAM H. WINSLOW HOUSE

The major external features are similarly related to the interior of the house as extensions of plan with T-square and set-square, so that it is possible to reconstruct a hypothetical grid. Although the volume of the house at the rear is broken down by the projection of the central bay over the dining room, and by the expression of the stair as a tower, the front and side elevations present a solid envelope that obscures the intentions of the plan. Instead of seeming to be part of the interior, the *porte cochere* appears to be stuck on, while the front terrace hardly suggests that the esplanade continues as a component of the interior.

It seems that Wright had yet to evolve a formal grammar that would enable him to convey a sense of the internal structure of an object from a view of its perimeter. With the Froebel patterns this was unnecessary because they could be seen from above. Wright was faced with the problem discussed by Le Corbusier in the opening pages of *Vers une Architecture* (*Towards a New Architecture*). If the plan was to be "the essence of sensation," he had to find a means of making the sensation appreciable to "eyes which are 5 feet 6 inches from the ground."[36] During the development of the Prairie Houses, innovations in appearance can often be interpreted in terms of this problem.

Internally the entrance hall is a distribution chamber from which the library, living room, and dining room can be reached. At first sight it is a deceptively simple box, but inspection reveals that its parts are knitted together in a way that anticipates the mature organization of later houses. One may regard the room simply as a container, but the rise in level suggests that the rear of the house is coordinated with the hall. It seems to have been drawn forward as a platform. This speculation is encouraged by the deep fireplace alcove projected out of the back of the room, which in turn reveals the flanking walls of adjacent lobbies. These relate to the flight of steps at the change of level, suggesting an interpenetration of space, and correspond to the banisters on each side to imply an extension of the cloakroom and stair landing into the hall. The part of the room at the lower level, immediately inside the front door, confirms the lateral axis established by the large openings with sliding doors into the library and living room. As in the Froebel exercises, the components subscribe to larger wholes within the discipline of a grid.

The hall is thus no simple box, but a place that anticipates those adjacent to it by presenting constituents that they apparently share. The lateral axis penetrating the hall is not located by coordinates in the library and living room; the outside walls make no response to the axis.

George Blossom House
Chicago, Illinois, 1892;
perspective and analysis of plan;
drawn by author

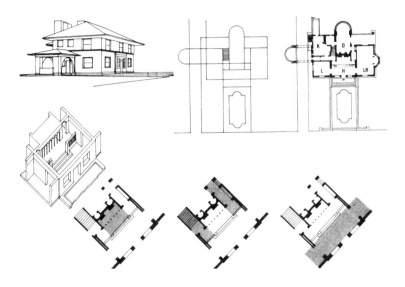

LLOYD JONES WINDMILL, "ROMEO AND JULIET"

The "Romeo and Juliet" Windmill has been praised for its structural ingenuity and even for its aerodynamic section,[37] an invalid appreciation since only the rotor, rather than the whole mill, revolves to face the wind. The mill is an exercise in geometry derived from Froebel and Sullivan. The tower supporting the rotor and the one supporting the observation platform are combined by the latent affinity of the octagon for the diamond. Both forms are fully appreciable but perfectly integrated. The octagon also culminates in a circle in the conical shingled roof. This transposition of content into essential pattern must have made Wright aware of how far he had to go to interpret the contents of houses in terms of the "inner nature of poetic principle ... according to my mother's kindergarten table ... the activating cause of all visible effects."[38]

ISIDORE HELLER HOUSE

In the Heller House, the transverse axis linking the living room to the entrance and stairs is embodied in the rooms themselves. This axis locates the middle of the living room and is the arm of a pinwheel (or a rotation in space) in relation to the dining room. In Sullivan's terms it is the "extension of form ... from the centre ... and from the periphery" of these rooms respectively.[39]

In his studio, built the year before the windmill, Wright managed to give the spaces to each side of the entrance their own external identity. Similarly, the cruciform plans of the Heller dining and living rooms not only accommodate their shared axis but expose their spatial components. The windows, with which Wright had been so dissatisfied in the Winslow House, saying, "I used to gloat over the beautiful buildings I could build if only it were unnecessary to cut windows in them,"[40] are no longer simply stuck on the building but have become an inherent part of the internal organization, submitting to the overall discipline.

A product of the way in which the dining room is organized is the sense of location that different functions assume in the room. The spatial compo-

William H. Winslow House
River Forest, Illinois, 1893; perspective, analysis of plan, and axonometric and plan analyses of entry foyer; drawn by author

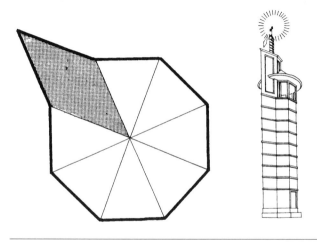

Lloyd-Jones Windmill,
"Romeo and Juliet"
1896; perspective and analysis of
plan; drawn by author

nents of hall and kitchen servery do not intrude on the dining space and sideboard. Wright's intention was not only to "represent the geometric idea of space but to create for the individual life, which unfolds itself, within that space, an accurately adjusted shell."[41]

JOSEPH W. HUSSER HOUSE

The correlated living and dining rooms of the Heller House hardly emerge in the external profile of the plan. With the spaces between them filled in with the staircase and the little reception chamber by the entrance, these organized constituents are lost within the amorphous whole.

In contrast, the first-floor plan of the Husser House is a marvelous clarification. The living area is entirely built up from integrated components so that, perhaps for the first time in Wright's houses, internal conditions and external appearance achieve identity as pattern, in the same sense as in the "Romeo and Juliet" Windmill.

The staircase that rises to the living area from the entrance below is an extension of one of the cross axes of the house. The lobby in the center of the plan establishes the width of the main axis, terminated by the fireplaces of the living room and the dining room. The volumes of these two rooms, which straddle the plan, are completely exposed externally by their windows; the giant bow of the dining room expands toward the view of Lake Michigan. The symmetrical stairs that lead to the bedroom floor are precisely located in the space (defined by the fireplace and lateral balustrades) between the living room and the inner core of the dining room, while the slots of space beside the main axis of the living area are provided with triangular terminals to meet the geometric condition requisite for attaching the porch, which echoes the octagonal form of the other projections.

Isidore Heller House
Chicago, Illinois, 1897; plan and
analysis of plan and dining room;
drawn by author

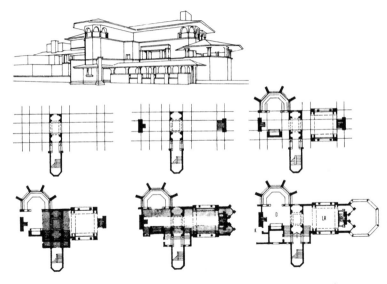

The Husser House develops the principle, employed in the Winslow reception hall and the Heller dining room, of establishing a grid as a substructure within the rooms, derived from the dimensions of their components. As in the former example, this idea has more than a merely geometric validity. Movement within such space assumes a particular quality. Each room is penetrated by spatial constituents of those adjacent so that, rather than pass from one to another and experience a moment of being in neither, one is carried through a succession of overlapping volumes.

RIVER FOREST GOLF CLUB

The Golf Club is the logical development of Wright's increasing tendency toward stratification. Apart from a distribution of piers, it has taken complete advantage of its timber construction to enable the windows to become a continuous strip—a possibility that had been inherent in American timber building throughout the nineteenth century.

For Wright this must have been an important discovery, for the strip window can be the perceptual reversal of the "hole in the wall" that he had found so unsatisfactory. By "a peculiar visual paradox,"[42] the hole in the wall, being a relatively small feature set against a plane, tends to be seen as a "figure," though it is supposed to look like a void. The discomfort can be overcome if the window is claimed as a figure by framing it with an architrave (like that of the Winslow House). But this condition means that the window aperture fails to disclose internal space. With the continuous strip window, the wall, aided perceptually by parapet extensions, is interpreted as figure and the window as ground. The wall becomes a screen enclosing the volume of the building; windows surrender their identity as objects.

The liberation of the wall, as strip, also had important consequences. Just as parts could grow from the internal grid on plan, a stratified arrangement in elevation could accommodate the parapets of porches, verandas, and balconies as an extension of intrinsic structure. This is why, even in Wright's timber houses, parapets are generally solid rather than openwork

Joseph W. Husser House
Chicago, Illinois, 1899;
perspective and analyses of plan;
drawn by author

balustrades. These open-air spaces outside bedrooms and living rooms were already a traditional part of American domestic architecture, and one can speculate that if the American climate had been less congenial, Wright might never have developed his aesthetic. For the extended roofs, balconies, and terraces of his work are equivalent to the play between the peripheral units and the innate structure of Froebel's patterns, or, in Sullivan's terms, "the efflorescence of residual power."[43]

FRANK THOMAS HOUSE

In the Husser House, the service quarters are arranged to the rear of the main living/dining room axis; externally they are seen as a continuation of the main volume of the house, but internally they are quite separate.

Similarly, in the smaller Thomas House, they are contained within the main two-story rectangular volume, and it is the family living spaces that generate the significant features of the exterior. Like the Heller and Husser houses, the Thomas House is penetrated by a long axis that connects the chief living rooms. Here it extends to include the open-air terrace.

The extension of form from the periphery of the main block is repeated by the dining room, so that the two suggest the arms of a pinwheel. For Sullivan the pinwheel was the basic alternative to developing the energy resident in the radials of a block. It was also the fundamental alternative to crosses and squares that were repeated in the Froebel patterns. For Wright this form had a continual attraction; it reoccurs throughout the span of his work.

This simple pinwheel is subtly elaborated by the open-air terrace and entrance that lie alongside its two arms. An effect of interweaving, which became a characteristic of later work, is evident in the relationships of the dining room to the main block, of the terrace to the dining room, and of the entrance axis to the terrace, each similarly abutting the other. It may have been to this that Wright was referring when he described the characteristic theme of the Thomas House as "unfolding."[44]

The longitudinal axis of the Husser House was set between two fire-places. Here it is revealed as a projection beyond the end of the terrace. Just as in the former the projections obtain a similar character by use of octagonal forms, here the resemblance between the two arms is completed by the cut back in the dining-room windows to provide flower boxes, which have the formal effect of revealing the stratum of the terrace in the absence of a balcony. The jutting profiles of the plans of the two arms of the Thomas House demonstrate Wright's development toward a grammar of external

River Forest Golf Club
River Forest, Illinois, 1901;
aerial perspective view

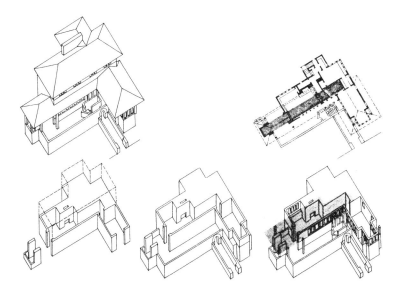

form that would enable him to suggest intrinsic organization, a significant advance from the plain facade of the Winslow House eight years before.

Further play with internal-external relationships is apparent in the way Wright uses the roof of the veranda. Externally it appears to penetrate the interior, and internally this illusion is satisfied by the distinction between the lower ceiling of the library alcove and the rest of the living area. The entrance lobby, which fills the space between the side of the house and the edge of this roof, also contributes to the effect of inner structure revealed. In combination with the veranda roof supports, it suggests an external plane stripped away to disclose the flank of the living room. The eaves of the roofs that cover the veranda and the dining room are each exactly aligned on one side with the eaves of the roof above, reaffirming the basic pinwheel principle.

CHARLES S. ROSS HOUSE

This small house is particularly simple and elegant in its conception. The cruciform ground plan contains the living areas, porch, and service quarters in its four extensions. Above, a cube with two lesser projections beneath the eaves contains the bedrooms.

The grid represents a schematic structure underlying the basic features of the house in much the same way that the plan of the Froebel "bath," discussed earlier, represents its three-dimensional projection as a model. In the Ross House, the grid is modified to produce a cross with another cross in it; three arms of the cross equivalently related to an underlying square give a discipline to the asymmetry of the figure. The subdivision of the main axis of the cruciform into an *a-b-a* module is a development of the internal substructure already discussed for the Winslow, Heller, and Husser houses.

The cube is a projection of the square at the intersection of the cruciform. It represents, schematically, the core of the house. The horizontal and vertical coordinates discipline the arrangement of the main features of the building. The actual core of the house is a pattern of solids and voids so derived. Even the first-floor casements open on the inner grid lines (creating

Frank Thomas House
Oak Park, Illinois, 1901;
axonometric and plan analyses;
drawn by author

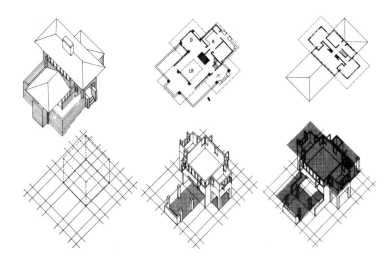

a spatial effect that Wright incorporated as a permanent feature in the John Pew House of 1940 by making square projections of roof over each pair of corner windows). From the core, the two roofs project and define the outer cruciform. Under the higher roof the two small bedrooms, with dining room and porch beneath them, project the inner cruciform. On the other axis the living room extends the wider module, but the inner part of the grid is embodied in the structural piers, the raised portion of the living room, and the punched-out veranda at the end. Thus the three main terminals of the house (as usual the service quarter is not enhanced) display the jutting profile observed in the Thomas House—an expression of intrinsic structure akin to the flat patterns made with the sixth gift.

The three arms of the living area are further unified by the weather-boarded parapet and podium to which their roofs have an equivalent relationship, as noted above. The integration of the podium is closely analogous to that of the Froebel "bath." Moreover, its relationship to the living room that it surrounds reflects the relationship of the upper roof to the projecting bedrooms. Thus it seems that Wright not only employed overhanging eaves for their peculiar aesthetic quality but recognized their capacity, like that of the podium, to project pattern and define space.

It was claimed at the beginning of the article that the Froebel patterns suggested to Wright an essentially abstract discipline unrelated to the nature of materials, and it is perhaps significant that the podium of the Ross House is completely sheathed (for appreciable formal reasons), suggesting a solid rather than a framed structure. The effect is strangely belied by the gaps between the boards and the gradual slope of the hill beneath.

GEORGE BARTON HOUSE

The Barton House is part of a comprehensive site plan including the Darwin D. Martin House and therefore makes concessions, in its organization, to the overall pattern of the site. Inspection of the plan reveals that it is based on a clear grid, comparable to that of the Ross House, exhibiting again the *a-b-a* structuring of the cruciform. However, the presence of the grid is much more strongly established in the living area than it was in the former exam-

Charles S. Ross House
Lake Delavan, Wisconsin, 1902;
axonometric and plan analyses;
drawn by author

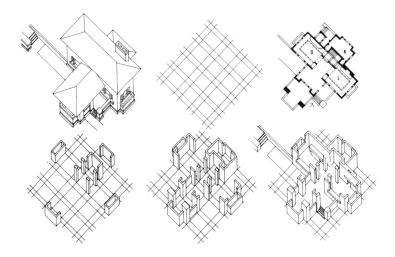

ple. It seems possible that this more overt approach could have been a consequence of Wright's experience in designing the contemporary Larkin
Building, with its consistent structural grid throughout.

Again, the inner cruciform, established by the structural piers at the center, is revealed in projections at the terminals of the plan: by flower boxes
under the dining and living room windows, by a projection from the end of
the entrance porch, and by a bay window accommodating the countertop in
the kitchen. It disciplines the arrangement of the windows and the position
of the staircase on the first floor. The outer cruciform is enclosed by the exterior walls that are further modulated by secondary axes. Into these, which
are the *b* of the *a-b-a* arrangement, the lateral windows of the dining room,
the living room, the sideboard, and fireplace are slotted. The other arm of
the cross accommodates the entrance, and the established subaxis continues as a feature of the garden beyond. The whole is crowned by the simple
intersection of the roofs, penetrated by the chimney.

F. F. TOMEK HOUSE

It is apparent that, by this time, Wright had to some extent established a successful formula for domestic design. Again, for the Tomek House the
T-square and the set-square established a grid that combined components
within it and extended into the house's surroundings.

The Tomek House adopts the second-floor living areas of the Thomas
and Heller houses and establishes an open-ended "deck," which was used in
the Robie House two years later. Rather than retain the open center of the
Heller and Barton houses, Wright subdivided the living area with an island
combining chimney and stair, through which the entrance axis penetrates
dramatically.

This internal cruciform is characteristically enclosed by the external walls
in such a way that three of its axes still project visibly; one may regard the plan
as an elongated version of the basic cross and square (without the subaxes
that differentiate dining and living rooms in the Heller and Barton houses).

The Tomek House distinguishes itself from those already illustrated in its
employment of a layer of structure outside the *a-b-a* module. This layer,

George Barton House
Buffalo, New York, 1903;
axonometric and plan analyses;
drawn by author

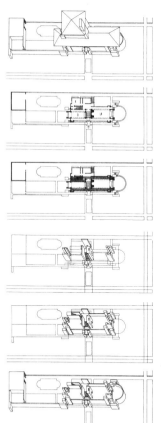

which is apparent chiefly from the front, functions as a screen wall to the yard and car turn around space, but its primary *raison d'être* seems to be a formal one. Where the continuity of the wall is broken in front of the house, there is a strong longitudinal field, reaffirming the effect of the other end projections and establishing the same tension between fact and implication. Perhaps Wright recognized the possibility in some of the exercises of the fifth gift, in which square or triangular fragments detach from the main body of the patterns but are inexorably held in mutual discipline by invisible lines of force.

This exhibition is so pronounced that the whole suburban corner lot, with its gridded sidewalls interlacing with the entrance axis, is employed in the pattern. It is in the idiom of Wright's earlier experiments with "quadruple block plans" for Prairie Houses, with the gardens combined into a foursquare pattern, with the houses projected in pinwheel formation from the corners, with the entrance paths, drives, and sidewalls interwoven, "the each in all and the all in each throughout."[45]

The first floor and service annex form a block that is related to the entrance axis in a peripheral rather than axial manner, tied in to the plan with the chimney and with the bedroom balcony, which is contained in a vertical extension of the end structure of the dining room. The internal subdivision returns to the relationship between uses observed in the Winslow entrance hall and the Husser dining room. By providing access in the lateral slots of space, the central band of the grid becomes a static zone distinct from those that embody movement.

ROBERT W. EVANS HOUSE

This house combines characteristics of several of those discussed. In addition to the familiar subdivisions of the grid, the figure bounded by the external walls is held, like that of the Tomek House, within a larger one suggested by the four massive corner piers, which have no function but to define the extent of the pattern of the plan. Again this grid seems to be of sufficient scale to engage the house with the road and sidewalk before it.

The Evans House illustrates Wright's achievement of "a harmonious relationship between ground plan and elevation ... considering the one as the solution and the other as an expression of the conditions of a problem."[46] The house consists of an almost square central block with a cross set into it, which can be interpreted as a development of the *parti* of the Blossom House. Openings are eliminated from the corner bays, which now clearly project the square component of the plan.[47] They appear to be the primary structure, but such vertical piers in Wright's houses, even where made of brick as in the Martin House, share the support of the roof with the timber window mullions. The central bays, which in the Blossom House had windows cut into them as holes, are here stratified into bands of windows and parapets to represent the full breadth of the internal axes.

This expression of the simple Froebel figure had been crystallized in the Unity Temple, with which, significantly, Wright claimed to have found "the first real expression of the idea that the space within the building is the reality of that building."[48] It seems that he was so pleased with the form, which

F. F. Tomek House
Riverside, Illinois, 1907;
axonometric and plan analyses;
drawn by author

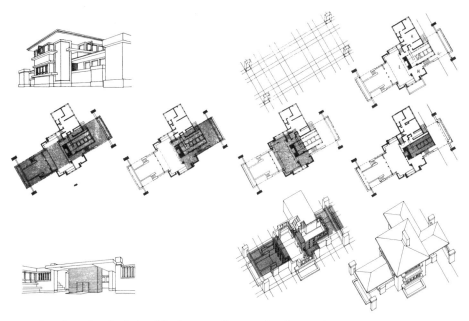

arose from functional relationships between the served and servant spaces, that he continued to employ it in other buildings where it could no longer express an organization of functions. The form is used in the project "A Fireproof House for $5000" of 1906, and in the Avery Coonley Playhouse built in Riverside, Illinois, in 1912. From this one must deduce that for Wright the relationship between interior and exterior had a formal significance, quite distinct from the European preoccupation with the "honest" expression of functional organization. Nevertheless the Evans House consists of more than merely pattern making. It displays the capacity of Wright's aesthetic to convey a hierarchy of places.

It is impossible to describe a moment of entry. A degree of access is perhaps experienced as soon as the field, exerted by the corner piers, is entered. Before one reaches the front door itself, further degrees of containment are encountered. Under the *porte cochere* an entry slot, flanked by a parapet, brings one up to the level of the living area via a short flight of steps. After this sequence, the front door becomes a relatively insignificant gesture of admission.

From outside, the extended roof over the ground floor may be interpreted as a continuous plane. Inside it is found to extend just beyond the entrance lobby, a space that is also contained within the central cube of the house, forming a place of transfer between interior and exterior. The view from inside the living room, with its higher ceiling, shows this penetrating roof of the *porte cochere*. Within the zone implied by this roof the dining area is defined by a gently dished ceiling and locked into position by the chimney.

Again the discipline of the grid has been employed for the subtle description of domestic functions in space. With this assembly of spaces and parts, characteristic of the mature Prairie period, Wright translated the patterns of the kindergarten into a three-dimensional system of architecture.

Robert W. Evans House
Chicago, Illinois, 1908; plan and axonometric analyses, exterior perspective and interior and living-room perspective; drawn by author

Enspacement:
The Main Sequence from 4 to 6
Analysis of Wright's
Steel Cathedral Project

BY OTTO ANTONIA GRAF

Only once during his long artistic life did Frank Lloyd Wright offer a small token of help for those interested in the workings of his compositional methods and energies: "And it is worthy of note in this connection that 9×9 equals 81 is just as simple as $2 + 2$ equals 4."[1]

$2 + 2$ defines the four corners of the square; 9×9 means the further subdivision of the square into 8×8 smaller squares. The Luxfer patents of December 1897, sometimes mentioned and routinely overlooked in regard to their architectural significance during Wright's life span, give, if used in combination of various twosomes or threesomes, all of his designs in sufficient detail, often down to the minute, albeit most telling, parts.

In 1923, Sullivan finally published his "seed germ" theory of ornament, which posits that patterns come from a primordial group of formative geometries. The theory has nothing to do with the seed of the maple or the lime, and even less so with Transcendentalism—instead it is the oldest primary pattern known to man through its systematically developed forms and variations since our earliest civilizations, including the Catal Höyük, Tell Halaf, and Susa A communities.

When creating and patenting patterns to cast into the glass of the Luxfer Glass Prism Company, Wright published his own, much more systematic attempt at formulating the basis of his compositional art (all the primary forms man had found to date), in the Official Gazette of the US Patent Office in December 1897. Surely one of the most outlandish repositories in architecture, it offers one of the very rare insights into the compositional workshop of all architectural history. The lamp of the Larkin Building produces the isometric version of patent 27992; the rest is incessant combination and recombination with the other forty designs, and the inevitable outcome twenty-five years later is the Steel Cathedral, a design for the largest known interior space of all history, usually shunned because of its apparent perplexity by the architectural historians' guild. Nothing more than the basic generic thought of the transposition and transformation of 4, the square and its spatial derivation, the cube, into the 6, the hexagon or isometric version of the cube and "seed germ" of the Steel Cathedral and almost each and every project and building until 1959, is necessary for all the riches of Wright's architec-

144

ture to appear before the thinking pen of the onlooker (all of which is illustrated in the following pages).

The division of the circle into twelve parts (the basis for our clock, found sometime during the fourth millennium in the Near East in a Neolithic cemetery below the great mosque of Samara) produces by sheer artistic necessity and experimenting curiosity the generative scheme for Hagia Sophia, commanding its "4^2" of the pattern included verbatim-formatim in the "5^2" of patent 27986. Wright's and Sullivan's arch pattern (the Schiller Building, uppermost story of the tower) may be deduced from the main sinuous line of the Magdalenian (the final cultural phase of the Paleolithic era), giving rise to almost every architectural process of composition. It may be seen in the lower church of San Francesco in Assisi: the Steel Cathedral arises out of it majestically if the patents 27986, 27995, and 27998 are combined, and some very few, happy lines of them elongated. Plan, enspacement, and elevation of the mountain of steel and glass appear in greatest and concise detail, together with the Mile High, the Guggenheim, and the plans for Baghdad. Wright, to his own confirmation, adds the basic 6 or isometry of the cube to both elevations in faint lines. The Beth Shalom Synagogue and the Trinity Chapel (an oscinian nightmare) show what could be saved from the most central and artistic design Wright put on paper after the Imperial Hotel.

Wright's patented world history of 1897 sets into motion the main sequence of the architect where every building has a specific place and function within the cosmic entirety, just as every glass pane, window, and lamp assumes a specific, individual function in the Dana House. There is no better way to envision the compositional method of Wright and his timely and morphological stretch in the world history of architectural composition since the seventh millennium. Why should he have explained anything about his composition or preached about his artistic independence and interdependence with the known and unknown world history after such a feat of imagination?

The patents of 1897 and the *House Beautiful* of the same year offer the fullest textbook of compositional morphology any architect has ever communicated and announced through the medium of his drawings, which are the lifeline of the art of building.

The often-feared subject of "geometry" in architecture, far from being the science from Euclid to modern mathematics, is nothing else than the identity of ornamentation and architectural composition. It is within that ancient cosmos that Wright must be studied and understood, not within the straitlaced confines of "modern" architecture alone. Then the observer sees how the patents are transformed into the Dana, the Dana into the Imperial, and how the Imperial and the Steel Cathedral emerge out of their generic precursors, to draw the most recent consequences of the Tell Halaf culture.

It should be remembered that Wright was the only great architect of the twentieth century not terrorized, traumatized, and totalitarianized through August 1914, a point that has escaped architectural critics completely, resulting in the strangest judgments completely beside any conceivable point. For all the rest, one of the first casualties of 1914 was ornament and its three-dimensional cosmos: the art of architecture.

Schiller Building
Louis Sullivan, Chicago, Ilinois, 1890; uppermost story of tower, frieze, and location of Wright's office beginning in the mid-1890s

Truncated Cube-Within-Cube
Wenzel Jamnitzer, *Perspectiva corporum regularium*, Nurnberg, 1568; this is a sixteenth-century example of the 4-side to 6-side geometry Wright employed in his Steel Cathedral plan

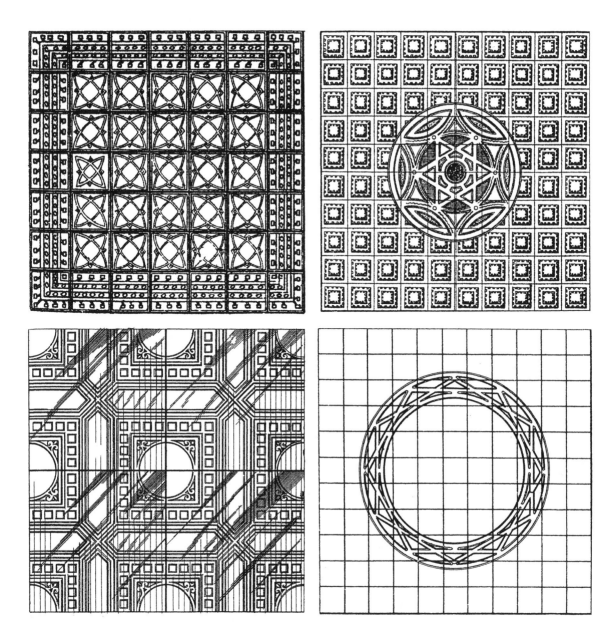

US Patent 27986
1896; Wright for Luxfer Glass
Prism Company, five times five
parts at center, within which one
may see the interlocking circles
that are divided into twelve parts

US Patent 27992
1896; Wright for Luxfer Glass
Prism Company, the lamp of the
Larkin Building is derived from
this pattern

US Patent 27995
1896; Wright for Luxfer Glass
Prism Company, division of the
circle into twelve parts

US Patent 27998
1896; Wright for Luxfer Glass
Prism Company, division of the
circle into six parts

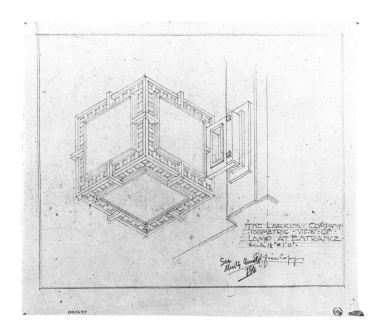

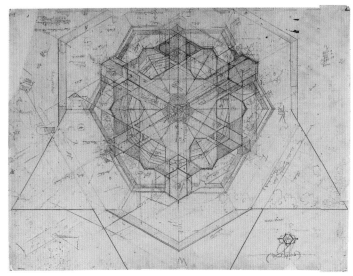

Larkin Building
Chicago, Illinois, 1902; isometric drawing of one of four lamps at entrance

Steel Cathedral
1926; plan, diagram of spatial structure

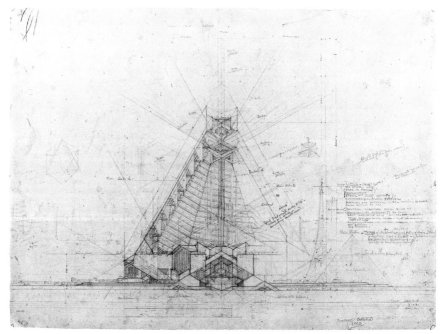

Steel Cathedral
elevation

Steel Cathedral
section

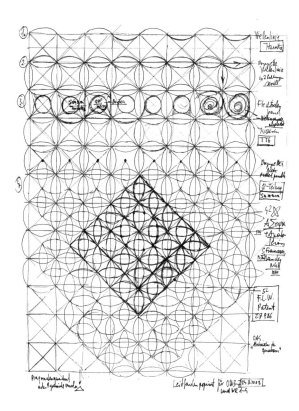

Hexagon
Louis Sullivan, *A System of Architectural Ornament*

Star of the Hexagon
Louis Sullivan, *A System of Architectural Ornament*

History of the Sinuous Curve of the Thirteenth Millennium
Wright patent 27986, within the lower part containing in its 5^2 parts the 4^2 of the matrix for Hagia Sophia; drawn by author

The sequence of diagrams on the following pages is the author's analysis of Wright's ordering geometries, for plan, section and ornament, indicating the direct relation of Wright's geometries to historical monuments and artifacts. The sequence explores the ancient system of formal order lying at the beginning of human civilization, and the manner in which Wright engaged it in all his designs. Each caption refers to the specific geometric elements and architectural examples being analyzed. All drawings are by the author.

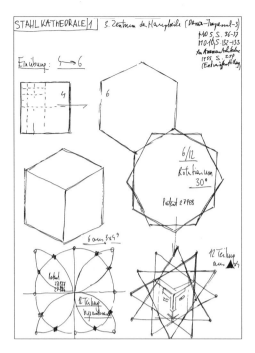

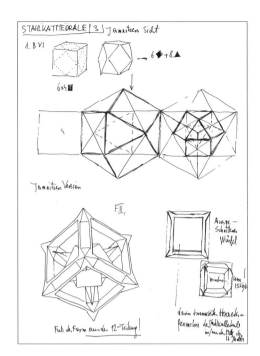

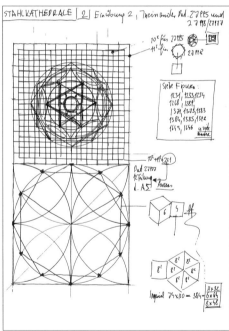

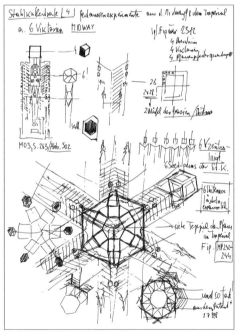

Steel Cathedral 1
basics of transition from "4" to "6" according to patent 27998
and division of the circle into twelve parts

Steel Cathedral 2
basics of combination of patents 27995 and 27922

Steel Cathedral 3
Jamnitzer's version of "4 to 6";

Steel Cathedral 4
four "Victories" (sculptures) from the Midway Gardens; 1913

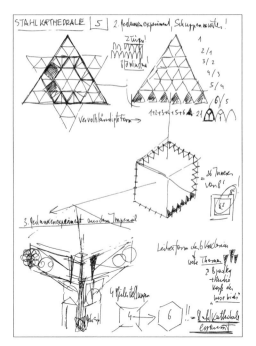

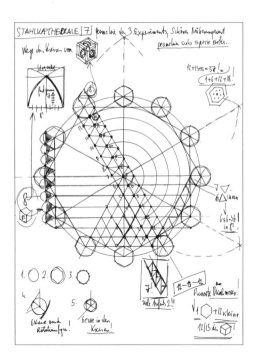

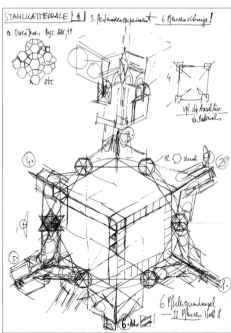

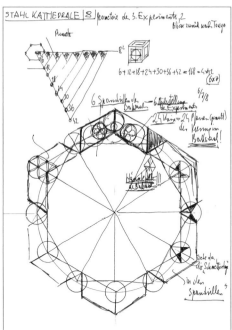

Steel Cathedral 5
the pattern of scales

Steel Cathedral 6
six "Peacock Kings" of the Imperial Hotel

Steel Cathedral 7
geometric derivation of the Steel Cathedral plan, step 1

Steel Cathedral 8
geometric derivation of the Steel Cathedral plan, step 2

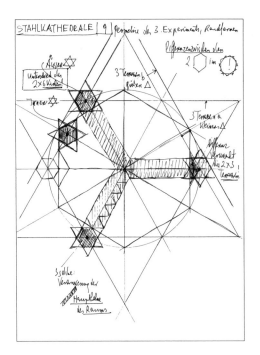

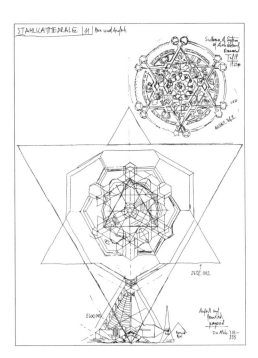

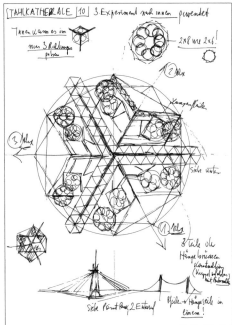

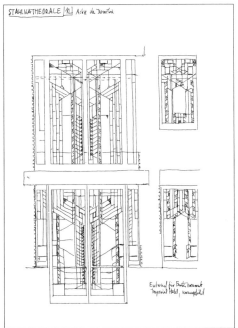

Steel Cathedral 9
geometric derivation of the forms at the border of the Steel Cathedral plan

Steel Cathedral 10
geometric derivation of Steel Cathedral plan, progression from edge to center

Steel Cathedral 11
plan and section of Steel Cathedral, compared to Sullivan's version of this same geometric form

Steel Cathedral 12
Imperial Hotel, drawing for a window, approximate geometry of the three main girders of the Steel Cathedral

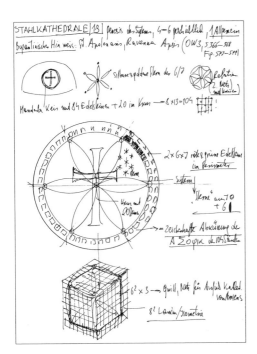

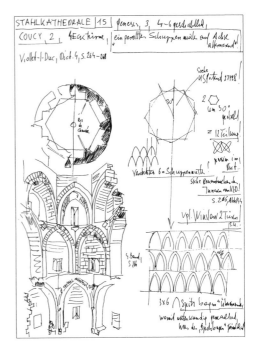

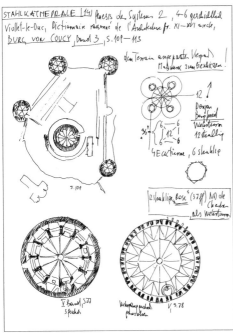

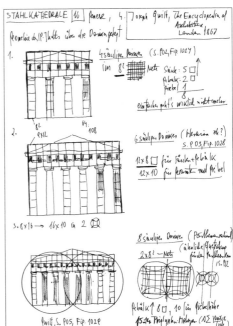

Steel Cathedral 13
apse at Sant Apolenaris, Ravenna, showing geometric sequence of 4 to 6

Steel Cathedral 14
Viollet-le-Duc, Fortress of Coucy, showing geometric sequence of 4 to 6

Steel Cathedral 15
Fortress of Coucy, towers, showing how the arches were constructed based upon the pattern of scale-shaped forms derived from the interlocking circles generating geometric sequence of 4 to 6

Steel Cathedral 16
matrices of the Doric order, from Joseph Gwilt's 1867 publication, indicating the underlying geometric sequence of 4 to 6

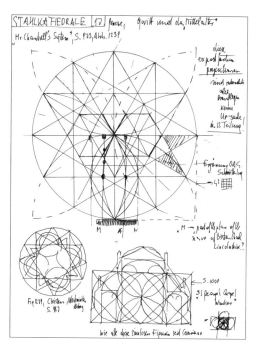

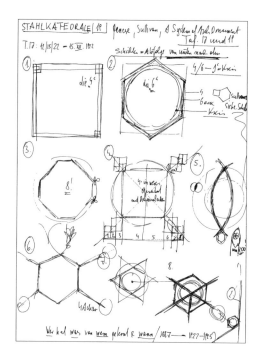

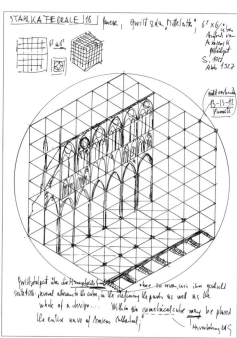

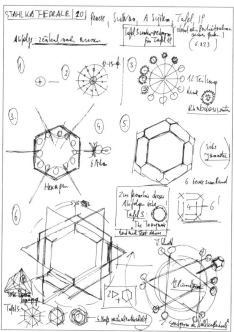

Steel Cathedral 17
medieval examples, plan and elevation, from Gwilt 1867, showing
use of forms derived from geometric sequence of 4 to 6

Steel Cathedral 18
Amiens Cathedral, isometry of the cube with six-fold division
containing interior elevation, from Gwilt 1867

Steel Cathedral 19
Sullivan, *A System of Architectural Ornament*, plates 17 and 19,
showing derivation from geometric sequence of square to
rotated cube, 4-sides to 6-sides

Steel Cathedral 20
Sullivan, plate 19, derivation from geometric sequence of 4 to 6

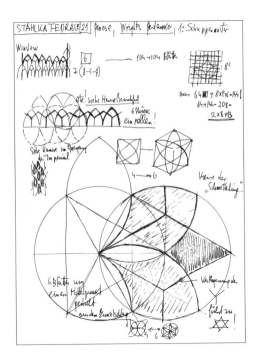

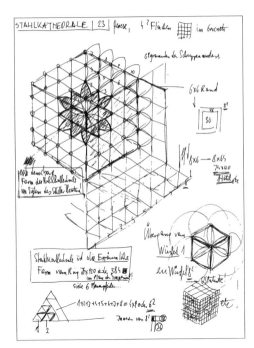

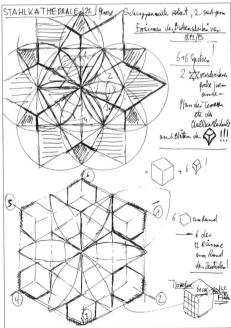

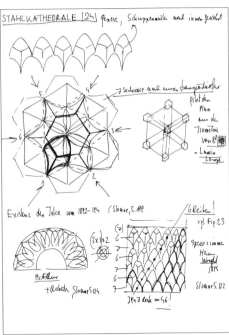

Steel Cathedral 21
derivation of pattern of scale-shaped forms derived from interlocking circles of geometric sequence of 4 to 6; Wright used pattern of scales in designing his dining room windows of 1889 as well as the William Winslow House of 1893

Steel Cathedral 22
rotation of pattern of scales around a center to produce basic diagram of Steel Cathedral plan

Steel Cathedral 23
4 times 4 sections, within matrix created by 6 times 6 sections, organized on hexagon or rotated cube, geometric matrix derived from 4 to 6

Steel Cathedral 24
pattern of scales rotated towards inner circle, indicating derivation of Steel Cathedral plan, related to McArthur House window of 1892 and Wright House window of 1889

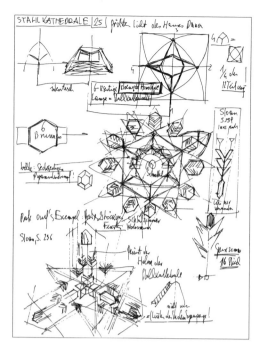

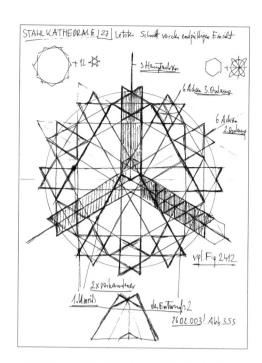

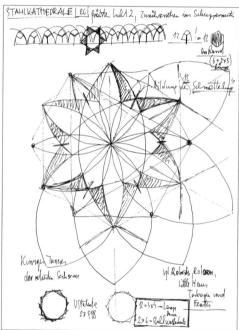

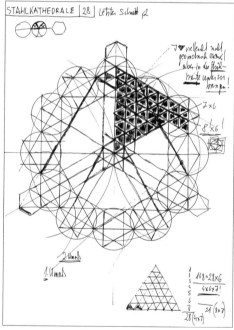

Steel Cathedral 25
lamps of the Susan Lawrence Dana House, 1902, showing that
it employs the same underlying geometric form as the Steel
Cathedral plan

Steel Cathedral 26
the pattern of scales extracted from Steel Cathedral and Dana
lamp plans

Steel Cathedral 27
derivation of Steel Cathedral plan and Dana House lamp from
geometric sequence of 4 to 6, step 1

Steel Cathedral, 28
derivation of Steel Cathedral plan and Dana House lamp from
geometric sequence of 4 to 6, step 2

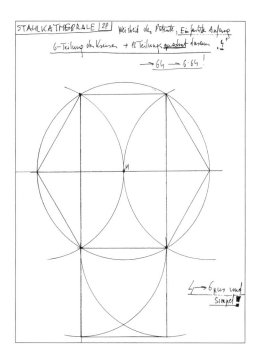

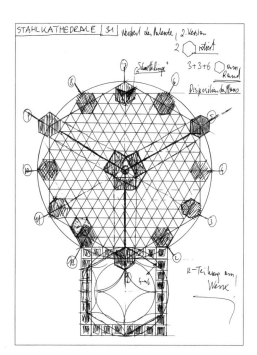

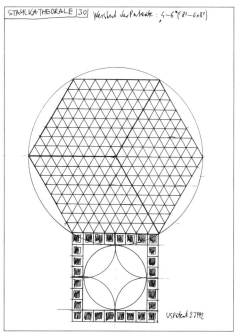

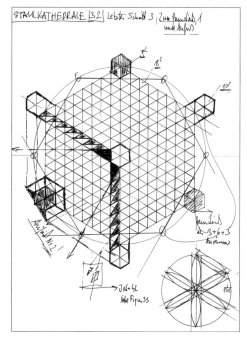

Steel Cathedral 29
derivation of Steel Cathedral plan, section and elevation from
underlying geometric sequence of 4 to 6 in Wright's Luxfer
Prism patent patterns

Steel Cathedral 30
geometry of the Luxfer Prism patent patterns, step 1,
4 to 6 = 8², below, to 6 x 8², above

Steel Cathedral 31
geometry of the Luxfer Prism patent patterns, derivation of Steel
Cathedral plan and section, step 2

Steel Cathedral 32
geometry of the Luxfer Prism patent patterns, derivation of Steel
Cathedral plan and section, step 3

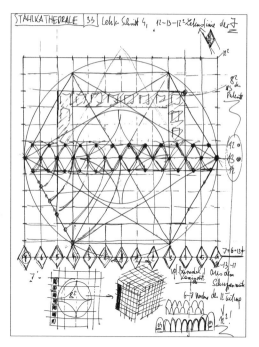

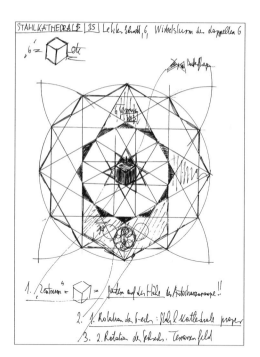

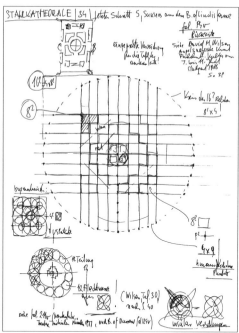

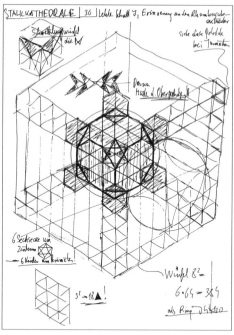

Steel Cathedral 33
geometry of the Luxfer Prism patent patterns, derivation of Steel
Cathedral plan, interlocking of geometries with 7 sections, step 4

Steel Cathedral 34
geometry of the Luxfer Prism patent patterns and Steel Cathedral
plan related to patterns from the *Book of Linisfarne*

Steel Cathedral 35
rotation of 2 x 6 to produce geometry of the Steel Cathedral

Steel Cathedral 36
rhombi-cube-octahedron related to plan of Steel Cathedral

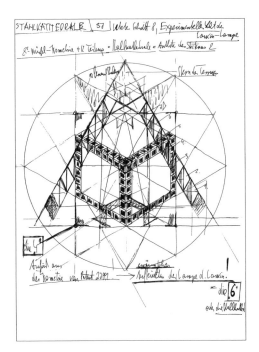

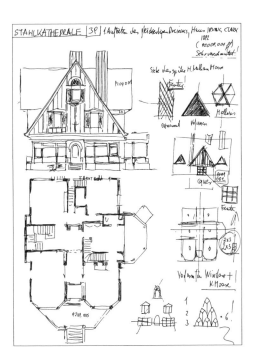

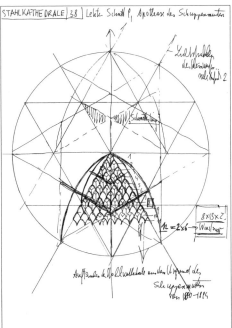

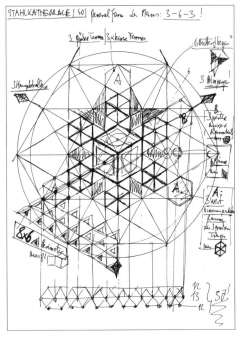

Steel Cathedral 37
Larkin Building lamp, as drawn by Wright, related to geometry of Steel Cathedral plan, section and elevation

Steel Cathedral 38
plan, elevation and section of Steel Cathedral related to pattern of scales and triangular segment

Steel Cathedral 39
Wright's first deployment of equilateral triangle in the Clark House, 1892

Steel Cathedral 40
basic geometries of the Steel Cathedral plan, constructed from equilateral triangles

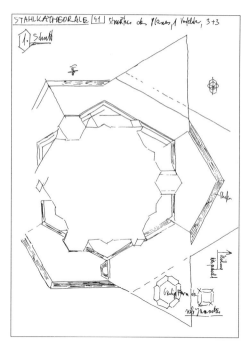

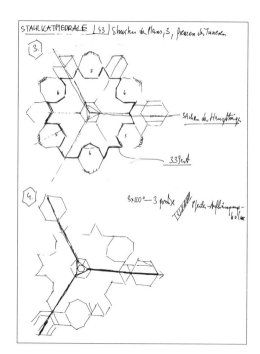

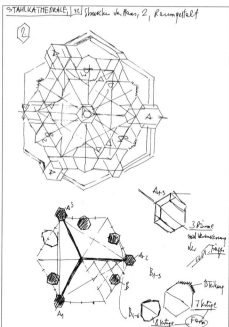

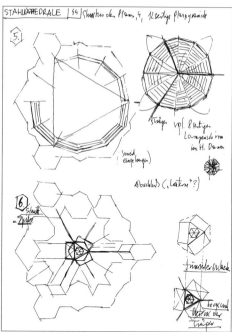

Steel Cathedral 41
geometric structure of building plan, site plan, and terraces of Steel Cathedral

Steel Cathedral 42
geometric structure of the plan, formation of enclosed space, Steel Cathedral

Steel Cathedral 43
geometric structure of the plan, formation of interior boundaries, Steel Cathedral

Steel Cathedral 44
geometric structure of the plan, formation of glass pyramid with 12 sides, Steel Cathedral

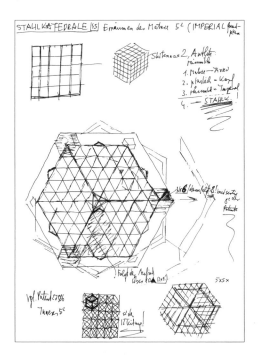

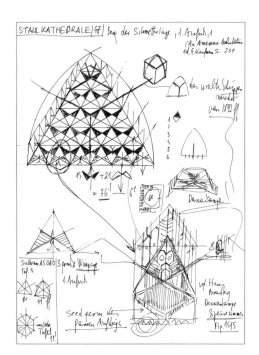

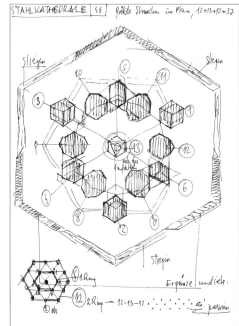

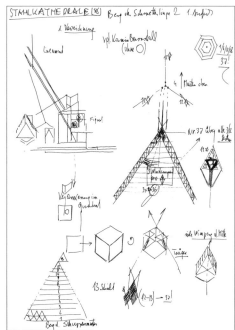

Steel Cathedral 45

enspacement, or enclosure and definition of space within
fundamental geometry, enspacement of matrix 5^2, five sections
times five sections used to generate geometric enclosure of
Steel Cathedral

Steel Cathedral 46

Steel Cathedral plan shown with outlying base structure, also
derived from geometric sequence of 4 to 6

Steel Cathedral 47

geometric formation found in first version of Steel Cathedral
elevation and in the Dana House lamp and window, related to
pattern of scales, division of equilateral triangle into series of
"butterfly shapes," forming a "mountain of butterflies," step 1

Steel Cathedral 48

first version of elevation of Steel Cathedral derived from
geometric form "mountain of butterflies," step 2

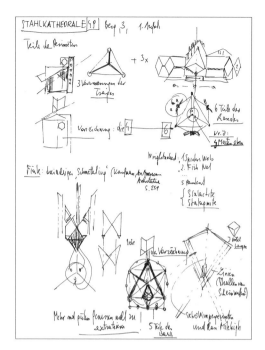

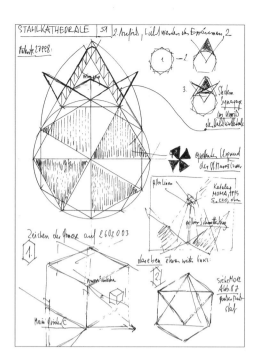

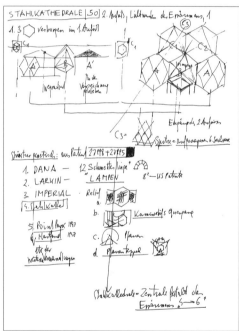

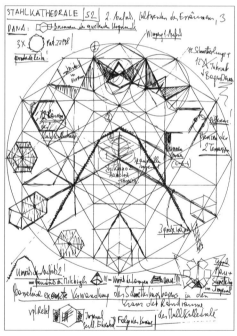

Steel Cathedral 49
first version of elevation of Steel Cathedral derived from geometric form "mountain of butterflies," step 3

Steel Cathedral 50
second version of elevation of Steel Cathedral derived from geometric sequence 4 to 6, enspacement related to Dana House light, step 1

Steel Cathedral 51
second version of elevation of Steel Cathedral derived from geometric sequence 4 to 6, enspacement related to Dana House light, step 2

Steel Cathedral 52
second version of elevation of Steel Cathedral derived from geometric sequence 4 to 6, enspacement related to Dana House light, step 3

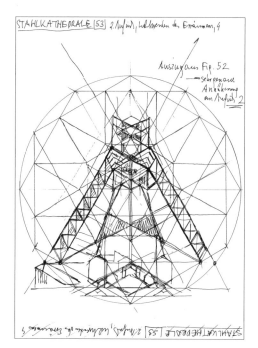

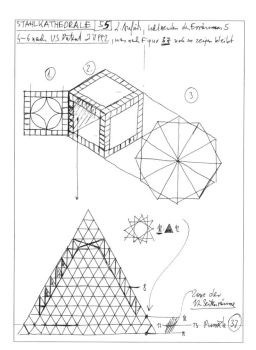

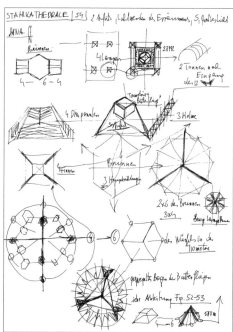

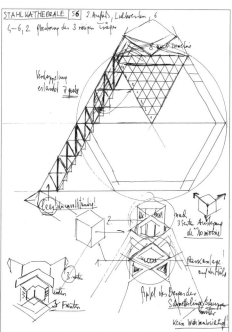

Steel Cathedral 53
second version of elevation of Steel Cathedral derived from
geometric sequence 4 to 6, enspacement related to Dana
House light, step 4

Steel Cathedral 54
second version of elevation of Steel Cathedral derived from
geometric sequence 4 to 6, enspacement related to Dana
House light, step 5

Steel Cathedral 55
second version of elevation of Steel Cathedral derived from
geometric sequence 4 to 6, enspacement related to Dana
House light, step 6

Steel Cathedral 56
second version of elevation of Steel Cathedral derived from
geometric sequence 4 to 6, enspacement related to Dana
House light, step 7

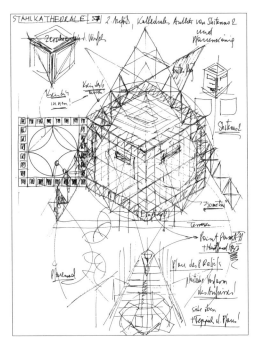

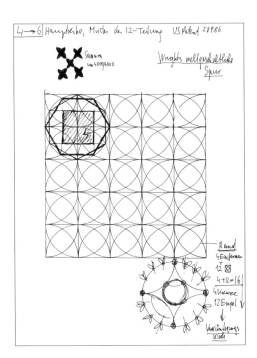

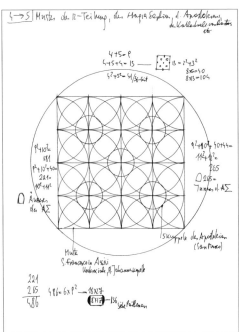

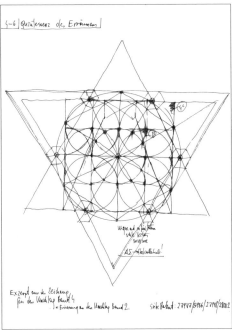

Steel Cathedral 57
second version of elevation of the Steel Cathedral, related to similar face of the Shitenno and Peacock King ornaments in the Imperial Hotel of 1916–22, as well as to Luxfer Prism pattern and Larkin Building lamp

Pattern of Division into Twelve Parts
resulting from geometric sequence of 4 to 6, as found in analysis three historic buildings, Hagia Sophia, Apostoleion, and San Francesco in Assisi

Pattern of Division into Twelve Parts
examples of Wright's work related to geometric sequence of 4 to 6 found throughout world history

Quintessence of Enspacement
showing how the same geometric pattern of the sequence from 4 to 6 underlies the plans of both the Steel Cathedral and Hagia Sophia, as well as the Luxfer Prism patent 27986

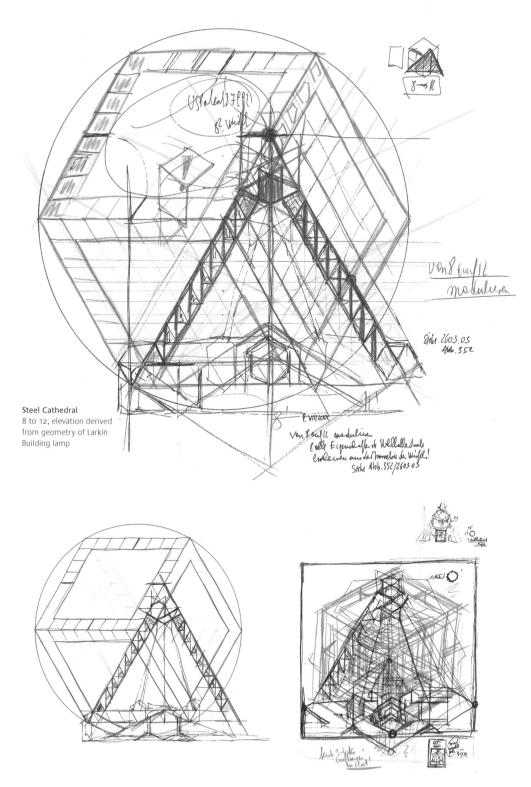

Steel Cathedral
8 to 12, elevation derived
from geometry of Larkin
Building lamp

Steel Cathedral
generation of the Steel Cathedral from
Larkin Lamp

Steel Cathedral
Larkin Lamp and Steel Cathedral

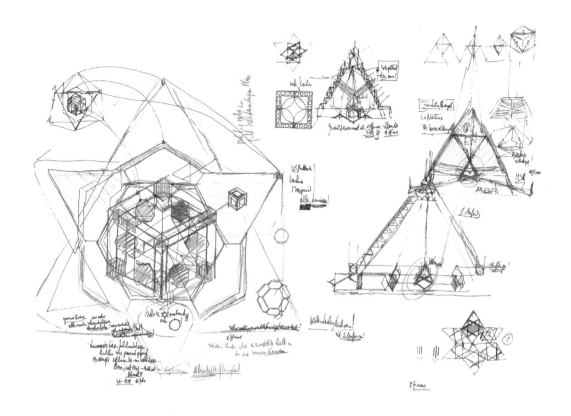

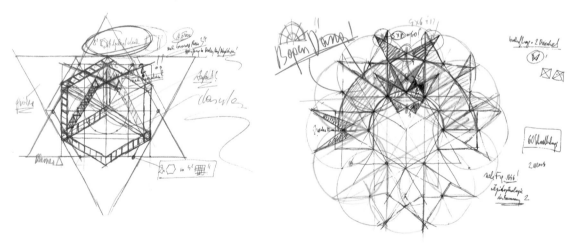

Steel Cathedral
geometry of plan, section and elevation
related to Luxfer Prism patterns

Steel Cathedral
plan and elevation out of isometric
of the Larkin Lamp, 1903–25

Sarah Lawrence Dana House
Springfield, Illinois, 1902; geometry
of the butterflies at entrance

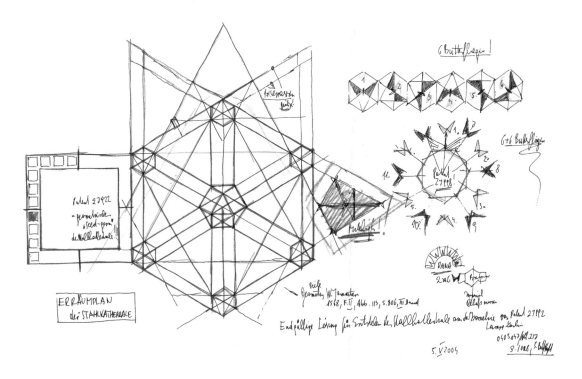

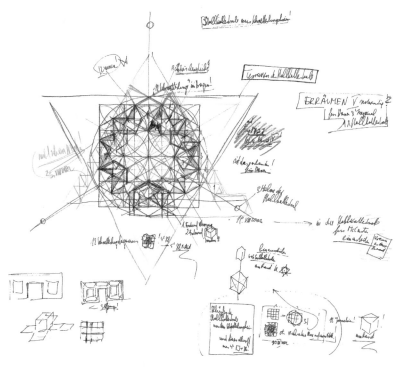

Steel Cathedral
tranformation of patent 27922 of 1897
into plan and elevation

Quintessence of Enspacement
second version, shared geometry of
plan of Steel Cathedral and Hagia
Sophia as well as Luxfer Prism patent
27986

"from
"4 → to 6"
MAIN SEQUENCE
1887 – 1959

Patents 1897 / Dana 1903 / Larkin 1904 / Imperial 1915–23 / Steel Cathedral

Patent
27992

4 LAMPS
LARKIN BLDS
1904

Central Vane of
Imperial
Entrance

Diana

Steel Cathedral
1925
plan elevation
out of one geometric
construction derived
from patents 27988 + 27992
otc (27986 – S. Francesco Assisi
+ ΑΣ OPIX

See: Otto Antonia Graf
Eräumen
zum Werk von Frank Lloyd Wright, III–IV
Vienna 2002, Verlag Böhlau

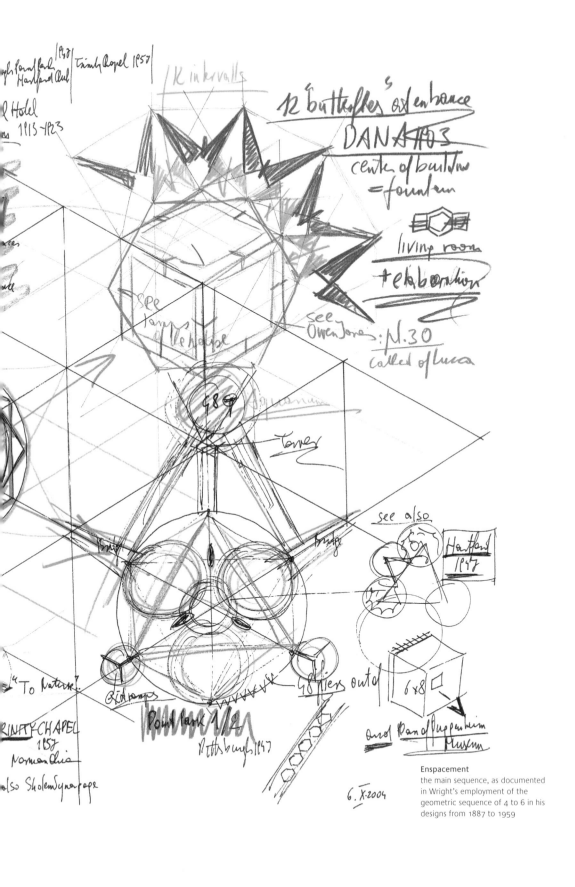

6. X.2004

Enspacement
the main sequence, as documented in Wright's employment of the geometric sequence of 4 to 6 in his designs from 1887 to 1959

The Text-Tile Tectonic
The Origin and Evolution of Wright's Woven Architecture

BY KENNETH FRAMPTON

"All the buildings I have ever built, large and small, are fabricated upon a unit system—as the pile of a rug is stitched into the warp. Thus each structure is an ordered fabric. Rhythm, consistent scale of parts, and an economy of construction are greatly facilitated by this simple expedient—a mechanical one absorbed in the final result to which it has given more consistent texture, a more tenuous quality as a whole."[1]
—*Frank Lloyd Wright*

THE TEUTONIC LEGACY

The fact that Frank Lloyd Wright always referred to Louis Sullivan as his *Lieber Meister* testifies to the strong hold that German culture exercised over Chicago during the last quarter of the nineteenth century. By the time of the Columbian Exhibition of 1893, Germans constituted a third of the city's population. In 1898, a survey of distinguished citizens of German origin listed seventeen architects, including August Bauer, Frederick Baumann, and Dankmar Adler, who was Sullivan's partner. Adler was a German émigré, and it is significant that Adler & Sullivan's Schiller Theatre of 1893 was built for the performance of plays in German, just as their canonical Auditorium Building of 1884 was largely devoted to opera, primarily that of Richard Wagner. Chicago boasted two daily newspapers in German and numerous German clubs and associations. Caught between his Beaux-Arts education and this omnipresent German environment, Sullivan included a number of French and German books in his library. Thus, as Barry Bergdoll has written:

> While neither Sullivan nor Wright read or understood German they were surrounded by people who did and who took an active interest in redefining the bases of architectural practice. In their own office in the Auditorium tower two of the principals were native Germans, Dankmar Adler and Paul Mueller, the young engineer from Stuttgart who later built many of Wright's most important designs. Sullivan, it should be remembered, had been exposed to German metaphysical philosophy already before joining Adler through his friend, the elusive John Edelman, who had spoken German since childhood and according to Sullivan's autobiography reinforced Sullivan's sympathy with American transcendentalist philosophy by long discourses on German Romantic

philosophy. In addition the entire office seems to have been interested in Wagner's music, the Auditorium building itself resonant with overtones of the Germanic notion of the Gesamtkunstverk and the possibility of dramatic art to lift the spectator to a higher realm of awareness.[2]

Bergdoll proceeds to show that the influence of the German theorist Gottfried Semper on late-nineteenth-century Chicago architecture was as intense as it was diffuse. It entered the architectural discourse from different quarters and was thus subject to somewhat varied interpretations. Two architects in particular seem to have assumed the main responsibility for the dissemination of Semper's views. These were the German émigré Frederick Baumann and the American John Wellborn Root.

Baumann would contribute to the development of the Chicago school in two completely different ways. In the first place, he would establish himself as a technician with his formula for constructing isolated pier foundations, made public through his pamphlet of 1873, *The Art of Preparing Foundations for all Kinds of Buildings with Particular Illustration of the Method of Isolated Piers*. In the second place, he would play a major public role in the interpretation of German architectural theory in translating Friedrich Adler's *Schinkelfest* of 1869 and in paraphrasing Semper's theories in his "Thoughts on Architecture," presented to the AIA in 1890, and his "Thoughts on Style," delivered to the AIA Convention in 1892. As Roula Geraniotis has remarked:

> The reasons why Baumann was so impressed by Semper are obvious: Semper was a profound thinker and a keen architectural critic, who had enjoyed a brilliant career as a designing architect. It is important to note that Semper's influence had reached Baumann directly through one of his former students; from 1969 to 1874 the foreman at the architectural office of Frederick Baumann and Eduard Baumann in Chicago was Carl Maximilian Heinzen, who had studied architecture under Gottfried Semper at the Eidgenössisches Polytechnikum (today's ETH) in Zurich. It is known that Semper was literally adored by his students and there is no doubt that Baumann shared fully the fascination that the young Heinzen had felt for his master.[3]

Baumann was not the sole figure to introduce Semper to the Chicago architectural scene. In late 1889 and again early in 1890, *Inland Architecture* published John Welborn Root's translations of Semper's 1869 essay "Über Baustile." The extreme closeness of theory and practice at this moment is borne out by the fact that Root made the translation in collaboration with his friend the German émigré Fritz Wagner, who happened to be an architect specializing in terra-cotta facing. It would be hard to imagine a more appropriate translator, since terra-cotta was a Semperian material *par excellence*, and exactly the material that Root would use in cladding his steel-framed Rand McNally Building, completed in 1890.[4]

Two aspects of Semper's theory were of special import for Baumann and for the development of the Chicago school in all its subsequent manifestations. First, the archetypal origin of all built form is textile production, with the knot serving as the primordial joint. Second, the art of building is anthropologically indebted to the aboriginal applied arts for many of its motifs.[5]

These hypotheses lead to Semper's theory of *Bekleidung* (cladding), wherein dress is seen as transposing itself across time into a form of permanent shelter. For Semper, the screenlike walls in permanent building were reminiscent of the tented nomadic textile form. As far as he was concerned, the terra-cotta facing and even brickwork were the cultural transposition of woven fabric.

While neither Wright nor Sullivan made any reference to Semper, we have every reason to suppose that they were aware of his theory, given that Chicago was so strongly subject to German cultural values and ideas. In any event, Sullivan would have heard Baumann's paper delivered to the Illinois State Association of Architects in 1887, wherein he paraphrased Semper's definition of style, "Style is the coincidence of a structure with the conditions of its origins."[6]

THE WRITING IN THE WALL

Among the more remarkable encounters in the prehistory of the Modem Movement is the meeting of the Welshman Owen Jones with Semper's close associate the young French architect Jules Goury. At the time of their encounter in Athens in 1831, Goury had already worked for seven months as Semper's research assistant; the direct object of their study was polychromatic decoration in Greek architecture. This concern for documenting aboriginal ornamentation led Jones and Goury to make a similar study of the Alhambra; their joint results were published in two volumes in 1836 and 1865, under the title *Plans, Elevations, Sections and Details of the Alhambra*.

Following Victor Hugo, Jones and Goury saw the Alhambra as a "palace that the [genies] have gilded like a dream filled with harmony." This romantic vision of an exotic alternative ran as a promise of cultural redemption throughout the rest of the century.[7] Jones, Sullivan, and Wright, all "outsiders" of Celtic origin, followed one another in this search for an "other" culture with which to overcome the spiritual bankruptcy of the West. Jones's *Grammar of Ornament*, published in 1856, served as a polemical guide for the pursuit of this goal; its transcultural, imperialist sweep through the world of ornament demonstrated by implication the relative inferiority of the European/Greco-Roman/medieval legacy compared with the riches of the Orient, the former appearing as palely tinted plates compared with the multicolored illustrations featuring exotic nonoccidental ornament. Over two-thirds of *The Grammar of Ornament* was devoted to these "other" cultures and these plates were beautifully printed in chromolithography, at considerable expense.

Jones's *magnum opus* led almost directly to Sullivan's own polychromatic ornament and to his richly colored "incantatory" system that was already fully elaborated by the time of his building for the Chicago Stock Exchange of 1894. This efflorescent enrichment reached its apotheosis in the midwestern banks designed towards the end of his career between 1906 and 1919. It is significant that almost all of these buildings were faced in rough-cut, tinted, pressed brick, a material that Sullivan regarded as a kind of textile. Thus he wrote in 1910:

> Manufacturers, by grinding the clay or shale course and by the use of cutting wires, produced on its face a new and most interesting texture, a tex-

Islamic Ornament Pattern
Owen Jones, *The Grammar of Ornament*

Celtic Ornament Pattern
Owen Jones, *The Grammar of Ornament*

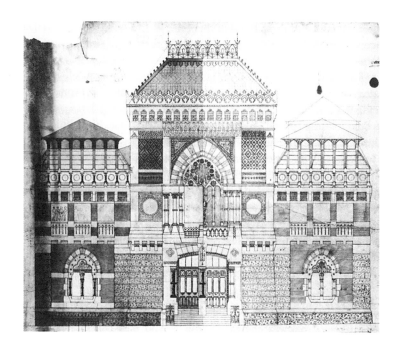

ture with a nap like effect, suggesting somewhat an Anatolian rug . . .
When [tinted bricks are] laid up promiscuously, especially if the surface is
large and care is taken to avoid patches of any one color, the general tone
suggests that of a very old Oriental rug.[8]

Wright made exactly the same analogy when writing of his textile block
system in 1927: "A building for the first time may be lightly fabricated, complete, of mono material—literally woven into a pattern or design as was the
oriental rug."[9]

Sullivan first came across the work of Jones through the Philadelphia
architect Frank Furness. Furness had been influenced by Jones, in part
through Cesar Daly's French translation of *The Grammar of Ornament* and
in part through contact with Jacob Grey Mould, who had been apprenticed
to Jones.[10] Furness evolved an orientalized Gothicism that was as evocative of
Moorish culture as the Alhambresque villas that Jones himself had realized
in Kensington Palace Gardens, London, in the late 1840s. Sullivan entered
into Furness's employ in 1873 at exactly that moment when the latter's orientalized neo-Gothic attained its maturity in his design for the Pennsylvania
Academy of Fine Arts.

While Sullivan unquestionably used sources other than Jones's
Grammar as the mainspring for his ornament, above all his own assiduous
scientific study of botanical form (see his intense study of Asa Gray's
Botany),[11] there is little doubt that many of Sullivan's philosophical ideas
find their correspondence in the numerous scholarly texts that accompanied Jones's compendium. Among these one may cite Jones's critical recognition of the cultural exhaustion of the West, condemned to the eternal
repetition of the same depleted formal syntax, and his insistence that we
need to return to nature as the Egyptians and the Greeks did rather than in
the manner of the Chinese and the Goths.[12] We also need to note Jones's

Pennsylvania Academy
of Fine Arts
Frank Furness, Philadelphia,
Pennsylvnia, 1871–76; elevation

introductory principles wherein he follows Semper in insisting on the primacy of tectonic form and urging that one decorate construction rather than construct decoration.[13] *The Grammar of Ornament* also contains J. O. Westwood's suggestion that Celtic art had its origin in the East, from which it may have been brought back by Irish missionaries; this must have provoked Sullivan, given his Irish background.[14] In a chapter dealing with the derivation of ornament from nature, Jones lays out the essence of Sullivan's own ornamental program:

> We think it impossible that a student fully impressed with the law of the universal fitness of things in nature, with the wonderful variety of form, yet all arranged around some few fixed laws, the proportionate distributions of areas, the tangential curvature of lines, and the radiation from the parent stem, whatever type he may borrow from Nature, if he will dismiss from his mind the desire to imitate it, but will only seek to follow still the path which it so plainly shows him, we doubt not that new forms of beauty will more readily arise under his hand, than can ever follow from a continuation in the prevailing fashion of vesting only the works of the past for present inspiration.[15]

Sullivan's *A System of Architectural Ornament According with a Philosophy of Man's Powers*, published in 1924, the year of his death, is a complex and subtle demonstration of Jones's hypothetical program. Sullivan elaborated those procedures that Jones outlined. What Sullivan demonstrated in documenting his method was a series of morphological and geometrical transformations in which the bipolar seed germ (the sycamore pod) was elaborated

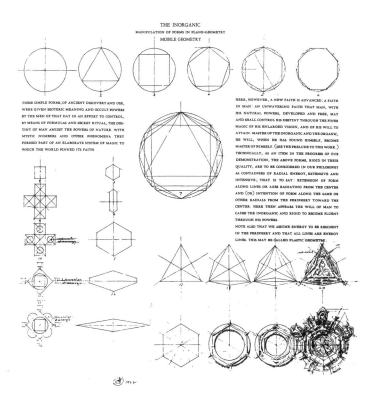

The Inorganic Manipulation of Forms in Plane Geometry and Mobile Geometry
Louis Sullivan, 1924

in ever more complex organic forms structured about simple Platonic armatures: the square, the circle, the triangle, etc. These forms are elaborated in their turn into complex, inorganic polyhedrons. The two procedures result in swirling, efflorescent exfoliations as may be found on the lower street facade of Sullivan's Schlesinger and Mayer Store of 1899 and on the banks that bring his career to a close. A form of quasi-scientific nature worship is latent in this pantheistic ornament. Perhaps this indirectly connects Sullivan's transcendentalism to the abstract universality of Islamic architecture. Sullivan's later ornament may be regarded as an incantatory assertion of cosmological faith, one that impregnates the entire surface of his structures like a magical tattoo, as is evident in the Guaranty Building, Buffalo, of 1895. This underlying intent is suggested by the brief text that accompanies his treatise on ornament:

> These simple forms of ancient discovery and use were given esoteric meaning and occult powers by the men of that day in an effort to control, by means of formulas and secret ritual, the destiny of man amidst the powers of nature. With mystic numbers and other phenomena they formed part of an elaborate system of magic to which the world pinned its faith. Here, however, a new faith is advanced; a faith in man: an unswerving faith that man, with his natural powers, developed and free, may and shall control his destiny through the finer magic of his enlarged vision and his will to attain.[16]

That the magical is still implied in this vision of a triumphant techno-scientific future is as significant as the mystical anthropomorphism that underlay everything Sullivan wrote. Sullivan saw creativity as the giver of both individual and collective identity and as the manifestation of some unnameable divinity.

Sullivan and Wright believed in the possibility of a modern civilization that would be comparable in its spiritual intensity to the great theocracies of the antique world. The implicit theology of their work, its intrinsic text, depended, in its reticulated surface, on the translation and iteration of organic morphological processes, on a conscious fusion of nature and culture. Thus a progressive pantheism came to be inscribed in everything they did, as a kind of cryptic language or as a petrified textile in which the walls were as much written as they were built. One is reminded at this juncture of Semper's account of cultural development as a kind of linguistic waxing and waning in which forms emerge and rise to high levels of articulation before degenerating into decadence. Within such a trajectory, Semper imagines primordial form as being an idiosyncratic syntactical inflection by which an entire nonverbal culture might be woven as a kind of rhythmic parallel to poetry or chant. Thus for Semper, as for Sullivan and Wright, architecture was closer to dance and music than to painting and sculpture.[17]

Jones illustrated the ornament of a number of nonrepresentational civilizations wherein a similar iteration amounted to a kind of incantatory inscription bordering at times on trancelike hallucination.[18] Within this context it is hardly an accident that Wright would be attracted to pre-Columbian and Japanese civilizations, as Sullivan had been drawn in his own time to Saracenic culture. In Islamic architecture, the written, the woven, and the tectonically inscribed are frequently fused together.

Guaranty Building
Louis Sullivan, Buffalo, New York, 1895; detail of column capital at street

Confirmation of this is found in Claude Humbert's study of Islamic ornament, wherein he writes:

> Writing, calligraphy and epigraphy are the testimony of a civilization. Not only do the ideas and deeds transcribed and communicated provide content, but the writing and the written page themselves constitute a form that can be analyzed graphically.... It is important to consider briefly here this script that forms an integral part of Arab design. Ornamental in itself, it quite naturally comes to be incorporated into other ornaments.... From an examination of all the forms of decorative and ornamental Islamic art, two quite distinct types emerge: polygonal ornamentation, characterized by a skilled and critical use of geometry; and plant and floral ornamentation, which, in contrast to polygonal design, are inspired by the natural world.[19]

Humbert cites numerous instances in which Kufic script appears as an ornament that is as much written as it is designed. He gives examples of motifs built up out of permutations of the word *Allah* or *Muhammad*, or of entire lines such as "There is no strength but that of God" that assume through abstraction the profile of an Islamic city, complete with minarets. Alternatively, the names Ali and Muhammad pinwheel about a solar cross. It is significant that something akin to a solar cross will appear in Wright's quadratic monogram and that this motif will be subjected to a series of permutations and patterned proliferations in Wright's concrete blocks.

DEUS EX CONGLOMERATUS

While it is unlikely that Wright was ever aware of Semper's essay "Science, Industry and Art" of 1852, certain parallels nonetheless exist between their respective views of the machine, particularly as Wright's view appears in his seminal address of 1901, "The Art and Craft of the Machine." Unlike his contemporary Adolf Loos, for whom the invention of ornament was an anathema, Frank Lloyd Wright attempted to derive an authentic ornament from the process of fabrication, irrespective of whether this entailed the mechanized manufacture of basic building blocks or the systematic assembly of prefabricated modular elements. Thus while Semper despaired of overcoming the newfound capacity of the machine to dissimulate or rather to simulate rich material effects in their absence. Wright regarded the machine as a phoenix that was destined to arise from the ashes of its current *kitsch* production to yield a future democratic culture, comparable to the ancient theocracies. After Victor Hugo's famous study of Notre Dame, Wright saw the rotary press as the *sine qua non* of the machine. Of the impact of mechanical reproduction on the preliterate text of architecture Wright wrote:

> Thus down to the time of Gutenberg architecture is the principle writing—the universal writing of humanity. In the great granite books of the Orient, continued by Greek and Roman antiquity, the middle ages wrote the last page.... In the fifteenth century everything changes. Human thought discovered a mode of perpetuating itself, not only more resisting than architecture, but still more simple and easy. Architecture is dethroned. Gutenberg's letters of lead are about to supercede Orpheus' letters of stone. The book is about to kill the edifice. The invention of

Islamic Ornament
calligraphic design based on and incorporating the names Muhammad and Ali

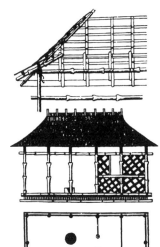

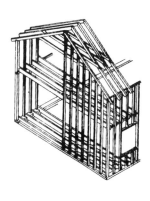

Ho-o-den Japanese
Exhibition Pavilion
World's Columbian Exposition,
Chicago, 1893

Indian Hut at the Trinidad
Exhibit
Great Exhibition, London, 1851;
drawing by Gottfried Semper

Balloon Frame System of
Timber Construction
George Washington Snow

printing was the greatest event in history. It was the first great machine, after the great city. It is human thought stripping off one mode and donning another.[20]

While recognizing the inevitable truth of Hugo's famous retrospective prophecy that this (the press) will kill that (architecture)—*ceci tuera cela*—Wright nonetheless argued for the employment of the liberative, mechanized potential lying dormant within the body politic of the late nineteenth century. As a corollary to this, Wright urged the reeducation and reintegration of all the various classes of modern manufacturers, from industrialists to craftsmen. He was prompt to recognize, however, that the laborsaving cultural potential of the machine would come into its own only if the machine was allowed to produce according to its own intrinsic order. Thus he wrote:

> The machine, by its wonderful cutting, shaping, and smoothing and repetitive capacity, has made it possible to so use it without waste that the poor as well as the rich may enjoy today beautiful surface treatments of clean, strong forms that the branch veneers of Sheraton and Chippendale only hinted at with dire extravagance, and which the middle ages utterly ignored. The machine has emancipated these beauties of nature in wood; made it possible to wipe out the mass of meaningless torment to which wood has been subjected since the world began, for it has been universally abused and maltreated by all peoples but the Japanese.[21]

Since he had yet to visit Japan, Wright was no doubt alluding here to the reassembled Ho-o-den Temples that appeared in the Columbian Exhibition of 1893. Bergdoll suggests that this work may well have had as great an impact on Wright as the Caribbean hut in the Great Exhibition of 1851 had on Semper. There seems to be a convergence here between Wright's appreciation for the repetitive yet variable order of Japanese domestic architecture and the vastly improved wood-milling capacity that had evolved in part out of the increasing demand for George Washington Snow's balloon-frame system of timber construction.[22] Thus Wright's early domestic architecture, executed in wood, is invariably conceived and machined according to a repetitive modular order and framed after Snow's invention. Seen in this light, Wright's early wooden architecture seems to be as modular as anything we will encounter in his later "textile block" construction.

Studding is invariably suppressed by cladding in the balloon-frame system, in part to provide a hermetic weatherproof sheath and, in part, to unify the surface, often in the cause of simulating more substantial forms of building. Wishing to express the fundamental framework and to exploit the tectonic virtues of advanced sawmill technology, Wright took the opposite tack of partially expressing the studwork through horizontal cover strips secured through the cladding into the studs. This "interwoven" tectonic was already evident in Wright's "Romeo and Juliet" Windmill of 1896, where it presented itself as a plaited fabric composed of timber shingles and horizontal wooden battening.

The "Romeo and Juliet" Windmill inaugurated that which Henry-Russell Hitchcock later identified as the "Forest period" of Wright's architecture, wherein he utilized a relatively inexpensive, all-timber mode of construction, a horizontal and greatly simplified version of the American shingle style. A number of works exemplify this short-lived episode in Wright's career, ranging from the River Forest Golf Club of 1901 to the Ross House built on Lake Delavan in 1902, and the Glasner House, completed at Glencoe, Illinois, in 1905. The summer cottages built for the Gerts family in Whitehall, Michigan, in 1902 also belong to this genre. In each instance a three-foot-square planning module was adopted, together with boarded sheathing, capped by horizontal battens at one-foot intervals. That these battens perform the same modulating role as recessed string courses in rusticated masonry is born out by the Arthur Heurtley House of 1902, where every fifth brick course is set in advance of the main wall.

A plaited approach to architectonic space, surely derived in some measure from the Froebel system, prevailed throughout Wright's long career. It assumed either a tartan or a simple quadratic form of varying modular dimension, ranging from the basic two-way, three-foot grid of the midwestern "Forest period" to the sixteen-inch-square grid of the Californian "textile block" period to the thirteen-inch recessed horizontal "battens" that striate the walls of the Usonian Houses of the 1930s and 40s. For Wright, this modular order varied according to local circumstance. At the same time, it was as much an economic, democratic, laborsaving device as it was an architectural concept.

Romeo and Juliet Windmill
Spring Green, Wisconsin, 1896;
period photograph

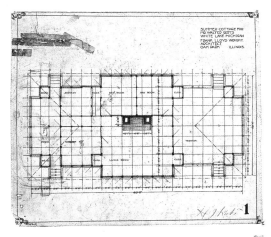

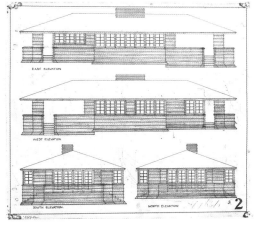

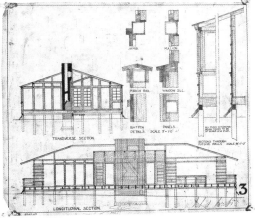

Walter Gerts Cottage
Whitehall, Michigan, 1902;
construction drawings, plan

Walter Gerts Cottage
construction drawings, elevations

Walter Gerts Cottage
construction drawings, sections

This tectonic method broke down when Wright had to confront the all-purpose, fireproof, durable material of his epoch: monolithic reinforced concrete, *cast in situ*. This is the material envisaged for his Village Bank prototype, projected, ironically enough, for the *Brickbuilder* in 1901, and this is the same material that will constitute the basic fabric of Unity Temple, completed in Oak Park in 1906. Even here Wright approached the entire design from the standpoint of building production. Thus he wrote of the temple:

> What shape? Well, the answer lay in the material. Why not make the wooden boxes or forms so the concrete could be cast in them as separate blocks or masses, these grouped about an interior space.... The wooden forms or molds in which concrete buildings must at that time be cast were always the chief item of expense, so to repeat the use of a single form as often as possible was necessary. Therefore a building, all four sides alike, looked like the thing. This reduced to simplest terms, meant a building square in plan. That would make their temple a cube—a noble form in masonry.[23]

Monolithic Concrete "Village Bank"
1901; perspective view from street

Unity Temple
Oak Park, Illinois, 1906; period photograph showing building under construction

However, like the French structural rationalist Anatole de Baudot in his Saint Jean de Montmartre Church of 1904, built of *ciment* as opposed to *béton armée*, Wright realized that monolithic concrete could not be accorded a convincing tectonic beacuse of its lack of inherent articulation. This fact is made explicit in his manifesto that appeared in *Architectural Record* in 1929: "Aesthetically concrete has neither a song nor any story. Nor is it easy to see in this conglomerate, in this mud pie, a high aesthetic property, because in itself it is amalgam, aggregate, compound. And cement, the binding medium, is characterless."[24] Later in the same passage, he writes of his invention of the textile block:

> I finally had found a simple mechanical means to produce a complete cladding that looks the way the machine made it, as much at least as any fabric need look. Tough, light, but not "thin," imperishable, plastic; no unnecessary lie about it anywhere and yet machine made, mechanically perfect. Standardization as the soul of the machine here for the first time may be seen in the hand of the architect, put squarely up to imagination, the limitations of imagination the only limitation of building.[25]

It is interesting to note that Wright made his first move away from monolithic reinforced concrete in the very year that Unity Temple was completed. This move came with a house designed for Harry E. Brown in 1906. In a later annotation attached to a drawing of this house, Wright claimed it as the first concrete-block house, projected some fifteen years before his use of the material in California. Tiled motifs set in plaster in the Avery Coonley House of 1908 and the patterned block capping to the A. D. German Warehouse of 1915 point in the same direction as do the terra-cotta blocks applied to Midway Gardens, Chicago, of 1915 and the carved ornamentation in Oya stone that appears in Wright's Japanese work from 1918–22. Wright finally tackled the idea of wire-reinforced, tessellated block construction (cf. de Baudot's wire-reinforced brickwork of 1904) with his 1921 study for a concrete-block house for Albert M. Johnson, in Death Valley, California.

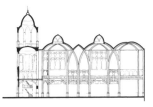

Unity Temple
view of exterior

Saint Jean de Montmartre Church
Anatole de Baudot, Paris, France, 1904; longitudinal section; redrawn under author's supervision

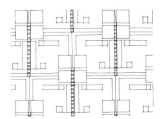

Harry Brown House
Genesco, Illinois, 1906; note at
bottom by Wright states, "First
block house"

Midway Gardens
Chicago, Illinois, 1913;
period photograph, view
from orchestra shell

Avery Coonley House
Riverside, Illinois, 1907; ceramic-
tile pattern on exterior walls

In terms of both panoramic form and grandiose program, this Egyptoid "cult" building entertained similar cultural aspirations as the complex that Wright designed for Aline Barnsdall at Olive Hill, Los Angeles, with which he was engaged intermittently from 1915 to 1920. However, Barnsdall's Hollyhock House was not built in concrete block, so the realization of "textile block" construction did not occur until Alice Millard's canonical "La Miniatura," built in Pasadena, California, in 1923. With typical metaphorical clarity, Wright set forth the economic/tectonic advantages of this method when he wrote in 1932:

> We would take that despised outcast of the building industry—the concrete block—out from underfoot or from the gutter—find hitherto unsuspected soul in it—make it live as a thing of beauty—textured like trees. Yes, the building would be made of the "blocks" as a kind of tree itself standing among other trees in its own native land. All we would have to do is to educate the concrete block, refine it and knit it together with steel in the joints and so construct the joints that they could be poured full of concrete after they were set up and a steel strand laid in them. The walls would thus become thin but solid reinforced slabs and yield to any desire imaginable. And common labor could do it all. We would make the walls double of course, one wall facing inside and the other wall facing outside, thus getting continual hollow spaces between, so the house would be cool in summer, warm in winter and dry always.[26]

Immediately after this passage, Wright referred to himself as the "weaver," thereby stressing, once again, his conception of the textile block as an all-enveloping woven membrane, suppressing at every turn those latent struc-

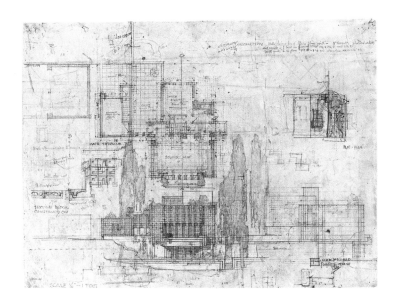

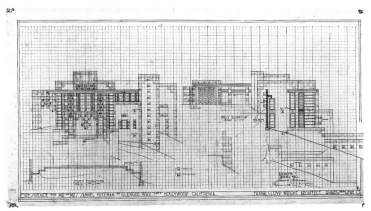

tural members that were equally essential to its constitution, that is to say those reinforced concrete beam and column sections essential to the stabilization of the thin tessellated walls. This suppression is evident from the fact that in almost all of the concrete block houses the floor depths do not coincide with the modular dimension of the system.

With its patterned, perforated, glass-filled apertures, La Miniatura already embodied the essential syntax of the "textile block" system that was employed, with subtle variations, in each of the subsequent block houses. With the exception of the Freeman House, where the textile blocks run into open glass corners and where the muntins seem to emerge directly from the joints between the blocks, Wright's Californian block houses—the Ennis and Storer houses—add little to the basic syntax of La Miniatura. The full implication of the Freeman innovation, the extension of the tessellated semisolid membrane into mitred glass corners and largely glazed surfaces, comes with Wright's National Life Insurance Offices, projected for Chicago in 1924. The unique nature of this curtain-wall system (following Wright's first curtain wall exercise for Luxfer Prism in 1895) comes from continuously "flowing"

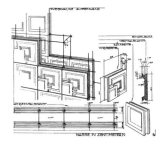

Alice Millard House
preliminary sketch study of plan and elevation

Samuel Freeman House
Los Angeles, California, 1923; south and west elevations, construction drawings; note use of square grid paper

Textile Block System
1923

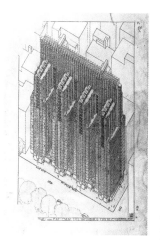

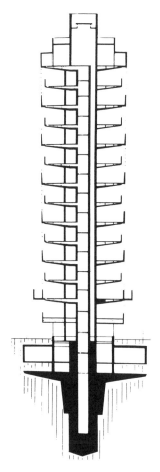

from copper sheathing to plate glass and back again, with hardly any formal transition. The equally nonhierarchical fusion and confusion of the textile block houses is overcome here through the total separation of the inner-cantilevered concrete armature from the outer membrane. The essential continuity *and* articulation of Wright's *magnum opus*—his masterly Johnson Wax Administration Building of 1936—is already implied in this dramatic articulation of structural and superficial form.

Wright's last concrete block house, built in 1929 in Tulsa, Oklahoma, for the Lloyd-Joneses, already appears as the transitional work, since here, the hitherto finely woven fabric of the textile block is abandoned in favor of a larger block formation, laid up as piers. Wright's unrealizable Egyptoid "ideal" of elevations without windows is now relinquished in favor of an alternating pattern of piers and slots that is as overtly solid as it is void. This passage from the sixteen-inch-square block pattern of Freeman House to the fifteen-by-twenty-inch plain-faced, straight-stack, bonded block pattern of the Lloyd-Jones House produces a paradoxical decrease in the apparent mass; the true scale remains misleading, since floor heights and openings are again suppressed. Apart from permitting a totally consistent alignment between block courses and window transoms, the larger block has many advantages, from the labor-saving in block laying to the filling of the hollow cores with cement and steel rods to produce the occasional reinforced-concrete column or the use of similar voids for the purpose of ventilation and other services. The Lloyd-Jones House suggests that the lack of "built-in" ducts in the textile block may have contributed to its abandonment, particularly since Wright was more preoccupied with the tectonic integration of services than any other architect of his generation.

Again, in his abortive work for Alexander Chandler, the romantic panorama of San Marcos–in–the–Desert of 1927, Wright attempted to render the textile block as a totally coherent form of prefabricated assembly by devising a system of modular floor beams. His simultaneous attempt to apply the Chandler "textile block" system to the design of a modest middle-class dwelling, the so-called Chandler Block House, already anticipates the Usonian typology that would emerge five years later.

This comprehensive work for Chandler reveals the two diametrically opposed faces of Wright's textile-block period. On the one hand we encounter the otherworldly, Xanadu-like grandeur of San Marcos–in–the–Desert, comparable in its "orientalism" to Wright's grandiose Doheny Ranch of 1921; on the other, we find the down-to-earth, democratic economy of the Chandler Block House. It is but a step from Wright's timber architecture of the turn of the century to this work, and the fact that this move comes with Wright's literal return to the Midwest should remind one of the regional inflection that was always latent as a creative impulse within Wright's work.

Wright's return to his roots led to the final phase of his textile tectonic—the self-styled Usonian House that endured in his work as a continuous vision and practice, up to his death in 1959.

The Usonian House emerged fully armed, as it were, in the Malcom Willey House projected for Minneapolis, Minnesota, in 1932, and built in modified form two years later. That Wright was well aware of the "break-

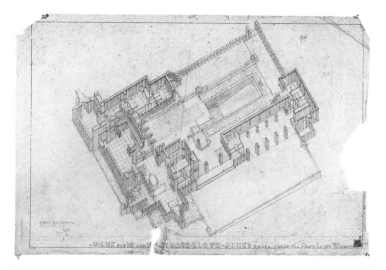

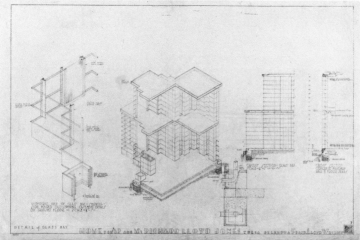

through" that this work represented is borne out by the following passage written in the same year:

> Now came clear an entirely new sense of architecture, a higher conception of architecture ... space enclosed ... this interior conception took architecture away from sculpture, away from painting and entirely away from architecture as it had been known in the antique. The building now became a creation of interior space in light. And as this sense of the interior space as the reality of the building began to work, walls as walls fell away.[27]

While this is not the place to enter into the vicissitudes of the Usonian House, it is nonetheless important to note that once again the generic prototype was conceived as having woven walls. Double-sided and triple-layered, these walls consisted of boards affixed to a continuous plywood core so as to produce horizontal recesses as opposed to the battens of Wright's "Forest style." Woven at more than one scale, the Usonian House was also conceived as a three-dimensional gridded cage in which the two-foot-by-four-foot or four-foot-square plan module yielded spatial layers that were interwoven with

Richard Lloyd-Jones House
Tulsa, Oklahoma, 1929; isometric view of plan with walls

Richard Lloyd-Jones House
construction details shown in isometric

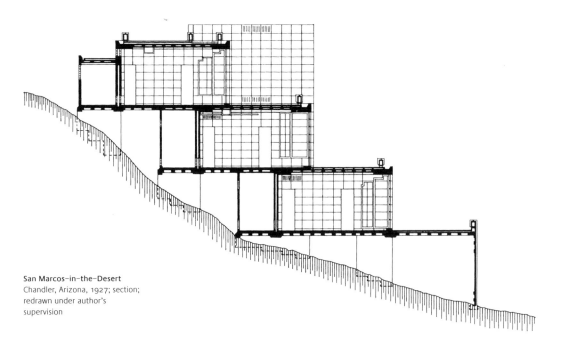

San Marcos-in-the-Desert
Chandler, Arizona, 1927; section;
redrawn under author's
supervision

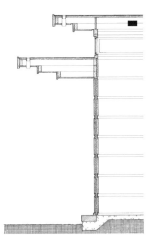

Typical Wooden Usonian House
wall section, redrawn under
author's supervision

Herbert Jacobs House
Madison, Wisconsin, 1936;
plan; redrawn under editor's
supervision

the vertical thirteen-inch layers governing the horizontal recesses, window transoms, door heights, and built-in furniture. The walls were given a thick warp and woof in which, as Wright put it in the sixth point of his famous *Architectural Forum* "manifesto" of 1938, "furniture, pictures, and bric-a-brac are unnecessary except as the walls can be made to include them or be them."[28] That the typical Usonian dwelling consisted of a three-dimensional matrix made up of interlocking locational "fixes" and layers is born out by Wright's provision of three separate plan cuts: one at floor level, one at door-head-clerestory height, and one at roof level. As John Sergeant has characterized it in his canonical study of the Usonian House, Wright's millwork is "interwoven like basketry."[29]

As far as was feasible, Wright eliminated field labor and reduced wastage in the cutting of timber by adopting a module that corresponded with standard mill dimensions. At the same time, Wright attempted to exploit the thermal flywheel effect of the *in situ* concrete site slab; it was warmer in winter and cooler in summer than the average wooden floor. With serpentine, small-bore heating pipes cast into the slab, a typical Usonian dwelling, when boosted with an open fire, would be comfortable in the winter rather than overheated; Wright stated that in severe weather people would simply have to wear warmer clothing. In high summer the ubiquitous clerestory window system provided ample cross-ventilation, as did the chimney flues, while the deep overhangs shielded the large areas of full glass from sun penetration in the middle of the day. Many liberative spatial sequences were built into the volume of the typical Usonian House, including ample continuous wall storage (the "thick-wall" concept), continuous seating, the proximity of the kitchen to the dining/living area, in both a physical and visual sense, and the nuanced zones of microspace throughout the house for every conceivable kind of activity.

From the beginning, Wright conceived of the Usonian system as a kit of parts that had to be ordered and assembled according to a particular sequence. His growing recognition of the economic and social need for many people to build their own houses led him to standardize many of the details in the Usonian system, and these, quite naturally, were repeated with variations from one house to the next. Borrowing its sequence and method of assembly from Japanese traditional house construction, the typical Usonian dwelling was built in a particular order. At each of its stages, this sequence reflected one of the four elements of Semper's general theory of 1852. One would first cast the floor slab and build the masonry chimney core and thus arrive at the first two elements of Semper's architectural hypothe-

Herbert Jacobs House
view from street, above, and view from garden, below

Herbert Jacobs House
interior view of living room

sis, the earthwork and the hearth. This was followed by Semper's third element, the framework and roof. The whole concluded with the application of a screenlike, infill wall, or *Wand*, as the German language so precisely puts it.

Apart from his masterworks realized in 1936—Fallingwater and the Johnson Wax Administration Building—Wright's architecture became increasingly grandiose and arbitrary as the years wore on, even, at times, descending into self-parody and *kitsch*. Here and there a particular commission, as the Guggenheim Museum or the Beth Sholom Synagogue, ignited the old fervor and conviction. However, in the main what remained of Wright's original New World vision came to be embodied in the Usonian House. This Usonian moment in Wright's long career reached its apotheosis during the New Deal decade from 1934 to 1944, when some twenty-five Usonian dwellings were realized by Wright. Built all over the country, these were designed not for a plutocracy but for an American exurban middle class and even lower middle class, to whom Wright's message had always been addressed. From "A Small House with 'Lots of Room in It'" of 1901 to the canonical Herbert Jacobs House, a Usonian dwelling built at Madison, Wisconsin, in 1936, the basic underlying, liberal, anarcho-socialist vision is always there. Along with the Usonian House went, in theory at least, the same densely cultivated and differentiated vision of society and the environment that was already present as a sociocultural model in Peter Kropotkin's *Factories, Fields and Workshops* of 1898.

The Usonian House, formulated when Wright was already sixty-three, is inseparable from the underlying thesis of Broadacre City, first broached by

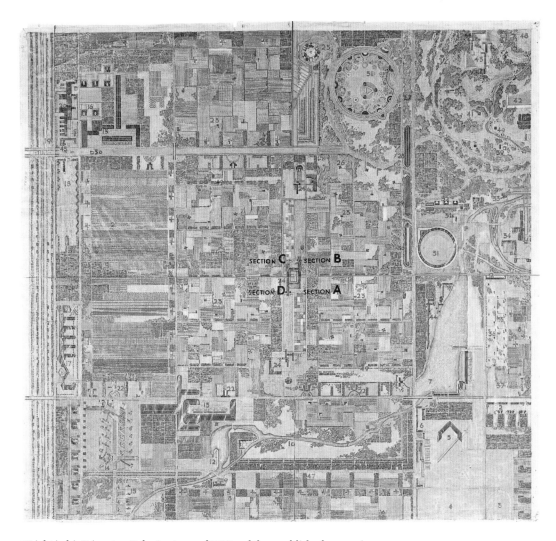

Wright in his Princeton Kahn Lectures of 1930 and then published as a socio-economic, exurban polemic in *The Disappearing City* of 1932. Broadacre City and the Usonian House shared a similar hypothetical socioeconomic basis; Wright's egalitarian vision was one acre reserved for every citizen at birth. In addition, the two were formally interrelated since the oversailing horizontal multiple roofs and outriding walls of the Usonian House would have layered the individual house into the new land-settlement pattern of the Broadacre City plan. Wright's Broadacre City, first exhibited in 1934, may be seen in retrospect as an infinite "oriental rug," as a cross-cultural, ecological tapestry writ large, as an oriental paradise garden combined with the Cartesian grid of the occident. This is Wright's textile tectonic literally inscribed into the earth, evoking that Edenic point where culture and agri-culture are inseparable, the natural home for the natural economy, the warp and the woof of a transhistorical time.

Broadacre City/Living City
1932–58; plan of typical
quarter section

Warp and Woof
A Spatial Analysis of Wright's Usonian Houses

BY JOHN SERGEANT

Any experience of Wright's domestic designs of the 1937–50 Usonian period shows a remarkable sense of naturalness and ease yet simultaneous conceptual rigor. Wright was able to conjure extraordinary spatial variety from minimal materials and dimensions. This ability was achieved through a structural vocabulary that was developed throughout his life. It consists of a three-dimensional field of grid lines through which the solid elements of the building are slid and located, and enables the voids, covered spaces, windows, other openings, and "no-form forms," such as terraces and car courts, to be both integral to the whole and equally meaningful. Indeed, the use of the grid allows what is implied by the perceived form, the building, to be as important as what is explicit. It is this quality that gives the houses their perceptual richness and meaning, that endears them so much to their owners.

The Usonian Houses develop and simplify the methods of grid planning that were first used in the Prairie Houses. Geometric systems had an obvious fascination for Wright, as can be seen in his earlier Sullivanian ornament and sketch plans. He himself suggested in the first book of his autobiography that the origins for this were his close childhood observation of plants, crystals, and rock formations. Wright's perception was already conditioned, however, by his kindergarten experience. Grant Manson, who first pointed out the formative nature of Froebel's precepts in Wright's early life, observed that "the child was encouraged to see that geometric forms underlie all natural objects."[1] Nevertheless an anomaly exists. The configuration of geometric grids is inorganic, and their use to create an "organic" architecture therefore presents a problem.

EARLY GRID PLANNING

It is impossible to overrate the importance of geometric organization in Wright's work. The origins of this design tool have been shown by MacCormac (chapter 6) to lie in the "gifts" of Froebel. As an educational pioneer, he may be compared to Maria Montessori, and his toy patterns were calculated to inculcate an appreciation of structure and expectation of unity into the world of the child. MacCormac showed that Wright derived a philosophy as well as a design discipline from the kindergarten. He had absorbed experiences with his hands and eyes, which were intended by Froebel to be an instrument in a system of education. This he based on a "pantheistic con-

John Storer House
Hollywood, California, 1923;
view from street

190

ception of nature." Its aim was to bring about an understanding of "Natural Law" that would simultaneously develop the powers of reason and convey a sense of the harmony and order of God: "God's works reflect the logic of his spirit and human education cannot do anything better than imitate the logic of nature."[2]

The basis of the patterns in the kindergarten handbooks was the geometry of crystallography, which Froebel had studied and which he took to be representative of the structure of all matter. Wright's inclination to look for unity in nature was confirmed for him by the writings of Herbert Spencer, which Sullivan gave him to read. The nineteenth-century confusion between organic and inorganic growth was articulated by Spencer, who as late as 1898 "could still assert that the growth of crystals and organisms was 'an essentially similar process.'"[3] MacCormac suggested that it was from the manuals of Froebel and the biological terms of Sullivan that Wright derived the characteristic meanings of some of his personal design vocabulary: he cited nature, organic, crystallization, integration, efflorescence, and structure.

When a child played with Froebel's blocks, he did so in a disciplined nineteenth-century manner on gridded boards and under rules that anticipated certain relationships. Similarly the mat making or plaiting "gifts" were carried out within an obvious operational discipline. MacCormac showed that Wright set out to build an architecture woven into a three-dimensional grid. He demonstrated that the Prairie Houses were a literal projection of their complex and often irregular planning grids. These took a "tartan" form, *a-b-a, a-b-a-c-a-d*, or *a-b-a-c-a-d-a-c-a-b-a*.

Wright was not concerned that the grid pattern should be symmetrical. It provided a means by which every element of the building could be coordinated into a whole. It also solved an endemic architectural problem: the potential divorce between the intellectual organization of the plan and the physical experience of an observer. With Wright they became one and the same, concept and experience. A vocabulary of forms was used to translate or express the grid at all points—the solid rather than pierced balconies, planters, bases of flower urns, clustered piers, even built-in seats were evocations of the underlying structure of a house. This process reached its most complex point in the rhythmic overlays and punctuating piers of the Martin House of 1904 in Buffalo, New York, and its most taut expression in the Evans House of 1908 in Chicago, Illinois, where the cruciform core of the plan (with the usual suppressed domestic quarter) was held as if magnetically between terminal piers.

SITES AND MOVEMENT PATTERNS

The early work, named after its region, the prairies, is for the most part placed on flat ground, within the enveloping grid of the city subdivisions. In organizing his clients' lots, which were themselves a subdivision of the block, into a mat of tartan grid lines, Wright was grounding an architecture of definition. The property boundary formed an enforced limit to a framing of activities and forms that spiraled into inglenook seats at the symbolic core of family hearth. It was an architecture that was organic in the sense of "the

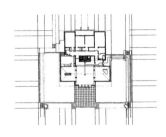

parts being integrated with the harmonious whole," but essentially inorganic, in the sense that it did not need to take account of nature's accidents. Almost the only exception is the Glasner House of 1905 in Glencoe, Illinois, with its bridge across a ravine to a teahouse, which may be seen as a point of departure for later developments. The grid planning of Usonians was to become looser by allowing nature to carry out a dialogue with the geometry of the house.

MacCormac gave a crucial insight into the grammar of Wright's design; however, one further element of the early work has not attracted attention: the use of a movement and careful organization of its pattern. This was to be an important element by which Wright sought to tie the geometry of the later designs into their sites. The plan of the Cheney House of 1904 in Oak Park, Illinois, is an instructive example of the use of the early tartan grid. This encompasses the whole site and controls the way in which the house makes contact with the streets around it. Their grid, in turn, is a part of the grid over the whole state of Illinois, of which Chicago is the climax, as well as a part of the one-mile grid of the nineteenth-century Continental Survey, which extends throughout the western United States. However, the house also displays a curiously wandering and shifting manner of approach. To reach the interior, a visitor is required to make many turns along paths that are deflected by such manifestations of the grid as steps and planters. At each turn, the house and its site are observed in a new relationship. The same process continues into the interior.

This way of moving and seeing has nothing to do with the axial, simplistic approach of the classical tradition but much in common with Eastern architecture. It was common practice in traditional Japanese urban housing to enter a small property by bridging a street water channel and traversing a minute forecourt or garden to the entrance. The first symbolized a transfer from public to private domain, and the second, involving careful planting and paving, meant experiencing an indirect approach through many kinds of texture and transparency. The dimensions for all this rarely exceeded five meters. In Versailles and the classical tradition, everything is subject to instant bombast. In traditional Japanese architecture, house and garden progressively reveal more of their nature as they are traversed.

Wright made his first contact with a culture that was to fascinate him for the rest of his life in the Japanese pavilion at the Columbian World's Fair in 1893. The Winslow House of that year in River Forest, Illinois, was his first mature design. It displays a simple axial, symmetrical approach, sustained within by a similarly balanced room plan. However, interior movement is circular around the central fireplace core, and the symmetry is eroded by a rear porch and the kitchen and *porte cochere*. The Heller House of 1897 and the Husser House of 1999, both in Chicago, were narrow, deep plans projected very clearly from tartan grids. However, the movement pattern of both designs was one of traversing strips in the grid between the offset symmetries of the main rooms. In the Waller project of 1898 in River Forest, Illinois, this movement pattern was used to combat a strongly axial plan that incorporated diagonals and an octagonal room—one of Wright's favorite devices of the time.

Edwin Cheney House
Oak Park, Illinois, 1903; plan analysis; the tartan grid is combined with a meandering movement pattern; drawing by author

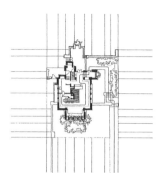

In 1905, Wright made his first visit to Japan. It is very likely that the insistent modular organization of traditional Japanese architecture, based on the *tatami* floor mat, reinforced his conviction of the need for grid planning. But his work after this date increasingly substituted a wandering, devious route pattern across and about the grid for the more simple progression up and down tartan strips of earlier designs. The six turns and spiral approach to the living-room seat of the Gale House of 1909 are matched in the Robie House and other work. This wandering effect is most clearly in evidence in the Emil Bach House of 1915 in Chicago, Illinois. This square-plan design shudders under the effect of the grid on it, indented, pier punctuated, and layered outside with trellises. The site is treated, albeit very quietly, as an obstacle course for the visitor to traverse. He is required to mount steps and negotiate garden elements that are all subterranean eruptions of the grid, before ricocheting through the overlapping spaces of the interior. By the time the spiral pull of the spaces have deposited him safely by the chimney core in the dining area, he has executed eleven turns.

By the time he left Chicago, Wright possessed a planning vocabulary of crystalline organization that contained a shifting manner of movement about it. He summarized his design process:

> In the logic of the plan what we call standardization is seen to be fundamental groundwork in architecture. All things in nature exhibit this tendency to crystallize; to form mathematically and then to conform, as we may see. There is the fluid, elastic period of becoming, as in the plan, when possibilities are infinite. New effects may then originate from the idea or principle that conceives. Once form is achieved, however, that possibility is dead so far as it is a positive creative flux.[4]

LATER DEVELOPMENTS

In Los Angeles, Wright was confronted by sites that were almost never flat. The Millard House of 1921 in Pasadena was embedded into the side of a ravine. The Storer House of 1922 lay on the acute bend of one of the contour

Emil Bach House
Chicago, Illinois, 1915; plan analysis; the intricate movement pattern is established at the sidewalk and continues into the interior—the plan is basically that of the one-zone Usonian House of 1934; drawing by author

Samuel Freeman House
Los Angeles, California, 1923; view from lower terrace

roads of the Hollywood Hills. The Freeman House of 1922, perched on the side of these hills, was entered from above with bedrooms below. The Ennis House of 1923 crowned a ridge in the Griffith Park area. Wright was obliged to extend his grid downward from the floor level of his designs (metaphorically speaking) to encounter local topography, and by this means he contrived to use terraces and retaining walls to tie his concept into the site. The vocabulary of these houses of the 1920s, of concrete block and paving, is therefore found all over the site, both above and up to fifty feet below them. At a functional level, this gives easy access to the house up the contours, or from the house to the terraces. At the conceptual level, it allows nature in the form of the demands of the site to penetrate Wright's geometric grid or "field," and to coexist there with the solid elements of the house.

The grid in these houses became a regular one determined by the module of block length horizontally and block course vertically. This construction system, named "textile block" by Wright, incorporated two-way steel reinforcement and could be given a patterned surface according to the mold used. It became a crucial stage in his struggle to unite inside space with outside space—to "break the box," as he termed it. It marked the transition from the mature and complex geometric organization of the Prairie Houses to the freer yet more rational ordering of space in the Usonian Houses. It was at this point that the reinforced block work dictated a vertical module corresponding regularly with the courses and enabled Wright to open up the corner, most dramatically in the Freeman House. Here the plate glass-to-glass corner windows run through two stories. They are framed with horizontal muntins, continuing the line of mortar joints course by course, and result in an extraordinary ambiguity where apparently weightless blocks intersect with the glass. In the Storer and Millard houses, Wright was able to dissolve the solids of his walls in a pierced, shimmering screen of textured, partially glazed blocks. They become a diaphanous membrane that sifted space flowing into and out of the interior.[5] The contrast with Wright's early description of his aspirations with this problem could not be greater. In 1908 he wrote: "I used to gloat over the beautiful buildings I could build if only it were unnecessary to cut holes in them."[6]

And in 1932 he declared with a sense of achievement:

Now came clear an entirely new sense of architecture, a higher conception of architecture . . . space enclosed . . . this interior conception took architecture entirely away from sculpture, away from painting and entirely away from architecture as it had been known in the antique. The building now became a creation of interior space in light. And as this sense of the interior space as the reality of the building began to work, walls as walls fell away.[7]

The advance in his grasp of spatial organization shown in the concrete block houses was clearest in the last building of this type, the Lloyd-Jones House of 1929 in Tulsa, Oklahoma. Its walls are made up equally of alternating vertical strips of glass and block work, the one divided by horizontal glazing bars and the other by cement courses. Faceted glass bays or prows plow through these walls as a literal crystallization of the planning grid. The artificial lighting and ventilation are integrated within pierced textile blocks.

Samuel Freeman House
perspective of corner; the three-dimensional grid of the "textile block" forms a cage within which solid and pierced blocks and windows are interwoven; drawing by author

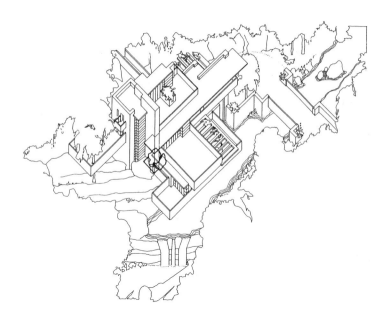

The Kaufmann weekend house, "Fallingwater," of 1935, built near Ohiopyle, Pennsylvania, is also important in the development of Wright's pre-Usonian designs. It is, of course, the most celebrated example in his work of the relationship between a house and its site. The spectacular form of the building, poised over its waterfall, has tended to obscure the nature of the strong contrast between the two and to substitute an image of conjunction of house and site. The house, although it is cantilevered from highly organic masses of stonework, is essentially composed of concrete horizontals with steel-framed glazing, both of which are inimical to the forms of the woods around it. Its grid planning, however, represents a turning point. It is a particularly lyrical example of the penetration of nature into the field of the house. Native rock is allowed to come through the floor, and this acts both as the base for the fire and as the psychological foundation for the design.

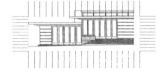

Fallingwater
Mill Run, Pennsylvania, 1936; axonometric view; Wright combined the horizontal grid of the Prairie Houses, the vertical grid of the Concrete Block Houses of the 1920s, and the exploitation of the site of his Usonian Houses—the native rock penetrates the floor and forms the hearth (shown in dark lines); drawing by author

Composite Elevation of Standard Usonian House Building Elements
Wright's "weaving" concept is carried literally into the wall details, battens flush with doorframes while boards lap over both; drawing by author

USONIAN GRID PLANNING

Usonian Houses were Wright's post-Depression solution to what he termed the "small house problem." Although each dwelling was designed for a particular site and client, it shared a common planning concept and constructional technique, or "grammar." The former consisted of a zoning of the plan into open and private areas, with a centralized service core; this was planned on ground level without basement and with easy access to terrace and garden and was called the "pollywog," or tadpole, plan by Wright. The latter included a colored concrete "floor mat," which eliminated conventional foundations and contained integral heating; roofs were heavy, compound slabs that shaded and insulated lightweight walls of glass and board-and-batten sandwich construction. The houses were cooled by cross-drafts through clerestory windows and were generally of L shape, allowing for easy expansion.

The three-dimensional grid of the Usonian Houses was regular and an inherent part of the locational process of their building. Grid lines were marked at the outset into the concrete floor mat. They were present both on drawings and on the house; they were numbered, and thus fundamental to communication with builders and others by telephone and to the intention of off-site prefabrication. Horizontal dimensions were two feet by four feet, or occasionally other subdivisions of the eight-foot by four-foot plywood sheet and other board materials. The vertical module was one foot one inch, or the distance between batten centers in the board-and-batten walls. Brick courses were laid to coincide with this dimension and were also a secondary vertical dimensioning system. The planning grid was therefore a "cage" made up of locational "fixes," which were in turn determined by practical considerations of building materials and process.

Both planes of the Usonian grid field were used to locate each element in space. They determined the broad enclosure of internal and external areas and every detail of interpenetration between the two. Wright's skill lay in the perfect coordination of horizontal and vertical systems to manipulate the character of every part of this "family" of houses. If a part of the structure rose above ceiling height, such as the chimney masses and raised clerestory roofs, it encountered the vertical grid. If a part of the concrete floor mat or brick base dropped to a lower level or to deal with a falling site, it again was gripped by the module and conditioned by it. This organization of the vertical dimension is a real advance on that of the Prairie Houses. In homes that are small, it gives a broad, unfussy appearance and unifies disparate elements. The one-foot-one-inch band forms a "layering" system of stripes. These control and regulate the heights of every visual element—the main structural features such as eaves and clerestory lines, planters and retaining walls, tops of doors and internal decks, and fittings such as built-in furniture, bookshelves, tables, and work tops. As a result, these all unite into an unobtrusive combination of calm horizontality, slipping past and apparently through brickwork and windows.

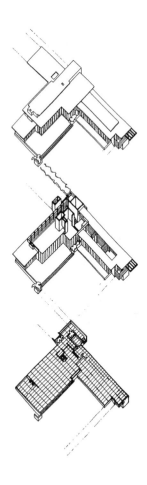

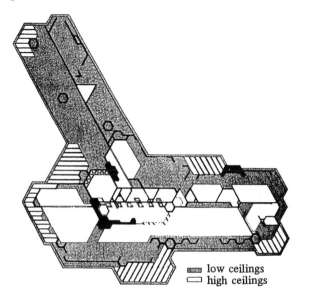

low ceilings
high ceilings

Stanley Rosenbaum House
Florence, Alabama, 1939; axonometric analysis; the three plan levels (floor, door-top sills or decks, ceiling), stepped roofs, and falling site are controlled by the planning grid; drawing by author

Paul and Jean Hanna House
Stanford, California, 1936; plan analysis; the configuration of the house door-top decks contrasts with the floor plan below and sloped ceiling above—in most flat-roofed Usonians the raised ceilings are in the clerestory lanterns; drawing by author

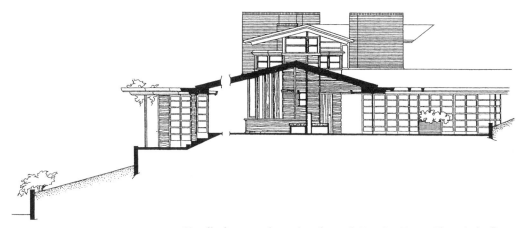

Usually there are three plans for each Usonian House. There is the floor plan; there is a "deck" plan at door-top height; and there is a high-level ceiling plan, which applies either to sloping ceilings or to raised clerestory areas depending on whether there is a pitched or flat roof. These plans do not necessarily coincide. The experience of Wright's interiors is one of immediate enclosure by means of walls, although these walls are more liberating than enveloping and always slip out of view toward some unseen point. The space that a person moves through is accompanied by a contrasting system that operates above his head. This is formed by Wright's characteristic "decks." These, like many of the elements of his architecture, originated in the Prairie Houses. They are flat ledges of wood construction normally about two feet in width and always some six feet six inches above the floor. They are an important component of Wrightian interiors, since they stream throughout the chief spaces at door-top height and visually unite areas whose boundaries may be complex. They carry the lighting system—concealed lights above to give indirect light reflected from the ceiling, and recessed downlights to wash the drapes and illuminate the perimeter of rooms. They incorporate track for drapes, provide a surface for bowls or decoration—this was where Wright placed his beloved pine boughs—and integrate inside with outside. The soffit of the deck continues above all windows to become the exterior roof overhang.

The upper-level ceilings have the property of dramatizing the main spaces of the Usonian Houses. In the post-1945 houses, these are often sloping and give a restful, containing "cap" to the interior. This is similar to what is popularly known in America as a "cathedral ceiling." With Wright the inner space always conforms to the exterior form; there is no such spatial "cheat" as a loft space. However, the majority of Usonian Houses have flat upper roofs, or lanterns, surrounded by clerestory windows. These give an open character to the space, akin to partially removing the roof, as the sky and nearby trees become visible inside. Moreover, the clerestory daylight is modified by the fretted plywood through which it filters. The interior is also animated by raking sunbeams that can be especially beautiful at the end of the day, when the lower part of the house may be in shadow.

The combined effect of architectural treatment at these three plan levels is to give Wright's space an extraordinary richness, which is simultaneously lucid, deceptively artless, and geometrically controlled. The lower part of his spaces is both containing and beckoning, leading the eye to a point beyond view. The decks give the interiors a sense of breadth and repose that corresponds with the overpowering horizontality of the exteriors. And twin scales of door and ceiling height provide contrast, which exaggerates the low character of intimate spaces and the height of living areas and convinces the eye that the house is larger than it actually is.

Wright demonstrated a final subtlety in the Usonian Houses that had cypress-boarded rather than plywood ceilings. He used the linear nature of the boards to emphasize the direction of movement through his spaces. The direction of the boarding corresponds with the flow of the space below so that the characteristic spiral movement pattern is dramatized by interlocking boards exercising a slow turn above. The result is analogous to sand ridges formed by the tide or current in water. The boards stream along above circulation areas, swirl around corners, and curl into backwaters over spaces of repose. In the living areas of the extended Sondern House and the Schwartz House, the safe, terminal nature of reaching the fireplace is emphasized, and in the Lloyd Lewis and Pew houses, the center of the room is delineated. The latter was an early feature of Prairie House rooms, which required a point of emphasis where the upper floor prevented any deep modulation of the ceiling. Dining rooms, such as that of the Evans House of 1908, contained leaded, stained-glass panels above the table. The Pew House has a similar effect, where beautifully miter-cut cypress forms a recessed vortex that holds down and occupies the center of a room with meandering boundaries. The only hexagonal Usonians having boarded ceilings are the Wall and Richardson houses of 1941. In the former, the boarding curls about sections of the main space like flower petals, and in the latter, it laps down and underlines the triangular form of the living area.

Bernard Schwartz House
Two Rivers, Wisconsin, 1939; view of exterior from garden

The grid plan became a conditioning and unifying structure. Wright increasingly exploited the potential ambiguity of overlapping different bands of the grid. This took architectural form both in the detailing and in the interpenetration of the masses of the houses. In the fenestration of the Hanna House of 1936, the hexagonal grid was mirrored in the glazing rhythm of the west facade. The existence of an external "boundary zone" is suggested by the universal overhanging eaves and trellises, and by such features as the corner "eyelids" of the Pew House of 1940, where each second-floor bedroom has a corner window shaded by an individual overhang. The same combination of a manifestation of the grid field with an environmental advantage occurs in an element common to all the Usonian designs. They display ranges of casement windows that are designed to open within and under the eaves overhang. In doing this, they reinforce the separate entity of the boundary zone and create a space that is both inside and out; in the case of the glazed doors this can be readily appreciated. They also change from being elements that lie along one plane of the grid, the facade, into those at right angles to it, modifying the relationship between interior and exterior. The practical result is windows in shade, which can be opened during the rain.

Bernard Schwartz House
interior view of living room

Gardens were conceived as an integral part of the grid format or as a continuation of the level system conditioned by it. This may be seen in the original Usonian models displayed at Hillside in Spring Green, Wisconsin, although not many of the designed schemes were realized. The Lloyd Lewis House of 1940, however, displays the intended "layering" of the garden, where the vertical rhythm of the brick piers of the loggia is continued in walks and parallel strips of flower planting. In the Hanna House, the grid successfully united the building with its surroundings, and then, as the owners' lifestyle required larger gatherings, it naturally ordered terraces and car-parking levels, built some twenty-five years later.

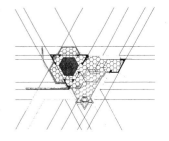

In the broad massing of Usonian Houses, Wright used the grid to unify and intersect the wings of his pollywog, or tadpole, plans. The brick base, capped by its rowlock course of brick headers, underlay everything and tied together the thirty-, sixty-, and ninety-degree angles of such plans as the Armstrong House of 1939. A falling plan like that of the Pope House of 1940 resulted in the entrance from the higher level being on the brick. Then to enter the lower living area, steps were cut down through the brick to reach the concrete floor mat of the main floor. Lower bedroom wings normally line through with the lower walls of living areas, while the latter are capped by higher ceilings on the clerestory strip windows. The houses can be read as low, wandering, boarded forms topped by clerestories or as a high, glazed living area into which lower wings were slid.

All these many elements were most eloquently combined in the 1941 project for the Sundt House in Madison, Wisconsin. The site, by the shore of one of the two Madison lakes, entered the grid field of the house by means of a triangular boat dock. The plan was broadly of V form, with the living area in the apex. It consisted of a superimposition of many triangles, some displaced and others interlocking in the manner of an afterimage. These allowed spaces to overlap in an unprecedented way. The carport was to be a part of the entry loggia but also a corner of the major triangle of the house. The design could be read as this basic format, with a lantern projected vertically from it over the living area and a bedroom wing projected horizontally. Or it could be read as a dominant living-room triangle with subservient outer triangles, some only partially stated, for sitting by the fire, writing, and eating.

The south terrace by the dining table can be viewed as part of an underlying base or symmetrical adjunct to the living area (emphasized by the raised, boarded ceiling), as a part of the driveway area, or as a central element of a half-stated triangular pond. The pond itself, as well as the driveway, suggests a system of greater triangles, forever moving out from the house. As the model at Hillside shows, the Sundt House would have matched these geometric abstractions with all the resources of Wright's Usonian vocabulary and would have been a spatial *tour de force*. Some idea of his intentions can be gained from the Richardson House, also planned in 1941, in Glen Ridge, New Jersey, which is similar but does not have such a strong geometric relationship with its site.

The elements of Usonian interiors combine to fulfill Wright's statement, "the reality of a room was to be found in the space enclosed by the roof and

Vigo Sundt House
Madison, Wisconsin, 1941;
analysis of plan; both the
modified lakeshore and driveway
are conditioned by the
overlapping system of the
triangular grid; drawn by author

walls, not in the roof and walls themselves." While this duality or ambiguity was Wright's architectural aim, he was unprepared and humbled to discover it already expressed in Eastern philosophy by Lao Tzu:

> The use of clay in molding pitchers
> comes from the hollow of its absence.
> Doors and windows in a house
> are used for their emptiness.
> Thus we are helped by what is not
> to use what is.[8]

Although calm, a Wrightian interior is not static, and its surfaces stream away beyond view. To comprehend the space, it is necessary to move around, and the fourth dimension of time and the observer's intellect are involved. Wright found this concept well described by Okakura, whose *Book of Tea* was a favorite of his: "True beauty could only be discovered by one who mentally completed the incomplete."[9] Usonian plans originate with their interior, of which their exterior is an expression, and their grid discipline reaches out into the landscape. Conceptually the dividing point between inside and outside can be discounted.

CELEBRATION OF THE SITE

There is an evident "fit" between the sites for Wright's Usonian Houses and the geometry he selected for them. The way in which movement patterns were integrated with this enabled him to relate the user to features of the site that were often at a great distance. The sensations were manipulated in the manner of stage handling, giving glimpses of selected points such as a rock, a tree, or a mountain and reserving the crowning view as a surprise, held back until the last. This occurred very clearly in the desert designs for the Pauson House of 1940 and for Wright's own home, Taliesin West. In the former, the house crowned a ridge and withheld dramatic views until a long stepped approach had been surmounted and the house itself entered. In the latter, the axes of the grid were fixed by Camelback, Tabletop, and Superstition mountains many miles away. The buildings form a smaller, more special place along the contours within this larger arena, and the many twists and turns in moving about the complex are intended to heighten an awareness of their interrelationship.

The rectilinear designs are, for the most part, a concession to the surroundings of urban sites and grid street plans. At times Wright used a rectangular grid in this context, but he set his house at a forty-five-degree angle to the street. This had the effect of improving orientation or view, as in the Pew and Schwartz houses, and of highlighting the individuality of the home. In all cases the geometry that was chosen—even in the circular cluster and one- and two-radius organizations of such later developments as the second Jacobs House of 1942 and the Sol Friedman House of 1949—achieves an inevitability that becomes truly marvelous in homes with dramatic sites.

The Palmer House of 1950, in Ann Arbor, Michigan, can stand for many others. The design is fused with a tiny hillock in thick woods, now somewhat suburban, and is of a V form. It has a twin-core plan based on the sixty-degree triangle, or one-sixth of the hexagon. The living area at its prow leads but to a gently falling slope, whereas the two wings, garage, and bedrooms slide along the edge of increasingly steep drops. The V is itself wrapped around the top of the hillock and also contains a car court. From the road below, a triangular pier (of the workshop) indicates the house above, and the driveway slopes up into the receiving arms of the car court and into the "field" of the grid. This grid has become an indissoluble part of the site, and, even some distance from the house itself, it can be encountered quite informally as a small triangle of brickwork or as a light. Outside the living room, a long step, made of the red-colored concrete of the floor mat, slips out of the grass and is revealed as a manifestation of the grid. The geometry of the design extends outward, not stopping at the walls of the building. Wright himself referred to this as "watching out for the ends" of a design. His treatment of house and site suggests that it would be possible to dig trenches anywhere in the site and discover the bones of the grid below ground level. His act of design grasps "force lines" or vectors, which, although unrecognized, always existed in the site. He perceives them as natural features, draws them quietly together, and knots them inexorably with the grid.

The achievement of Wright's Usonian Houses in the grammar of his architecture was to develop a quite abstract geometric planning grid that ordered all the spaces and parts to the whole. The discrepancies and opportunities of nature, in the form of the features of each site, were allowed to "invade" this grid and to carry out a dialogue with it. The houses were the result of both. In 1957, looking back at what he had done, Wright summarized his design process:

> Kindergarten training, as I have shown, proved an unforeseen asset; for one thing, because all my planning was devised on a properly proportional unit system. I found this would keep all to scale, ensure consistent proportion throughout the edifice, large or small, which thus became— like tapestry—a consistent fabric woven of interdependent, related units, however various.
>
> So from the very first this system of "fabrication" was, applied to planning even in minor buildings. Later, I found technological advantages when this system was applied to heights. In elevation, therefore, soon came the vertical module as experience might dictate. All this was very much like laying warp on the loom. The woof [substance] was practically the same as if stretched upon this predetermined warp. This basic practice has proved indispensable and good machine technique must yield its advantages. Invariably it appears in organic architecture as visible features in the fabric of the design—insuring unity of proportion. The harmony of texture is thus, with the scale of all parts, within the complete ensemble.[10]

From the Prairie House to Fallingwater

BY BERNHARD HOESLI

Why Fallingwater? At a time that has been acclaimed as postmodern, one may indeed ask if this once-remarkable work of the Modern Movement can still attract our interest and, if so, for what reason? Today it seems no doubt a classic as remote as the Capella Pazzi, the Santa Maria della Consolazione at Todi, "L'Arlesienne" by Picasso, or a still life of 1913 by Braque.

I remember that I first saw photographs of Fallingwater after World War II in the exhibit "USA Builds" that traveled in 1946 to Switzerland and elsewhere in Europe. I also found it in *Built in USA: A Survey of Contemporary American Architecture* from the Museum of Modern Art, New York, in 1945. It was unexpected and unique in the work of Wright, and it remains as outstanding today as when it was built [sixty-nine years ago].

Looking back almost [three-quarters] of a century, one still marvels at the singularity of Fallingwater. It appeared as a mutation sprung into existence. Fallingwater still stands out as a unique achievement in the career of a distinguished architect, and it would also seem that in 1936 nothing in Frank Lloyd Wright's previous work had prepared one to expect it. There is a surprising lack of ornamental detailing in the stark plainness of the balconies extending into space and the demonstrative use of cantilever construction in the reinforced-concrete slabs that appear to hover like abstract planes in space. The orthogonal constellation of few, separate, space-defining walls that characterizes the first floor in particular and also prevails within the restrictions that bedrooms and baths prescribe in the other floors had previously made a tentative and only local appearance in the plans of the Boynton House of 1908 and the projects for the Wright Studio House of 1903 and the Gerts House of 1906.[1]

These walls, constellated in space, boldly characterize the spatial organization of the entire building, and the orthogonal projection of this constellation resembles the famous painting *Russian Dance* by Theo van Doesburg (1918), which in turn has been generally associated with the plan for the Brick Country House project of 1923 by Mies van der Rohe.[2]

[I]

In 1945, I was only halfway through my work toward an architect's degree at the Swiss Federal Institute of Technology in Zurich. I think that by studying

Fallingwater
Mill Run, Pennsylvania, 1936;
general view from downstream

Fallingwater
exterior perspective, view
from below

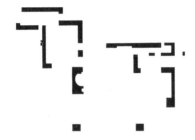

Fallingwater
analysis of the first floor plan;
drawn by author

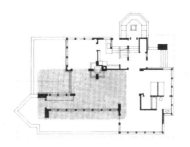

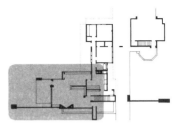

Studio for an Artist
Oak Park, Illinois, 1903; analysis of
plan; drawn by author

Walter Gerts House
Glencoe, Illinois, 1906; analysis of
plan; drawn by author

E. E. Boynton House
Rochester, New York, 1908;
analysis of plan; drawn by author

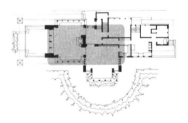

architecture at that time, my fellow students and I were among the first belonging to a new generation of architects; the "roots of modern architecture"[3] were not only remote but obscured. We were removed from the heroic age of the Modern Movement, and though its pioneers and protagonists were still alive and active, they could no longer be seen and understood as our contemporaries. We discovered their work as one rediscovers something of the past. I had understood, for instance, Le Corbusier's villas around Paris as harbingers of a world to come, and it was with a feeling of shocked recognition that I found them as modern ruins when I visited in the summer of 1946. An architectural past was the future, and at the same time the present was also the past. This experience impressed itself deeply on my consciousness.

At that time, and well into the end of the 1950s, the three great protagonists of modern architecture—Wright, Le Corbusier, and Mies—were universally seen and critically acclaimed as representing distinct and opposed embodiments in the spirit of modernity. Admirers, architects, and critics seemed to cluster in distinct and opposing camps. The work of these great men was what stars are for navigation: datum marks in relation to which students as well as professionals could and must determine their own positions and courses.

When I started teaching at the School of Architecture, University of Texas, Austin, in the fall of 1951, I became progressively dissatisfied with the prevalent and undisputed insistence on the obvious differences among Wright, Le Corbusier, and Mies. Critics as well as practicing architects explained the differences as both personal in nature and as fundamental and irreconcilable variations among the conceptual bases of their architecture. More and more I became interested in the issue: If not to the contrary, there must exist a common base of those obvious differences—a common denominator among the work of Wright, Le Corbusier, and Mies that could be used not only to distinguish the perceptibly obvious differences but to understand the less apparent but significant conceptual differences in their work.[4]

[II]

The plane as an element of volumetric organization made its first appearance in Wright's work from 1893 to 1911. It appeared as a tangible possibility as early as 1899 at the Husser House, and more and more it characterized the Prairie Houses in a long line of empirical development: the River Forest Golf Club, the *Ladies' Home Journal* houses, the Fricke House, the Thomas and Willits houses, the Yahara Boat Club, the Robie House, and finally—not merely in the form of the horizontal undersides of the projecting and seemingly hovering roofs but as a dominant and integral, even exclusive, element of volumetric organization for the entire building—the Gale House of 1909.

With the Gale House, a remarkable synthesis had occurred. At the Winslow House of 1893, an elementary theme of form organization occurred: a solid masonry mass rising from the ground and a horizontal roof or plane above it. It is much more explicitly stated at the Williams House of 1895 and deliberately contrasted to vertical prisms at the Heller House of

Hillside Home School
Spring Green, Wisconsin, 1902;
analysis of southeast exterior
corner; drawn by author

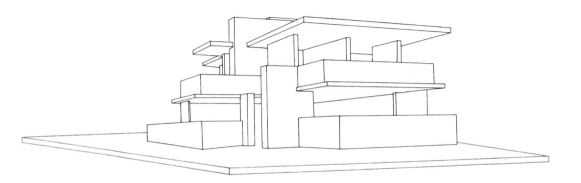

1897. At the well-known southeast corner of the Hillside Home School of 1902 at Taliesin, *this theme is demonstrated* in almost abstract purity. There is a dominant sculpture of constellated prisms of masonry as the major element, and the bold horizontal plane of the projecting roof that is varied as the minor element in the slabs topping the masonry piers. We find variations of this in the masonry part of the Dana House of 1903; it is the dominant feature of the volumetric organization of the Larkin Building of 1904; and it shows itself in the most elaborate and magnificent orchestration at the Martin House of the same year.

And then the Gale House of 1909 is built. The spandrels and balcony parapets become continuous horizontal bands, and, like the wall enclosing the terrace below, they are seen as edges of rather thick horizontal slabs. These slabs—the roof slab, the prisms, and planes of the walls—are constellated orthogonally in space. Take away the trim and we have the same form elements and the same volumetric organization as with Fallingwater. Or, if a somewhat anachronistic metaphor is permitted, it is as if the volumetric elements of a composition by Vantongerloo had become fused with the planar elements of a composition by van Doesburg. Mass is interpreted in terms of plane, and the plane is interpreted in terms of volume, working together to define space.

[III]

These exercises in the development and organization of the mass are marked by a gradual development in the *concept of continuous space.* Through one remarkable decade at the turn of the century, we can follow almost day by day a continuous process. This process starts at the Blossom House of 1892, where space is obviously conceived as an entity that is singular, local, and the whole of the spatial system is a composition of highly individualized and intrinsically separate parts. Then, already in the Winslow House of 1893, some of the interior walls are replaced by sliding doors, and the volumes of library–hall–living room are linked to form a continuity of shaped space. In the Hickox House of 1900, the music room–living room–dining room is one space with only rudimentary indication of a division into three parts. Furthermore, and this will prove the significant anticipation of a further development, a walled terrace extends at a right angle from the mass of the building. In the Bradley House of 1900, we find this

Mrs. Thomas Gale House
Oak Park, Illinois, 1909; analysis; drawn by author

Fallingwater
view of west living-room balcony

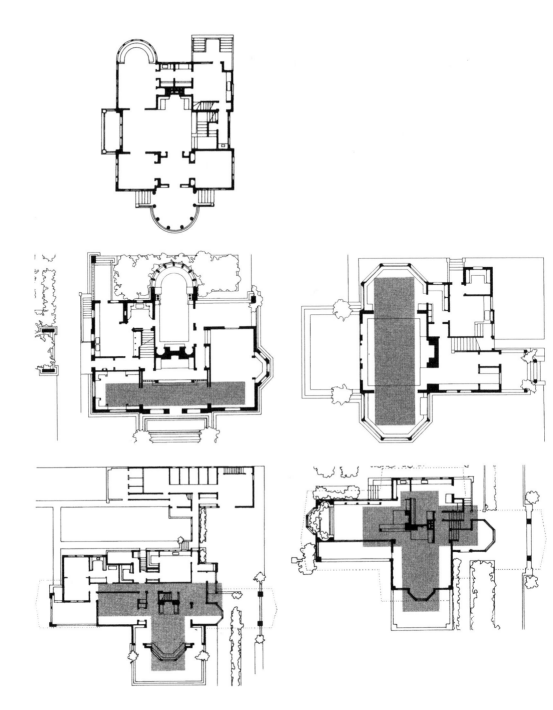

Plan Analyses
George Blossom House, 1892,
top, William Winslow House,
1893, center left, Warren Hickox
House, 1900, center right,
Bradley House, 1900, bottom left,
"A Small House with 'Lots of
Room in It,'" 1900, bottom right;
drawn by author

same protruding terrace but now the volume of the house follows it. *Diagonal* views are invited and encouraged and the *shift of the spaces* make them to be *individualized areas of one continuous space.* In the "Small House With 'Lots of Room in it'" of 1900, we find the cruciform plan that announced itself in the Bradley House vigorously affirmed; the major spaces are the arms of a cross extending outward into space from the root of the fireplace like spokes from the hub of a wheel. Mass and space interlock; and since the outer walls are replaced to a considerable degree by window openings and rows of windows, "inside" space and "outside" space become connected in an unprecedented way. The articulation in terms of use, entry–living–dining–cooking, is identical with the articulation in terms of volume and space. The second-floor spaces consciously echo this manner of simply defining space.

The Willits House of 1902 is the superb culminating statement, summing up and demonstrating what has been accomplished: the interlocking of mass and space and unification of inner and outer areas. The house's spaces can be understood as *differentiated parts* of the same uninterrupted, *continuous medium.* There is only a small step to the Martin House of 1904, where the implied possibilities have become a manifest reality and demonstration of all the consequences. It is the conclusion of Wright's empirical road to the *concept of continuous space* in architecture: individual space-defining piers or constellations are arranged to define architectural area, and "interior" and "exterior" space are but complementary aspects of the same continuous medium.

The concept of continuous space is now not only a possible but a *constitutive aspect of modern architecture* and intrinsically characteristic for its protagonists and their work. Architectural space must be defined through the intervention of space-defining elements in terms of the physical and mathematical area, a part of it thus becoming qualified through this creative intervention. Space became the elementary material to which the architect gave shape. Space became the medium in which and through which architecture existed and, above all else, was endowed with significance.

Picasso and Braque had come to similar and analogous conclusions in terms of picture space during the development of cubism from 1909 to 1914. It is coincidence that in 1910 Wright's work was exhibited in Berlin and published by Wasmuth. Perhaps Mondrian's development from early experiments, from his study of analytical cubism to the establishment of his own iconography in the early 1920s, is an empirical process not unlike Wright's. The enunciations of the de Stijl *Manifesto* of 1917 are certainly the announcement of a theory *that presupposes the concept of space as a continuous medium* in which to operate.

It is a matter of historical record that Mies as well as Le Corbusier had his contact with de Stijl. And if *Mies* availed himself rather deliberately, radically, and systematically to the new possibilities based implicitly on the concept of continuous space, *Le Corbusier* could possibly emancipate himself in 1923 from dominant structural and empirical concerns under the influence of the de Stijl exhibit in Paris, 1923, and concentrate on the ideal of manipulating space. But this only meant that a recessive interest became dominant. His

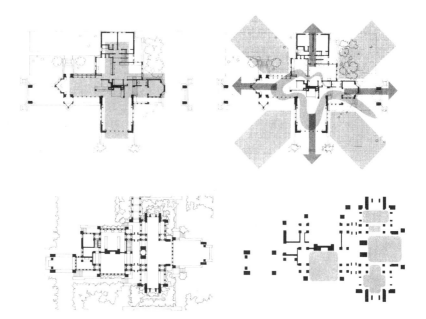

evocative passage about the Pompeian House from *Vers une architecture* is revealing: "There are no other architectural elements internally: light, and its reflection in a great flood by the walls and the floor, which is really a horizontal wall." "*The floor, which is really a horizontal wall*" is a statement that would be strange, incomprehensible as well as incredible, if one did not assume a distinct concept of space.

Thus neither wall nor floor (nor ceiling for that matter) is addressed empirically or pragmatically in terms of its obvious use and significance for sensual recognition. Both are addressed, or seen, as space-defining elements disposed in unqualified (continuous) space that is essentially isotropic, without orientation and isomorphous throughout. Up, down, left, right, here and there, what's called floor or wall, are qualities that must be defined in terms of man.

It adds some encouragement and interest but no new substance to our insight that one can point out that this seems to be thoroughly in the tradition of French rationalism. Choisy, in his famous treatise,[5] routinely presents buildings in a plan-section-axonometric composite as if seen floating in space like a NASA vehicle.

[IV]

If we then can be permitted and encouraged to assume a consciously adopted or unconsciously presupposed *vision or concept of space* that is constitutive for modern architecture, we can enjoy the pleasure of having a base and common denominator that enables us to distinguish and unite Wright, Le Corbusier, and Mies, to understand what could constitute the architectural essence of the Modern Movement, with all its dissimilarities, incoherence, undercurrents, orthodoxy, and heresies.

Frank Lloyd Wright was to discover empirically the *continuity of space*; but he never got seduced by the more ideal and abstract possibilities this

Ward Willits House
Highland Park, Illinois, 1902; analysis of plan, top left, and analysis of plan and site, top right; drawn by author

Darwin Martin House
Buffalo, New York, 1904; analyses of plan, bottom left and right; drawn by author

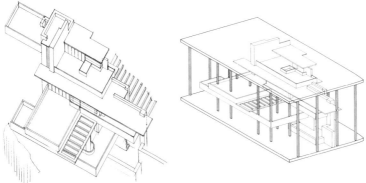

concept of space made possible. He never abandoned the tectonic reference "from the ground up." He always interpreted any possible abstract quality of elements arranged in continuous space in "the nature of materials" and in terms of the tectonic base of construction. During his European career, Mies's first manifestation in space is to presuppose a horizontal slab of space parallel to the ground, to define its perimeter, and to proceed to organizing it, neglecting any other possibility. Le Corbusier, the great dialectic, interprets again and again the two possible elementary assertive gestures in space: the vertical slab of space of the Citrohan Type or the horizontal slab of the Domino Type. These are primary interventions in isotropic continuity of space. Within the structural frame, he then elaborates expressive space, contrasting it to structure in a dialectic rapport in which space and structure mutually affirm one another. Wright never accepted frame construction; in

Fallingwater
view from entry bridge toward
east living-room balcony

Fallingwater
axonometric view from above;
drawn by author

Le Corbusier's Structural Frame
axonometric view of the Villa
Stein at Garches, superimposed
on the planes of Wright's
Fallingwater; drawn by author

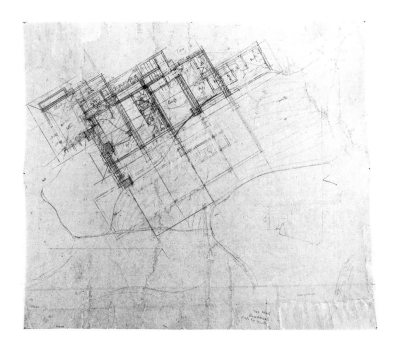

his work, space and structure are identical. Frank Lloyd Wright was never much interested in the more intellectual aspect of architecture or in any speculation on the possible problem of defining its nature that now generates so much of the activity and efforts of architects today.

[V]

So Fallingwater stands alone—an incredible and lone pinnacle, a crystallization or sediment in the flow of architectural events, a hardly conscious reminder of Heraclites' *Panta rhei*. Uniquely personal as well as universal, it is a timeless leftover of human aspiration and endeavor.

Fallingwater is a sculpture in space—anchored with constellations of solid prisms of stone masonry in the wooded hillside above stream and waterfall—and at the same time an almost abstract demonstration of man's possible "taking possession of his earth" through defining and organizing space, an elegant and seeming effortless tour de force posing as *legerdemain*, like the smiling acrobat whose flawless performance makes us forget the hours of practice and instant effort behind it. But above all it is a life-enhancing place to live in, shaped space that appeals to senses and mind. A possible illustration of David Hume's "All probable knowledge is but a species of sensation."

The "New World of Space"[6] has vanished; it seems irretrievably lost. One is tempted to conceive of it as a myth like Atlantis—were not a handful of buildings to prove that it did exist, buildings that are palpably material and make us almost violently feel the *condition humaine*.

It is the space of the "Moment of Cubism"[7] that fills us with the kind of admiration and love we reserve to what we once had—we suffer and enjoy the sweetness of memory spiced with a drop of bitterness. There *was not a promised ideal*; there remains the sensation of the possible.

Fallingwater
first sketch of floor plans by
Wright from September 1935

Fallingwater
interior view of bedroom of Edgar Kaufmann, with glass set directly into channels in the rock wall; this view shows very tellingly what is meant by continuity of space—the identity of "inside" and "outside" space—so that there is no longer the difference of "inside" and "outside" space

Fallingwater
interior view from kitchen looking out to west living-room balcony

A Beat of the Rhythmic Clock of Nature
Wright's Waterfall Buildings

BY KATHRYN SMITH

> That sweep of river which lulled and soothed me is but the visible link in the endless chain of being; it was the seen moment in the unseen round of existence, a segment in the divine circle of law, a beat of the rhythmic clock of nature.—*Jenkin Lloyd-Jones, "The River of Life"*[1]

Fallingwater—Frank Lloyd Wright's consummate union of architecture and nature—has long been recognized as a unique building in his prodigious seventy-year career. Yet the very device that distinguishes Fallingwater, the lyrical integration of a waterfall as a part of the architectural composition, was used by Wright in numerous commissions both before and after the completion of the country house at Bear Run, Pennsylvania.[2] The juxtaposition of building and waterfall was not new in Wright's work; rather, it was the result of almost three decades of experimentation and refinement that would have profound implications for his later work. Among the antecedents, there is a palatial house perched on a bluff in Lake Forest, Illinois, with views over Lake Michigan; a cultural center spiraling from a mountaintop in Maryland; and a resort hotel nestled in a meadow at the base of the Rocky Mountains in Colorado. The function of each project is distinctly different; and, although the incorporation of water into the plan is in response to landscape conditions, there is no consistency in whether water appears on the site naturally or is introduced by the architect.

The program and location of each project point to their differences. But the common use of the waterfall motif reveals an underlying theme that began to dominate Wright's work as he moved away from the suburban limitations of the Prairie House to embrace a more profound view of the spiritual value of nature. The pragmatic constraints of the Prairie House, centered as they were on the demands of the American family, were obstacles to the attainment of the transcendent relation between building and landscape. In the last years of the Oak Park Studio, movement toward this new thematic dimension led Wright away from the fireplace as the central focus of the plan. Instead, the buildings began to look outward toward vistas into the landscape, and, increasingly, these views were of water. Turning away from suburbia and toward nature, Wright found that water in architecture symbolized, as fire did not, man's place in the physical universe.

Hatsune Falls
Nikko, Japan, before 1905, Frank Lloyd Wright photo album, possible postcard view

The introduction of the new motif was a direct result of a journey of transition, growth, and intellectual development that Wright made during a trip to Japan in 1905 with his wife, Catherine, and clients Mr. and Mrs. Ward Willits.[3] While he maintained later that the main purpose of his trip was to buy Japanese woodblock prints at their source, it is clear from his extensive travel throughout Japan that his intention was to see and experience temples and Imperial residences within the context of their landscaped gardens.

Little is known of the preparation Wright made both before his departure and after his arrival, but it is safe to say that he clearly consulted both books and friends.[4] While several scholars have made note of the fact that Wright had most certainly studied the classic primer *Japanese Homes and Their Surroundings* (1886), by Edward Morse, no mention has been made of the equally obvious source, Josiah Conder's *Landscape Gardening in Japan* (1893; revised 1912).[5] Conder provided a historical overview of the Japanese garden and devoted chapters to elements such as garden stones, water basins, wells, bridges, vegetation, and five types of gardens: hill and water gardens, flat gardens, ceremonial teahouse gardens, passage gardens, and fancy gardens. Ninety-two drawings by a Japanese illustrator were supplemented with forty photographs.

There is no evidence that Wright had read the oldest and most famous Japanese garden manual, *Sakuteiki* (Records of Garden Making), believed to have been written in the mid-eleventh century. However, Conder listed it as one of the thirteen original Japanese sources that he consulted. *Sakuteiki* laid out the tenets of the *shinden zukuri*, an architectural and garden style of the Heian era (784–1185) devoted to water gardens heavily influenced by Chinese models. The basic principles of the *shinden zukuri* garden (comprising the key elements of rivers, waterfalls, lakes, and islands) is outlined by Conder in his chapter "Ornamental Water." Of particular interest is the description given for garden cascades—in other words, waterfalls—where Conder, following the *Sakuteiki*, listed ten different types by visual characteristics.

There is evidence that Wright was both aware of and deeply impressed with Japanese aesthetics, especially the sophisticated observation of natural phenomena such as waterfalls. During his journey from mid-February to April 1905, he systematically sought out temples and Imperial residences, recording them with his camera. On his return home, he compiled fifty-five of these photographic images into a small album. Although the majority are architectural, fourteen photographs, or twenty-five-percent of the album, are of waterfalls.[6] Exhibiting knowledge of Japanese landscape gardening, Wright assembled images that described variations of type as Conder had outlined. Examples of "Right-and-left-falling" (waterfall dividing on two sides), "Stepped-falling" (waterfall broken into steps like a torrent), and "Heaven-falling" (a waterfall of great elevation in which the water tumbles in layers), among others, appear in the album. Wright's fascination with waterfalls is a clue to his impatience with the confines of the suburban plot and his eagerness to move into a greater landscape setting. The influence of Wright's trip to Japan, however, was not immediate; it did not find germination until several years later.

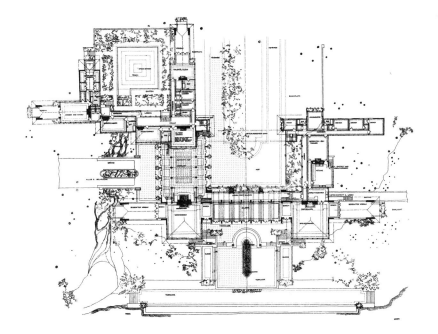

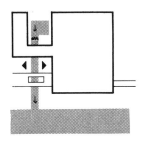

Wright first introduced the device of a waterfall in the Harold McCormick House of 1908 in Lake Forest, Illinois. The U-shaped plan is perched on a steeply precipitous point of land overlooking Lake Michigan. The building occupies its promontory like an island separated from the plateaus around it by ravines and from the lake below by a steep cliff. Enclosed by the bedroom wing on the left-hand side, a large square fountain spills its overflow down the ravine, creating a series of cascades as the land drops off to the shore below. To overcome the fact that the waterfall remains a minor incident in the landscape, Wright draws attention to it by spanning the watercourse with an elegant bridge; its destination—a belvedere—a secluded lookout affording panoramic views of the sea and sky. The sight and sound of the brook is revealed through an opening in the bridge, heightening the viewer's awareness of the falls during the promenade.

Harold McCormick House
Lake Bluff, Illinois, 1908;
perspective view of exterior, top

Harold McCormick House
plan; note on the far left, the
man-made stream flows down
the ravine from a square pool
until it meets the lake below,
bottom left

Harold McCormick House
diagrammatic analysis of plan,
bottom right; drawn under
author's supervision

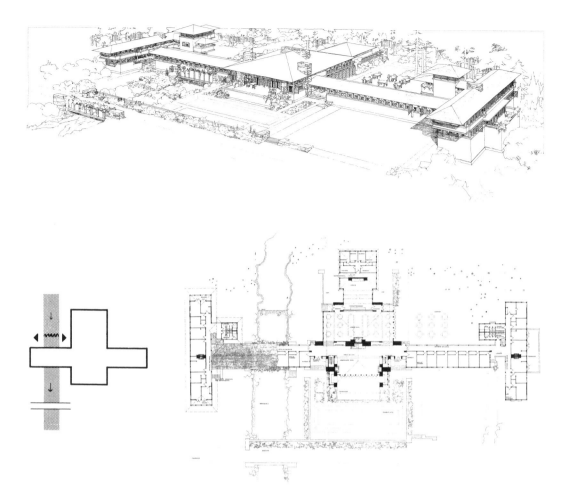

Horseshoe Inn
Estes Park, Colorado, 1908;
perspective view of exterior, top

Horseshoe Inn
diagrammatic analysis of plan,
bottom left; drawn under
author's supervision

Horseshoe Inn
plan, bottom right

In the same year, 1908, Wright designed a resort hotel in the wilderness at the base of the Rocky Mountains near Estes Park, Colorado.[7] The site of Horseshoe Inn, located in what is today Rocky Mountain National Park, is an ancient lake bed encircled on three sides by one of the most imposing mountain ranges in the United States. Beneath mountain peaks that rise to between eleven and fourteen thousand feet, the Fall River weaves through a meadow of juniper and alder, providing water for the elk and mule deer that forage nearby. Despite this dramatic juxtaposition of mountains and water, Wright merely repeated the forms of the Prairie style, joining a low primary mass to two secondary masses by long horizontal galleries, placing a low hip roof overall. However, the integration of the waterfall into the plan of Horseshoe Inn indicates that Wright used the motif to serve more than one architectural purpose. To integrate the building with an existing waterway, Wright sited the building over the Fall River on one side and abandoned the lateral bridge of the McCormick House for a bridge that became an important ceremonial feature of entrance. Horseshoe Inn introduced a new development in Wright's use of the waterfall motif. The stream acts as a line of demarcation between the outside and inside; the connection between the two worlds is celebrated as a passage over water. Yet the waterfall remains a lesser element in the composition; it is at some distance from the bridge and hardly visible when one enters.

The idea of integrating the landscape into the experience of entrance became more explicit at Taliesin, Wright's own studio-residence, built in 1911 near Spring Green, Wisconsin.[8] With the purchase of 31.5 acres of rural land threaded by a spring-fed stream, Wright had, for the first time since his return from Japan, both the opportunity and the means to introduce a waterfall into his architectural composition. Wright's site is located in a valley that is bounded on the east by three softly contoured hills and on the west by three less equal hills.[9] Down its center flows Lowery Creek, "winding and doubling upon itself," as Wright explained, "on its way to the river with fine disregard of time and distance."[10] To the north, the stream meets the Wisconsin River at the edge of the valley. Wright's house and studio, taking full advantage of this water feature, was sited around the extended ridge of the northernmost hill, providing an elevated view of the twists and turns of the creek. Yet Wright did not leave this landscape undisturbed; instead, he manipulated the elements to create a powerful integration of architecture and landscape. The major alteration to the site was the construction of a masonry wall that extended across the stream, forming a dam. The wall continued at an oblique angle, forming a ceremonial entrance with wooden gates.

The damming of the stream accomplished multiple ends. Primarily, it created what Wright described on the original plot plan as a "Water Garden," a pond with such natural contours that a spit of land was formed with access from the shore by a small bridge. But more important, the dam created a flat sheet of water that tumbled onto the staggered stones below in a spray of white water and foam. Thus all the elements of the *shinden-zukuri* water garden appear: the stream, the pond, the island and its bridge, and, of course, the waterfall.

The waterfall was placed directly opposite a small stone bridge that spanned the stream. These elements combined together with the Wisconsin

Taliesin I
Spring Green, Wisconsin, before 1913; plot plan

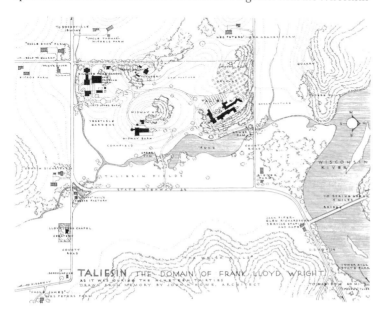

Taliesin Valley
Spring Green, Wisconsin, ca. 1930s; plot plan

River to create a double passage over water to Taliesin, providing layers of transition from the public realm to the private domain. From the nearby town of Spring Green, it is first necessary to cross a bridge spanning the river, at which point a vista of the entire valley and embracing hill masses unfurls directly ahead. This experience is repeated on a smaller scale at the entrance to Taliesin. The visitor must cross over the stone bridge spanning the stream before making a sharp turn to face the imposing masonry wall.[11] The dam, with its cascading waterfall, was placed so that it would be visible along the entire 180-degree arc from the bridge to the entrance gates.

With the exception of Fallingwater, Taliesin represents the only built example of the waterfall motif; it is also one of Wright's most potent uses of the device. Since the waterfall was placed directly in view of the entrance

Taliesin I
waterfall at entrance

Taliesin I
view of main house

bridge, it takes on enormous architectural weight and symbolic power. Taliesin is separated from the rest of the valley by the boundary line of the stream and from the world outside the valley by the Wisconsin River. At the same time, the stream links Wright's domain to the larger world of nature by its confluence with the river.

In the next few years, the basic elements of the waterfall entrance motif reappeared in the first scheme for the Sherman Booth House of 1911 in Glencoe, Illinois, and at the unbuilt Odawara Hotel of 1917 in Odawara, Japan. With the Odawara Hotel, Wright introduced an important innovation that he would repeat in the first scheme for the Director's House for Aline Barnsdall's Olive Hill in 1919. In both plans, the entrance bridge and waterfall become lateral extensions of the building itself. Resolving the incidental character of the earlier McCormick project with the scheme for the Odawara Hotel, Wright had struck on a solution that incorporated landscape as a major element of the building plan. Through the use of water, and the element of the waterfall in particular, Wright had discovered a way to re-create the preindustrial connection between architecture and nature while satisfying a modern program.

The Director's House was part of a larger master plan for Barnsdall's theater community, Olive Hill, in Hollywood, California. The hilltop, which had been planted as an olive grove in the 1890s, rose gently above the plain of Hollywood at the base of the Santa Monica Mountains. Although, ultimately, there were two master plans for the site (the last one only partially completed in 1921 according to Wright's design), it is the lesser-known original plan of 1919 that is pertinent to this study. The earlier plan included a 2,500-seat theater, an apartment building for the acting company, a house for the company's director, and a large residence, Hollyhock House, for Barnsdall. To unify the plan and respond to the topography, Wright introduced an ornamental watercourse, which originated within a springhouse, emerged as a meandering stream, and flowed down the hill between the Director's House and the theater, until it met flat ground.

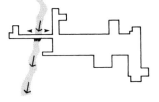

Odawara Hotel
Odawara, Japan, 1917;
perspective view from below

Odawara Hotel
diagrammatic analysis of plan;
drawn under author's supervision

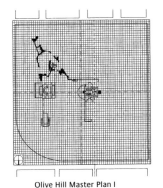

Olive Hill Master Plan I
Los Angeles, California, 1920; plot
plan; the water elements—stream
and waterfalls—indicated in black;
drawn under author's supervision

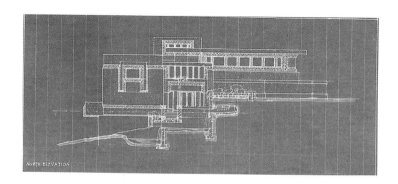

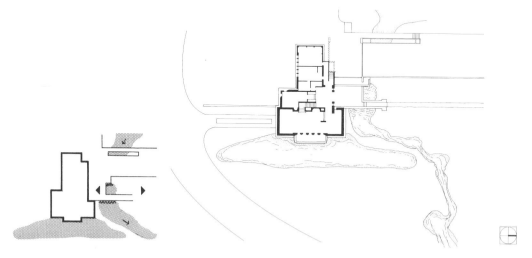

Director's House, Olive Hill
elevation, top

Director's House, Olive Hill
diagrammatic analysis of plan;
drawn under author's supervision,
bottom left

Director's House, Olive Hill
plot plan, bottom right

Wright's experimentation with the waterfall motif at Olive Hill produced a plan that would portend refinements he would carry out at Fallingwater over a decade later. The Director's House was sited to the south of the theater and was connected to it by a walkway and a narrow bridge. The bridge, repeating the precedent of the Odawara Hotel, led to the building's entrance. However, foreshadowing the natural site conditions at Bear Run, Wright introduced two waterfalls: one, elevated five feet above the bridge, clearly visible during entry; the other, splashing over the edge of a small pond directly beneath the bridge. Up the slope from the Director's House, theatergoers could stroll across a paved terrace in front of the theater, gaining a view of the stream below through a wide slot in the pavement. This void inserted into a solid to make the rushing water more immediate recalls the McCormick House bridge and portends the hatchway cut into the living room floor of Fallingwater.

Wright's use of the waterfall motif increased between 1923 and 1925, when he produced three plans using the device. These include House "C" for the Edward L. Doheny Ranch Development of 1923 in Beverly Hills, California; the Lodge-Type Cabin plan of 1923 for Emerald Bay in Lake Tahoe, California; and the Gordon Strong Automobile Objective of 1925 in Sugarloaf Mountain, Maryland. The spiral ramp of the Automobile Objective rises from the flat summit of the mountain, creating a man-made pinnacle to

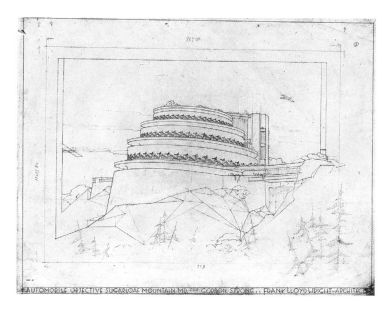

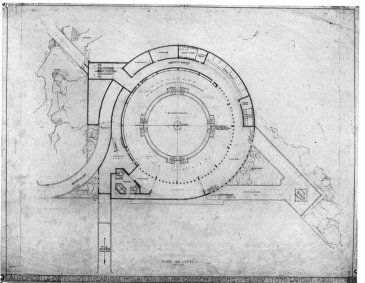

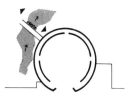

complete the natural formation.[12] Cars approach and exit from one side of the building, while on the opposite side, a pedestrian bridge traverses a steep waterfall that drops from a narrow ravine like a thick sheet of glass. Like the McCormick project, this bridge becomes a viewing platform affording a 270-degree panorama of the countryside accompanied by the sight and sound of the falls below.

Unfortunately, the speculative nature of designing a hotel, cabins, and houseboats for Emerald Bay prevented Wright from taking full advantage of the most spectacular site of wilderness he had been presented since Horseshoe Inn.[13] An inlet of Lake Tahoe on the west, Emerald Bay possesses all the features of a watery paradise.[14] Cradled in a deep basin formed by towering mountain peaks, some rising as high as nine thousand feet,

Gordon Strong Automobile Objective
Sugarloaf Mountain, Maryland, 1925; exterior perspective, top

Gordon Strong Automobile Objective
plan, bottom left

Gordon Strong Automobile Objective
diagrammatic analysis of plan, bottom right; drawn under author's supervision

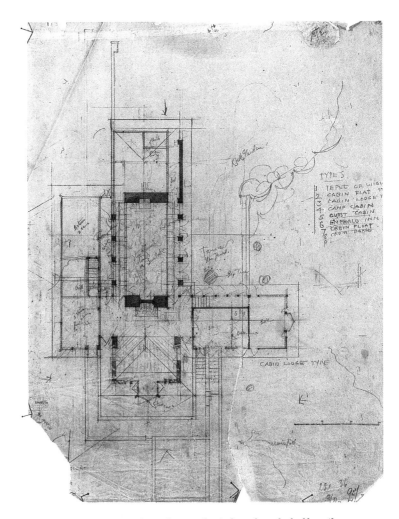

TYPES

1 TEPEE OR WIGU
2 CABIN FLAT T
3 CABIN LODGE T
4 CAMP CABIN
5 GUEST CABIN
6 EMERALD INN
7 CABIN FLOAT
8 CABIN BARGE

CABIN LODGE TYPE

Emerald Bay, Lodge Type Cabin
Emerald Bay, California, 1923;
plan; at the lower right corner
see Wright's note: "waterfall"

Emerald Bay measures about three miles in length and a half a mile across
and opens to Lake Tahoe through a narrow channel approximately a quarter
of a mile wide. Dotting the bay, diminutive Fannette Island is perched off the
northwestern shoreline. From the edge of the water, a pine-covered slope
rises approximately two hundred feet to a road circling the bay. Directly to
the west, cascading Eagle Falls plummets to a rocky ledge and from this basin
descends to meet the still waters below. A notation on the plan for the Lodge-
Type Cabin indicates that Wright intended to site one of the houses next to
Eagle Falls, but the project was abandoned before he could work out the
necessary details.

   Although there is no further development in the waterfall motif with
these two projects, a radical alteration had appeared with the earlier
Edward L. Doheny Ranch Development in 1923.[15] It is likely that the unique
topographical and geological conditions of the site are what prompted
Wright's daring poetic response. Hillside houses to be built on speculation
planned for several narrow canyons that penetrate the Santa Monica
Mountains just east of the Beverly Hills Hotel. Water was naturally present
on the property in the form of spring-fed caves.[16] The most prophetic house

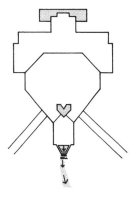

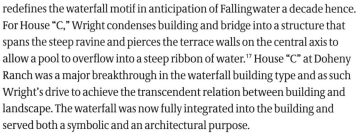

redefines the waterfall motif in anticipation of Fallingwater a decade hence. For House "C," Wright condenses building and bridge into a structure that spans the steep ravine and pierces the terrace walls on the central axis to allow a pool to overflow into a steep ribbon of water.[17] House "C" at Doheny Ranch was a major breakthrough in the waterfall building type and as such Wright's drive to achieve the transcendent relation between building and landscape. The waterfall was now fully integrated into the building and served both a symbolic and an architectural purpose.

Wright was presented with few commissions in the next decade; but the implications of House "C" were realized in a novel form when, after a destructive fire, Wright initiated an extensive new building program at Taliesin between 1925 and 1926. Directly next to the waterfall at the entrance

Edward Doheny Ranch, House "C"
1923; perspective with plan
below

Edward Doheny Ranch, House "C"
diagrammatic analysis of plan;
drawn under author's supervision

Hydro House, Taliesin III
Spring Green, Wisconsin, 1926;
period photograph

gates, Wright placed a graceful structure housing a hydroelectric plant, which provided power for his house and studio. The juxtaposition of waterfall and building existed until the early 1930s, when the surging waters of a spring thaw washed the powerhouse away.[18]

In December 1934, when the Kaufmanns, father and son, presented Wright with the location for the family's new country house, it was the first time since 1923 at Emerald Bay that he had been given a commission to design a building for a site with a waterfall. The family's favorite spot was buried deep in a wooded glen and was characterized by large sandstone outcroppings, which exhibited a rustic, even ancient, appearance. The stream contained two waterfalls (as Wright had designed at Olive Hill); but they crossed the stream on the diagonal (at Olive Hill, he had placed the waterfalls at right angles to the stream), providing greater potential for a dynamic spatial composition. The falls were not uniform; one fell to a drop of almost twenty-five feet, the other almost ten. Because of the irregularities of the broken ledges, the falls did not have a formal appearance. Upstream, some distance above the first waterfall, a small wooden bridge spanned the creek. On his return to Taliesin, Wright is reported to have written Kaufmann, "the visit to the waterfall in the woods stays with me and a domicile has taken vague shape in my mind to the music of the stream."[19]

As he had been prone to do since the Doheny project of 1923, Wright placed the building, not the bridge, next to the falls. And in so doing, he abandoned the association of the waterfall with the entrance and clearly brought the house into intimate contact with transcendent nature. As Fallingwater dramatically cantilevers over the first waterfall, like the Doheny project, it condenses elements of building and bridge. And as he did with the bridge for Harold McCormick and with the terrace at Olive Hill, Wright carved an opening in the living-room floor and terrace to bring the movement of the water beneath the building within sight. But Fallingwater is more intricate than either of these earlier examples because the hatchway is more than a simple void. The stream can be viewed in layers of spatial transition: from both inside the building, while in the living room; and outside, while on the terrace. And from the living room, it is possible to descend a staircase under the glass-covered hatch and be within view of the water below and the sky above.

Fallingwater is the realization of the new development in the waterfall building, which began with the Doheny Ranch project, House "C." By placing the house at the head of the upper waterfall rather than between the two falls (as he had at Olive Hill), Wright guaranteed that the building and water elements would form one sublime union rather than a composition of disparate parts. He further reinforced the relationship by mimicking the form of the waterfalls in the building. As Bear Run flows downstream to the west, the broken ledges of the first waterfall direct the water on a diagonal primarily to the south, and the stream then continues to flow in a westerly path, spilling over the second tier of ledges. As a result, when viewed from a central vantage point downstream, the two waterfalls appear to flow at ninety-degree angles to each other. This configuration is repeated in the projecting living-room and bedroom parapets, which crisscross at a ninety-degree angle echoing the waterfalls below. With increasing frequency after the Prairie House, abstraction had replaced pictorialism in the depiction of natural motifs: Wright had substituted symbolism for decoration.[20]

Fallingwater illustrates more clearly perhaps than any of Wright's other waterfall buildings, either before or after, his effort to forge a spiritual unity between architecture and nature. With the exception of Eagle Falls at Lake Tahoe, where real-estate speculation prevented him from specifically addressing the site, only Bear Run provided the necessary elements—the stream, the rocks, and the falls—in their natural state. The transcendent quality of Bear Run serves as a perfect counterpoint for the virtuosity of Wright's geometric grammar. While the building differentiates itself from its surroundings and retains its identity as a man-made object, it is perceived as a complement to nature, and, as a result, each ennobles the other by its presence.

The perception of the transcendent relationship between building and landscape is related to the pursuit of a spiritual relationship between man and the physical universe. Unity, deriving from a parallelism between man's order and the order of the natural universe, was manifest in the waterfall motif. While Wright endowed waterfalls with architectural weight and presence, they also carried with them associations of the water cycle—the infinite progression of evaporation, condensation, and precipitation that completes the circle of nature. "The cycle guarantees that all water is connected in a continuous global chain," Charles W. Moore has written in *Water and Architecture*, "so that water never remains an isolated incident and never exclusively belongs to any specific time or place. Even the tiniest drop of water shares a heritage with the greatest ocean."[21] Fallingwater compresses all these levels of meaning into one powerful metaphor; comprehension is immediate yet, at that same time, sublime.

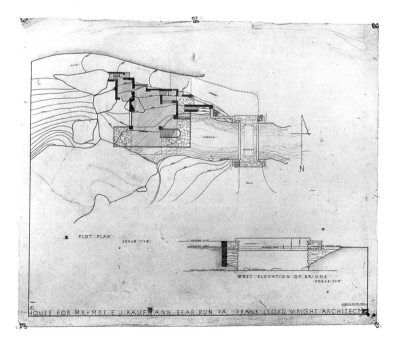

Fallingwater
Mill Run, Pennsylvania, 1936;
plot plan

Fallingwater
diagrammatic analysis of plan;
drawn under author's supervision

Ralph Jester House
Palos Verdes, Califnornia, 1938;
model

Ralph Jester House
diagrammatic analysis of plan;
drawn under author's supervision

Wright would never again receive a site like Bear Run. However, only two years after the completion of Fallingwater, Wright designed the Ralph Jester House of 1938 in Palos Verdes, California, using the overflow from the swimming pool to create a curtain of water spilling down the cliffside site.[22] Like the Doheny project, the Jester House integrates the waterfall into the building plan, but here it serves a recreational as well as a romantic purpose. With a 270-degree vista across the Pacific Ocean to the horizon, the line of sight from the edge of the pool to the ocean beyond links the two bodies of water in one continuous image. The literal and virtual relationship is reinforced by the action of the water falling toward the ocean.

The development of the waterfall motif culminates in 1947 with Pittsburgh Point Park Civic Center, planned for a triangular point of land at the confluence of the Allegheny and Monongahela rivers. Wright's megastructure consists of two circular buildings: a large one of fifteen stories, housing cultural and civic functions, and a smaller building, four stories in height, containing two aquariums, a restaurant, and a public swimming pool. With a sense of bravado and daring, Wright proposed to take the waters of the two adjoining rivers and, as he did on a tiny scale with the Taliesin powerhouse, use them to generate electricity. The water would be released on the roof gardens in the form of monumental jets, fountains, and overflow and return to its source as a circular drapery of water falling at the confluence of the building and two rivers.

Although designed under the patronage of the same client, Edgar Kaufmann Sr., Fallingwater and Pittsburgh Point Civic Center illustrate the incongruities Wright was able to reconcile by the end of his career. His facility with water, and waterfalls in particular, provided him with the means to address a diversity of sites, from the naturally sublime to the industrially ravaged, and reestablish the seminal connection with a higher order of nature.[23] The element of water, then, provides, as fire did for the Prairie House, a means of understanding the profound thematic dimension that characterized Wright's mature career.

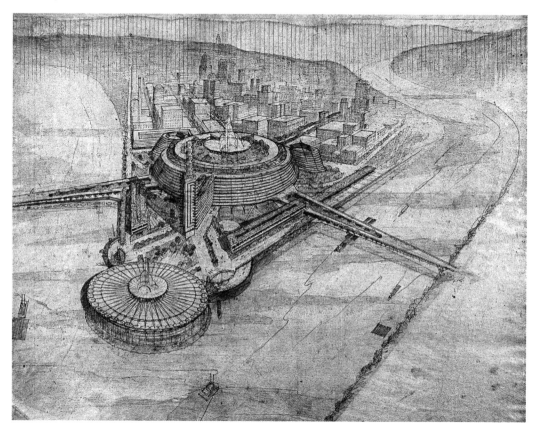

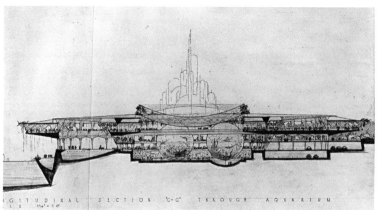

Pittsburgh Point Civic Center
Pittsburgh, Pennsylvania, 1947;
perspective

Pittsburgh Point Civic Center
section

Pittsburgh Point Civic Center
diagrammatic analysis of plan;
drawn under author's supervision

Frank Lloyd Wright's Diagonal Planning Revisited

BY NEIL LEVINE

Despite the development of a much greater understanding of Frank Lloyd Wright's architecture since the publication of Bruce Pfeiffer's *Monograph* in the mid-1980s and the rapid growth of archival-based research and scholarship following that, it is fair to say that an unthinking acceptance of Philip Johnson's now nearly fifty-year-old characterization of Wright as "the greatest architect of the nineteenth century" still serves to obscure the coherency and continuity of Wright's career as a whole.[1] His early work, from 1889 to 1909, is generally lauded as a major precursor of twentieth-century modernism, while his later work, after 1932, is viewed in rather negative terms as something quite removed from and even at odds with it. In between is a fallow period, called by Reyner Banham the "wilderness years" and more recently by Anthony Alofsin the "lost years."[2] Where historians and architects alike seem transfixed by the stunning originality, uniformity, and exemplary force of the buildings of the so-called Oak Park years, the later work is all too often perceived as inconsistent, idiosyncratic, and lacking any discernible overall principle of design.

The Wasmuth portfolio of 1910, which served as a retrospective of the Oak Park years, presented a demonstrative image of coherence from the point of view of planning, but the same can hardly be said for the two issues of *Architectural Forum* that were devoted to Wright, in January 1938 and January 1948. While the German publication gave such an impression of discipline and unity that it could soon be accepted as a textbook of modern architecture, the later collections offer an almost bewildering variety of geometric forms. Gone is the rigorous orthogonal plaiting that informed the earlier public and private buildings and gave the architect's planning an almost mesmerizing sense of logical necessity. Instead, there is Fallingwater, with its open series of staggered, rectilinear elements; the Hanna House, with its hexagonal grid fanning out in a pattern of reflex movement; Taliesin West, with its spiky projections from an elongated spine; the Guggenheim Museum, with its spiraling, closed, circular forms; and, finally, Florida Southern College, with its rotated, multilayered square grid, edged by angular paths pivoting on circles and projecting into space. The radically different geometries emphasize the particularity of each project and appear to deny

any form of consistency. But their very use depends on an underlying principle of order, having its source in Wright's earlier work and common to all his later work, which is the diagonal axis.[3] Whether or not the diagonality is made explicit in the geometry of the plan, as in the Hanna House or Florida Southern, it is always implicit in determining the spatial experience of the building and its relation to the site.

"When Dad builds," wrote Wright's son John in 1946, "he sees things out of the corner of his eye. He never looks straight at them."[4] In his Prairie-style buildings, Wright's desire for free-flowing space led him to open up the corner and deny its role of containing and bounding interior space. By the mid-1920s, he found a way to systematize these effects on a geometric basis. The diagonal axis then became the positive organizing principle of his planning, bringing a new depth and meaning to the architecture of his later career.[5] The supple principle of diagonality allowed for the new sense of freedom, breadth, and connection to nature that Wright sought after leaving the suburban world of Oak Park and moving to Taliesin in the hills of southern Wisconsin. When seen against the background of his early work, the full elaboration of the principle of diagonality helps chart the course of Wright's career more accurately and clarifies the changing values of his architecture.

FROM THE OAK PARK YEARS THROUGH THE LATE TEENS

While it is true that the diagonal axis has played an important role in planning throughout history—and here one immediately thinks of the Acropolis in Athens, Hadrian's Villa, and the radiating avenues of baroque cities and gardens—it must also be noted that its systematic use in the design of buildings themselves is a relatively modern development. One might have resorted to the diagonal when faced with the structural problem of a dome, or a particularly difficult site, or, especially as the eighteenth century evolved, in order to produce an intricate and animated solution; but, to the classically trained Western architect, the diagonal implied irregularity and irrationality. Its use in the rib vaults, canted piers, and flying buttresses of medieval cathedrals was a major reason for the traditional criticism of Gothic architecture.[6] However, by the later nineteenth century, following the Gothic Revival, the desire for more picturesqueness and casualness, particularly in domestic architecture, made the use of diagonal shifts in axis almost common practice in America, until the renewal of classicism in the 1890s redirected the shingle style toward greater discipline and order. It is in this context, as Vincent Scully pointed out long ago, that we can understand Wright's early work and its singular resolution of the opposed pressures toward freedom and order.[7]

Wright employed diagonal shifts in axis from the very beginning of his career as a way of opening up the plan and giving direction to the interior space. The house he apparently designed in 1887 and showed Louis Sullivan when applying for a job, which he proposed to build three years later for the Cooper family in La Grange, Illinois, has three wings projecting at forty-five-degree angles from the corners of a square central hall. The "butterfly plan," as it was called in late-Victorian England, had an obvious source in the project for a town house by Viollet-le-Duc published in his seventeenth *entretien*

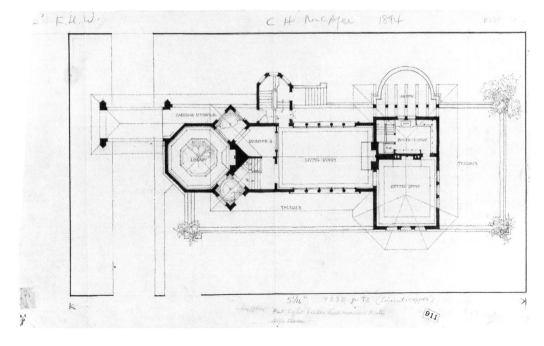

in 1872 and in Bucknall's English translation in 1881.[8] It was used almost immediately by McKim, Mead, & White, first in the Colonial-detailed Appleton House at Lenox, Massachusetts, built in 1883–84, and then in the shingled house for John Cowdin at Far Rockaway, Long Island, built a year or so later and likewise published in Sheldon's *Artistic Country Seats* in 1886–87.[9] In Wright's design, the loose and picturesque handling of the parts is tightened up, and the changes in direction are articulated with greater clarity and assertiveness. The hall, with its fireplace on axis, is preceded by a partially enclosed garden, gently skewed toward the corner entrance; and each separate wing is assured privacy as well as light on three sides.

Wright's drive to give ever-greater focus and order to his architecture soon led him away from the dispersive tendencies of the "butterfly plan" toward much more compact solutions. In the Blossom House in Chicago, of 1892, and especially the Winslow House in River Forest, Illinois, of the following year, the rooms are grouped around a central fireplace. Oblique views from room to room break up the apparent symmetry and give a dynamic, pinwheeling effect to the space, as in the house and studio he built for himself in Oak Park in 1889–90. But directly following the almost classical statement of the Winslow House, Wright designed two other houses in the Sullivanesque mode in which he returned to the explicit use of forty-five-degree angles. The projects for both the McAfee House of 1894 and the Devin House of 1896 were designed for narrow lots on the shore of Lake Michigan, and angled projections were provided to take advantage of the view. In the McAfee House, the shifts in axis are integrally related to the spatial movement of the plan, giving it a dynamic pistol-like shape. The two square vestibules, rotated within the reentrant angles of the octagonal library and entrance area, provide a fork in the main axis and echo at a distance the symmetrical projections of the dining room and arbor.

A. C. McAfee House
Kenilworth, Illinois, 1894; plan

By the turn of the century, as his work matured, Wright began to eliminate any such graphic representation of axial inflection but continued to use the rotated square as the terminating projection of the orthogonal axes themselves. A fully developed instance of this is the Willits House in Highland Park, Illinois, of 1902–03. The main axis of the dining room ends in a triangular bay; a cross axis projects through the low front wall of the porch to form a conservatory just under the edge of the overhanging eaves. Since the apex of the dining-room bay window lines up with the far wall of the porch, half the view from that room is directed outward to the garden, while the other half is contained within the open porch. In this way, the pointed axial terminations extend the interior out into a half-indoors, half-outdoors space. Their diagonal shape gives physical form to the idea of manipulating space as the plastic medium of architecture. Indeed, it is as if the interior space had literally been pulled out from the center and stretched taut between one's thumb and forefinger.

The Robie House in Chicago, of 1907–10, culminated Wright's use of the diagonally set bay to define and extend the spatial axes. Here, both the living room and the dining room are pulled out from the central fireplace into prowlike extensions under the extended eaves. Inside, the effect is rather like that of classical one-point perspective. The angled planes of the projecting bay establish a vanishing point, and the three pairs of piers, set parallel to the direction of the space, recede into depth, enforcing the telescopic effect. While the corner is in fact denied its role of containment, the eye is not allowed to look out on the diagonal. The slots of space created by the inset piers *in antis* give the illusion of space seeping out at the corners while actu-

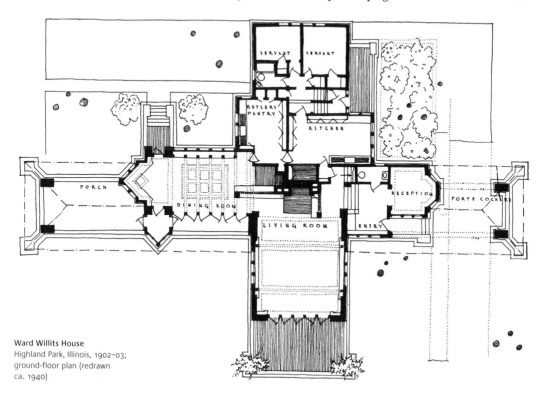

Ward Willits House
Highland Park, Illinois, 1902–03;
ground-floor plan (redrawn
ca. 1940)

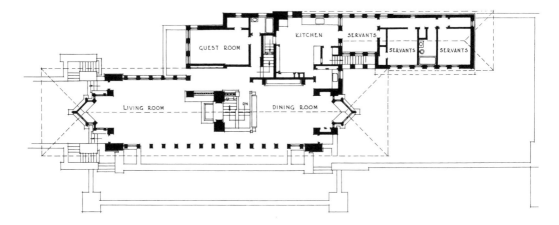

ally channeling the view and focusing it on the center. This method of giving a feeling of openness and extension to the interior space through the use of inset piers and corner slots of space was characteristic of Wright's Prairie style and could occur with or without the diagonally set projections. The effect is fundamentally unidirectional and relates to classical methods of Beaux-Arts axial composition and framing, exemplified in Sullivan's teacher Emile Vaudremer's plans for the Parisian churches of Saint-Pierre de Montrouge (1864–75) and Notre-Dame d'Auteuil (1876–83).[10]

There were, however, a few instances during these early years when Wright made more radical use of the diagonal axis. It is perhaps no coincidence that the Glasner House in Glencoe, Illinois, of 1905, which is often cited as a prototype for the later Usonian Houses with their combined living-dining space, has a plan that develops along two main diagonal axes, realizing, as it were, the full implications of the earlier McAfee project. The eccentrically placed living-room fireplace is located on a forty-five-degree line of sight from the corner entry, and the same angle defines the diagonal disposition of the bedrooms and octagonal sewing room that step out over the ravine site. A longitudinal axis defined by the two larger octagons of the library and projected teahouse, however, stabilizes the plan in a rectilinear fashion.

Still more radical in their employment of the diagonal axis and rotated square, as well as more prophetic of later developments in Wright's work, are the Hillside Home School addition, built for his two aunts Jane and Ellen in Hillside, Wisconsin (later the site of Taliesin), in 1901–03, and a Studio House planned for himself around the time the school was being finished. In the former, Wright rotated a square balcony forty-five degrees within the main square space of the assembly hall. The aggressively diagonal spatial cut causes the ceiling to appear unsupported at the corners and the space to expand out in all directions. In the Studio House project of 1903, Wright set the dining room, living room, and studio all on a forty-five-degree diagonal perpendicular to the diagonal axis from the entry hall to the porch, and then expressed the diagonal deflection of the space by an eccentrically placed fireplace, open at three of its four corners.[11] The experimental quality of this very personal design was obviously subdued for the Glasner House, just as

Frederick Robie House
plan, second floor (redrawn
ca. 1940)

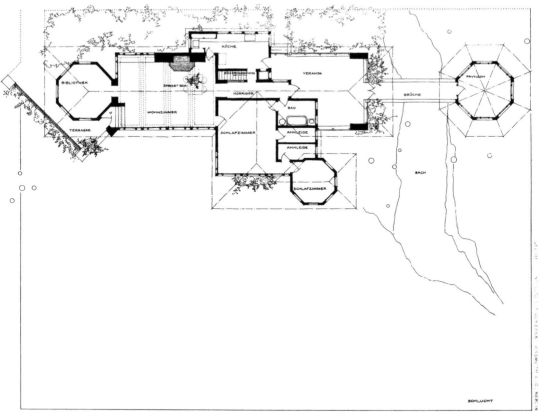

the aggressiveness of the Hillside Home School assembly hall was modulated in the sanctuary space of Unity Temple (1905–08).

It is quite apparent that at this point in his career Wright considered the use of diagonality rather unconventional and confined its overt expression mainly to buildings for himself and his family. This is even more true in the decade following his return from Europe. Between 1910 and 1920, Wright's planning generally became more and more classical, emphasizing rectilinearity, closure, and formality. While the symmetrical courtyard plans of Midway Gardens in Chicago of 1913–14 and the Imperial Hotel in Tokyo of 1913–23 are the most notable examples, this development can also be seen in the architect's domestic work, beginning with the Coonley Playhouse in Riverside, Illinois, of 1911–12, and culminating in Hollyhock House, built for Aline Barnsdall in Los Angeles, in 1919–21. The summer house for the Bagley family at Grand Beach, Michigan, of 1916 gives perhaps the best indication of the extent to which Wright tried to impose an abstract geometric order of a highly formalized sort regardless of program or site. Functions are zoned in separate pavilions, which are all connected at their corners. The five symmetrically disposed pavilions describe a right-angle triangle, which thus contrasts in its complete regularity with the openly casual arrangement of the Glasner House or the 1903 Studio House project.

A few houses of this period, however, such as the projects for Arthur Cutten and Sherman Booth of 1911 or the second Little House at Wayzata, Minnesota, of 1912–14, display a more freewheeling relation to the site. But the casualness is once again a pale reflection of the assertive diagonality of a building Wright designed for his own use. Taliesin, built in 1911 on a hill just to the north of the Hillside Home School (and rebuilt and enlarged after fires in 1914 and 1924), stands out from all his other work of the period in the way it blends in with the landscape and almost literally becomes part of it. It is organized around a court in a loosely connected series of wings following the contours of the hill, just below its crown, to form, as Wright explained, "the 'brow' of the hill" itself.[12] The rough stone laid up in strata imitates the outcrops of the surrounding hills, while the fundamental sense of oneness

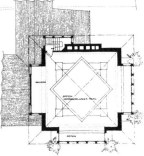

W. A. Glasner House
Glencoe, Illinois, 1905;
perspective and plan, opposite

Hillside Home School Addition
Spring Green, Wisconsin,
1901–03; photograph of
assembly hall

Hillside Home School Addition
assembly hall, plan

Wright Studio House
Oak Park, Illinois, 1903; plan
(redrawn ca. 1940)

Joseph Bagley House
Grand Beach, Michigan, 1916;
plan (redrawn ca. 1940)

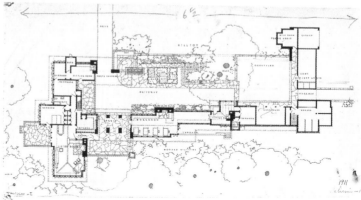

with the land is most fully expressed in the commanding view from the living room out over the valley below.

The rectangular living room, perched out over the hillside, is entered through a loggia off the corner of the court diagonally opposite the main view. The great fireplace and bookshelf seat, forming a nook in the path of entry, immediately define the implied diagonal axis, while the notched corner and diagonally placed piano at the far end of the fireplace wall reinforce the angled line of sight. When the residential area of Taliesin was rebuilt after the tragic 1914 fire, Wright thought to increase the importance of the implied diagonal by pushing the window-wall opposite the fireplace out two bays. And after the fire of 1925, he even further increased the effect of the diagonal by setting a stone pier just inside the far corner and opening the corner out onto a balcony. He also enlarged the farm buildings and set them at a forty-five-degree angle, echoing the visual axis of the living room.

The view on entering the living room now cuts across the space and over the hills in one great, effortless, arching movement that seems to follow the curve of the earth itself, as the stone fireplace to the rear mirrors the pier in the far corner and anchors the vista back in the hill behind. The kitty-cornered placement of the stone uprights helps give the impression of shearing along the diagonal; and, with the planes of the hipped ceiling spreading above and the floor sliding out toward the light, one has the boundless sense of being in the center of things, in a space turned inside out. Recalling the times when as a boy he would pick flowers on the hillside now occupied by the house, Wright later described how, "when you are on the low hill-crown, you have the feeling of being out in mid-air as though swinging in a plane, the Valley . . . dropping away from you leaving the treetops standing below all about you."[13] In this house built for himself on his family's former farmland, it would seem that Wright had consciously set himself the task of creating an architectural equivalent for nature. The underlying diagonal axis was critical to this effort.

THE TWENTIES IN CALIFORNIA AND ARIZONA

For whatever reasons, Wright was not to offer a client anything quite like Taliesin until Fallingwater, in the mid-1930s. But in the mountains and desert of California, for which he developed the textile-block method of construction just after returning from Japan, Wright began to experiment more and more with diagonal planning until it became the norm rather than the exception in his work.[14] The first indications are the impressive projects for the Doheny Ranch Development in Los Angeles, of 1923, the Tahoe Summer Colony at Lake Tahoe in the Sierra Nevada Mountains, designed in 1923–24, and the Johnson Desert Compound in Death Valley, of 1924–25. The multiple concrete-block houses that form the terraced hillsides of the Doheny project take their cue from Taliesin in leaving, as Wright noted, the "contours of the hills undisturbed."[15] Some become arched bridges over ravines, others stretch out in long horizontal platforms, while still others emerge like natural promontories from an existing gully. Wright obviously felt that a non-orthogonal geometry was more accommodating to such a terrain. One of the most spectacular houses develops around an open court defined by the splayed, angled walls of a natural cleft. The chamfered square court is rotated forty-five degrees and then set like a cut diamond in the hillside. The diagonals define the major axes. The transverse one forms terraces to the left and right, following the contours of the hill, while the longitudinal one reaches out from the fireplace, itself set in a pool deep in the cavelike living room, to a projecting hexagonal terrace.[16] The wedgelike shape of the pool reflects the conical hill behind while, below, its angled planes split to allow a mountain stream running under the court to cascade down the ravine.

In the project for the Tahoe Summer Colony, Wright pursued the obtuse

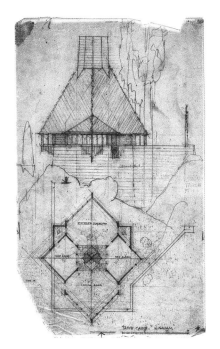

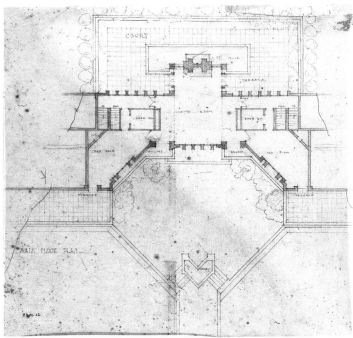

geometry and open-angled plan in a number of the shore cabins. In others, he went even further in developing some of the implications of the forty-five-degree angle that had appeared in his work prior to 1909. The Big Tree (or Wigwam) Type Cabin, for instance, is composed of a square rotated forty-five degrees within another, like the assembly hall at the Hillside Home School, but here the rotated square projects through the outer casing to emphasize the extent of the diagonal. The Family Barge, with its double prow, restates the central shape of the Robie House plan, while the smaller Barge for Two is composed of three interlocking hexagons, with the central axis extending from point to point. Now also, for the first time, the diagonal geometry is not limited to the plans but is reflected in the sections and elevations as well, thus echoing the shape of the surrounding conifers and referring to traditional forms of nomadic shelter.

The Johnson Desert Compound is far and away the most original and consequential of the three projects.[17] Planned as a winter retreat for a remote canyon high above the desert floor and with views across the valley to the opposite mountain range, the multiple structures of battered, striated textile block are unified into a single megastructure that is more like an earthwork than a building. The L-shaped living quarters to the left are cranked thirty degrees off the main east–west axis to point in the direction of the descending canyon. The raised diagonal causeway leading to the living quarters picks up the angle of deflection as it pivots off the main road up the canyon to direct the eye toward the vista while creating a terraced area for cultivation within the resultant thirty/sixty-degree triangular forecourt. In the process, the driveway/embankment becomes a dam, or sluice gate, to control the water irrigating the gardens and collecting on both sides of it in a series of angled pools.

Lake Tahoe Summer Colony
Lake Tahoe, California, 1923–24;
Big Tree (Wigwam) Cabin, plan
and elevation

Doheny Ranch, House "C"
Los Angeles, California, 1923;
plan

The radical and unprecedented asymmetry of the diagonal geometry provides a degree of openness and air of contingency to the architecture that causes one to read the relationship between building and landscape in a newly interdependent way. The structure's extruded, fluid forms appear to have been shaped and laid low over time by the very process of erosion that made the valley. Indeed, the triangular bed of irrigated land, kept in check by the pivoting causeway, holds in suspension the image of an alluvial fan in the making. The angle of the dam, as it responds to the pressure of earth and water against its upper edge, reveals an unprecedented symbiotic relationship between architecture and nature. The resolution of the conflict between force and resistance occurs along the elastic and responsive line of the diagonal that Wright likened to a natural "reflex" and believed to be particularly appropriate to the desert.[18]

Wright's experiments with diagonal planning in California were partially realized in two buildings that form a watershed in the development outlined so far. The first, the Community Playhouse designed for the Barnsdall estate on Olive Hill in 1923 and called the Little Dipper because of its shape, was barely begun before it was altered out of recognition.[19] The second, the Freeman House, also in Los Angeles, was built in 1924–25. Both were designed

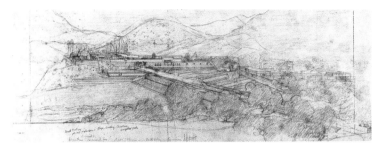

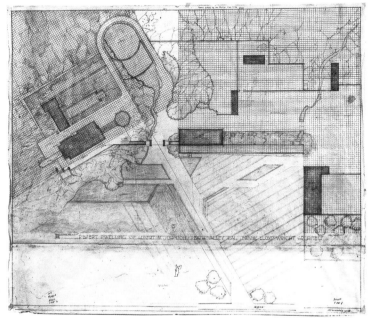

Johnson Desert Compound
Death Valley, California, 1924–25;
preliminary perspective, from
south

Johnson Desert Compound
final site plan

for precipitously sloping sites, and both were constructed of sixteen-inch-square concrete blocks set into a square grid of steel reinforcing rods.

The Little Dipper was sited, halfway down the slope from Hollyhock House to the Studio Residence B, at a forty-five-degree diagonal to the main east–west axis of the estate. The schoolroom angles out from the hill and is entered on the diagonal down a narrow ledge connecting it to the driveway above. The plan, while obviously deriving from the Hillside Home School and the Tahoe Big Tree Cabin, represents the most complex expression of diagonality Wright had achieved so far. Movement down the slope is gently deflected by a series of three forty-five-degree bends. Two offset, elongated hexagons define the overall length of the building and determine the first two forty-five-degree shifts. Then, at the crossing of the two major hexagons, within the deformed square of the schoolroom, the axis is once again shifted forty-five degrees to angle out through the corner opened up by two diagonally placed piers.

The main axis of the schoolroom, under the clerestoried central section, opens out at either end in vertical slots of perforated concrete block as in the preliminary project for the much later First Unitarian Church in Madison, Wisconsin, of 1946–52. The cross axis reaches back into the deep-set fireplace to carry the eye out through the corner hexagonal pool and surrounding sand box in an arc of two hundred-seventy degrees over the bowl of seats defining the southern horizon.[20] The connection of fire and water to earth and sky along the diagonal axis resembles the Doheny House project described above; and one must assume that Wright felt that the thrust of the diagonal into space provided the means to effect that natural union at the scale of the landscape itself.

While the diagonal axis could be a carrier of elemental meanings, the sense of depth it projects could also be translated onto the domestic plane to produce a more dynamic spatial experience of openness and breadth. The Freeman House is a perfect case in point. It terraces down the hillside, like the Little Dipper, but in the form of a square ladle. Its narrow entry passage also aligns with the rear wall of the main space to become the back of a fireplace. But whereas the entry into the Little Dipper was deflected forty-five degrees along the side of one hexagon and the fireplace was set on the diagonal in the corner of another, the entry into the living room of the Freeman House is through a corner, and the fireplace is located in the middle of one side of an absolutely square room.

Piers on either side of the fireplace support deep beams that extend across the space to the large expanse of windows overlooking Los Angeles. The piers opposite the fireplace are matched by others along the side walls inset equidistantly from the corners. The corners are left completely open; the horizontal sheets of plate glass are butted directly, with no vertical mullion, in one of Wright's first true corner windows.[21] The view from the entry out the far corner is thus unimpeded and has an immediate and powerful impact. The diagonals of the square define the axes of the space, like an early Gothic rib vault, extending the space outward beyond the perimeter of the square. The room takes on the virtual shape of the Little Dipper schoolroom, something one can imagine by making the rotated square balcony of the

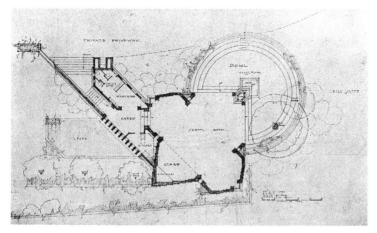

Hillside Home School equal in size to the room itself, as Wright had just done the year before in the Big Tree Cabin.

The spatial experience of virtual, or implied, diagonality in the Freeman House recalls Piet Mondrian's contemporary Diamond paintings, just as the explicit diagonality of the Little Dipper reminds one of Theo van Doesburg's diagonal "countercompositions" of 1924–25. Mondrian adopted the diamond format as early as 1918–19 for a series of grid paintings continuing through 1921. Then, in 1925–26, perhaps in reaction to van Doesburg, who was the spokesman for the de Stijl group, Mondrian produced another group of four works in which the square central space projects a sense of dynamic continuity but without forsaking the orthogonal structure of vertical and horizontal lines. Van Doesburg, on the other hand, just after completing a series of architectural designs with Cornelis van Eesteren in 1923, translated the forty-five-degree geometry of their axonometric projections onto the flat, rectangular picture plane and declared the resulting diagonality the basis of a new Elementarism.[22] The issue of explicit diagonality became so divisive that Mondrian left the de Stijl group in 1925.

It is important to remember in this context that the second major European publication of Wright's work occurred at just this time, in the Dutch magazine *Wendingen* in 1925. Although the relation between

Little Dipper Community
Playhouse
Los Angeles, California, 1923;
perspective

Little Dipper Community
Playhouse
plan

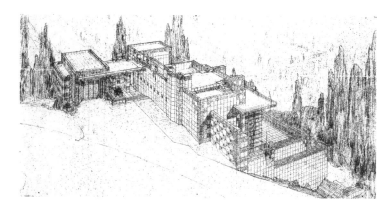

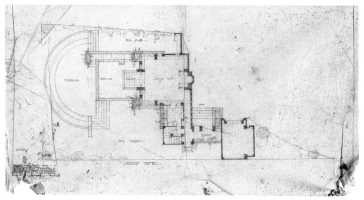

Wright's bird's-eye perspective of the orthogonal Freeman House and the explicitly diagonal plan of the Little Dipper makes one think of van Doesburg's strikingly similar translation of axonometric projection, it should be noted that for Wright explicit and implicit diagonality were not mutually exclusive and, indeed, would continue to coexist throughout his work as they did in the Little Dipper and Freeman House. Moreover, diagonality was never a polemical issue for Wright as it was for the Dutch. Van Doesburg ascribed to its dynamic form a spiritual, "space-time" dimension and believed that its incorporation in works of art would help break down the traditional barriers between art and life.[23] While such ideas were hardly inimical to Wright, as evidenced by his 1926 project for a pyramidal Steel Cathedral for a Million People for New York City, he did not adopt the principle of diagonality for theoretical or ideological reasons. The diagonal had always been for him, even in its restricted use in the Prairie House, a very practical means for cutting across the boundary between indoors and outdoors and establishing, as he eventually would in Taliesin, a more direct relationship between building and landscape. In effect, it was the specific topographical conditions he faced in California in the early 1920s and the means of construction he developed in response to those conditions that led him to formalize a spatial idea in a method of planning that had previously appeared only sporadically and unsystematically in his work. Once he began to use a modular system, with the square grid directly expressed in the lines of the adjoining blocks of the floor, it was almost a natural reflex to draw the

Samuel Freeman House
Los Angeles, California, 1924–25;
perspective, from entrance side
on north

Samuel Freeman House
plan, main (upper) floor

diagonal from corner to corner to define the greatest internal dimension.

The next stage in this development came about as a result of working in another desert environment of the Southwest. In 1928, while in Arizona to help his former student Albert Chase McArthur on the design of the Arizona Biltmore Hotel, Wright met Alexander Chandler, who commissioned a project for a winter resort hotel to be called San Marcos–in–the–Desert. In response to the local topography, Wright returned to the thirty/sixty-degree triangle he had used in Death Valley. In the temporary camp he built for himself at the base of the Phoenix South Mountains in the following year, which he named Ocatilla after the spindly, scarlet-flowered cactus that dotted the area, a group of small wood and canvas structures were connected by a continuous low wall that angled in and out, following the contours of a barrow-like rocky mound and rising in the center to a triangular campfire. In his *Autobiography*, Wright explained that the thirty/sixty-degree geometry was directly inspired by the shapes of the surrounding mountains: "The one-two triangle is the cross-section of the talus at their bases. This triangle is reflected in the general forms of all the cabins as well as the general plan."[24]

For the San Marcos hotel, Wright used the thirty/sixty-degree geometry to make, as he said, "a far-flung, long-drawn-out building" rather than an enclosure. The textile-block structure was to become a form of "great nature-masonry rising from the great mesa floor [like] an abstraction of this mountain region itself."[25] Two lateral wings, stepped back in three terraces against the mountainside, branch off a central volume, which contains the public spaces of the hotel and bridges the wash that serves as the driveway and lower-level entrance court. The wing of rooms to the right, or east, takes a straight path from the lobby at an angle of one hundred-twenty degrees to it; the one on the left initially takes the same angle to the southwest along the ridge of the wash before cranking north in a thirty/sixty-degree triangle to round the spur following the contours of the hillside. The diagonal section of the two terraced wings provides for a maximum degree of sunlight, privacy, and vista.

In conjunction with the main hotel, Wright also designed a group of private houses either adjoined to it or in close proximity to it. In the one for Owen D. Young, the rectangular geometry of the enclosed spaces is set off against the diagonal projection of an elongated hexagonal terrace, while the diamond pattern of the concrete blocks echoes the distant mountain peaks. In the house for Wellington and Ralph Cudney, called the "Sahuaro," the plan is based on a diagonal grid, making the house appear to be an extension of the jagged cliffface behind. As in the rest of the hotel and Ocatilla as well, the diagonal serves both to echo in the building the natural shapes of the environment and to direct the eye outward to those shapes across the vast expanse of the desert.

Wright eventually was to favor the thirty/sixty-degree triangle over the right-angle triangle for the more dynamic, more varied, and more supple relations it allowed. Its characteristic effect on his work can be seen in one other major project he undertook before the Depression, the St. Mark's Towers for New York City, of 1928–30. Here, within the constrictions of an urban situation, the architect gave new life to the Tahoe Big Tree Cabin para-

Painting I
Piet Mondrian, 1926

Counter-Composition V
Theo van Doesburg, 1924

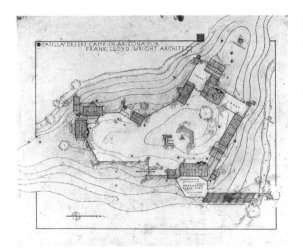

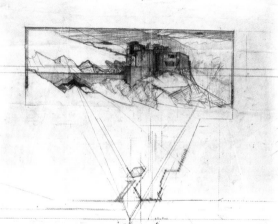

digm of a square rotated within a square by reducing the degree of rotation from forty-five to thirty degrees. The gaps are used for exterior balconies and projecting fire stairs. The apparent shift and dislocation of each duplex apartment, with its mezzanine balcony set at a thirty/sixty-degree angle, gives an effect of great variety and sweep to the interior space, as can be appreciated in the similar apartments in the Price Tower, built in Bartlesville, Oklahoma, in 1952–56.

THE LATER WORK

The Depression cut short Wright's activity in the Southwest as well as such projects as the St. Mark's Towers. The final phase of his career, which often used to be referred to as his "renaissance," began in 1932 with the establishment of the Taliesin Fellowship and the commission for the Willey House in Minneapolis. These coincided with the International Style exhibition held at New York's Museum of Modern Art in the fall of that year. While Wright's work of the 1930s, '40s, and '50s grew directly out of his embrace of diagonality in the previous decade, there now appeared a much greater degree of complexity in the intersection of implied axes and a much looser relationship between them and the actual definition of spatial boundaries. The increased flexibility and openness undoubtedly owed something to the example of European modernism, and in particular to Mies, but it also must be understood in terms of the extraordinary facility Wright had attained by that time in the shaping of architectural space.[26]

The Willey House is located on a small lot at the southern end of a north–south street on a bluff overlooking the Mississippi River, which flows on a diagonal from the northwest to the southeast. The first project, which proved too costly, called for a two-story building with the living room and dining alcove raised on a base of bedrooms and opening out onto a cantilevered terrace with splayed sides. Sited east–west, the house has floor-to-ceiling glass doors running the entire length of the south-facing living room and wrapping around both ends, with indented corner windows containing planters in the reentrant angles. From the entry into the living room at the top of the stairs, the view continues straight across the space, through a pair

Ocatilla (Wright Camp)
Phoenix South (formerly Salt River) Mountains, Phoenix, Arizona, 1929; plan

San-Marcos-in-the-Desert Hotel Project
Chandler, Aizona, 1929; sketch, perspective, and plan, Cudney House ("Sahuaro")

of glass doors, over a walled garden on the east. The fireplace is positioned at a forty-five-degree angle to the southwest corner of the room and at a sixty-degree angle to the southeast corner window. The northeast corner of the living room is entirely closed by the fireplace and wraparound seat. The view out from this corner, toward the Mississippi River to the southwest, follows an arc whose chord is the major diagonal axis of the space. The axis runs from the far northwest corner of the dining room, at a thirty-degree angle, out through the southeast corner window, paralleling the river below and thus tying the small house to the horizon.

To meet the demands of the budget, Wright completely redesigned the house over the next two years, making use of a thirty/sixty-degree geometry that first made its appearance in the previous decade and that he had just recently employed in a project, only partially realized, to expand the Hillside Home School to accommodate the Taliesin Fellowship Buildings (begun 1932–33).[27] The only feature the two designs for the Willey House have in common is the diagonal axis that relates the house to its site and the river below, but even that was given an entirely different definition. The house was reduced to a single story, with the walled garden turned into a bedroom wing forming an ell, and the living room and dining alcove combined into one open space at the center. From the street, a series of steps, decreasing in width at an angle of thirty degrees, rises up to a level brick walk to form a monumental processional entrance. Just before the door, to the right of a planter, the brick mat angles out thirty degrees into a triangular terrace carrying the eye out to the end of a brick wall at the eastern edge of the lot. From the entrance to the living room, a diagonal axis carries the eye straight to the corner fireplace. The view through the passage to the bedrooms is at an angle of thirty degrees, literally mirroring the view along the edge of the outside terrace. The opposing diagonal, defined by the projecting pier of the fireplace, parallels the thirty/sixty-degree angle of the terrace, thus skewing the space of the room toward the southwest. As you turn around in that direction, the terrace appears to swing out from under your feet as if hinged to the edge of the brick walk; and the diagonal vista it opens up extends the view out far beyond the confines of both house and garden. The edge of the terrace parallels the course of the river below and thus locks the house into the site, causing the one to pass through the other and, as it were, making the space of the house an aspect of a much larger whole. "Itself parallel to the ground, companion to the horizon," is the way Wright described the effect in the 1938 *Architectural Forum*.[28]

San-Marcos-in-the-Desert Hotel Project
aerial perspective

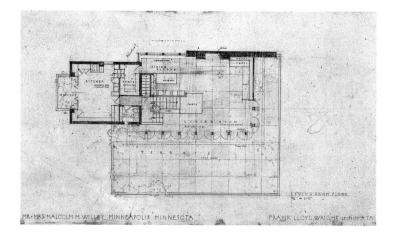

The Willey House introduced a new development in Wright's use of diagonality while at the same time giving prominence to another that had appeared only once before. The novelty is the multiplication of visual axes and their overlapping in space, resulting in a constant shifting of focus. One can now begin to distinguish not only between explicit and implicit axes but also between the objective, or compositional, axis and the subjective, or experiential, one. The subjective experience of space is no longer coextensive with the axial definition of that space. As the former Taliesin apprentice Curtis Besinger remarked, "the vistas are generally oblique to and—in effect—independent of the geometry of the house. This independence suggests to the occupant a freedom of movement in any direction [for now] the occupant is always the center of the space and not an onlooker."[29]

The other significant aspect of the Willey House, clearly relating to the first while ultimately deriving from the Death Valley project, is the substitution of pivoting, or swinging, for the rotation of a plane around a central axis. With the point of deflection now moved to the perimeter, the centrifugal power of the core—be it solid or space, fireplace or hollow—finally disappears from Wright's work and is replaced by a progressively expanding space. The Willey House is the first instance in which the edge of the pivoted terrace is perceived as a portion of the radius of a circle containing the house in a sector and having for its circumference the horizon.

The idea of pivoting soon became the basis of the project for the Marcus House in Dallas, Texas, of 1934–36; the Johnson House, called "Wingspread," just north of Racine, Wisconsin, of 1937; and Wright's own desert compound of Taliesin West in Scottsdale, Arizona, begun in 1938. In all these cases, the terraces pivot thirty or forty-five degrees to expand the interior space out into the landscape. In the plan of Florida Southern College of 1938, the buildings themselves act as either the hinges or the leading edges of space. But in Fallingwater, the weekend house designed for the Kaufmann family in Mill Run, Pennsylvania, in 1934–36, Wright reversed the roles of building and terrace to effect an unparalleled integration of architecture and nature. Instead of pivoting a terrace out from the house, he pivoted the house itself out from the rocky cliff, angling it thirty degrees to the southeast over the water to create, as he said, "an extension of the cliff beside a mountain stream."[30] The

Malcolm Willey House
Minneapolis, Minnesota, 1932–34; first scheme, 1932; plan, upper floor (redrawn ca. 1940)

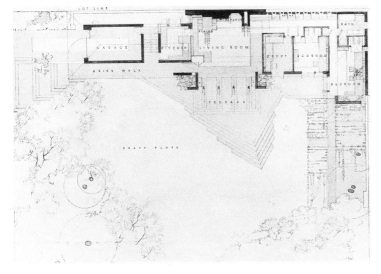

house becomes a stack of indoor–outdoor terraces projecting from a stone wall that parallels the rocky ledge behind and seems to be an integral part of the site itself. All the floors are flagstone, inside and out, and the sense of a plane angling back into the earth is literally expressed at the fireplace, where a boulder projects through the floor to form the hearth.

The diagonality of the plan of Fallingwater is extremely subtle. The staggered, rectilinear elements create a rhythmic pattern that seems at first closer to the International Style of Mies, as in the Barcelona Pavilion (1928–29) or the Tugendhat House (1928–30), than to anything earlier in Wright's own work. No doubt sensitive to any such charge of influence from the younger generation of Europeans, Wright highlighted the precedents in his own work for the plan of Fallingwater in the text and layout of the January 1938 issue of *Architectural Forum*, where the Kaufmann House was featured. The section devoted to it follows right after the Willey House, but between them Wright inserted two projects that could have no other purpose than to make his development of diagonal planning the link. First is a perspective and plan of the Little Dipper, drawings never previously published in the United States. Following that is a project of 1937 for the Memorial to the Soil, a chapel designed in southern Wisconsin whose diagonally sliced space and asymmetricality Wright contrasted with the rectilinearity of the earlier Unity Temple.[31] The first two images of Fallingwater are a

Malcolm Willey House
perspective, second scheme

Malcolm Willey House
plan, second scheme

raking-angle view of the open corner window to the left of the chimney mass and a distant view on the diagonal taken from below the first waterfall, similar to the celebrated perspective. The Little Dipper and the Memorial to the Soil mark the poles of explicit and implicit diagonality in Wright's planning; the corner window immediately recalls the Freeman House, which, along with Taliesin, is the clearest precedent for Fallingwater.

Like the Freeman House, the weekend house for the Kaufmann family is a two-sided building, presenting a nearly solid face to the hill behind and a series of terraces overlapping down the slope. Both are entered from the rear and then open out into a sweeping diagonal vista across the main living space. In Fallingwater, a series of crevices in the stone wall lead to the entry where you turn left, go up three steps, and then look out across the space of the living room along a forty-five-degree diagonal, which is extended beyond the confines of the room by the terrace projecting out over the ravine. The raised stone floor and recessed ceiling give a lift to that diagonal, recalling the great arching vista of the Taliesin living room. But the basic shape of the one at Fallingwater, as in the Freeman House, is a square, here expressed in the form of an atrium by the four stone piers (the fourth being the fireplace) supporting the indirectly lit coved ceiling. Unlike the Freeman House, the square is off center, shifted back toward the commanding corner fireplace. Set diagonally opposite the hatch leading down through the floor to the water below, its semicircular cavity is reflected in the curve of the parapet enclosing the stairway on the east terrace. The corresponding half circles, both resulting from a late change in the design, accentuate the link between the two elements as defining the thirty/sixty-degree cross axis of the main living space.

The two major diagonals—from entry to west terrace and from fireplace to hatch—do not intersect in the center of the square at ninety degrees, as in the Freeman House. The plan of Fallingwater is more complex than those of the 1920s in maintaining the continuity of interior and exterior space. The main diagonal axis from the entry follows the course of the stream below; while the thirty/sixty-degree cross-axial diagonal, running due east–west, following the rocky ledge and drive, parallels the datum line from which the house was originally pivoted into position. This suggests the metaphorical content Wright had already ascribed to the diagonal axis in the Little Dipper

Fallingwater
Mill Run, Pennsylvania, 1934–37;
perspective, from above

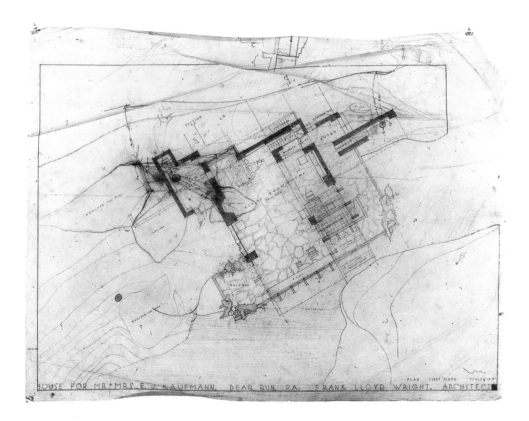

and perhaps explains why he chose to introduce Fallingwater through that image. A single straight line joins all elements in the earlier building, but in Fallingwater the diagonal from the entry to the far west terrace connects the rocky earth ledge, from which the house springs, to the sky, while the cross axis joins the elements of fire and water on a line that internalizes the conjunction of architecture and nature. Both more dynamic and more subjective than the relationships established in the Little Dipper, the meaning of Fallingwater nonetheless grows out of that background, just as the idea of placing the house over a waterfall can be traced to the contemporaneous Doheny House C project.

Fallingwater derives its unique immediacy of impact and oneness with the landscape from the overriding force of the diagonal axis. While the special circumstances of such a commission produced a highly charged symbolism, the house's formal principles could be reused by Wright whenever he was presented with such a tight, steeply sloping site that the only way to relate a building to it was to dramatize the situation and ensure continuity through the purely visual effects of implied diagonal axes. Among the group of Usonian Houses known by their owners as "Little Fallingwaters," the Sturges House in Brentwood Heights, California, of 1939–40, may be the most dramatic, but the Pew House in Shorewood Hills, Wisconsin, of 1938–40, is the most moving.

Perched precariously at the edge of Lake Mendota, the Pew House is set diagonally on its site to take fullest advantage of a mere seventy-five-foot frontage. The house is planned, based on Fallingwater, as a series of rectan-

Fallingwater
preliminary plan, ground floor

gles overlapping a square. The roof terrace, living room, and lower terrace slide out from under the top bedroom story and are offset on a thirty-degree diagonal pointing in the direction of the lake. The house is tiny, but the scale is gigantic. The living room is only twenty-six feet long by sixteen feet wide. The sense of space and its extension into the landscape are due to the powerful action of the main diagonal axis linking the house at its very foundations in the hillside to the distant horizon. An uninterrupted visual axis runs from the rear corner of the stone dining nook, out across the fireplace, on a continuous thirty-degree diagonal course, through the corner window of the living room to the far shore of the lake. The eye traverses this space in a flash and perceives in an instant the sense of oneness with the landscape. The diagonal, as at Fallingwater, cuts across boundaries and makes connections immediate.

For more typical sites, Wright would ask, "Where does the garden leave off and the house begin?" and then answer, "Where the garden begins and the house leaves off."[32] The near-seamless integration of interior and exterior in the diagonal planning of his later Usonian Houses could be expressed through whatever geometric module seemed most appropriate. The first two Usonian Houses, the Jacobs House in Madison, Wisconsin, and the Hanna House in Palo Alto, California, were both designed in 1936 and completed the following year. The Jacobs is based on a double-square-rectangle module, etched in the concrete floor mat, and the Hanna on a hexagonal one. Like the Little Dipper and the Freeman House, the one is the obverse of the other.

The first house Wright built for the Jacobs family is sited on a suburban corner lot. It turns its back to the street and opens out in an ell to the south, enclosing a garden between the living and bedroom wings. The basically rectangular shape of the living room is sheared into thirds along a thirty/sixty-degree diagonal, with the upper part pushing out toward the garden terrace through wraparound floor-to-ceiling glass doors, and the lower part, closed to the street, sliding back in toward the entry. This shearing creates a virtual rhomboid out of the rectangle, with its two thirty/sixty-degree diagonal axes—the one from the entry to the upper corner of the living room, and the other from the dining nook to the lower corner—crossing just in front of the fireplace. While the diagonal from the entry gives a sense of openness and direction to the relatively small communal space of the house, the cross-axial diagonal leads the eye back across the fireplace to the bedrooms, thus tying the two wings of the house together at their hinge in the utility core. That same axis is extended to define the jog of the bedroom corridor out to the lot line, while parallel axes drawn due east from the offsets of the living room—the first from the glass slot between the L-shaped pier and the flat one, and the second from the outside corner of the brick mat of the terrace—locate the two main setbacks of the bedrooms and define an imaginary thirty/sixty-degree triangle between the two garden fronts. The hypotenuse of that triangle stretches across the garden from east to west, embracing the southern horizon and making the house "itself parallel to the ground, companion to the horizon." It is as if the house had spread out like a fan hinged at its utility core.

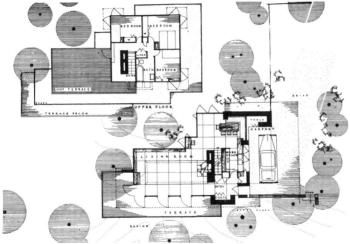

The method used in planning the Jacobs House remained characteristic of all Wright's later domestic work. Sometimes, the rectangular shape of the house might be set diagonally on its site in order to take advantage of a particular view, as in the Pew House or the house built for Alma Goetsch and Kathrine Winckler in Okemos, Michigan, in 1939–40; at other times, it might be aligned on the diagonal in order to create a sense of vista and expanse where there was none, as in the Adelman House at Fox Point, Wisconsin, of 1947–48, or the Zimmerman House in Manchester, New Hampshire, of 1949–52. The Jacobs House, however, physically conforms to its orthogonal suburban lot. The larger-scaled, superimposed diamond grid of sixty/one hundred-twenty degrees, defined by the intersecting diagonal axes, is only virtual. Its actual effect, however, can be visualized in Wright's bird's-eye perspectives, which seem almost to illustrate the ways in which an explicitly diagonal grid, such as he was to use in many of the later houses, would allow

John C. Pew House
Shorewood Hills, Wisconsin,
1938–40; living room looking
toward Lake Mendota

John C. Pew House
plan

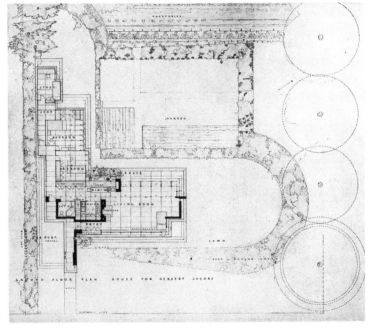

Herbert Jacobs House
Madison, Wisconsin, 1936–37;
perspectives from street side and
from garden side

Herbert Jacobs House
plan

the wings to fan out one hundred-twenty degrees or fold in sixty degrees in response to more irregular sites.

The hexagonal plan of the Hanna House, as its fans open from its utility core to embrace the hillside, makes explicit the shearing of space in the Jacobs House. "Here," Wright noted, "the thesis changes, not in content but in expression."[33] The obtuse angles have a "reflex" action, causing the plan to appear to flip in and out of perspective. The impression is that of looking at a flattened-out axonometric projection of a rectilinear pattern, much as van Doesburg had done in his paintings of the 1920s, and uncannily related to Wright's own typical bird's-eye perspectives. Clearly, Wright's most important reason for adopting an explicitly diagonal module was to fit the house more snugly into its environment. The Hanna House site presented the broad-sloping arc of a hillside, and the one hundred-twenty-degree angle of the court allows the house to follow its contours in a gently accommodating fashion. The existing trees were left untouched, and the house cuts in and around them like a Japanese screen, producing, according to Wright, an effect of great "repose."[34] For the Bazett House in Hillsborough, California, of 1939, located at the point of a steep hill, Wright set the two wings sixty degrees to one another to enclose a garden at the apex of the rising triangular piece of land; and at the Wall House in Plymouth, Michigan, of 1941, the hexagonal living room and terrace form a headland above a lake while the open one hundred-twenty-degree angle of the court cups the broad plateau behind.

The thoroughgoing expression of diagonality in the Hanna House through the use of a nonrectilinear module indicates Wright's increasing insistence on the organic integration of building and landscape—most strikingly realized in Fallingwater—along with the corollary idea of the building itself growing and expanding like nature—first given tentative expression in the Death Valley project and then more fully in the diagonal pivoting of the Willey House. Wright compared the hexagonal grid of the Hanna House to "a cross-section of honeycomb" and maintained that its "flow and movement" give a reflexiveness to the space, allowing it to open and close, expand and contract, and, indeed, almost to return back on itself in a continuous curve.[35] The angled space between the two hinged wings of the typical Usonian House, be it sixty, ninety, or one hundred-twenty degrees, is understood as the sector of a circle, and it is therefore not surprising that, the year after the completion of the Hanna House, Wright returned to the circular plan, for the first time since the Gordon Strong Automobile Objective project of 1924–25, as a logical extension of the principle of diagonality.[36]

Implied diagonal axes almost always determine the internal organization of Wright's circular buildings as well as their relation to the site. A preliminary sketch for the Jester House for Palos Verdes, California, a project of

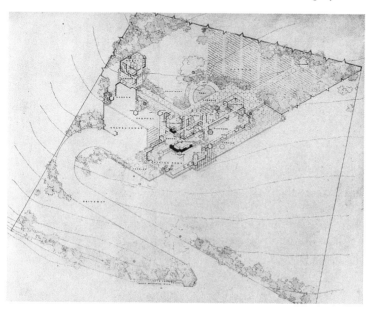

Jean and Paul Hanna House
Stanford, California, 1936–37;
plan

1938–39 and the first of these designs, shows how the positions of the different cylindrical volumes were established by two contiguous thirty/sixty-degree triangles. The first has its long side forming the diameter of the pool and its hypotenuse running from the servant's room to the living room through the center of the dining room; the second has its hypotenuse along the gate and its long side defining the axis from the bedroom to the dining room. In the final project, the patio was widened and the living room set back fifteen degrees on a diagonal perpendicular to the main forty-five-degree axis extending from the bedroom at the rear of the house across the swimming pool and down the length of the valley opening out into the Pacific Ocean.

In 1938, Wright also produced the master plan for Florida Southern College, using circular and semicircular forms to articulate the joints of the diagonal covered walks. The Roux Library, completed in 1941 and the first of Wright's circular designs to be built, is located at the entrance to the campus in the sixty-degree angle formed by the main axis leading to the Pfeiffer Chapel and central triangular plaza. For this pivotal spot, Wright reused the Little Dipper plan, aligning the axial walkway with the hexagonal school-room, placing the periodical shelves where the fireplace was, and enclosing the bowl of seats to form a circular reading room around the projecting hexagonal reference desk that replaces the earlier pool and sandbox.

The Florida Southern library graphically illustrates the direct link between Wright's diagonal planning and his later circular designs. Few of these were ever to be as explicit in their diagonality. More characteristic is the Guggenheim Museum, built in 1956–59 though originally designed in 1943–45, where only traces of the diagonal remain in the implied axes that orient the visitor and relate the building to the site. The integral expression of the circular form is overriding, yet one of the first studies of 1943–44 shows the building as a hexagon rotated thirty degrees around an interior hexagonal court. A circular ramp, the same size as the court, overlaps the left wall of the main hexagon; its projecting half is treated as a dodecagon, matching the dodecagonal administration wing at the far corner of the site. Where the Florida Southern library conjoins circular and hexagonal spaces as in the

Ralph Jester House
Palos Verdes, California, 1938;
sketch plan and elevation

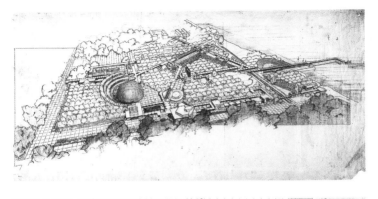

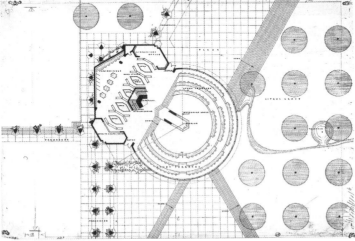

earlier Little Dipper, this preliminary design for the Guggenheim Museum illustrates the progressive transformation of the hexagon into a circle through a process of continuous rotation that ultimately resulted in a completely circular design.

The cylindrical volumes of the final design—varying in size from those containing the restrooms and ducts, through the small administration building known as the Monitor, to the main gallery itself—are related to one another along the lines of overlapping thirty/sixty-degree triangles, and the final plan is a mirror image of the Jester House. From the entrance between the main gallery and the Monitor, the axis is defined at a thirty/sixty-degree angle to the Fifth Avenue sidewalk by the two-tiered opening into the double-height Grand Gallery. This is crossed in the center of the space by another thirty/sixty-degree axis, extending from the end of the ramp and elevator to the southwest corner of the building, where a large window provides the only view out and point of orientation. Otherwise, the spiraling form of the museum is a closed circuit, rotating around a vertical axis. The sense of infinite extension in space is thus linked to a feeling of suspension in time. Wright used a natural metaphor to describe the phenomenon. The quality of "complete repose known only in movement that characterizes this building," he said, is "similar to that made by a still wave, never breaking, never offering finality to vision."[37]

Florida Southern College
Lakeland, Florida, begun 1938; aerial perspective

Florida Southern College
1941; plan of Roux Library

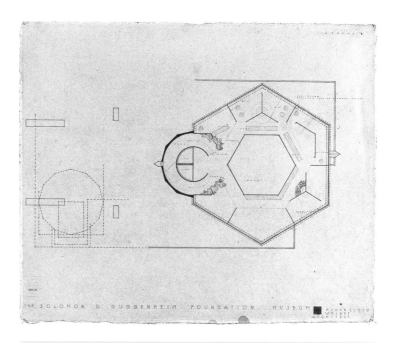

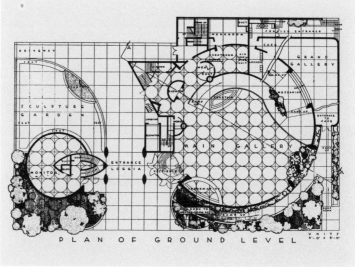

Following the examples of the Jester House, Florida Southern, and the Guggenheim Museum, Wright designed many of his later public buildings and urban projects using circular forms that are controlled and articulated by diagonal axes to integrate functions and relate the structures more intimately to their sites. The most significant of these include the projects for the Pittsburgh Point Park Civic Center of 1947, the Baghdad Opera House and Cultural Center of 1957–58, and the Marin County Civic Center in San Rafael, California, designed in 1957–58 and completed in 1970, a little over a decade after the architect's death. Still other projects, like the one for an inn and visitor center at Meteor Crater, Arizona, of 1948, the Masieri Memorial student hostel for Venice of 1952–55, and the Mile-High Illinois skyscraper for the Chicago lake shore of 1956, rely exclusively on diagonal geometry for their plans. In the case of the Meteor Crater and Mile-High designs, the principle of diagonality also plays a key role in shaping the structural and symbolic forms of the buildings.

Of all Wright's later designs, however, the work that most fully and most profoundly expresses the meaning that diagonal planning held for him since the 1920s is, perhaps not surprisingly, the winter home and headquarters he began building for himself and the Taliesin Fellowship in 1938 in the desert of Paradise Valley, northeast of the city of Phoenix. Taliesin West was meant to be the architect's definitive expression of the desert—a space "beyond the reach of the finite mind"—and to look as if it belonged "to the Arizona desert as though it had stood there for centuries."[38] The site rises above the floor of the valley, just beneath the McDowell Mountains. The tentlike structures branch off both sides of an elongated circulation spine paralleling the range of mountains. The main working and living quarters face south off the hypotenuse of a large triangular terrace that swings out over the desert to the southwest, its hinge marked by a prehistoric Native-American petro-glyph boulder set on a small prow-shaped ledge immediately to the right of the steps at the entrance. The upper part of the apprentices' court twists in response to this movement, while the pivoting of the main diagonal axis is checked at forty-five degrees by the counterbalancing office/study, at the top of the entrance court, and the shop building, which echoes and amplifies it at the court's base. The continually changing angles of approach, the slope of the exposed redwood trusses of the canvas roofs, and the canted "desert stone" walls all echo the shapes of the surrounding mountains, while the right-angle triangle of the terrace seems to reflect the image of Thompson Peak onto the plane of the desert below.

The forty-five-degree diagonal that pivots off the boulder at the entrance forms the leading edge of the triangular terrace linking the complex of buildings to the surrounding landscape through the panorama of desert and mountains it literally brings into view. This is made to happen suddenly and, as it were, instantaneously. It occurs only after one proceeds down the long

Taliesin West
Scotsdale, Arizona, begun 1938;
aerial photograph looking east

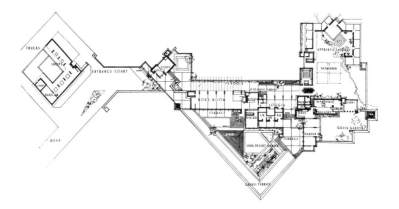

covered pergola behind the drafting room and out through the loggia.[39] Concealed by the drafting room and the depths of the loggia, the desert appears following a series of twists and turns ending in a final forty-five-degree shift in axis that brings one out into the light and carries the eye across the desert down the length of the terrace to the point where the prow seems to dissolve into space. Wright wanted the experience to recapture his first impression of the site as "a look over the rim of the world."[40] "Just imagine," he said, "what it would be like on top of the world looking over the universe at sunrise or at sunset with clear sky in between. Light and air bathing all the worlds of creation in all the color there ever was . . . nothing to imagine—all beyond the reach of the finite mind"[41] The diagonal links everything together in a glance—buildings, mountains, desert—and in its arc produces what Wright conceived of as "an esthetic, even ascetic, idealization of space . . . a sweep that was a spiritual cathartic for Time if indeed Time continued to exist in such circumstances."[42]

The diagonal fans out across the horizon and makes the slice of space palpable and its measure of distance perspicuous. The space is sensed in depth, not through an intellectually reconstructed series of layers or planes perpendicular to the line of sight, but immediately, instantaneously.[43] It was this absolute experience of space as depth and the consequent immediacy of the connection with the landscape that Wright ultimately sought to achieve through the use of the diagonal axis. Beginning with his first exposure to the desert in the 1920s, in Death Valley and the Phoenix South Mountains, Wright saw a spiritual factor in the space opened up by the diagonal axis and, indeed, like his contemporary van Doesburg, attributed a temporal dimension to it. But in Wright's work, the concept of "space-time" never became an abstract simultaneity, ultimately deriving from cubist painting. Rather, as he translated the axonometric vision of simultaneous points of view into the reality of diagonally defined space, Wright was able to create in his architecture of the 1930s, '40s, and '50s an expression of instantaneity assimilable to the condition of nature itself.

Taliesin West clearly retraces the various stages in Wright's development of the concept of diagonality, thereby vividly summarizing the overall pattern of his life's work. The forty-five-degree shifts in axis, though now pro-

Taliesin West
plan (redrawn ca. 1940)

gressive and linear, go right back to the plan for the Cooper House of 1890, supposedly based on the one he showed to Sullivan in 1887. The rotated squares and prowlike projections, though now disconnected and dispersed, find their source in the Willits House and the Hillside Home School of 1901–03. The canted roofs and swinging, shifting diagonals in plan immediately recall Death Valley, San Marcos–in–the–Desert, and Ocatilla, indeed, all those many designs of the 1920s in which Wright laid the groundwork for his later work. And, finally, there is the pivoted terrace, open plan, sheared space, and reflex diagonal of the Willey House, Fallingwater, and Jacobs and Hanna Houses, all directly preceding it.

Clearly, there is a consistency and continuity in Wright's work over the course of his long career. While it is not to be presumed that the principle of diagonality explains all, it can surely be seen as a powerful measure of the coherence of his work after 1920. As such, it goes a long way toward explaining the shift in emphasis that took place in his architecture after his flight from Oak Park to Europe in 1909 and the creative interregnum of the following two decades. If the Oak Park years may be characterized as a search for types—images of the home, work, or worship—the later work, in fact beginning with Taliesin, reveals a quest for a more profound synthesis of architecture and nature. The shift represents a turning outward, from a focus on the inner workings of things to their integration in the larger order of nature. The emergence of an explicit diagonality in the work after 1920 also ties Wright's architecture firmly to the developing modernist tradition. The diagonal axis represented for Wright a way to go beyond the confines of the symmetry, formal order, and orthogonal rigidity of "the major-axis and the minor-axis of classical architecture," as he described the premodern, traditional method he inherited.[44] The diagonal gave Wright's architecture a flexibility, an immediacy, an openness, and a reflexivity that are uniquely and quintessentially modern, making it incumbent on us to find the ways to resituate his work within the mainstream of modernism it was so seminal in helping to define in the first place.

Taliesin West
terrace prow looking southwest

Consecrated Space
Wright's Public Buildings

BY JONATHAN LIPMAN

Frank Lloyd Wright's great urban, nonresidential buildings—the Larkin Building, Unity Temple, Midway Gardens, the Imperial Hotel, the Johnson Wax Administration Building, the Solomon R. Guggenheim Museum, Beth Sholom Synagogue, Annunciation Greek Orthodox Church, and the Marin County Civic Center—are seemingly very different from one another.[1] Yet in fact they are variations on a single, remarkably specific architectural device that establishes, in the strongest possible architectural language, a functional and symbolic focus for the group consciousness of the building's users—in Wright's words, "consecrated space." Wright described his architectural intentions when he wrote: "The building as architecture is born out of the heart of man, permanent consort to the ground, comrade to the trees, true reflection of man in the realm of his own spirit. His building is therefore consecrated space wherein he seeks refuge, recreation and repose for body, but especially mind."[2]

While it is clear that Wright fulfilled these intentions in his finest domestic designs located in the natural landscape (such as Taliesin and Fallingwater), it may not be so apparent how this statement of intent motivated Wright's designs for public buildings on urban sites.[3] Nonetheless, I believe that it did. Whether or not an entire building or its site might be considered "consecrated," Wright determined that the main activity occurring in a public building should be housed in a consecrated space, that is, one that would provide a symbolic and ennobling focus for the group consciousness of its occupants. To permit the building's honest expression, such a space should read clearly as the main mass of the building; to accomplish this, Wright housed almost all of the building's other, supporting activities in a second, subordinate mass. To emphasize the significance of the primary mass, Wright physically separated the two masses, placing the building's entry zone between them. This causes people entering the building to distinguish clearly between the consecrated space and the supporting spaces.

To make the major space emphatically primary, Wright employed a series of architectural techniques. First, he made the space symmetrical and located it at one end of the building's primary axis. Second, he flooded it from above with sunlight, the one element of the natural world that exists

inviolate in the city. This effectively increases the space's dramatic impact, on being reached from a lower, darker intermediary space. Third, although one approaches the great room on axis, Wright placed an obstacle in one's parh at the point of entry into the room, further separating the room from its environment. Fourth, the room was ringed with one or more mezzanine, which emphasizes the room's separateness by buffering the space from the profane urban surroundings. Finally, the room's removal from its environs was reaffirmed by its spiraling circulation path from the street.

These devices are used in the nine buildings discussed, and in six of these buildings, Wright detailed the great room to express what he considered to be the underlying nature or concept of the building. These architectural devices create buildings that speak of their purpose, buildings whose circulation emphasizes the room that embodies the building's purpose, and finally, buildings in which the room itself proclaims in space and detailing its consecrated nature.

FRANK LLOYD WRIGHT'S OAK PARK STUDIO

We find the antecedents to these ideas in Wright's first independently executed nonresidential building, his own Oak Park, Illinois, architectural studio of 1895, designed when he was twenty-eight. In plan and massing, the building contains three zones: on the right is an almost freestanding octagonal library, in the center is an entry and circulation zone, and on the left is the drafting room, Wright's first multistory, mezzanine-ringed, clerestory-lit space.

The octagonal library competes in importance with the larger, two-story studio space. To accord equal importance to two spaces is an ambiguity in the *parti* that distinguishes this early design from all of Wright's later public buildings. The scheme's bipolar nature suggests that two distinct important activities occurred in the building. Of course, the primary activity, drafting, occurred in the studio. But David Van Zanten speculates that the library was far more important than its name suggests, that it was in fact a museum/laboratory filled with beautiful objects intended to inspire and instruct his draftsmen.[4] Windowless at eye level, focusing one's attention on the central table (the only piece of furniture in the room), the library seems to have also

Oak Park Studio
Oak Pak, Illinois, 1895; analysis, *parti* diagram of plan; drawn by author

Oak Park Studio
plan and perspective from street

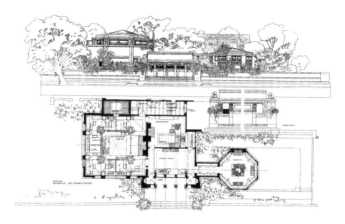

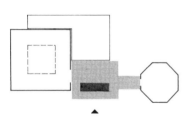

been used for the indoctrination of clients by the eloquent Wright.

Wright tantalizes us as we contemplate the origin of this *parti*: on the four piers framing the studio's entry loggia, Wright prominently located bas-reliefs that feature a floor plan apparently taken, with liberties, from the Roman Baths of Caracalla, 211–17 AD. This plan, which it seems Wright wished one to contemplate as one entered his studio, is strikingly similar to the plan of the studio itself. This is one of the very few times Wright overtly encouraged that his architecture be seen in a historical context.

THE LARKIN BUILDING

Wright's first major built urban, nonresidential building was the Larkin Building (design begun in 1902, building completed in 1906) in Buffalo, New York.[5] It has been hailed as an early and influential landmark of modern architecture; its brutal massing, nonhistoricist facades, clear expression of structure, and the articulated prominence given to its air handling shafts and stair towers established it as a seminal building.

However, a deeper understanding of the building is gained when we examine its *parti*: the building is clearly composed of two distinct masses,

Oak Park Studio
view of drafting room

Oak Park Studio
bas-relief sculpture on entry

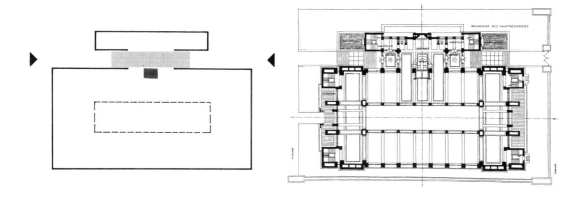

separated by a narrow circulation zone. The smaller mass contains a variety of miscellaneous functions—public lobby, locker area, toilets, lounge, library, and classroom—while the major mass is devoted to the building's primary function, seating the company's 1,800 clerical workers and executives. This mass is biaxially symmetrical, its center occupied by a six-story, mezzanine-ringed light court.

The typology of a mezzanine-ringed light court is not new with the Larkin Building. It is a logical building type that permits all occupants to receive adequate sunlight from up to four sides. Jack Quinan notes that during preliminary negotiations for the Larkin commission, Wright urged company executive Darwin Martin to view D. H. Burnham's recently completed store for the Marshall Field Company in Chicago, with a thirteen-story mezzanine-ringed light well.[6] The Larkin Building's distant antecedents are Roman *insulae* and courtyard-ringing Renaissance palazzi. The palazzo, its court now covered with plate glass, was the prototype for a number of nineteenth-century office buildings.

In his design for the Larkin building, Wright made at least two large advances on this building type. First, he moved the staircases from their traditional location near the light-court into articulated stair towers. Second, he moved most of the building's support functions into the semi detached secondary mass. This caused the building's main function to correlate with the dominant mass of the building. This was a brilliant, if abstract, example of *architecture parlante*, or "talking architecture." The form of the building proclaimed, "Look at this great primary mass, this is what is significant in the building; whatever is in the secondary mass is not so important."

However, the *parti* had two even greater implications for the building's interior. First, it permitted all of the clerical and executive workers to share a single space, working either on the main floor at the bottom of the light court or on mezzanines overlooking it. Working in a single room, with the company's executives—seated on the main floor—visible below and among them, was surely intended to reinforce the family-like nature of the firm, if not as owner John D. Larkin saw it, then certainly as Wright saw it. A company dining area that occupied the fifth-level mezzanine of the main space reinforced employees' sociability. However, Wright carried the notion far beyond the level of a *parti*. Jack Quinan has written:

Larkin Building
Chicago, Illinois, 1902; analysis, *parti* diagram of plan; drawn by author

Larkin Building
first floor plan

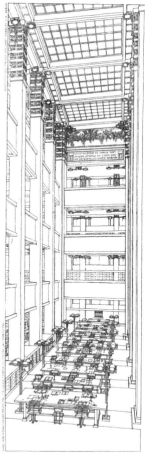

In its final form Wright's Larkin light court represented an analog to Ralph Waldo Emerson's belief in the aspiration of all matter to a spiritual ideal and in the unity of all things in nature. Simple brick-faced piers were carried 76 feet from the main floor of the light court to a gridded skylight through which diffused sunlight—Wright's medium of transformation—flooded into the space. The fifth-floor balcony fronts were set back in order to maximize the apparent dissolution of the pier tops into small scintillant sculptural fragments. Those same balcony fronts carried . . . inspiration inscriptions whose gilded letters shone brightly down upon the balconies and main floor below. Two conservatories on the sixth floor . . . held potted palms, ferns, and vines under the brighter light of that single-shelled portion of the roof and in visual conjunction with the fragmented [and gilded] pier tops. Wright's progression from solid piers to exfoliated capitals to living plants and then, by way of the dematerializing power of sunlight and the suggestiveness of the inscriptions, to the realm of ideas, is wholly Emersonian in its origins.[7]

Elsewhere Quinan has written that "the light court exemplifies Emerson's belief in the unity of all things in nature and the aspiration of all matter to a spiritual ideal."[8] On the basis of Quinan's persuasive arguments, I propose that Wright detailed the Larkin Building light court specifically to make a place for transcendental experience. Quinan argues that Wright selected an architectural vocabulary to express an Emersonian worldview because both Wright and his Larkin Company clients were enthusiastic proponents of Emerson's ideas. The Larkin Building light court thus became Wright's first nonresidential consecrated space.

Larkin Building
exterior perspective view
from street

Larkin Building
interior perspective of central
light court

As Wright was designing the Larkin Building, he received the commission to create a new church for his Oak Park, Illinois, Unitarian congregation. As this building, Unity Temple of 1904, and the Larkin Building were two urban, nonresidential buildings of similar size in plan and were on Wright's drafting boards at the same time, it would not be surprising if the two designs shared some resemblance. Nonetheless, the degree of similarity in plan between the two buildings is noteworthy. Like the Larkin Building, Unity Temple is a symmetrical building composed of a minor mass, a narrow circulation zone, and a major mass. Once again, the minor mass houses the building's auxiliary functions, in this case a Sunday school, a kitchen, and a meeting area, and the major mass is a mezzanine-ringed, skylit single space, devoted to the building's primary function, a sanctuary. Charles White, who was a draftsman in Wright's studio as the buildings were being designed, observed in 1905: "The motif [of Unity Temple] is an evolution of Wright's studio. An entrance in a link connecting a dominant, and subordinate mass."[9]

Wright himself went so far as to call the two masses by separate names, "Unity Temple" and "Unity House." He described his application of the *parti* to the commission in straightforward but suggestive language:

> The site was noisy. Therefore it seemed best to keep the building closed on the three front sides and enter it from a court to the rear at the center of the lot . . . But there was a secular side to Universalist church activities— entertainment often, Sunday school, feasts, and so on. To embody these with the temple would spoil the simplicity of the room—the noble Room in the service of man for the worship of God. So I finally put the secular space designated as "Unity House," a long free space to the rear of the lot, as a separate building . . . but harmonious with the temple—the entrance to both to be the connecting link between them.[10]

In spite of a formal kinship, Unity Temple looks very different from the Larkin Building because the masses and spaces of the two buildings differ in proportion, and the buildings are detailed differently. The primary mass of the brick Larkin Building is vertical, its verticality reinforced by projecting piers on the build's main facades. Wright was aware that his administration building would be dwarfed by the Larkin Company's factory across the street. To lend his comparatively small building the stature appropriate to

Unity Temple
Oak Park Illinois, 1906; analysis, *parti* diagram of plan; drawn by author

Unity Temple
composite plan of first floor and mezzanine level

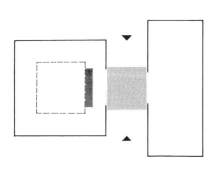
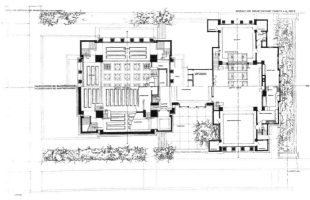

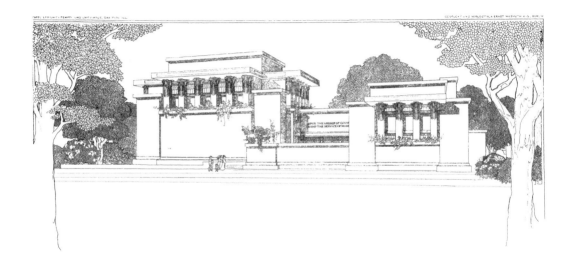

the headquarters of the large firm, he manipulated massing and detail to make it appear tall.

Unity Temple had no such oversize neighbors, and the main mass of the building is a cube. In his autobiography, Wright derived the square plan of Unity Temple's sanctuary on economic grounds: a low budget suggested an exposed reinforced concrete structure—a radical idea at the time—and the expense of wood forms would be minimized by repeating their use in a cube. This argument appears to be born out by a construction photo of Unity Temple, published prominently by Wright in *Ausgeführte Bauten*, that reveals one exterior wall of the sanctuary already poured, its forms removed and erected on an identical adjacent wall. Nonetheless, an equally plausible reason for Wright to design a cube-shaped sanctuary is that the square, a less axial form than the rectangle, appropriately suggests that the congregant, rather than God or the pastor, is central to Unitarian worship.

I have argued that the shape of the main rooms in the Larkin Building and Unity Temple expressed an abstract notion that reinforced the group consciousness of the buildings' users. As he did in the Larkin Building, Wright reinforced this notion through the detailing of Unity Temple's sanctuary. A striking feature of the sanctuary is that Wright consistently pulled moldings away from the corners of the rooms' surfaces, painting the areas enclosed by the moldings different colors from the areas outside of them. This has the effect of obfuscating the boundaries of piers, spandrels, and other architectural details. In contradistinction to his designs for the Larkin Building or other structurally expressive buildings, Wright went to great lengths to obscure the physical reality of structure, surface, and edge in Unity Temple. Wright later wrote that "the Unitarian abstract is the modern essence," that is, that the transcendental level of existence, Wright's "inner Nature," is central to life. In fact, the sanctuary is an essay in abstraction. Through Wright's detailing the physical elements that constitute the room are decomposed, whereby an analogue of the "Unitarian abstract" is rendered palpable.

Unity Temple
exterior perspective with sanctuary, left, and classroom building, right

Unity Temple
interior view of sanctuary, looking
toward altar and organ

Unity Temple
interior view of entry foyer
between sanctuary and classroom
building, directly ahead

According to Wright, when he received the commission for Midway Gardens, Chicago, in 1913, he was asked in unusually explicit and expressive language to create a consecrated space. As told in Wright's autobiography, client Edward C. Waller Jr. offered him the commission by saying, "In all this black old town there's no place to go that isn't bare and ugly unless it's cheap and nasty. *I want to put a garden in this wilderness* of smoky dens, car-tracks, and saloons."[11]

The commission was serendipitous: as a summer beer garden, outdoor restaurant, and music pavilion, the structure required virtually no roof. Midway Gardens was not merely a skylit transformation of the walled para-dise, it was a garden in fact, open to the sky—Wright's own Garden of Eden existing joyously within the profane urban environment. As such it was his most essential rendering of the consecrated public space.

The major axial garden space was composed of a series of landscaped dining terraces that stepped down to a bank shell. This space was sur-rounded by two-story arcades, open-air equivalents to the mezzanines sur-rounding the main spaces of his indoor public buildings. An auxiliary building that Wright called a winter garden housed indoor dining and danc-ing areas, toilets, and a tavern. A large central kitchen and service area occu-pied the basement located beneath the winter garden and a portion of the terrace. Characteristically, an outdoor circulation terrace separated the major summer garden from the smaller winter garden, but intriguingly a parallel interior circulation spine, which terminated in entrance pavilions, skewered the winter garden. As a foul-weather substitute for the main out-door garden, the winter garden also contained its own mezzanine-ringed central space. In naming the mezzanine-ringed dining structure a winter gar-den, Wright revealed the Edenic conception behind his public urban spaces.

The design for Midway Gardens is a remarkably elegant and subtle scheme. Nonetheless, it was based on the simple binuclear *parti* of his earlier public buildings, allowing him to write, "The thing had simply shaken itself out of my sleeve. In a remarkable short time there it was on paper."[12]

Wright records that in their first conversation his client predicted, "I believe Chicago would appreciate a beautiful garden resort ... [with] light, color, music, movement—gay place!" Whether this language was real or invented by Wright, he responded to his charge by vigorously attempting to

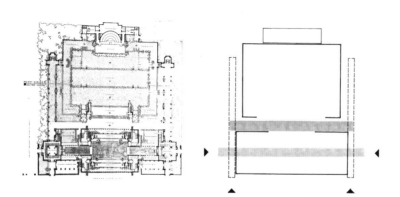

Midway Gardens
Chicago, Illinois, 1913; plan of ground level

Midway Gardens
analysis, *parti* diagram of plan; drawn by author

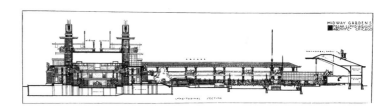

orchestrate every element of the environment to a degree almost unknown in his career, bringing "painting and sculpture in to heighten and carry all still further into the realm of the Lamp in the same Spirit. A synthesis of all the Arts."[13] Geometrical bas-reliefs and sculptures by artists Richard Bock and Alfonso Ianelli and abstract murals by Wright and Chicago Art Institute instructors punctuated walls, parapets, and soffits. Wright designed lamps and even china with a confetti-like motif. A tight budget prevented inlaying decorative colored glass in the ornamental concrete tiles; trees and shrubs, festive furniture, and hundreds of colored helium balloons were also cut from the project.

All of the ornaments and forms that Wright designed for Midway Gardens were based on simple geometry, "pure form in everything ... Forms could be made into a festival for the eye no less than music made a festival for the ear."[14] Period photographs reveal that the carefully orchestrated, brightly colored abstract designs that were realized produced a festive environment, conducive to dining, dancing, and enjoying entertainment. In its celebration of all the arts Midway Gardens was Wright's greatest *Gesamtkunstwerk*, and a brilliant, consecrated space dedicated to entertainment.

THE IMPERIAL HOTEL

Wright considered the Imperial Hotel of 1913–14 in Tokyo, Japan, the high-point of his architectural career.[15] Its plan, in which two guestroom wings enclose a rigidly symmetrical, axial sequence of public spaces and gardens, appears at first glance to have more in common with Palladio's expanded plan for Villa Barbaro than with the *parti* of Wright's earlier public buildings. However, the hotel's de facto circulation urges another surprising reading of the plan. The more commonly used, as opposed to ceremonial, entrance to the hotel was at one end of what appears to be a secondary circulation spine. With this understood, one observes a primary volume, containing three major public spaces—the cabaret, auditorium, and banquet hall—stacked one on the other. The functionally primary circulation spine separates this volume from the hotel lobby and dining room. Louis Sullivan concurred with this reading when he observed that "At the level of the main floor of the theatre the entire structure is traversed and in a manner *bisected* by a grand promenade twenty feet in width and three-hundred feet in length. This promenade brings the two long wings of guest rooms in touch with the central group and acts as a foyer from which are entered the theatre, [etc.]"[16] Early in the twentieth century such an interior promenade, from which guests might view and greet each other, was central to the social life of a large hotel.

It is to be expected that the much larger and far more complicated Imperial Hotel should have a more complex *parti* than do Unity Temple and the Larkin Building, but nonetheless, the plans have a remarkably similar underlying order. Kenneth Frampton has observed that the Imperial Hotel is derived in both plan and section from Midway Gardens. Actually, the two commissions overlapped in time, so it is unclear which was begun earlier. Nonetheless, it is stimulating to consider Frampton's thesis that "the restau-

Imperial Hotel
Tokyo, Japan, 1914–22;
ground-floor plan

Imperial Hotel
main-floor plan

Imperial Hotel
analysis, *parti* diagram of plan;
drawn by author

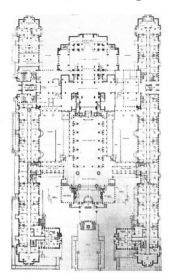
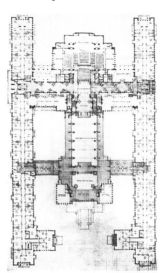
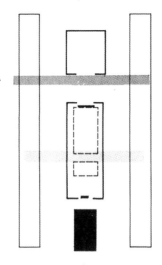

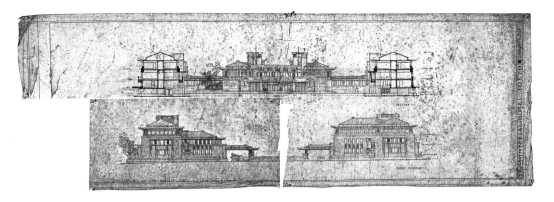

rant/winter garden of the Chicago complex reappeared as the auditorium and lobby of the hotel, while the flanking arcades of the gardens themselves became transformed into its residential wings. The internal murals and reliefs also extended Midway themes, while the galleried access ways of the hotel recalled the café terraces of the Midway layout."[17]

What were the underlying ideas latent in the Imperial Hotel commission that Wright used to generate the hotel's massing and detailing? Wright wrote that "the building was intended to harmonize with those around the moat across the part before it [that is, the Imperial Palace complex]. . . . There was a tradition there worthy of respect and I felt it my duty as well as privilege to make the building belong to them so far as I might."[18]

Indeed, the hotel had such strong stylistic similarities to the Imperial Palace's nearby feudal Edo Castle that one might call the Imperial Hotel "contextual." The two buildings had very similar roofs, with shallow pitches and distinct vertical striations. Both roofs extended almost horizontally to a corresponding degree over deep eaves, with almost identical upturned corners. Wright also designed finials at the ends of each roof ridge very similar to those in the Imperial Castle.[19]

The exterior walls of both buildings featured similarly oversize string courses immediately above and below deep-set windows, which were often grouped and separated by similar narrow piers flush with the wall. The walls of the hotel were battered, mirroring the moat wall on which the castle sat.

In keeping with its stylistic affinity to the nearby Imperial Castle, the Imperial Hotel was less hermetic and introverted than Wright's other public buildings. The hotel was closed to its environment on three sides, but in the fourth direction its massing cascaded exuberantly toward the Imperial Palace grounds. This reflects Wright's attempt to make the hotel "belong" to the Palace complex. It also explains why the hotel's public rooms were not skylit, unlike those in the other buildings discussed in this paper; where profaned environments led him to create introverted buildings centered around skylit interior spaces, it appears that the more sublime surroundings of the Imperial Hotel led him to open the public rooms outward.

In Japan, at the time Wright was designing the Imperial Hotel, ornament was associated with power, and the more status or power possessed by the owner or user of a public building, the more ornate the building. Because this hotel was associated with the emperor, it was therefore appropriate that

Imperial Hotel
elevation and sections

Imperial Palace
fifteenth century, Tokyo, Japan;
view of feudal Edo Castle and
moat on grounds; drawn
by author

Wright designed its public rooms as the most ornate interiors of his career.[20] In contrast, traditional private residences of all segments of Japanese society, including the emperor's, were spare and unornamented. This was reflected in Wright's treatment of the unornamented, residential guestrooms that echo the plain grammar of the traditional Japanese residential interior, composed of an expressed post-and-beam structure with screen infill.

JOHNSON WAX ADMINISTRATION BUILDING

In the Johnson Wax Administration Building of 1936 in Racine, Wisconsin, Wright again employed a mezzanine-ringed, skylit major space, returning to the unambiguous binuclear scheme of the Larkin headquarters. He acknowledged the two designs' conceptual similarities and differing systems of detailing when he wrote that the Larkin Building was the masculine sire of the more feminine Johnson Building.

Wright and client Herbert Johnson shared the desire to locate the company's clerical workers in a single room. Though this was an unusual strategy for the time, it had a practical basis. Wright laid out the departments to promote the most efficient flow of information through the room. Paperwork followed a linear route, related departments were near one another, and departments used by all employees were centrally placed. An independent study concluded that the efficiency of the company's office operations improved significantly when the administration moved into the new building.

Psychologically, and perhaps spiritually, the Great Workroom (as Wright named it) was equally successful. The Johnson Company was—and remains—family owned, and was actively managed in 1936 by the grandson of the company's founder. The company had always been run as a benevolent patriarchy, with management exhibiting an unusual degree of loyalty to employees.[21] The Great Workroom was appropriate for the family-like firm, as the large room not only was efficient but strengthened the employees' already present collective consciousness. In this respect it functioned as the sanctuary in an ecclesiastical building does: a beautiful room in which to gather for worship uplifts a group and reinforces group consciousness. Wright, still an Emersonian, considered work as a spiritual and uplifting activity. He saw no conflict in celebrating work in an ecclesiastical-like space

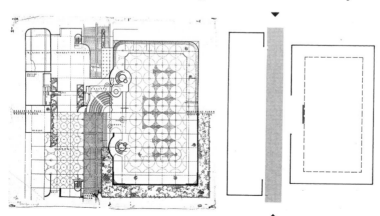

Johnson Wax Building
Racine, Wisconsin, 1936;
composite first floor and
mezzanine level plan

Johnson Wax Building
analysis, *parti* diagram of plan;
drawn by author

Johnson Wax Building
interior view of Great Workroom

and wrote, "This great building is as inspiring a place to work in as any cathedral ever was in which to worship."[22]

The company's executive offices were located in a penthouse above the Great Workroom and were visually and spatially connected to the clerical workers below via the lobby's three-story light well. Midlevel managers were located on a mezzanine surrounding the skylit Great Workroom.

An outdoor vehicular and pedestrian circulation spine separated the lobby/penthouse/Great Workroom mass from a low secondary mass. Characteristically, it contained a series of supporting functions: carport, maintenance garage, exercise deck, and squash court.

Would Wright identify, as in Unity Temple and the Larkin Building, a deeper, latent meaning in the commission that he shared with his client, and then express that meaning through the massing and detailing of the design? Johnson, a young, wealthy businessman, and the older, virtually unemployed Wright seemed to share very little at first. After their initial meeting, Johnson recalled, "[Wright] insulted me about everything, and I insulted him. He had a Lincoln-Zephyr, and I had one—that was the only thing we agreed on. On all other matters we were at each other's throats."[23]

Remarkably, the single item that the two men agreed on, the Lincoln-Zephyr, was sufficient grounds for Wright to generate a grammar for the building. The Lincoln-Zephyr was America's first successful mass-produced, streamlined automobile, and it had been released only the year before. The grammar of streamlining had been recently created by designers of airplanes and ships, who attempted to devise forms that would encounter the minimum of resistance from air and water. Because of their success, employ-

278   JONATHAN LIPMAN

ing curved vertical corners and horizontal striations as a design motif became a symbol of industrial progress by the mid-1930s. The nation came to associate cleanly curved lines with the apparent triumph of new technology over the forces of nature.

Consequently, the two men may have felt a measure of self-affirmation as each discovered that the other was, like himself, on the "cutting edge" of taste; Wright chose to design a streamlined building, his first, for the Johnson Company. Wright tightly integrated all of his streamlined elements into the fabric of the design. Some of the streamlined details were unarguably practical, such as curved desktops that acknowledged the natural, curvilinear path of circulation in a room. As such, Wright succeeded in transcending the current moderne fashion, allowing himself to write of his design, "High time to give our hungry American public something truly 'streamlined.'"

Wright reinforced this concept by making the building's secondary mass a carport, serving as a streamlined backdrop for employees' (presumably) streamlined vehicles, which by implication extended the design motif of the building into the landscape.

SOLOMON R. GUGGENHEIM MUSEUM

In 1943, four years after he completed the Johnson Building, Wright began designing the Solomon R. Guggenheim Museum in New York. Although the design proceeded through a series of alternatives and modifications before construction began in 1956, the final scheme remained quite similar to the original. In the Guggenheim, perhaps Wright's best-known public building, the great skylit room (in this case an art gallery) is encircled by a continuous six-story ramp. The smaller three-story secondary mass, which Wright called a "Monitor," contains the museum's offices. Until the building was altered, the main gallery and the Monitor were separated by a *porte cochere* and a pedestrian entry, as in the Johnson Wax Administration Building.

Johnson Wax Building
exterior view of main entrance

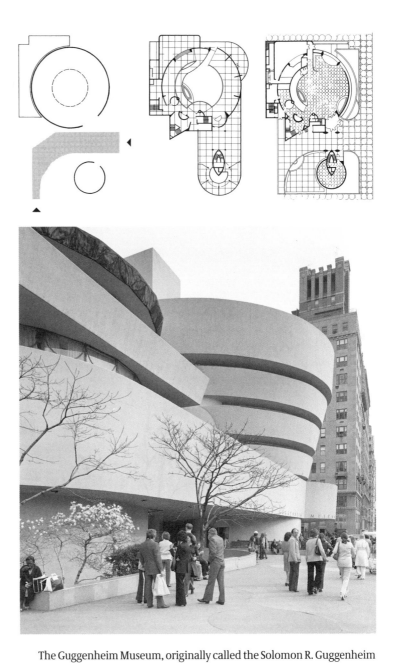

The Guggenheim Museum, originally called the Solomon R. Guggenheim
Collection of Non-Objective Painting, began as a private collection of paintings by Wassily Kandinsky, Rudolf Bauer, and other twentieth-century
avant-garde artists. The collection's director, Baroness Hilla Rebay von
Ehrenweisen, proposed that Wright's building be "a Temple of Non-
Objectivity," and it is clear that Wright adapted his now-familiar *parti* to
meet this charge. The building is treated as a large, curvilinear sculptural
mass. During its construction Wright said: "For the first time a building has
been designed which destroys everything square, rectilinear. It destroys the
rectilinear frame of reference."[24] Wright's "temple of non-objectivity" was so
convincing that Lewis Mumford wrote, "you may go into this building to see

Kandinsky or Jackson Pollock; you remain to see Frank Lloyd Wright."[25]

In designing this "temple of non-objectivity," it is understandable that Wright did not make it strictly axial or symmetrical. But in all other respects, its organizing principles are those of the earlier public buildings. In fact, the *parti* of the Guggenheim Museum is remarkably similar to that of Wright's 1895 Oak Park Studio. However, while the studio's library competed with the studio space as a primary element, the library's equivalent at the Guggenheim, the Monitor, is clearly secondary to the gallery. Also, Wright located an auditorium directly beneath the main gallery in the Guggenheim. This seemingly minor architectural decision presaged a new direction in subsequent public building designs.

ANNUNCIATION GREEK ORTHODOX CHURCH

In the Annunciation Greek Orthodox Church of 1956 in Wauwatosa, Wisconsin, the great mezzanine-ringed room is elevated into the air, with the auxiliary spaces—the church's offices and Sunday school—underground and the entry to the building on grade between them. It is as though Wright

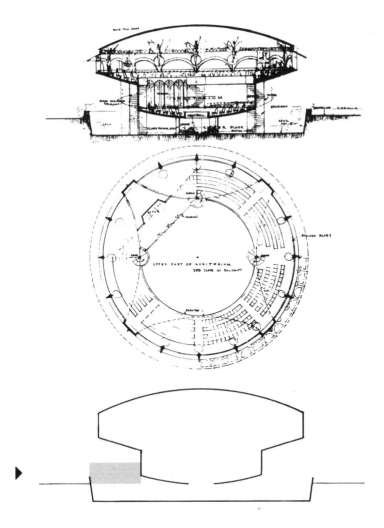

Annunciation Church
Wauwatosa, Wisconsin, 1956;
preliminary section and plan

Annunciation Church
analysis, *parti* diagram of section;
drawn by author

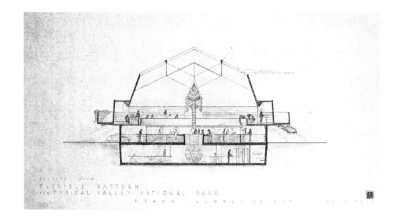

turned his earlier *parti* on its side, from a plan concept to a sectional concept.[26] This strategy makes the composition of the building clear. There can now be no question as to which room constitutes the building's statement, because one room is all one sees.

What appears to be Wright's first use of this *parti* is his little-known, unbuilt Valley National Bank for Tucson, Arizona, of 1947. The design consists of a single two-story, skylit, mezzanine-ringed room. Entry, teller counters, and two private offices are on the main floor, and the mezzanine contains unenclosed office space. An opening in the center of the floor on the main level provides a view of the underground vault and vault lobby. Curved ramps provide both public and private vertical circulation, and an external vehicular ramp serves a drive-in window on the mezzanine level. The building was to be a hemicycle, its roof a faceted glass or plastic dome that would have flooded the space with sunlight. Wright called the design the "Daylight Bank."[27]

In the Greek Orthodox Church the sanctuary, which occupies the entire aboveground mass, is composed in plan of the combination of a circle and Greek cross, two traditional symbols in the Greek Orthodox faith.[28] This is an evolutionary step beyond Wright's earlier notion of applying details or ornament to express the deeper value in the building. In this late design, the very structure of the building signifies the building's meaning.

BETH SHOLOM SYNAGOGUE

The ultimate example of Wright's one-room buildings is Beth Sholom Synagogue of 1954 in Elkins Park, Pennsylvania. The above-ground building consists solely of a one-hundred-foot-tall pyramidal room whose translucent skin is supported by a three-legged structural frame. In the synagogue, whose auxiliary rooms are underground beneath the space, the entire visible building is the space that corresponds to the main or consecrated purpose of the building, and thereby the building directly represents its purpose and is a symbol for itself.

Wright also treated Beth Sholom Synagogue as a symbol for itself in a more ambiguous, and perhaps richer, fashion. The congregation's rabbi, Mortimer Cohen, apparently specifically asked Wright to create an edifice that was truly an American synagogue by invoking symbols of both Judaism

Valley National Bank
Tucson, Arizona, 1947; section

and America. Thus, the building resembles a high-tech tepee because it is meant to suggest a tepee; as a Native American form Wright considered it an appropriate form to borrow for a new American building. At the same time, the shape of the building suggests much more, as this building/symbol is not only American but also Jewish. Rabbi Cohen also requested a "traveling Mount Sinai . . . mountain of light,"[29] from which Moses received the Torah amid "lightning, fire and thunder."

At its base the building has not three but six sides, suggesting the Star of David. The hexagonal sloping floor of the sanctuary approximates the concave shape formed by a pair of hands held together slightly cupped, with palms up and thumbs out—in the palms of these hands rests Mount Sinai.

If the glowing, pyramidal form expresses the idea that the Torah is light and Mount Sinai is a mountain of light, then on entering the building one is surely in the celestial regions of light. One gazes up into an expansive, palpable space, whose bounding surfaces are so luminous and abstract as to be otherworldly.

The religious symbolism of the building is reinforced by layers of symbolic details. For example, the three main structural posts signify the three patriarchs of the Jewish faith, and seven projecting lights, which represent the traditional seven-branched candelabra, or *menorah*, are located on the exterior of each post. Throughout the sanctuary, hexagons, which suggest both the Jewish star and the plan of the building, are used as a design motif. Other ornamental designs apparently have Aztec inspiration, reminding one again that this is a specifically American synagogue.

Over the main entrance is a canopy that takes the form of a biblical priest's outstretched hands, joined together as he recites a benediction. By having congregants enter under these hands, Wright suggested that the congregants are blessed on entering the space.[30]

Beth Sholom Synagogue
Elkins Park, Pennsylvania, 1954;
interior view of sanctuary

Beth Sholom Synagogue
analysis, *parti* diagram of section;
drawn by author

Beth Sholom Synagogue
exterior view at night

Like the forms of the two preceding buildings of the mid-1950s, the form of the Marin County, California, Civic Center of 1957 speaks to us about its meaning. Among the government facilities in the quarter-mile-long building are courtrooms and a jail. Courthouses and jails are frequently treated by architects as imposing, dominant forms, evoking authoritarian connotations. Wright, however, did not acknowledge this in his design. In fact, the courthouses and jails are concealed, rather than expressed, in the megastructure. Instead, an exuberant, ornamented radio tower (concealing a smokestack) and a domed public library are the two forms that break out of the linear structure of the building. Radio stations and libraries signify the dissemination of knowledge, rather than control over society. The arched, blue-topped building strongly conjures up the image of a Roman aqueduct. Might not this form be meant to suggest that it is first of all a conduit of useful knowledge to the public? By celebrating the radio tower and library, and failing to give significance to courtrooms, a jail, or government offices, Wright was surely stating his well-known preference for a government that assists rather than controls the public.

Though by far the largest of Wright's public buildings, the Marin County government complex is an ambiguous footnote to the main thesis of this article. In each of the previously discussed public buildings, Wright created a primary mass to contain the major, consecrated space. This dovetailed with his treatment of the buildings as hermetic universes that rejected their profaned urban surroundings.[31] However, in the Marin County Civic Center, Wright was faced with a rural site, not an urban one, and he responded with an ambivalent scheme in which the building's occupants' attention is drawn both inward and outward. A narrow light well or "mall," lined with two corridors that each serve an outside zone of offices, runs through almost the entire length of the megabuilding. Depending on where movable office partitions are placed, office users may view either the surrounding countryside, the mall, or both.

Compared with the previous buildings, the Civic Center's *parti* is relatively weak because the building is neither clearly centripetal, like the other public buildings, nor centrifugal, like so many of his Prairie Houses. The centrifugal houses draw their users' attention to nature, that is, the landscaped

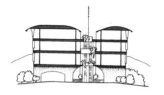

Marin County Civic Center
San Rafael, California, 1957–59; lateral section prior to posthumous alterations, drawn by author

Marin County Civic Center
aerial perspective view

site, with a series of views and perimeter extensions, while the great central spaces of his centripetal public buildings reinforce and inwardly focus the group consciousness of their users.

In the Marin County Civic Center, the central space, although mezzanine-ringed and skylit (and intended by Wright to be unglazed), is not overwhelmingly important because no activity essential to the nature of the building occurs in it. As the space is open to the ground below, perhaps its symbolic purpose is to communicate that the government is accessible to the public. Functionally, the narrow space serves solely to provide circulation and admit sunlight to offices. As such, while the view down the mall does succeed in imparting a sense of the whole building to its users, it only modestly focuses and strengthens the group consciousness of the civic enterprise; thus the mall may not be considered an ennobled or consecrated space because it fails to provide a symbolic focus for the group consciousness of its occupants.

Johnson Wax Company retirees have movingly recalled how enthusiastic they felt about working in the Johnson Administration building when it opened in 1939,[32] and I recall the ennobling atmosphere I have experienced in meetings held in the sanctuary of Unity Temple. In fact it is the absence of convincingly consecrated space in the Marin County Civic Center that allows us to reflect on the power of this device, used so effectively in each of Wright's earlier public buildings.

Marin County Civic Center
view down central light well
or mall

The Integrated Ideal
Ordering Principles
in Wright's Architecture

BY ROBERT MCCARTER

"We must make the shapes, and can only effect this by mastering the principles." —*Horatio Greenough (1853)*[1]

Frank Lloyd Wright wrote relatively little about his process of design, preferring to state his intentions in terms of general principles. While these principles were present both in the design process and in the resulting building, there was no revelation on Wright's part of how he went, as he said, from the general to the particular—from the abstract principle to the concrete building. In this Wright is certainly not unusual; few architects have ever attempted to reveal the process by which general principles or ideals are made present in space and form. It is something that cannot be adequately explained in words; it can only be brought forth in the act of designing and constructing. As Ralph Waldo Emerson said, "No answer in words can reply to a question of things."[2]

In this investigation of the way in which principles act to *order* architecture, Wright's own words may clarify our understanding, but the insights into the process of making must be drawn first from *things*: the buildings themselves. Analysis and design are here understood to be reciprocal; by subjecting Wright's designs to formal and spatial analyses, we may reveal the marks of their making. Wright's process of design went from the general to the particular, therefore analysis should go from the particular (building) to the general (principle). Thus we may work our way "backward," attempting to draw out from the architecture the ordering principles that shaped it. As Goethe wrote, "We ought to talk less and draw more. I personally should like to renounce speech altogether and, like organic nature, communicate everything I have to say in sketches."[3]

Two parallel investigations are undertaken here: The first in both occurrence in time and relative importance is the analysis of the hand—the diagrammatic sketches. These are the first step back from the particular design to the general principle; it is an *engaged* method, one that attempts to remain close to Wright in the act of designing. The sketches were undertaken in the belief that the more closely and precisely one examines particular artifacts, the nearer one comes to understanding the ideas that they

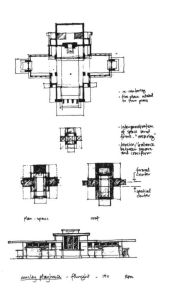

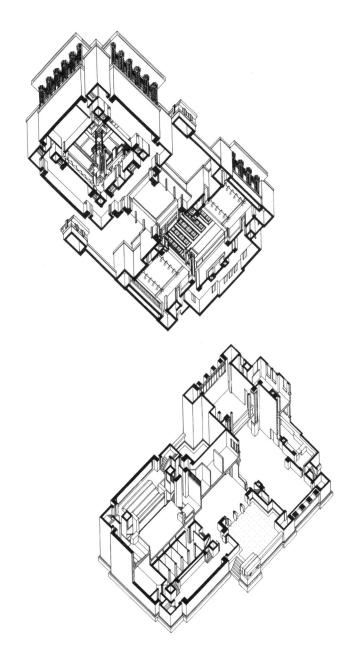

embody and the order that formed them. These extraordinary buildings cannot be grasped completely by any analysis—they are matters of thoughtful experience. Yet we pay appropriate homage in the attempt; as Ludwig Wittgenstein wrote, "My hands feels tempted to draw them: that would be a definition of the beautiful."[4]

The second investigation is the written analysis that draws conclusions from the diagrammatic analyses, relating them to certain biographical information and to Wright's own writings in order to gain a clearer understanding of the general principles *at work* in the work. Here we must be careful in attempting to put Wright's principles into any hierarchical order, as they are in reality much more complexly interrelated, constantly circling about and leading both backward and forward. There is certainly no linear sequence to be followed; rather, there are many principles working all at the same time, affecting each other, even conflicting at times, but held in balance by the ideal of an integrated order. This is a matter of the spirit, and though it is not possible to fully document, and it can never be "scholarly," as Wittgenstein wrote, "It is a great temptation to try to make the spirit explicit."[5]

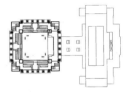

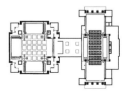

THE MIND AT WORK

> "Of course what is vitally important in all that I have tried to say and explain cannot be explained at all. . . . But here in this searching process may be seen the architect's mind at work."—*Frank Lloyd Wright*[6]

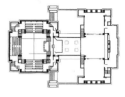

Wright left few sketches from the early stages of the design process; while many were doubtlessly lost or destroyed by fire, the few drawings that survive hint at the real reason for this curious absence. These drawings have often been worked and reworked many times by Wright, but the basic order and form of the design was clearly set before the drawing was begun. Even the sketches dashed off on the back of envelopes are fully developed—they frequently have dimensions already indicated. In fact, all Wright's design sketches that do exist cannot be called "conceptual" or initial studies—they are designs already developed before they appeared on paper.

This conclusion is supported by the many stories told by Wright's apprentices of designs appearing fully formed in the first drawing; Wright drew the design for Fallingwater from scratch in the two hours it took the client to drive to Taliesin, and the finished house is virtually identical to this initial set of sketches.[7] One cannot escape the feeling when studying Wright that he was able to visualize forms and spaces to an uncanny degree—rotating and projecting, folding and unfolding, disassembling and reassembling, seeing outside and inside, all in his mind—so that what eventually emerged on paper is more in the nature of a recording or double-checking than what is normally thought of as a conceptual design sketch. Wright confirmed this in writing in 1928:

> Therefore conceive the building in the imagination, not on paper but in the mind, thoroughly—before touching paper. Let it live there—gradually taking more definite form before committing it to the drawing board. When a thing lives for you—start to plan it with tools. Not before. To draw during conception or sketch, as we say, experimenting with practical adjustments to scale, is well enough if the concept is clear enough to be firmly held. It is best to cultivate the imagination to construct and complete the building before working on it with the T square and triangle.[8]

The kind of mind that can, without drawing, "construct and complete" the extraordinarily complex spaces and forms we find in Wright's buildings is not easy for other architects to understand, much less those who have not themselves struggled in the process of design. Wright was obsessed with space and form, trained since an early age in their manipulation and order; as he said, "It is perhaps a gift—but it may be attained by practice."[9] Wright was certainly gifted, yet he constantly practiced—analyzing and projecting

Unity Temple
plan and reflected ceiling-plan layers; redrawn under supervision of author

Avery Coonley House
Riverside, Illinois, 1908; period
photograph looking from living
room to stair and dining room

Exhibition of Japanese Prints
Art Institute of Chicago, 1908;
designed and installed by Wright

his vision of an integration of space, form and experience. When he commissioned photographs of his buildings on completion of construction, he positioned the furnishings to achieve a sense of dynamic spatial organization—even the rugs overlap and run across room divisions and through doorways to indicate the spatial interpenetrations that result from the movements of the occupants. In his designs for the exhibition of Japanese wood-block prints at theArt Institute of Chicago in 1908, he constructed display cases that ran through the existing doorways, occupying two rooms at once, and he interlaced the system of wooden wall strips and wires used to hang the prints so that they became part of a larger composition of lines and planes defining the rooms.

Wright was constantly engaged in perfecting his capacity to visualize and compose space and forms, seeing no difference between his work and his everyday life in this regard. In addition to the "night labor at the drawing board," which he treated as a normal occurrence, he used any opportunity to design, no matter how ephemeral the outcome. While living in Oak Park, Wright would bring home gas-filled balloons for his children, then spend hours in the vaulted playroom helping the children arrange the brightly colored spheres in different patterns by tying them to furniture and playing out their strings to varying lengths; the colored glass windows of Wright's 1911 Avery Coonley Playhouse reflect this hands-on "practice." Wright's family tells of the difficulties encountered getting dinner started on time; Wright not only has designed the room, the table, the chairs, the tablecloth, and the napkins, but he also insisted on arranging and then rearranging these and the plates, glasses, and utensils in ever new and ever more dynamic design compositions on the tabletop.

A series of photographs composed and taken by Wright, an avid photographer, over a span of seventy years, depict an ever-changing layout of furnishings and artworks in the interiors of his own residences in Oak Park and Spring Green—Wright "practiced" on whatever material lay closest at hand. In the midst of the busy workday, Wright would send the office apprentices

Taliesin I
Spring Green, Wisconsin, 1911; photograph taken by Wright; view of dining room with furniture arranged by Wright—note how rug runs through doorway and ceiling interlocks with adjacent spaces, left

Taliesin II
Spring Green, Wisconsin, 1914; period photograph taken by Wright, view of loggia with furniture arranged by Wright, above

out into the fields to collect wildflowers, which he then composed into skillful arrays that showed his deep knowledge of the Japanese art of floral
arrangement.[10] Finally, many friends and clients have related similar stories
about Wright's visits to their homes; after bidding Wright good night and
retiring to their rooms, the homeowners would hear much noise and
activity well into the night. In the morning, they would find that Wright
had left them with a completely new furniture arrangement—a gift from
their architect.

THE DISCIPLINE OF IDEALS

Wright's process of conceiving a "thought-built building" did not end when
the design was committed to paper. The relentless pursuit of an ideal order
that may be discerned in the layers of lines worked into the Ullman House
plan of 1904 continued throughout the process of design, development,
presentation, construction, and publication. Wright was exhaustive in his
endeavors to achieve a building that completely embodied his principles,
and the research took place in his own work. He constantly reevaluated his
own designs and attempted to improve them during design and construction, and he utilized later commissions to pursue the perfection of each
design idea. As Wright wrote, "These studies never seem to end, and in this
sense no organic building may ever be 'finished.' The complete goal of the
ideal of organic architecture is never reached. Nor need be. What worthwhile ideal is ever reached?"[11]

In design, Wright engaged in an arduous intellectual effort to develop
every aspect of each project. His drawings were covered with small perspectives and axonometrics, developing in three dimensions every corner and
intersection in plan and section. After designing the Larkin Building of 1903,
including its innovative furniture, wall-hung toilets, air-conditioning system, plantings, sculpture, lighting, leaded glass, fountains, engraved slo-
gans, and even certain construction processes (such as a special concrete
mix used for floors, trim, and desktops), Wright was disappointed not to
be allowed to redesign the telephones. Wright recalled the thirty-four separate, completely resolved studies that he made before he achieved an
acceptable fit between the sanctuary of Unity Temple and its classroom
annex, Unity House:

> The ideal of an organic architecture is often terribly severe discipline for
> the imagination. I came to know that full well. And, always, some minor
> concordance takes more time, taxes concentration more than all besides.
> Any minor element may become a major problem to vex the architect.
> How many schemes I have thrown away because some one minor feature
> would not come true to form![12]

While we might expect such exacting determination during the designing of
a project (though we also know that this kind of dedication to an ideal is in
fact rarely the case), for Wright the beginning of construction marked no
end to the process of design. Of particular interest are Wright's many statements about how much he learned from the contractor and the construction workers, and how often this new knowledge allowed him to change and
improve the design during construction. At other times, as the forms rose

Exhibition of the Work of
Frank Lloyd Wright
Art Institute of Chicago, 1907;
designed and installed by Wright
with a composition of multiple,
overlapping layers

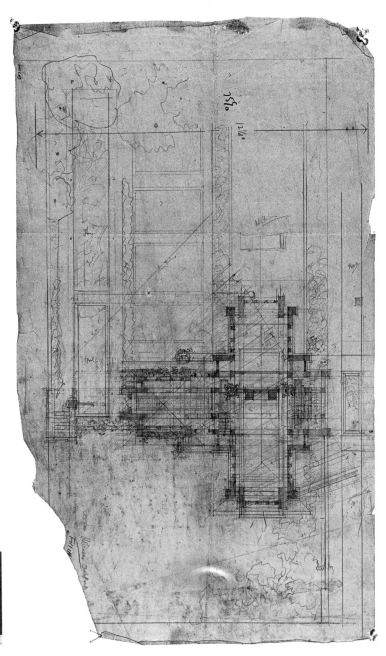

H. J. Ullman House
Oak Park, Illinois, 1904; sketch plan
(Wright's handwritten
identification on sheet), top

Unity Temple
cast and carved plaster model,
with interior space, below

under construction, he saw new spatial opportunities that had not been apparent during design even to his perceptive inner eye, such as the openings he had cut in the balcony floor of the Robie House of 1908, to give the court below both more light and a view of the cantilevers overhead—taking advantage of the steel frame embedded in the structure of the house.[13]

In his own home and studio in Oak Park, Wright experimented continually with space and form, and experienced the results. During the time he lived in Oak Park, from 1889 to 1909, he made numerous renovations, additions, and alternations, including a playroom added to the second floor, and

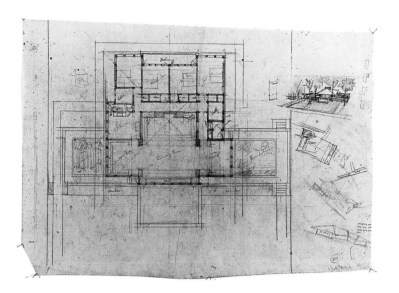

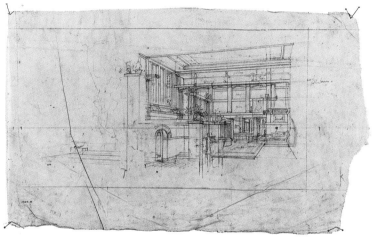

the studio, office, and library added to the side in 1895. Even after he moved to Taliesin, Wright continued renovating the Oak Park complex, dividing the studio into apartments. Because of Wright's continuous experimentation with his own house, recent efforts to "restore" the ensemble have been complicated by the fact that, during its twenty years of use by Wright, the complex had no "typical" or long-lasting organization. Following this firsthand experience with the development of houses that can change as their occupants change in Oak Park and Taliesin, Wright planned his later Usonian Houses with additions in mind, understanding that this offered him an opportunity to continue to improve and perfect the design even after it was built.

So even the building as built was never quite right in Wright's mind. During the Prairie period, Wright's "presentation" of a design often involved the following: plan, elevation, and perspective drawings for the client; a model as "check" for the public commissions; construction with its in-process changes; photographs of the built work (carefully set up and framed by Wright); and perspectives drawn for publication, made by tracing over

Edwin Cheney House
Oak Park, Illinois, 1903; sketch plan with small perspective view of exterior, right

Susan Lawrence Dana House
Springfield, Illinois, 1902; sketch perspective of entry hall

the photographs. These final perspective drawings often enlarged and perfected the actual views captured in the photograph, eliminating or adding furniture and trees, opening doorways and walls for broader, more comprehensive views of interior spaces. Similarly, the plans that Wright published in the 1910 Wasmuth portfolio were frequently "improved," even if the house had been built according to an earlier, less perfect plan; in his Wasmuth site plan, Wright "perfected"—made rectangular—the irregularly shaped site of the Darwin Martin House of 1904. Wright was also known to regularly draw over old drawings in his archives, improving them, even reusing them for later commissions—scandalizing his apprentices and art historians by treating his earlier designs not as historical artifacts but as living things, free to develop further. As Wright wrote, "I would watch sequences fascinated, seeing other sequences in those consequences already in evidence. I occasionally look through such early studies as I made at this period, fascinated by implications. They seem, even now, generic."[14]

Finally, and perhaps most important, Wright considered individual designs and buildings to be parts of a sequence—as steadily perfected variations on a theme. Each of Wright's designs *in-formed* those that followed—they were developments of precise formal and spatial types that approached ever more closely an ideal order. Thus, while his individual buildings were

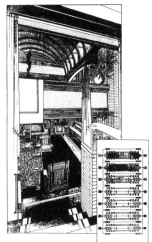

Susan Lawrence Dana House
interior perspective of library and gallery traced from photograph with the view expanded in all four directions

Susan Lawrence Dana House
period photograph of interior of library and gallery

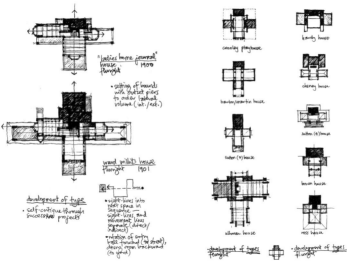

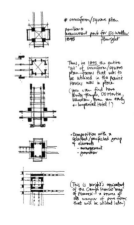

resolved to an astonishing degree, Wright was never satisfied with them: "There is no discipline so severe as the perfect integration of the correlation in any human endeavor."[15] The ideal of *perfection* permeates and illuminates all of Wright's works: it is the key to understanding Wright. He was searching for perfection and believed it was possible to approach, if not to realize. Such a bold endeavor to achieve an ideal, so plainly stated, should give us pause, for in our contemporary period it is rare indeed. Wright sought a discipline of design that would allow him to seek a perfection of form and space. As he said, "The method in itself does not of necessity produce a beautiful building, but it does provide a framework as a basis which has an organic integrity, susceptible to the architect's imagination."[16]

Wright's "system" of design, achieving its full capacity in the Prairie Period after 1900, was directed toward the development of a process of formal composition that would have a sense of both inevitability and harmony. Already mentioned was the development of the houses as *types*—in sequence. Yet all of Wright's buildings share certain elements and methods of assembly or composition. Wright himself called attention to the similarity between this design discipline and musical composition; certain constants control the development of variations resulting from the differences in each project—site, climate, client, material, and structure.

Wright understood the making of architecture to be an act of *construction*, not creation. The architect was not a creator but *a maker*, and his works were things constructed in a particular place of specific materials, formal elements, and spatial relationships, according to the discipline of integral order. In describing his design process for Unity Temple of 1906, Wright observed, "what has actually taken place is only reasoned arrangement."[17] Froebel training, which Wright had been taught as a child, and which he taught his own children in the last years of the nineteenth century, involved the child's arranging a given set of blocks, tiles, or lines to construct geometric forms. *Ikebana*, the Japanese art of floral arrangement that Wright greatly admired and practiced, was similarly predicated on making a com-

Development of Spatial Type through Successive Projects
analysis, variation on a theme; "A Small House with 'Lots of Room in It,'" 1900, and Ward Willits House, 1901; drawn by author

Prairie Period
analysis, development of pure cruciform and compressed cruciform plan types; drawn by author

Wolf Lake Amusement Park
Chicago, Illinois, 1895; analysis of pavilions; this project includes plan types for later Prairie period designs; drawn by author

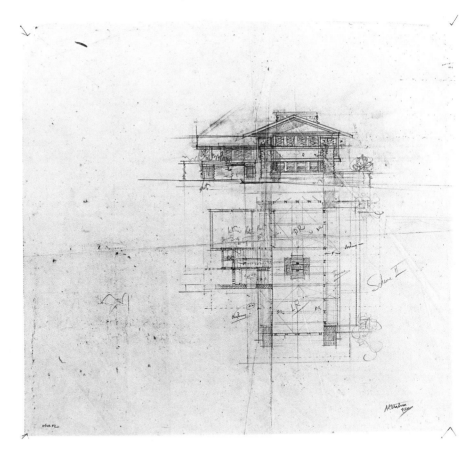

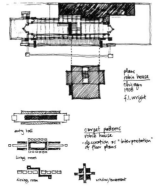

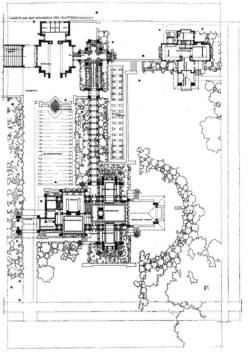

P. A. Beachy House
Oak Park, Illinois, 1906; sketch
plan and elevation, top

Frederick Robie House
analysis, main and bedroom floor
plans, above, and carpet patterns,
below; carpet patterns as
"interpretation" of main-floor
plan, bottom left; drawn by
author

**Darwin Martin House and
George Barton House**
1903–05; site plan as redrawn for
1910 and 1911 publications; plan
cut at standing eye level (five
feet), where there are few solid
walls; "floricycle," semicircle of
flowering plants, at lower right,
on axis with living room-terrace,
bottom left

position from a selected group of elements. It is in this sense of architecture as the "reasoned arrangement" of spaces constructed from a given set of elements that Wright spoke of a grammar of architecture: "*Grammar*, in this sense, means the same thing in any construction—whether it be of words or stone or wood. It is the shape-relationship between the various elements that enter into the constitution of the thing."[18] And of his own buildings, Wright wrote, "I have tried to make their grammar perfect in its way and to give their forms and proportions an integrity that will bear study."[19]

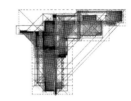

The analytical diagrams that parallel this text are predominantly drawn from Wright's floor plans. The *plan* was of preeminent importance in Wright's work—the plan came first and determined the development of the entire design. The building was conceived as being generated from the plan—it gave form and order to the space within to be lived in. The plan was the "solution" and the elevation was the "expression" of an organic, integrated whole.[20] Even the building's ornamentation was often generated by and related to the plan; in this we should note the rug designs for the Robie House, where Wright provides three "interpretations" of the floor plan.

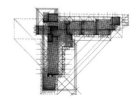

In the Taliesin drafting room, Wright had a copy of the Wasmuth portfolio Darwin Martin House plan of 1903 prominently displayed on the wall for over fifty years. This plan represented for Wright a kind of perfection to be sought in all projects, as well as itself being generative of new designs; it is possible to construct close approximations of the much later Usonian House plans by folding this plan along its symmetrical axes. The unity of Wright's ordering principles across time may be understood in the fact that the Usonian House plans were developed from the earlier Prairie House plans, despite the evident differences in the spatial character and scale of the two types; in the Prairie Houses, space is *projected*, while in the Usonian Houses, space is *unfolded*.

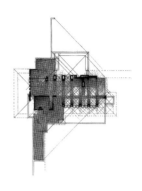

Wright's plans were carefully drawn and cut to show particular interpretations of the space he was defining and constructing. Wright believed that if the floor plan was not beautiful, neither could be the building that rose from it, and that the architect's plan was his most telling drawing: "To judge the architect one need only look at his ground plan. He is the master then and there, or never. Were all the elevations of the genuine buildings of the world lost and the ground plans saved, each building would construct itself again. Because before a plan is a plan it is a concept in some creative mind."[21]

THE COUNTENANCE OF PRINCIPLE

The plan shaped and formed space, and the only reason to shape space was for the experience of people. Architecture, for Wright, was first and foremost concerned with the presentation of mankind. Architecture gave order to peoples' experience and thus made them present in the world—in space conceived and formed as being occupied. Wright stated, "Architecture is man's great sense of himself embodied in a world of his own creation."[22] Wright understood buildings to be the "background or framework" for human life; architecture was not placed at the center of the stage—architecture was the stage itself, allowing the rituals of daily life to take place in its spaces. Thus the various means of creating order that I shall shortly examine

Plans of Three Usonian Houses
Herbert Jacobs, 1936; Stanley Rosenbaum, 1939; and Bernard Schwartz, 1939; all derived from Darwin Martin House plan, these analyses also illustrate Wright's "woven" conception of architecture and plan making; drawn under supervision of author

were measured by, scaled by, or controlled by the human body and its experience—Wright's often-labeled "abstract" system of design was in fact calibrated precisely to the human figure.

The dynamic spatial development of Wright's architecture originated in his understanding of inhabitation and experience as nonstatic events. Henri Bergson, Wright's contemporary, wrote: "We attribute to motion the divisibility of the space which it traverses, forgetting that it is quite possible to divide an object, but not an act."[23] People inhabit architecture through movement; space and material are woven together to become the setting for daily life. Here I want to emphasize that Wright's principles of order were determined by experience. The ordering ideas were the means; the inhabitant's experience was the end. As Emerson wrote, "People forget that the eye makes the horizon."[24]

The dynamic movement involved in experience led Wright to make subtle adjustments to his "abstract" system of design—meeting what Joseph Connors has called "the requirements of the eye."[25] The plan generated the three-dimensional order, but Wright utilized his skill in perspective sketching to check the visual experience against the pure form derived from the

Darwin Martin House
Buffalo, New York, 1904; period photograph of interior, view of living room with doors to terrace to right

Darwin Martin House
sketch perspective of exterior, view from street

idealized plan. Wright made adjustments to balance the requirements of the eye and geometric order, but never designed from the perspective: "A perspective may be proof but it is no nurture."[26]

Wright based his method of constructing and assessing form and space on empathy and abstraction rather than on preconceived "knowledge" derived from existing sources or models. There was thus nothing "typical" about Wright's buildings, yet they were immediately understandable in experience. Wright constructed spaces that clearly showed the manner in which the occupant might *be* in them: "form became feeling," as Wright stated.[27] His architecture appealed at a fundamental level to the occupant's sense of embodied presence and bodily movement—interpreted through experience. As Sullivan had written, "It is the perfect concrete analysis of the senses and sympathies that serves as a basis for the abstract analyses of the intellect."[28]

It was this balance between abstraction and empathy that allowed Wright to construct architecture that was both geometrically pure and experientially determined. The abstract concept of scale was directly related to the concrete ideal of comfort—the human body was the measure for both. While the geometric rigor of Wright's planning is well known, the esteem in which he held *use* and *comfort* is not as widely understood. When Wright modified Sullivan's "form follows function" (after Greenough) to "form and function are one," it was not only a more integrated concept but one in which architecture's "function" was interpreted as the spiritual quality of daily life. This is captured in a statement of Mrs. Coonley, who noted that she and her husband chose Wright to be their architect because his buildings "bore the countenance of principle."[29] In Wright's architecture, the intellectual and formal order of the plan was balanced by the physical and spiritual engagement of the inhabitant; for Wright concept and experience were one and the same.

Unity Temple
sketch perspective of interior of sanctuary, with final design of details

"Therefore the first great necessity of modern architecture is this keen sense of order as integral. That is to say, the *form* itself in orderly relationship with purpose or function: the *parts* themselves in order with the form: the materials and methods of work in order with both: a kind of natural integrity."—*Frank Lloyd Wright*[30]

For Wright, *integrity* remained the most important principle in his work. It suffused all that he did and, it held in balance the many contradictory or dichotomous concepts he attempted to resolve. Integrity gave rise to the primary ideals of *elemental independence* and *spatial fusion* that defined and determined his efforts to make architecture. Wright saw integral order as an essential source of the architectural discipline that had ordered the great architecture of the past, and that would be applied to his own work. Integral order allowed the development of the design's overall form and grammar to which the various parts were related; it required a consistency of expression. Repose, a simultaneous sense of completeness and of belonging to a place, was for Wright the result of experiencing integrity in architecture. Space, form, and experience were fused in Wright's work through this principle of integral order made constitutional in the plan. Wright wrote in 1908:

> In laying out the ground plans for even the more insignificant of these buildings a simple axial law and order and the ordered spacing upon a system of certain structural units definitely established for each structure in accord with its scheme of practical construction and aesthetic proportion, is practiced as an expedient to simplify the technical difficulties of execution, and, although the symmetry may not be obvious always the balance is maintained.[31]

GRID, SCALE, AND PROPORTION

The grid or unit system that underlay all of Wright's designs operated as both an "expedient" in construction and an essential compositional method needed to achieve the integral order that gave beauty. Wright wrote, "In the

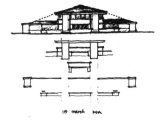

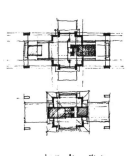

Robert W. Evans House
Chicago, Illinois, 1908; analysis of elevation, pyramidal massing, and nesting of horizontal planes, above; and analysis of plan, below; drawn by author

Robert W. Evans House
period photograph of exterior, view from street

logic of the plan what we call standardization is seen to be fundamental groundwork in architecture. All things in nature exhibit this tendency to crystallize: to form mathematically and then to conform."[32] The grid gave a basic stability that allowed variations within the matrix. Wright manipulated the uniform repetitive grid to produce modulated form, and the resulting "tartan" or *a-b-a* spacing was the foundation for his designs throughout his career. The minor, smaller spacings were the structure and service zones, and the major, larger spacings were the spaces structured and served by the secondary zones—in this, as in so many ways, Wright had a direct influence on the thinking of Louis I. Kahn, who would later develop his concept of "servant" and "served" spaces.

Wright considered the uniform grid to be the means by which every element and space in the composition could be coordinated and integrated into a whole. To emphasize the importance of this unit system in his work, Wright in 1928 published a series of his Prairie-period plans with the underlying grids redrawn.[33] In both earlier and later working drawings, the grid appeared as a way of eliminating and dimension lines and making the modular construction evident; this culminated with Wright's having the grid scored into the concrete floor slabs of the Usonian Houses before the walls were erected.

The relationship between the grid and the predominant material of construction, a relationship wherein the grid was either determined by the material (the two-by-four-foot grid of the Usonian Houses, based on the standard wood component's dimensions) or determined by the material's dimensions (the sixteen-inch-square grid of the concrete block houses, where the blocks were manufactured on site using custom-designed molds), will be further explored later. The relationship of the grid to enclosed, occupied space is equally important; Wright considered the modular volumes of each space capable of being articulated individually—as he wrote, the different rooms "may thus become small buildings in themselves,"[34] each with its own structure and symmetrical order. (This was also later taken up and developed by Louis I. Kahn). Wright's Prairie-period buildings were frequently composed of several large, strictly symmetrical rooms that are interlocked to form either a symmetrical or asymmetrical "balanced" whole;[35] examples include the Darwin Martin House and Robie House, respectively. The grid was used by Wright to organize and hold together these interlocking masses, thus making possible the expression of interior volumes in exterior form, and expression of paramount importance in Wright's architecture.

Wright used the unit system of design to "keep all to scale, ensure consistent proportion throughout the edifice, large or small, which thus became—like tapestry—a consistent fabric woven of independent related units, however, various."[36] Wright was arguably more attentive to and accomplished in the adjustment of spaces to human scale than any other architect in modern times. I shall later examine more closely the way in which he constructed rooms of carefully scaled horizontal layers of space and form, so that the movement from a standing to a seated position resulted in an entirely different experience of the space. Wright's understanding of scale

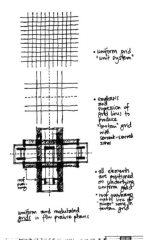

• uniform grid "unit system"

• emphasis and suppression of grid lines to produce "tartan" grid with servant-served zones

• all elements are positioned on underlying uniform grid
• roof overhangs mark line of minor zone in tartan grid

uniform and modulated grids in few prairie plans

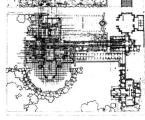

1928 re-publication by FLW w/grids re-drawn

Darwin Martin House
analysis, uniform "unit system" square grid and its modulation to produce "tartan" or *a-b-a* planning grid, above; drawn by author, and Wright's republication (1928) of the Martin House with square grid, below

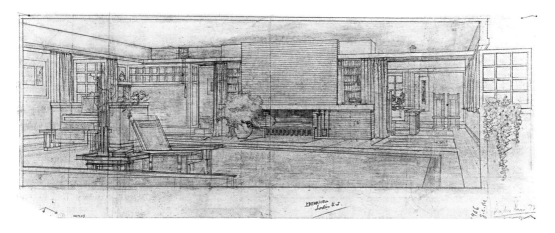

involved the specific size of the human figure, so that his own fairly short stature had considerable effect on the dimensions of the various ceilings and soffits in his buildings. Wright was overheard directing his six-foot-four-inch apprentice William Wesley Peters to sit down at Taliesin gatherings, for, when standing, Peters was "destroying the scale" of the room.[37]

Wright understood that people responded to differing scales and experienced space and form by way of empathic experience; the fireplaces at the centers of his houses, with their crouching stance, hulking mass, and low mantels, combined with the low ceilings to make the occupants feel taller, more in command of the space and the vistas they could see beyond the low overhanging eaves.

Wright designed form and space at widely varying scales, while always employing the same ordering principles. His furniture, freestanding and built-in, was often developed as an "interpretation" of the building as a whole—for example, the wooden sideboard in the Robie House dining room is a reduced scale version of the main street elevation of the house. As Wright wrote, "scale is really proportion," here utilizing the concept of hierarchy, ordered by the underlying grid or unit system.[38]

"A Fireproof House for $5,000"
1906; *Ladies' Home Journal*, interior sketch perspective of living room with dining room to right of fireplace

Frederick Robie House
period photograph of dining room; all furnishings designed by Wright

Wright "nested" one form and space inside another, so that his buildings were composed of similar elements repeated at varying scales. During the Prairie period, the major structural piers in Wright's designs were inevitably paired, and the wall between them was defined by a smaller, inset pair of piers; or a smaller cubic mass projected from the center of the major cubic mass. In this way, the set of elements at varying scales reinforced each other, and the building seemed to have been generated by some inner crystallization.

The elements in plan were proportional in scale to their height in elevation; the larger piers in plan were the taller, the smaller piers in plan were the shorter. In this Wright was no different from the designers of the ancient classical monuments, whose inheritance he acknowledged. For Wright, the plan remained generative: "A good plan is the beginning and the end . . . its development in all directions is inherent—inevitable."[39]

GEOMETRY, AXIS, AND MOVEMENT

Wright's designs were constructed of individually articulated pure forms—independent geometric shapes and spaces that were then fused into larger compositions. The exterior clearly exhibited the shapes taken by the interior spaces. This geometric purity found confirmation in Wright's studies of the forms of nature, wherein he "observed that nature usually perfects her forms; the individuality of the attribute is seldom sacrificed: that is, deformed or mutilated by co-operative parts."[40] Geometric order was Wright's primary method of producing structured space; it was this structure that enabled the spaces to be both independent, as pure geometric forms, and interdependent, as part of a woven or continuous whole. As Wright wrote, "Geometry is the grammar, so to speak, of the form. It is its architectural principle."[41]

This geometric purity presents itself most forcefully when Wright's designs are examined as abstract forms, yet the experience of their spaces makes us aware of the complementary fusion of their interdependent parts. David Van Zanten has observed that what Wright was trying to achieve was not geometric purity as an end in itself; rather, "geometric purity was a means to expedite assembly, achieving a kind of mechanical self-generation in architectural composition."[42]

Wright utilized the square and the cube as primary geometric proportional "units" in his Prairie-period compositions. In the plan and section of Unity Temple, the primary volume of the sanctuary is a pure cube (1:1:1 in plan and section), and the secondary spaces—entry cloisters and balconies to either side of the main space—are smaller double cubes (1:2:1 in plan and section); the secondary spaces are dependent on the primary one, both functionally and proportionally. Wright assembled these proportional units into basic spatial cells, either directed outward from a central point to form a cruciform or spiraling around a center to form a pinwheel. These, along with other combinations of the square unit, were organized along axes and cross axes to form larger compositions, such as those found in the Larkin Building and the Darwin Martin House complex.

Wright referred to "a simple axial law and order" and to a symmetry that, although not always obvious, maintained an overall balance in space

Edward Schroeder House
Milwaukee, Wisconsin, 1911; analysis of elevation, above, showing "nesting" of similar forms at different scales; general analysis of "nesting" in Wright's work, below; drawings by author

and form. There was, however, nothing simple or conventional about Wright's use of axial planning and symmetry. While the volumes and forms of his Prairie-period buildings were frequently bi-axially symmetrical, the occupant never moved along the axis of symmetry (as was inevitably true in contemporary Beaux-Arts neoclassical buildings) but along the edges of the space. Openings between spaces occurred at the corners, resulting in diagonal views to adjacent spaces.

The center of the elevation and of the room was almost always blocked to physical passage, though often open to partial view (as the Robie House fireplace), making the occupant aware of the differences between the paths and experiences of the eye and those of the body—between the visual and the haptic. When there were banks of doors opening onto a terrace, the center door was often drawn as fixed in a closed position on the plan. In the period photograph of the living room of the Darwin Martin House, Wright placed a piece of furniture set squarely in front of the central terrace door, blocking its use for physical passage but still allowing views out. Wright often placed a column, window post, or wall directly on the center axis of the elevation—a clue to its "impassable" nature. The entry to Wright's own studio and office in Oak Park does not allow axial entry: one must choose between two equal doors in an entryway charged with unexpected tension.

Entry to Wright's buildings is anything but "obvious." Confronted with the symmetrical, axial exterior form, where the primary volume is always clearly evident, the person wishing to enter searches for a way in, moving along the edges of the exterior and interior volumes, spiraling inward until the central volume is again discovered. These entry sequences are intentionally obscured, and penetration into the building requires a conscious effort to decipher the underlying order of the design.

Unity Temple
square/cube and double-square/
cube proportioning system
employed by Wright to develop
plan, left, and
elevations/sections, right; drawn
by author

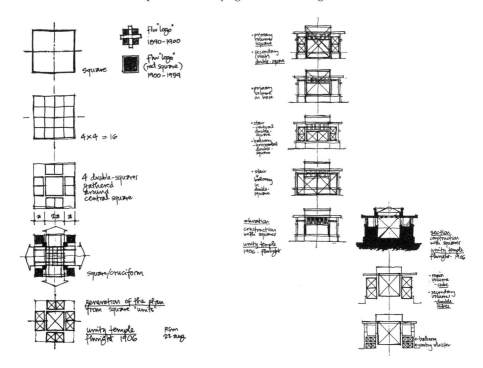

Wright utilized axial symmetry in a way that made entry more difficult than expected; he intentionally lengthened the path, increased the number of different angles from which the building was seen, and varied the space, material, and light along the entryway in contrast to those characterizing the final goal—a dark, compressed, circuitous, peripheral route leads to a bright, high, open, central space. There is a sense that no goal is worth attaining without effort, and the desirability of the goal increases—as does the tension—with each new barrier to our reaching it. The entry sequence was only one of many ways in which Wright designed the movement of the occupant to be a counterpoint to the pure geometries, modular grid, and axial symmetry of his designs. For Wright, the occupant's *position* was as important as the formal *composition* in determining the experience of his architecture.

SPACE, ELEMENT, AND CONTINUITY

Wright believed the construction of the room was the primary intent of architecture; he paraphrased the ancient philosopher Lao Tzu (as paraphrased by the author Kakuzo Okakura), "The reality of the building does not consist in the walls and the roof but in the space within to be lived in."[43] The room was the generator of the architectural form: all other ordering ideas were subordinated to this principle. The room was the focus of Wright's spatial investigations because of its essential part in the experience of the inhabitant; the room was the place where man was truly embodied in a world of his own making.

Rather than employ a stable, pure form for the room, Wright constructed a dynamic repose through the balanced fusion of interdependent volumes. There were two fundamental spatial plan forms for Wright. The first is the *pinwheel*, four volumes that spin around a solid center (unfolding space). The second is the *cruciform*, two volumes that interpenetrate to form a stable square at the center (projecting space). In his earliest work, Wright held these compositions within a larger square, of which they were understood as subdivisions.

Unity Temple is more powerful as an experience than its simple cubic center would lead one to expect; this is because its volume is actually con-

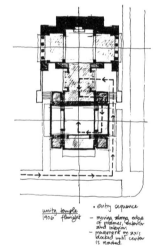

Oak Park Studio
Oak Park, Illinois, 1895;
perspective view from street and
plan of entry loggia

Unity Temple
entry sequence of seven turns to
arrive at center; drawn bu author

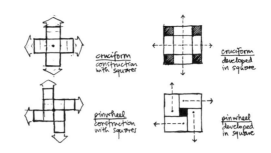

cruciform construction with squares

cruciform developed in square

pinwheel construction with squares

pinwheel developed in square

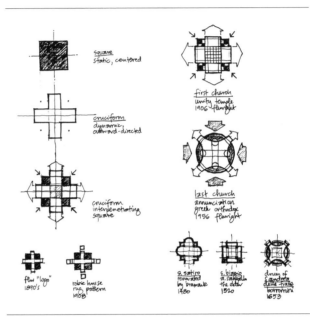

square static, centered

cruciform dynamic, outward-directed

cruciform interpenetrating square

first church unity temple 1906 flwright

last church annunciation greek orthodox 1956 flwright

flw "logo" 1890's

robie house rug pattern 1908

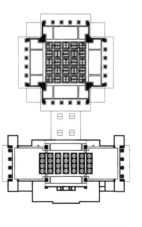

s. satiro remodeled by bramante 1480

s. biagio a. sangallo the elder 1520

drum of s. andrea della fratte borromini 1653

Prairie House Plan-types
pinwheel and cruciform plans, constructed of squares and developed from square; drawn by author

Woven Spaces
analysis, plan forms of cruciform interpenetrating square; Wright's first church (1906) and last church (1956) share this basic plan; drawn by author

Unity Temple
plan of entry level, left, and reflected ceiling plans of sanctuary and classroom buildings, right; drawn under author's supervision

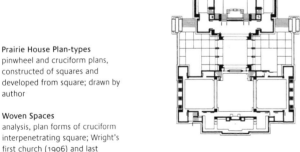

composite plan (entry/sanctuary)

composite reflected ceiling plan

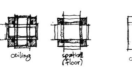

ceiling

spatial (floor)

centrality

extension

interpenetration

structed of several spaces woven together and held in tension. The cruciform interpenetrating the square is one of the most typical plan-forms of Wright's Prairie period; the dynamic outward-directed cruciform complements and balances the static centered square. Here Wright is closer to the baroque architects than to those of the Renaissance, despite the similarity of his geometric forms to the latter; Wright created a tense fusion of opposite spatial forms (static and dynamic; infolding and exfoliating) rather than a simple addition of static forms. It is no coincidence that Wright's first and last churches, designed and built fifty years apart, are both composed of a static form interpenetrated by a dynamic form.

The room, for Wright, was defined by the resolution of a dichotomy: elemental independence and spatial fusion. Wright separated and articulated the components of the room—floors, walls, ceilings, piers, windows, doors, stairs, even furniture—by giving them independence as elements so they might be used to structure space more precisely. These independent elements were ordered by the underlying grid, on which Wright moved them into a variety of positions (as pieces on a chessboard, an analogy Louis I. Kahn would later employ). By disconnecting walls, ceilings, and floors and using them as independent elements, Wright simultaneously *defined* spaces more precisely and *fused* them into larger and more ambiguous compositions. For example, Wright raised and lowered the ceilings of his houses to respond to the specific activities that took place in each space—low at the fireplace and dining area where people were seated and high at the living room and the stair where people were standing or walking. This precision of definition resulted in the creation of several ceiling heights, each defining a different space, yet all within a single space.

The order of a space in Wright's buildings was never in question, yet the experience of that space was often full of mystery and discovery. The fusion of several interpenetrating spaces led to a *continuity* of space, an integration of traditionally separate rooms—an integration requiring the occupant to decipher, through personal experience, the definitions of space. Multiple spatial interpretations and, consequently, a richer, more engaging experience resulted. Usually characterized as being more "open," Wright's spaces are in reality more mysterious; spaces are joined by obstacles that must be moved around (such as the fireplace in the Robie House); the resulting rooms are private and yet ambiguously bounded.

In the definition of both exterior and interior volumes, Wright employed multiple boundaries and ambiguous spatial layers that belong to more than one volume, being both inside and outside—the spaces under the roof overhangs are one of the more obvious "in-between" zones, where casement windows swing open to literally extend the interior space outside and to bring the exterior inside. This ambiguous rendering of space continues to the surfaces that form the interior space itself. As Wright wrote:

> I call it *continuity*. It is easy to see it in the folded plane. . . . The folded plane enters here emphasized by lines merging wall and ceiling into one. Let walls, ceilings, floors now become not only party to each other, but part of each other, reacting upon and within one another; continuity in all.[44]

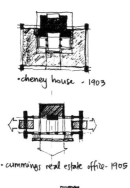

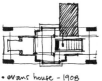

· cummings real estate office- 1905

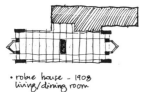

· evans house - 1908

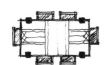

· robie house - 1908
living/dining room

· robie house dining table
w/ linen designed by flw

setting the bounds
·implication of spatial field

Spatial Fields
analysis at various scales in
Wright's work, from furniture to
room to building to landscape;
drawn by author

Wright used plaster and concrete to render ceilings and walls as homogeneous planes that appear to have been "folded" to make enclosures. Unity Temple is the most astonishing example of this method; wood strips or trim boards were utilized to define, explain, indicate, divide, and relate the surfaces—to articulate the continuity of surface around corners and between ceilings and walls. The continuity of planar surfaces indicates a similar continuity and a plastic manipulation, or folding, of the spaces defined by the planes. There is a constant play between monolithic massive planes and thin, eloquent articulation of wood stripping that outlines openings, joins planes, and gives an interpretation of the space. The wood strips are one example of Wright's idea of integral ornament understood as the underlying structure-pattern of the space made visible by and articulated as a rhythm of the form.

The rooms in Wright's houses are banded by the horizontal projecting planes and trim that ring the room just above head height. In addition to aligning the tops of all doors and windows, this soffit plane ties the room together as a spatial entity (allowing the walls below the plane to be more freely disposed) and fuses the ceiling with the upper part of the wall above the plane (which is frequently a line of clerestory windows, allowing the ceiling to merge with the roof soffit outside, giving a generous sense of space overhead). In this development, as in so many others, Wright learned from traditional Japanese architecture, with its screen walls that do not reach the ceiling—free to move below the beam that ran at door-top height. Yet Wright pushed this method much further in designs such as the Darwin Martin House, where plans of the floor, the soffit plane and its beams (many free-spanning through the spaces), and the ceiling give three completely different definitions of the same volumes. The resulting rooms are far more complexly layered than their relatively low height would lead one to expect.

A dynamic balance of the horizontal and the vertical defined Wright's rooms. The horizontal lines, parallel to the horizon, identify themselves with the earth. The vertical lines, aligned with the tree trunks, identify themselves with the sky. The general dominance of the horizontal in Wright's houses is complemented by the more subtle vertical patterning of the glass, the proportions of the casement windows and the posts between them, the upward thrust of the piers and fireplace, and, of course, the presence of the standing human figure. The resolution of this dichotomy—earth and sky, horizontal and vertical—is experienced in the house interiors, where the light plaster ceilings with their floating folded planes, free-spanning beams, and skylights hover over and gather around the heavy dark fireplace anchored to the earth.

Wright wrote of rooms that were both caves and tents. This spatial resolution bonded two conceptions of the house—a dark, earthbound, anchored and protected center of collective ritual, with its huge hearth, and a centrifugal expansion of space and view to the distant horizon in all directions, with its sense of freedom and individual independence. The walls belong to the earth, the roof belongs to the sky. Wright wrote: "In the way the walls rose from the plan and the spaces were roofed over was the chief interest of the house."[45]

The "walls that rose from the plan" are often clusters of piers with low infill panels between, and the roof floats over all. The piers Wright utilized

Unity Temple
interior view of sanctuary balconies, light fixtures, and leaded-glass windows

Avery Coonley Playhouse
period photograph of interior

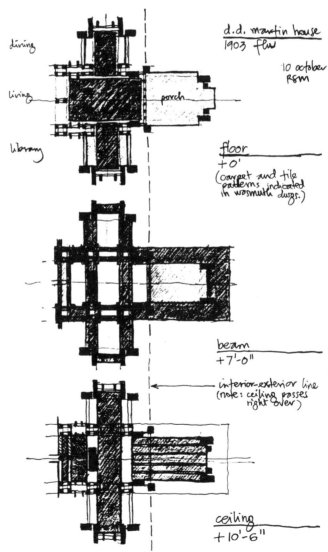

Japanese Print Showing Interior
note similar organization of door-top beams, with walls fixed and closed above, sliding and open below; print likely from Wright's own collection, included as illustration in Wright's 1912 book, *The Japanese Print: An Interpretation*

Darwin Martin House
three differing definitions of interior space at floor, door-top beams, and ceiling; drawn by author

dining

living

library

porch

d.d. martin house
1903 flw

10 october
RSM

floor
+ 0'
(carpet and tile patterns indicated in wasmuth dwgs.)

beam
+7'-0"

interior-exterior line
(note: ceiling passes right over)

ceiling
+10'-6"

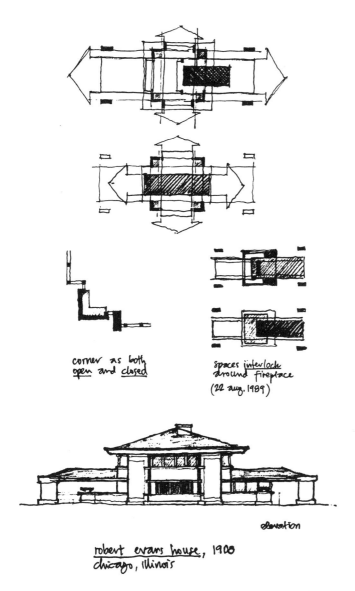

corner as both
<u>open</u> and <u>closed</u>

spaces <u>interlock</u>
<u>around</u> fireplace
(22 aug. 1989)

elevation

<u>robert evans house</u>, 1908
chicago, illinois

are ambiguous elements both structurally (as shall be discussed later) and spatially. As something between a wall and a column, the pier not only stands as an isolated element but also gives direction to space. In the interpenetrating and layering of interior space, these piers interlock varied spaces. They link floor to ceiling and reinforce the primary axis with which they are aligned, aiding the occupants' interpretation and understanding of complex volumes.

Because of this close connection between spatial form and human experience, Wright was acutely sensitive to "formal" problems—the many studies he did to resolve the relatively "minor" concordance in the design of Unity Temple are an example. In this, perhaps the best example is the classic *corner* problem that Renaissance architects spent considerable time endeavoring to resolve. This problem arose in the attempt to make interior courtyard elevations by folding the flat exterior facades and arcades of the classical

Robert W. Evans House
plan, above, and elevation, below; simultaneous anchorage and extension; drawn by author

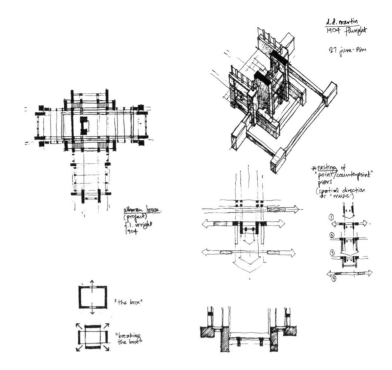

d.d. martin
1904 Plurplot

27 june - Rom

*nesting of
"point/counterpoint"
piers
(spatial direction
or "muse")

uherman house
(project)
f.l. wright
1904

"the box"

"breaking
the box"

Roman ruins; the critical element was the solution of the inner corner. The similarity to Wright's formal interests is clear, and the timeless nature of such formal problems is also evident in the parallels between Wright's work and that of these ancient predecessors.

Wright's reinterpretations of the basic elements of architecture were not undertaken to oppose the history of the discipline but to continue it—his reinterpretations were inventive, liberative, and fundamentally concerned with the precise definition of inhabited space. These "formal" and spatial problems were experientially determined: They were the opposite of disengaged form making. Much has been made, primarily because of his own rhetoric, of Wright's "destruction of the box" or traditional room;[46] yet a closer study of his work reveals that such singular interpretations are misleading—though no doubt highly effective for Wright's polemical purposes. While he redefined walls, floors, ceilings, and other elements to allow the corners of rooms to be opened, he also designed solid walls and closed corners when they served his larger spatial intentions.

Wright was interested not in limiting his formal choices but in expanding them; his work was not an attack on the idea of *room* but an enrichment of it. While he manipulated the elements that composed the room, he never sacrificed the *definition* of the room—he strengthened it and made it more complex. It would perhaps be better to say that what Wright destroyed was not the room-as-box but, rather, any singular interpretation of the room; in this he engaged issues of space making and inhabitation, grappling with the questions of how one defines a volume, a place, an experience in space. Wright characterized and distinguished spaces according to their use through reinterpretations of these fundamental space-making elements

Wright's Definition of the Room
analysis; drawn by author

derived from an analysis of the room. For example, rather than uniformly eliminating the corner, Wright manipulated it to define the nature of each space within the larger order of the building.

In the ground-floor, public rooms of the Prairie Houses, Wright usually strengthened the corner and made it more prominent as a definer and container of space; see, for example, the Darwin Martin House, where the corners are composed of double and quadruple pier groups that protrude into the rooms to form the cruciform-shaped spaces. In the upper-floor, private bedrooms, open corners with glass wrap around in such a way that the corner, having no presence in the room and allowing view and space to open outward, seems to disappear. Thus, contrary to expectations, the public rooms have central openings and closed corners, while the private rooms have windows wrapping around three sides and open corners.

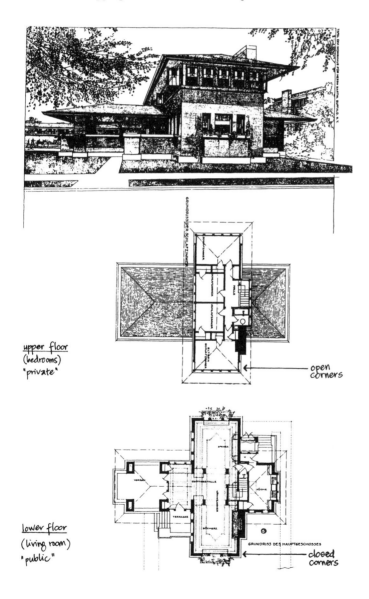

upper floor
(bedrooms)
"private"

← open corners

lower floor
(living room)
"public"

← closed corners

George Barton House
Buffalo, New York, 1903;
perspective, above, upper
(bedroom) floor plan, center,
and main living-floor plan, below;
"public" lower floor has closed
corners, while "private" upper
floor has open corners; notations
by author

In the Martin House and neighboring Barton House, the public rooms on the ground floor required protection from the intrusion of outside views, yet the nature of the rooms (reception, living, dining, library) demanded openness to nature and to the outside world for those inside. Wright constructed these rooms of two seemingly contradictory elements: massive masonry piers and walls, and large sheets of glass. The masonry comes forward and the glass stands back, almost unseen in the protective shadows of the walls and roof. The masonry walls are low, and the glass runs high up above these walls and in thin vertical slots between the piers. From the relative darkness of the interior there is a surprising degree of transparency, while from the brighter exterior there are deep shadows behind heavy protective masses; the inability to see into the house from outside is complemented by the ability to see out from within the house.[47]

The plan for the lower, public floor of the Darwin Martin House Wright published in the Wasmuth portfolio is cut at eye level and shows an extraordinary open quality—there appear to be only piers, with no walls in the traditional sense. Yet by simply sitting down, one finds oneself within a protective enclosure of low masonry walls and solid built-in oak cabinetry, with views limited to the interior realm. The difference between standing and sitting is astonishing; for Wright the drawn plan was only one of many horizontal layers of space carefully modulated to human scale, the occupant's activity, and the resulting position of the eye.

The private bedrooms of the Prairie Houses required protection from the outside world, yet their position on the upper floor allowed for openness. Wright constructed these spaces by extending the first-floor piers and walls up to form protective parapets (with deep built-in cabinets and balcony planters) and by cantilevering the roof all around. The glazed corners and rows of continuous horizontal windows make the bedrooms surprisingly open, and when standing, one has broad views out in three directions. Yet the deep setback behind the parapets shields the bedrooms, and the roof overhang casts protective shadows, so that from the street it is not possible to see anyone in these bedrooms.

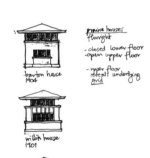

Darwin Martin House
period photograph of dining room; all furnishings designed by Wright

Prairie House Elevations
closed massive lower floor and open framed upper floor; drawn by author

There are other ways in which Wright made distinctions between public and private spaces within the Prairie House. By continuing the wall from foundation to second-story sill height, the ground floor is aggrandized in exterior massing, while the continuous windows above are recessed, so that the bedrooms recede into the shadows of the overhanging roof. The resulting massing tends to be vertical for the public volumes of the house and horizontal for the private volumes. The public rooms are fused or interpenetrated, while the private and service areas remain enclosed and separate from each other. The windows on the public lower floor frame the axis of symmetry (with posts or piers to either side), while the windows on the private upper floor either close the axis with a post set on center or disperse it by revealing the underlying omni-directional modular grid. The resulting dialectic between lower public floor (closed corners, open center, vertical, solid massing) and the upper private floor (open corners, blocked center, horizontal, light framing) typifies Wright's manner of designing—a fusion of opposites—and mirrors Wright's treatment of variations in building *type*.

Wright's public buildings throughout his career invariably focused on introspective, top-lit, central spaces, protected by solid walls that deny eye-level views outward. Although introverted at ground level with their closed exteriors and open centers, the buildings are primarily vertical in orientation and open up and out in section and massing, being directed toward the sky. In addition, Wright's Prairie-period public buildings are cubic in form, composed of pure geometries with clear, distinct edges and boundaries.

Wright's private houses throughout his career were extroverted, opening outward with views in several directions, and anchored by the heavy, solid hearths at their centers. With their exteriors open under overhanging eaves, their closed centers, and their predominantly horizontal orientations, they open down and out in section and massing, being directed toward the horizon, the earth-line. In addition, Wright's Prairie-period houses were pyramidal in form, often composed of incomplete or interrupted geometries with multiple edges and ambiguous, overlapping boundaries.

The clarity with which Wright distinguished ways of ordering space in public and private buildings is complemented by those elements shared by the two types. The fusion or interpenetration of the primary volumes is achieved by utilizing many of the same forms, such as squares and cruciforms, and ordering systems, such as symmetrical axes and tartan grid organizations. The entry sequence to both building types invariably is developed as a concealed, spiraling, unfolding, revelatory experience, reinforcing the sacred character of the center—the hearth as altar and central space as nave. Unity Temple, with its classroom annex (called by Wright "Unity House"), shows the manner in which Wright articulated a hierarchy of public and private spaces within the public building similar to that characterizing the private house, with the vertical public (sanctuary) volume centered on the introverted space and the horizontal private (classroom) volume centered on the fireplace.

In his designs for public and private buildings, Wright often utilized similar formal elements ordered in dissimilar ways. For example, the pier clusters of the Darwin Martin House have the exact same plan as the sanctuary

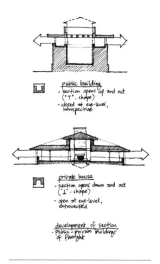

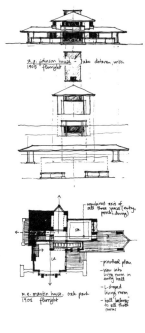

Prairie Period Buildings
analysis, development of opposite section types for public and private; drawn by author

Wright Prairie Houses
analysis, pyramidal, extroverted, solid masonry center, opening outward at eyelevel; drawn by author

volume of Unity Temple. The former measures six feet six inches square and is centered on a radiator with a lay-light above and surrounded on four sides by bookcases, while the latter is sixty-five feet square and centered on the sanctuary with skylights above and surrounded on four sides by two levels of balcony seating. The fact that the Unity Temple plan is precisely ten times the size of the Martin House piers cluster-plan is hardly coincidental. In Wright's work, geometric form is universally applied irrespective of building type, but scale and use determine the nature of the space.

The organization and formal expression of the service zones reveal the spatial hierarchies underlying Wright's buildings. In his public buildings, the service zones are collected into an "annex," a less perfect form, symmetrical along only one axis (as opposed to the main space, symmetrical along both axes), which is separated from the pure geometric form of the main space, to which it relates along its single axis of symmetry. The elevations of these annex spaces, often with simple punched windows and unarticulated wall surfaces, are not as rigorously composed as those of the main space—the rear of the Unity House is an example. This imperfect form, unarticulated elevations, and smaller size and mass result in the service volume having an appropriate deference toward and dependence on the primary volume.

In Wright's private houses, the service volumes are often ordered by a different compositional logic than the rest of the building. Typically in the Prairie period, the kitchens are ruled out of the order that organizes the primary rooms of the house within pure geometric forms; instead, the service spaces are collected in a nongeometric, disordered back side of the house, away from public view from the street. In the Robert Evans House, Wright placed the kitchen and service volumes outside the spatial bounds set by the four terminal piers that order the rest of the house. In addition, this service zone interrupts the pure cubic form of the central volume, engulfing one

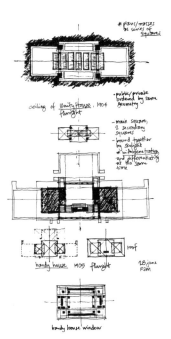
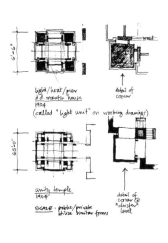

Wright's Public and Private
Prairie-period Buildings
analysis of similar forms at
dissimilar scales; drawn by author

corner as it attaches itself to the house. At the second floor, the bedrooms are held inside the central cubic volume of the house, but their more informal planning suggests their secondary importance relative to the rigorously ordered and axially aligned public rooms of the ground floor.

Rather than being a mistake or the result of careless disinterest on Wright's part, as it has been incorrectly characterized, this distinction between the geometrically and axially ordered primary volumes and the more casually or loosely organized service spaces in the Prairie Houses is clearly intentional. Wright, with his astonishing formal skills and relentless pursuit of perfection, could relatively easily have placed the kitchen and other service elements within the same geometrically and axially ordered envelope that held the primary volumes of the house. But if he had done so, our ability to recognize and experience the relationship between the service spaces and the primary spaces they served would have been lost. In all his buildings, Wright constructed a hierarchy of public, private, and service spaces, giving spatial form to this hierarchy in plan, interior volume, and exterior form.

Darwin Martin House
period photograph of a typical pier cluster, containing structural piers, bookcases, leaded-glass windows, lay lights, electric lamps, poles for curtains separating rooms, and radiator heating unit at center

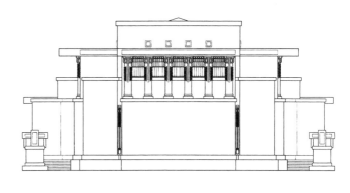

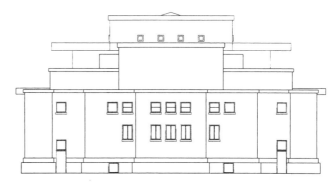

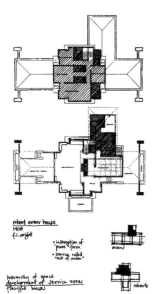

robert evans house
1908
f.l.wright

· interruption of
pure form

· service noted
"out of order"

hierarchy of space
development of service zones
(wright house)

Unity Temple
north elevation of sanctuary
(front public entry and street)
and south elevation of classroom
building (back and service);
drawn under supervision of
author

Robert W. Evans House
analysis, hierarchy of space—
public, private, and service;
service zone is placed outside of
primary geometric order; drawn
by author

FORM, STRUCTURE, AND MATERIAL

A particularly complex aspect of Wright's architecture is the relationship
between the two most fundamental components of the act of building—the
space/form and the structure/material with which it is made. As Wright's
contemporary Paul Valery wrote in 1894, "What we call space is relative to
the existence of whatever structures we may choose to conceive. The architectural structure interprets space, and leads to hypotheses on the nature of
space."[48] Throughout his career, Wright engaged in a constant search for a
comprehensive order that would encompass both *composition* and *construction*, and order similar to the fusion of structure, material, form, and
space that Wright found in his studies of nature. The internally integrated
forms of natural objects such as the crystalline geometries of rock formations, which Wright called "proof of nature's matchless architectural principles," and the dynamic structure of the sahuaro cactus, which Wright called
"a perfect example of reinforced building construction," exhibit the simplicity that results from a coherence of composition and construction order.[49] As
Wright wrote, "There is only one way to get that simplicity.... And that way
is, on principle, by way of *construction* developed as architecture."[50]

This principle can be seen throughout Wright's career as he developed
forms from the order inherent in each particular system of construction he
engaged. In the cottage built for Walter Gerts in 1902, typical of the wood-
clad Prairie Houses, a formal and structural tension is developed between
the one-story wood frame of the vertical four-inch square posts spaced at

three-foot intervals (exposed on the interior between plastered panels and on the exterior between the windows that run in a continuous band under the roof) and the exterior cladding of horizontal wood boards one foot in width.

In the Samuel Freeman House of 1923, typical of the California concrete-block houses, the sixteen-inch grid of the reinforced concrete-block wall system organizes, both horizontally and vertically, the spacing of everything, including the steel window mullions, the wood floor and roof joists, the concrete floor joints, and the wood-panel ceilings.

In the Herbert Jacobs House of 1936, typical of the early Usonian Houses, the roof is supported by a composite wall system that includes brick piers, wood posts between full-height glazed doors, and solid wood panels made of a plywood core with board and batten siding on both sides. These materials are both structure and finish and are exposed inside and out.

In the house built for Raymond Carlson in 1950, a late Usonian House that reveals the continued influence of traditional Japanese architecture on Wright's work, Wright returned to the four-inch-square wood frame, spaced both horizontally and vertically on a four-foot-four-inch grid (or a half-module, two-foot two-inch) and exposed on exterior and interior between insulated infill panels and glass.

Yet Wright did not always literally reveal all structural members, as he did in the above examples; in fact, he continually experimented throughout his career with different building systems and materials, searching for those that would respond plastically to his spatial ideas, often resulting in the buildings exhibiting more ambiguous "readings" of their underlying constructive order.

In the Ward Willits House of 1901 and the Thomas Hardy House of 1905, typical of the plaster-clad Prairie Houses, the posts between the continuous windows at the second floor reveal the wood "balloon" or braced frames

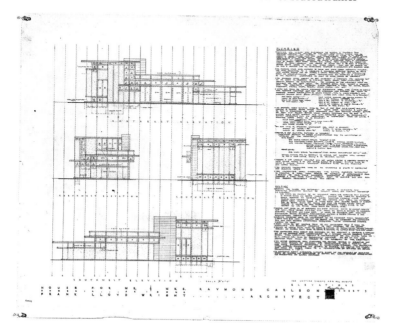

Raymond Carlson House
Phoenix, Arizona, 1950;
elevations showing wood frame
exposed on exterior, with stucco
plaster panels and glazing
between

with which these houses were structured. And yet, unlike the Gerts and Carlson houses mentioned above, this "revelation" is not complete; that is, the upper window posts reveal only a portion of the framing, the major part of it remaining hidden beneath the sheathing and plaster, inside and out. When it is also noted that the floor line between the two stories of the houses is suppressed, these houses may be understood to reveal the order of—rather than literally expose—the balloon-frame system: the regular spaced rhythm of continuous vertical wood members running vertically from foundation to roof, past the upper floor joists. Wright applied vertical wood-trim boards on the houses' exteriors, over the plaster, aligned with and nailed through to the matching vertical framing members underneath, reinforcing the ambiguity of the resulting form as being both monolithic and articulated.

Wright's efforts to base his architecture on the order inherent in the system of building construction were inflected by his simultaneous attempts to resolve both monolithic mass and articulated elements within a single form. The ambiguity that thereby characterized many of his works was intentional and recalls Friedrich Froebel's requirement that forms "must be simple and multiform."[51] The manner in which a building was constructed and the materials of which it was made were bound up in this endeavor; it is therefore not surprising that Wright so frequently turned to composite systems of construction, often combining wood and brick, brick and steel, steel and concrete, among others.

Wright's architecture engaged both earth and sky—the heavy, homogeneous, stereotomic mass complemented the light, heterogeneous, and tectonic elements. Wright bonded these seemingly opposed ways of building with occupied, experienced space. It is interesting to note here that the two architectures Wright admired most, the heavy, earthbound Maya and the light, articulately framed Japanese, share the characteristic of being without glass; in both, space is continuous from exterior to interior, palpably present in the shadow of the masonry lintel and the frame roof.

Thomas Hardy House
Racine, Wisconsin, 1905; view
from street

Darwin Martin House
period photograph of exterior,
view from the street

Larkin Building
Chicago, Illinois, 1902; period
photograph of exterior, view
from street

In Wright's work the resolution of monolithic mass and articulated elements reached a peak in the brick, steel, and concrete constructions of the Larkin Building of 1902 and the Darwin Martin House of 1903, which not coincidentally mark the arrival of Wright's mature system of design. Both buildings are composed of and structured by piers, with beams and floors spanning between them. There are no punched openings: glass is deeply set in between piers or part of a screen running under the roof overhang—always in shadow. The *piers* that Wright utilized so often, and built of many materials, are wonderfully ambiguous elements: both *column* and *wall*. When, as in both these buildings, the piers are constructed of brick, with its strong horizontal articulation, they can rise vertically straight to the roof yet simultaneously be fused horizontally to the neighboring brick walls.

The potential for invention inherent in these ambiguous elements can be seen in the Larkin Building, where the piers at the four corners of the preliminary design were expanded to become freestanding stairs and ventilation shafts in the development of the design. According to Wright, this joining of structure and service, made possible by the ambiguous character of the pier, saved the building as architecture.[52] The idea that structure could contain service space was of great significance for Wright's work and is apparent in the double beams housing ventilation ducts in the Larkin Building, the pier clusters housing heating units in the Darwin Martin House, the four corner piers housing ventilation shafts in Unity Temple, the central structural shaft housing all services in the "tap-root" skyscrapers, and the service-filled structures of the Usonian Houses, among others. (This concept would have similar importance in the later work of Louis I. Kahn.)

Wright's brick Prairie buildings most clearly exhibit the structural ambiguities that resulted from his attempted resolution of mass and frame. The Larkin Building had a composite structural system, with exterior piers of load-bearing brick and an interior steel-frame structure, horizontal and vertical, which for formal as much as safety reasons was entirely encased in brick or concrete, except for the steel beams of the glass-roofed conservatory, which are left exposed. The result was a building that was structurally "expressive" yet did not reveal the actual steel structure—nor did Wright feel it necessary that it should. Wright's concept of the coherence between (spatial) composition and (structural) construction did not require the literal exposure of structure. As Wright wrote, "Why should you always expose structure? I call it *indecent exposure*."[53]

This is perhaps best seen in the way Wright constructed the many examples of what he felt to be his great structural rediscovery and contribution to modern building: the cantilever. He valued the cantilever for the *space* it at once liberated and defined, not for any revelation of literal structure it might allow. In the Robie House, the heroic extension of the roof cantilever above the main floor is made possible structurally by steel beams hidden within the depth of the roof. Though unexposed, these steel beams are subtly present in the dropped ceilings along each edge of the extended living-dining room: on both exterior and interior, the steel beams are transformed into a spatial experience. This is related to Joseph Connors's statement "Wright's reputation as a great innovator in the realm of structure has obscured the

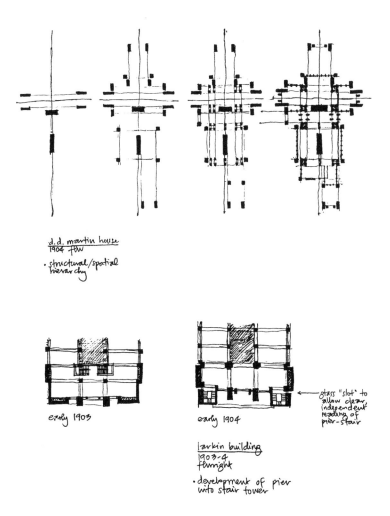

d.d. martin house
1904 flw

· structural/spatial
hierarchy

early 1903

early 1904

glass "slot" to
allow clear,
independent
reading of
pier-stair

larkin building
1903-4
flwright

· development of pier
into stair tower

fact that he was also a brilliant visual psychologist."[54]

The steel that frames all the horizontal planes of the Robie House is never exposed; it is revealed through the spatial freedom it allows. The uppermost floor, which floats over the flowing horizontal planes of the main floor, the balcony that effortlessly spans the enormous length of the street facade, and the roof that cantilevers at its ends are all examples of the structural steel frame made present as space for inhabitation in the Robie House.

Wright did not see structure itself as separate and different from or more important than the other materials of construction. He used the term "structure" to refer to geometric formal and spatial order; load-bearing elements were undifferentiated from construction in general. Wright wrote: "In design, that element we call structure is primarily the pure form, an organization in a very definite manner of parts and elements into a larger unity."[55] Thus all building material, including structural material, was to be *structured* by the underlying spatial order of the design.

Wright said he worked "in the nature of materials,"[56] but this "nature" was profoundly inflected by the overall spatial and experiential intention of the design. In the Robie House, there is a wonderful play between the vertical,

Martin House
analysis, pier as space-making device, above; drawn by author

Larkin Building
evolution of corner design, below; drawn by author

Frederick Robie House
exterior view from street corner
to southwest

Larkin Building
period photograph of interior of
central light court

load-bearing brick piers and the brick-clad balcony, which appears to be a type of beam leaping across the distance between the piers. This great span is clearly an "unnatural" use of brick, which has no inherent spanning capacity when laid in a running bond; the steel that is doing the real work of supporting the span is not seen. Wright was not interested in the literal expression of a material's constructive nature. (In this aspect alone, Louis I. Kahn, who otherwise was perhaps Wright's truest disciple, would not follow Wright, for Kahn felt exposure of structure in construction was an ethical imperative.)

What Wright did employ, with unmatched skill, was the capacity of each material to characterize spatial experience. Wright used an extremely long and thin brick (called "Roman brick"), and he had the vertical joints finished flush to the face of the brick and used brick-colored mortar, effectively making the vertical joint disappear, while he had the horizontal joints raked or cut in deeply, resulting in the subtle but all-pervasive horizontal shadow pattern. For Wright, this exaggerated horizontal expression was the more architectural interpretation of the "nature" of the brick, characterizing space and experience within the larger order of the design, and occasionally contradicting expectations that he himself had set up; the vertical brick piers of the Robie House demonstrated a "normative," load-bearing use of brick and as such served as the perfect foil for the mysteriously floating brick balcony that spanned between them.

One material proved perfectly "plastic," able to be formed into any shape, and fully self-supporting: reinforced concrete. In Unity Temple, Wright constructed a building of a single material that was completely responsive to his formal and spatial ideas. This remarkable building gives evidence of Wright's affinity for the homogeneous plastic nature of concrete: The fusion of horizontal and vertical elements, the continuous folded surfaces woven together by the lines of wood trim, the monolithic material exposed both inside and outside all make Unity Temple the most perfect expression of Wright's design system in the Prairie period.

Yet Wright was often critical of concrete's inherent lack of integral order; the type of modular order evident in the brick that he had utilized to combine the monolithic and the elemental. In 1928, twenty years after the completion of Unity Temple, Wright wrote, "Here in the conglomerate named *concrete* we find a plastic material that yet has found no medium of expression that would allow it to take plastic form."[57] Though the walls of Unity Temple had in fact been cast in repetitively used wooden forms, Wright sought a more direct revelation of the construction module and the rhythm of the hidden steel bars—the internal balance between the tensile (steel) and compressive (concrete) components. He achieved this with the elemental building components and modular construction grid of his precast concrete-block system, initially conceived in 1906 for the Harry Brown House project and first utilized by Wright in his California concrete-block houses of 1923. [58]

Wright returned to reinforced cast-in-place concrete as a monolithic plastic mass where, as he wrote, "the unit-system may be abandoned,"[59] in such 1950s structures as the Guggenheim Museum, the Annunciation Greek Orthodox Church, the Kalita Humphreys Theatre, and the Marin County Civic Center. Yet, in the Usonian Houses of the same period, Wright utilized concrete block, brick, or wood as their primary construction materials, and here the unit-system was retained. In his late work, Wright invariably constructed public buildings of monolithic cast-in-place concrete, while private houses were constructed of elemental, modular materials.

The almost total lack of human scale, order, and formal control that has been noted in Wright's late public buildings (and more extravagant private commissions) is unquestionably related to the unlimited formal capacity and lack of integral modular order of the cast concrete used in their construction. At the same time, the balance of subtlety, invention, order, and human scale maintained by the Usonian Houses must be related to the integral modular order characteristic of their materials: concrete block, brick, and wood.

Only when he combined concrete with modular materials, such as in the Johnson Wax Buildings and the Price Tower, was Wright able to attain the same balance in the larger buildings that he continually maintained in the Usonian Houses. We should remember that in Fallingwater, the large house that paralleled the development of the first Usonian House, Wright employed both cast-in-place concrete slabs and locally quarried stone walls, giving the house its famous combination of internal intimacy and external expansion into nature. In the columns of the workroom at Johnson Wax, cast-in-place concrete reached a level of structural ingenuity and formal brilliance rarely matched in Wright's work or that of any other architect. It is not coincidental that these columns were cast as modular elements rather than as parts of a monolithic mass.

Unity Temple remains the only large building constructed completely of cast-in-place concrete to achieve spatial and formal perfection. According to Wright's principles, material was to be structured by an underlying spatial order. Only the remarkably rigorous geometric order of Wright's Prairie period proved capable of controlling and directing the limitless formal possibilities of cast-in-place concrete.

The modular grid present in Wright's best work is used as a method of both *formal* and *economic* control. His descriptions of Unity Temple made clear the economic intentions: "The wooden forms or molds in which concrete buildings must at that time be cast were always the chief item of expense, so to repeat the use of a single [concrete] form as often as possible was necessary." Wright also held that appropriate ornament came from the revelation of the nature of the material, the method of its making, and its integral structural module: "Ornament meaning not only *surface qualified by human imagination* but imagination giving *natural pattern* to structure."[60]

Wright was concerned with how to put things together, how to construct architecture. Such construction required a spatial structure that evolved out of the programmatic activities and intended experience of the design and that reflected the modular rhythm natural to the materials of construction. It was in this sense that Wright wrote, "All form is a matter of structure."[61]

DWELLING, ARCHITECTURE, AND NATURE

For Wright, dwelling took place between earth and sky—on the horizon. The house was the place of dwelling, and it was made by creating a sense of *shelter*. The roof established the horizon line, what Wright called "the true

Unity Temple
exterior detail of sanctuary
corner

Unity Temple
interior view of sanctuary from
behind pulpit

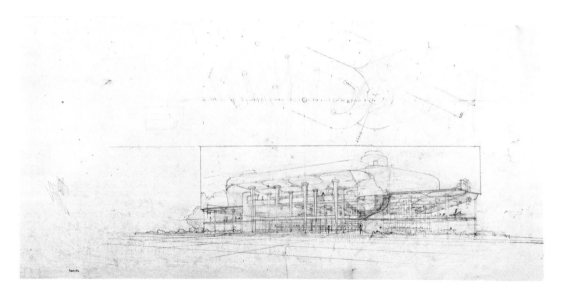

earth-line of human life, indicative of freedom,"[62] and acted as a datum that allowed variation underneath: the roof protected, enclosed, and freed the inhabitants. The low, overhanging roof was balanced by the tall, vertical chimney, and, as Wright wrote, the shadows within set off the sparkling light of "the fire burning deep in the masonry of the house itself."[63] By bringing the horizon into architecture with his long, low walls and overspreading roof, anchored by the vertical piers and hearth, Wright's houses merged with nature. As Wright wrote, "Buildings perform their highest function in relation to human life within and the natural efflorescence without; and to develop and maintain the harmony for a true chord between them, making the building in this sense a sure foil for life."[64] Architecture, the work of mankind, and landscape, the work of nature, were thus joined in form and fused in experience.

The only photograph of a building not designed by Wright himself that he displayed on the wall of his Taliesin studio was one portraying the Potala, the Dalai Lama's residence in Lhasa, Tibet.[65] It showed the building's masonry walls rising up from the shear face of the natural rock bluff, the window openings developing as vertical scorings in the wall and becoming continuous bands under the overhanging horizontal roofs. The massing of the whole, with its terminal towers and layered roofs, seemed to have grown naturally from the site: it is hardly surprising that Wright deeply admired this great structure.

The boundary between inside and outside was obscured or multiplied by Wright. In his houses, the various elements that define the edges are not held within a precise pure form; while the massing is often pyramidal, with walls decreasing in height with their distance from the central hearth, the boundaries demarcated by the roof, windows, piers, walls, and terraces are all at varying distances from the hearth, resulting in an interpenetration and interdependence of interior and exterior space: the definition of a place without bounds. Wright gave the entire site a geometric order; the low walls, terraces, stairs, piers, and planters anchored the house to the earth, project-

Johnson Wax Building
Racine, Wisconsin, 1936; section · perspective study, showing "dendriform" columns of Great Workroom

Dalai Lama's Palace
Potala, Lhasa, Tibet, ca. 1600; the only photograph of a work of architecture by another that Wright had hung on the walls of his Taliesin drafting room

ing the grid of the house out into the landscape and simultaneously pulling the landscape into the house.

These outreaching walls and stairs, punctuated by terminal piers with planters, allow a slow and incremental entry sequence by which one is taken into the house step by step. The house is woven into the site through the varying views one is given during this spiraling sequence and in the haptic experience of moving along the walls and under the roofs. The ends of these elements establish various boundaries and thresholds, or, as Wright wrote, "Terminal masses are most important as to form. Nature will show this to you in her own fabrications. Take good care of the terminals the rest will take care of itself."[66] This may be understood as a marking of the ground, an establishment of territory and bounds within which overlapping interiors can be formed.

Wright utilized roofs as shadow makers and defined the place of inhabitation as the space made by the shadows on the earth. Wright's domestic interiors were relatively dimly lit, not flooded with light. In his houses there are large amounts of glass, but the shadows cast by overhanging roofs and deep-set piers allow an increase in openness without simultaneous increase

John Pew House
Shorewood Hills, Wisconsin, 1938; perspective view from lake, showing house anchored to landscape by outlying walls

Lloyd Lewis House
Libertyville, Illinois, 1939; aerial perspective, showing garden penetrating into space under house

in light level. Both the pinwheel and cruciform plan shapes are directed toward the extension of single rooms out into nature, giving light, views, and spatial extension on three sides. As Wright wrote, "I began to see a building primarily not as a cave but as broad shelter in the open, related to vista; vista without and vista within."[67] The vista without is limited by the leaded- and stained-glass windows, which allow light in but distort views out. These prismatic designs capture and retain light, holding it within their sparkling geometries, so that the enclosure limiting the vista within is perceived as lines woven in space.

"Shadow itself is of the light," Wright wrote.[68] This particular quality of light and shadow is related to the Japanese culture of "half-light" described by Juni-chiro Tanizaki; it is interesting that in his book *In Praise of Shadows*, Tanizaki mentions only one building by name—Wright's Imperial Hotel in Tokyo—which he praises for its "indirect lighting."[69] The important part played by light in characterizing the experience of Wright's public buildings may be exemplified by the contrast between the dimly lit entry "cloisters" of Unity Temple and the bright, top-lit sanctuary space; the person entering can see into the main space without being seen and thus can make a discreet and comfortable entrance.

In Wright's work there is a distinction between urban and suburban buildings. His various apartment-house designs for urban settings tend to have the cubic massing typical of his public buildings. The few individual houses built in urban settings reveal the complicated relationship between ordering concepts and site situations in Wright's work. The Thomas Hardy House presents a sheer vertical facade to the street, and projects walls and terraces as it opens to the lake behind. In the Emil Bach House of 1915, Wright collected the public spaces of the lower floor into a compact closed cube and sent the bedrooms on the upper floor sailing out in cantilevers to either side. This intersection between public and private is summarized and

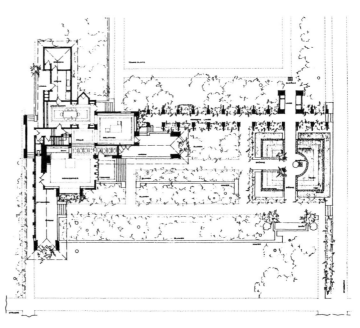

W. E. Martin House
Oak Park, Illinois, 1902; site plan as published; note manner in which house is set to the side, left, and garden takes up center of composition; entry sequence starts at sidewalk, lower right, and ends in dining room, upper left

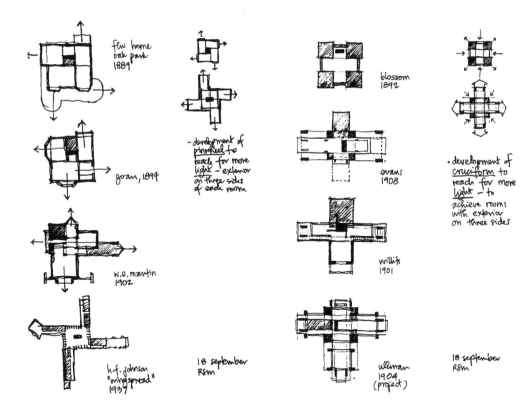

few home
oak park
1889

blossom
1892

— development of
cruciform to
reach for more
light — to
achieve rooms
with exterior
on three sides

goan, 1894

— development of
pinwheel to
reach for more
light — exterior
on three sides
of each room

evans
1908

w.e. martin
1902

willits
1901

h.f. johnson
"wingspread"
1937

18 september
RSM

ullman
1904
(project)

18 september
RSM

perfected in the Usonian Houses, with the tight, closed elevations on the street and their open, fully glazed elevations in the rear, wrapped around their gardens.

Wright was continuously interested in the development of the American city and suburb; as early as 1901, simultaneous to the publication of the *Ladies' Home Journal* houses and the design of the first Prairie Houses, Wright made his first proposal for the design of a suburban community. The extraordinary quadruple Block Plan envisioned a fully developed suburb for railway and automobile commuter living—this only a few years after the invention of the automobile. This plan, with its subtle social compositions based on the pinwheel arrangements of groups of houses, is one of the richest spatial visions ever proposed for the American way of life.

Other suburb plans followed, and Wright's individual house commissions were utilized to test out these collective ordering ideas. Wright engaged the American planning grid, the streets, and the rectangular building lots in his house plans, giving the landscape, with its driveways, garages, gardens, terraces, pavilions, porte cocheres, and sidewalks, an order linked to the house. This interest in the community as an organic part of the landscape culminated in Wright's Broadacre City proposal of 1932 and the hundreds of Usonian Houses designed and built during the next thirty years. The spatial and social richness of all these proposals sets Wright apart from every other American architect practicing during this century, and the loss of the opportunity to give the developing suburbs an appropriate and precise spatial and social definition is only now being fully felt.

Development of Pinwheel and
Cruciform Plan Types
analysis, relation to landscape
and sunlight; drawn by author

Thomas Hardy House
perspective view from lake below
house, top

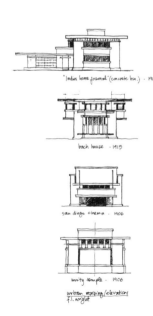

**Urban Buildings from
Prairie Period**
analysis, elevations; drawn by
author, bottom left

Emil Bach House
Chicago, Illinois 1915; period
photograph of exterior view from
street, bottom right

"The intellect is a whole and demands integrity in every work. This is resisted equally by a man's devotion to a single thought and by his ambition to combine too many."—*Ralph Waldo Emerson*[70]

The ordering principles that lie behind Wright's work represent a comprehensive, idealized view of the world and the place of mankind within it. For Wright, these principles "in-form" the making of architecture, a discipline to be pursued relentlessly with what Leonardo da Vinci called "obstinate rigor."[71] Perfection is possible only within the limits of a discipline: the "law and order" of architecture to which Wright frequently referred.[72] Wright understood that buildings are embodiments of ideals, spirit, and character; that people's motives are made visible in the works that they build. Integrity, for Wright, was sought in architecture as in life, for "architecture is life; or at least it is life itself taking form and therefore it is the truest record of life as it was lived in the world yesterday, as it is lived today, or ever will be lived."[73]

For Wright, the experience of architecture was a spiritual matter: "Reality is spirit—the essence brooding just behind all aspect. Seize it!"[74] His vision of life was not "symbolized" in his buildings; it was embodied and brought into being by the occupation of space. The meanings of Wright's buildings are made present in the experience of their spaces; the buildings do not "re-present" some absent or displaced meanings but engage the rituals of daily life. Wright's principles have both formal and ethical meaning, and his ideals have a timeless validity.

Some may believe that Wright's work is not relevant to us today, that mankind's situation changes and therefore mankind changes. Indeed, many contemporary concepts of space and inhabitation exhibit an unsettling spiritual vacuity; space is formed and generated not by the life of mankind but by forces of economic production thinly disguised as fashion and heavily armed with "theory." Wright's buildings are an indictment of our ever-

Quadruple Block Plan
1903; pinwheel configuration of four houses on shared square block; layering from public street to private house, with views from houses directed away from immediate neighbors

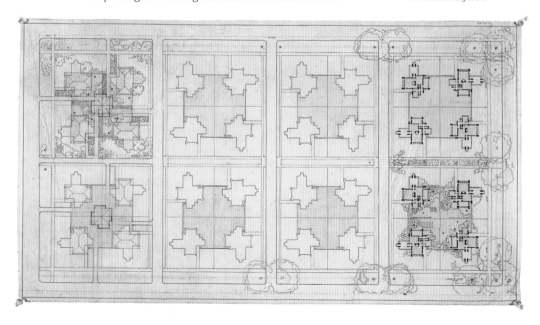

expanding "pluralism," our incessant style-changes, and our increasingly "disturbed plans,"[75] all indicative of an almost complete absence of principles and ideals. Wright's buildings, through their reinterpretations of and reverence for the great architecture of the past, remind us that the nature of mankind remains the same.

This does not mean, however, that new forms may not evolve: in this, Wright's work is exemplary. While the principles underlying the designs are eternal and exact, as Wright wrote, the formal possibilities are infinite: "There is a fluid, elastic period of becoming, as in the plan, when possibilities

are infinite. New effects may then originate from the idea or principle that conceives."[76] Architecture began again, in that Wright constructed new forms for ancient meanings: he was "original," both in returning to origins and in creating something new and unique.

Wright's genius lay in resolving the contradictory demands of elemental and integrative design intentions. By balancing and resolving spatial and experiential dichotomies, Wright gave form to his vision of life. He designed by resolving opposed ideas, and all the great oppositions or paradoxes of architecture may be seen in his work: horizontal/vertical; monolithic/articulated; heavy/light; solid/void; static/dynamic; open/closed; inside/outside; architecture/nature; public/private; order/experience; and many others. Wright's achievement of such paradoxical resolutions in his work remains astonishing.[77] Emerson wrote, "An inevitable dualism bisects nature, so that each thing is a half, and suggests another thing to make it whole."[78]

In the entry to the Oak Park Studio, Wright confronted the visitor with two doors exactly alike at opposite ends of a loggia. On entry, by occupying the space between, the inhabitant resolved the paradox: mankind's experience forms the center, giving space its meaning. Wright himself quoted Emerson as saying, "Excess of contrast, in genius, brings about a mighty equilibrium."[79] In Wright's architecture, the boundless is achieved through the bounded, the immeasurable is achieved through the measurable, and freedom is achieved through order. It is only through the resolution of these paradoxes in space and experience that mankind is able to truly dwell on earth. As Wright wrote:

> What is the reality here in this so familiar object we call the drinking glass? The answer is, reality is the space within into which you can put something. In other words, the idea. And so it is with architecture; so it is with your lives; and so it is with everything you can experience as reality.[80]

Oak Park Studio
interior view from entry foyer toward studio, with Wright's private office door to right and public entry from street to left

By Frank Lloyd Wright

In the Cause of Architecture
First Published: *Architectural Record*, March 1908

Radical though it be, the work here illustrated is dedicated to a cause conservative in the best sense of the word. At no point does it involve denial of the elemental law and order inherent in all great architecture; rather it is a declaration of love for the spirit of that law and order and a reverential recognition of the elements that made its ancient letter in its time vital and beautiful.

Primarily, Nature furnished the materials for architectural motifs out of which the architectural forms as we know them today have been developed, and, although our practice for centuries has been for the most part to turn from her, seeking inspiration in books and adhering slavishly to dead formulae, her wealth of suggestion is inexhaustible; her riches greater than any man's desire. I know with what suspicion the man is regarded who refers matters of fine art back to Nature. I know, that it is usually an ill advised return that is attempted, for Nature in external, obvious aspect is the usually accepted sense of the term and the nature that is reached. But given inherent vision there is no source so fertile, so suggestive, so helpful aesthetically for the architect as a comprehension of natural law. As Nature is never right for a picture so is she never right for the architect—that is, not readymade. Nevertheless, she has a practical school beneath her more obvious forms in which a sense of proportion may be cultivated, when Vignola and Vitruvius fail as they must always fail. It is there that he may develop that sense of reality that translated to his own field in terms of his own work will lift him far above the realistic in his art; there he will be inspired by sentiment that will never degenerate to sentimentality and he will learn to draw with a surer hand the ever-perplexing line between the curious and the beautiful.

A sense of the organic is indispensable to an architect; where can he develop it so surely as in this school? A knowledge of the relations of form and function lies at the root of his practice; where else can he find the pertinent object lessons Nature so readily furnishes? Where can he study the differentiations of form that go to determine character as he can study them in the trees? Where can that sense of inevitableness characteristic of a work of art be quickened as it may be by intercourse with nature in this sense?

Japanese art knows this school more intimately than that of any people. In common use in their language there are many words like the word edaburi which, translated as near as may be, means the formative arrangement of the branches of a tree. We have no such word in English, we are not yet sufficiently civilized to think in such terms, but the architect must not only learn to think in such terms but he must learn in this school to fashion his vocabulary for himself and furnish it in a comprehensive way with useful words as significant as this one.

For seven years it was my good fortune to be the understudy of a great teacher and a great architect, to my mind the greatest of his time Mr. Louis H. Sullivan.

Principles are not invented, they are not evolved by one man or one age, but Mr. Sullivan's perception and practice of them amounted to a revelation at a time when they were commercially inexpedient and all but lost to sight in current practice. The fine art sense of the profession was at that time practically dead; only glimmerings were perceptible in the work of Richardson and of Root.

Adler and Sullivan had little time to design residences. The few that were unavoidable fell to my lot outside of office hours. So largely, it remained for me to carry into the field of domestic architecture the battle they had begun in commercial building. During the early years of my own practice I found this lonesome work. Sympathizers of any kind were then few, and they were not found among the architects. I well remember how "the message" burned within me, how I longed for comradeship until I began to know the younger men and how welcome was Robert Spencer, and then Myron Hunt, and Dwight Perkins, Arthur Heun, George Dean, and Hugh Garden. Inspiring days they were, I am sure, for us all. Of late we have been too busy to see one another often, but the "New School of the Middle West" is beginning to be talked about and perhaps some day it is to be. For why not the same "Life" and blood in architecture that is the essence of all true art?

In 1894, with this text from Carlyle at the top of the page—"The Ideal is within thyself, the condition is but the stuff thou art to shape that same Ideal out of"—I formulated the following "propositions." I set them down here much as they were written then, although in the light of experience they might be stated more completely and succinctly.

Simplicity and Repose are qualities that measure the true value of any work of art.

But simplicity is not in itself an end nor is it a matter of the side of a barn but rather an entity with a graceful beauty in its integrity from which discord, and all that is meaningless, has been eliminated. A wildflower is truly simple. Therefore:

1. A building should contain as few rooms as will meet the conditions which give it rise and under which we live and which the architect should strive continually to simplify; then the ensemble of the rooms should be carefully considered that comfort and utility may go hand in hand with beauty. Beside the entry and necessary work rooms there need be but three rooms on the ground floor of any house, living room, dining room, and kitchen, with the possible addition of a "social office"; really there need be but one room, the living room, with requirements otherwise sequestered from it or screened within it by means of architectural contrivances.

2. Openings should occur as integral features of the structure and form, if possible, its natural ornamentation.

3. An excessive love of detail has ruined more fine things from the standpoint of fine art or fine living than any one human shortcoming—it is hopelessly vulgar. Too many houses, when they are not little stage settings or scene paintings, are mere notion stores, bazaars, or junk shops. Decoration is dangerous unless you understand it thoroughly and are satisfied that it means something good in the scheme as a whole, for the present you are usually better off without it. Merely that it "looks rich" is no justification for the use of ornament.

4. Appliances or fixtures as such are undesirable. Assimilate them together with all appurtenances into the design of the structure.

5. Pictures deface walls oftener than they decorate them. Pictures should be decorative and incorporated in the general scheme as decoration.

6. The most truly satisfactory apartments are those in which most or all of the furniture is built in as a part of the original scheme considering the whole as an integral unit.

[II]

There should be as many kinds (styles) of houses as there are kinds (styles) of people and as many differentiations as there are different individuals. A man who has individuality (and what man lacks it?) has a right to its expression in his own environment.

[III]

A building should appear to grow easily from its site and be shaped to harmonize with its surroundings if Nature is manifest there, and if not try to make it as quiet, substantial and organic as She would have been were the opportunity Hers. (In this I had in mind the barren town lots devoid of tree or natural incident, townhouses and board walks in evidence.)

We of the Middle West are living on the prairie. The prairie has a beauty of its own, and we should recognize and accentuate this natural beauty, its quiet level. Hence, gently sloping roofs, low proportions, quiet skylines, suppressed heavyset chimneys and sheltering overhangs, low terraces and outreaching walls sequestering private gardens.

[IV]

Colors require the same conventionalizing process to make them fit to live with that natural forms do; so go to the woods and fields for color schemes. Use the soft, warm, optimistic tones of earths and autumn leaves in preference to the pessimistic blues, purples, or cold greens and grays of the ribbon counter; they are more wholesome and better adapted in most cases to good decoration.

[V]

Bring out the nature of the materials, let their nature intimately into your scheme. Strip the wood of varnish and let it alone—stain it. Develop the natural texture of the plastering and stain it. Reveal the nature of the wood, plaster, brick, or stone in your designs, they are all by nature friendly and beautiful. No treatment can be really a matter of fine art when these natural characteristics are, or their nature is, outraged or neglected.

[VI]

A house that has character stands a good chance of growing more valuable as it grows older while a house in the prevailing mode, whatever that mode may be, is soon out of fashion, stale, and unprofitable.

Buildings like people must first be sincere, must be true, and then withal as gracious and lovable as may be.

Above all, integrity. The machine is the normal tool of our civilization, give it work that it can do well—nothing is of greater importance. To do this will be to formulate new industrial ideals, sadly needed.

These propositions are chiefly interesting because for some strange reason they were novel when formulated in the face of conditions hostile to them and because the ideals they phrase have been practically embodied in the buildings that were built to live up to them. The buildings of recent years have not only been true to them, but are in many cases a further development of the simple propositions so positively stated then.

Happily, these ideals are more commonplace now. Then the skylines of our domestic architecture were fantastic abortions, tortured by features that disrupted the distorted roof surfaces from which attenuated chimneys like lean fingers threatened the sky; the invariably tall interiors were cut up into box like compartments, the more boxes the finer the house, and "Architecture" chiefly consisted in healing over the edges of the curious collection of holes that had to be cut in the walls for light and air and to permit the occupant to get in or out. These interiors were always slaughtered with the butt and slash of the old plinth and corner block trim, of dubious origin, and finally smothered with horrible millinery.

That individuality in a building was possible for each homemaker, or desirable, seemed at that time to rise to the dignity of an idea. Even cultured men and women care so little for the spiritual integrity of their environment; except in rare cases they are not touched, they simply do not care for the matter so long as their dwellings are fashionable or as good as those of their neighbors and keep them dry and warm. A structure has no more meaning to them aesthetically than has the stable to the horse. And this came to me in the early years as a definite discouragement. There are exceptions, and I found them chiefly among American men of business with unspoiled instincts and untainted ideals. A man of this type usually has the faculty of judging for himself. He has rather liked the "idea" and much of the encouragement this work receives comes straight from him because the "common sense" of the thing appeals to him. While the "cultured" are still content with their small chateaux, colonial wedding cakes, English affectations, or French millinery, he prefers a poor thing but his own. He errs on the side of character, at least, and when the test of time has tried his country's development architecturally, he will have contributed his quota, small enough in the final outcome though it be; he will be regarded as a true conservator.

In the hope that some day America may live her own life in her own buildings, in her own way, that is, that we may make the best of what we have for what it honestly is or may become, I have endeavored in this work to establish a harmonious relationship between ground plan and elevation of these buildings, considering the one as a solution and the other an expression of the conditions of a problem of which the whole is a project. I have tried to establish an organic integrity to begin with, forming the basis for the subsequent working out of a significant grammatical expression and making the whole, as nearly as I could, consistent.

What quality of style the buildings may possess is due to the artistry with which the conventionalization as a solution and an artistic expression of a specific problem within these limitations has been handled. The types are largely a matter of personal taste and may have much or little to do with the American architecture for which we hope.

From the beginning of my practice, the question uppermost in my mind has been not "what style?" but "what is style?" and it is my belief that the chief value of the work illustrated here will be found in the fact that if in the face of our present day conditions any given type may be treated independently and imbued with the quality of style, then a truly noble architecture is a definite possibility, so soon as Americans really demand it of the architects of the rising generation.

I do not believe we will ever again have the uniformity of type which has characterized the so-called great "styles." Conditions have changed; our ideal is Democracy,

the highest possible expression of the individual as a unit not inconsistent with a harmonious whole. The average of human intelligence rises steadily, and as the individual unit grows more and more to be trusted we will have an architecture with richer variety in unity than has ever arisen before; but the forms must be born out of our changed conditions, they must be true forms, otherwise the best that tradition has to offer is only an inglorious masquerade, devoid of vital significance or true spiritual value.

The trials of the early days were many and at this distance picturesque. Workmen seldom like to think, especially if there is financial risk entailed; at your peril do you disturb their established processes mental or technical. To do anything in an unusual, even if in a better and simpler way, is to complicate the situation at once. Simple things at that time in any industrial field were nowhere at hand. A piece of wood without a molding was an anomaly; a plain wooden slat instead of a turned baluster a joke, the omission of the merchantable "grille" a crime; plain fabrics for hangings or floor covering were nowhere to be found in stock.

To become the recognized enemy of the established industrial order was no light matter, for soon whenever a set of my drawings was presented to a Chicago mill man for figures he would willingly enough unroll it, read the architect's name, shake his head, and return it with the remark that he was "not hunting for trouble"; sagacious owners and general contractors tried cutting out the name, but in vain, his perspicacity was rat-like, he had come to know "the look of the thing." So, in addition to the special preparation in any case necessary for every little matter of construction and finishing, special detail drawings were necessary merely to allow the things to be left off or not done and not only studied designs for every part had to be made but quantity surveys and schedules of millwork finished the contractors beside. This, in a year or two, brought the architect face to face with the fact that the fee for his service "established" by the American Institute of Architects was intended for something stock and shop, for it would not even pay for the bare drawings necessary for conscientious work.

The relation of the architect to the economic and industrial movement of his time, in any fine art sense, is still an affair so sadly out of joint that no one may easily reconcile it. All agree that something has gone wrong and except the architect be a plain factory magnate, who has reduced his art to a philosophy of old clothes and sells misfit or made over-ready to wear garments with commercial aplomb and social distinction, he cannot succeed on the present basis established by common practice. So, in addition to a situation already complicated for them, a necessarily increased fee stared in the face the clients who dared. But some did dare, as the illustrations prove.

The struggle then was and still is to make "good architecture," "good business." It is perhaps significant that in the beginning it was very difficult to secure a building loan on any terms upon one of these houses, now it is easy to secure a better loan than ordinary; but how far success has attended this ambition the owners of these buildings alone can testify. Their trials have been many, but each, I think, feels that he has as much house for his money as any of his neighbors, with something in the home intrinsically valuable besides, which will not be out of fashion in one lifetime and which contributes steadily to his dignity and his pleasure as an individual.

It would not be useful to dwell further upon difficulties encountered, for it is the common story of simple progression everywhere in any field; I merely wish to trace here the "motif" behind the types. A study of the illustrations will show that the buildings presented fall readily into three groups having a family resemblance; the low pitched hip roofs, heaped together in pyramidal fashion or presenting quiet, unbroken skylines; the low roofs with simple pediments countering on long ridges; and those topped with a simple slab. Of the first type, the Winslow, Henderson, Willits, Thomas, Heurtley, Heath, Cheney, Martin, Little, Gridley, Millard, Tomek, Coonley, and Westcott houses, the Hillside Home School and the Pettit Memorial Chapel are typical. Of the second type, the Bradley, Hickox, Davenport and Dana houses are typical. Of the third, atelier for Richard Bock, Unity Church, the concrete house of *The Ladies' Home Journal*, and other designs in process of execution. The Larkin Building is a simple, dignified utterance of a plain, utilitarian type, with sheer brick walls and simple stone copings. The studio is merely an early experiment in "articulation."

Photographs do not adequately present these subjects. A building has a presence, as has a person, that defies the photographer, and the color so necessary to the complete expression of the form is necessarily lacking; but it will be noticed that all the structures stand upon their foundations to the eye as well as physically. There is good, substantial preparation at the ground for all the buildings and it is the first grammatical expression of all the types. This preparation, or water table, is to these buildings, what the stylobate was to the ancient Greek temple. To gain it, it was necessary to reverse the established practice of setting the supports of the building to the outside of the wall and to set them to the inside, so as to leave the necessary support for the outer base. This was natural enough and good enough construction but many an owner was disturbed by private information from the practical contractor to the effect that he would have his whole house in the cellar if he submitted to it. This was at the time a marked innovation though the most natural thing in the world and to me, to this day, indispensable.

With this innovation established, one horizontal stripe of raw material, the foundation wall above ground, was eliminated and the complete grammar of type one made possible. A simple, unbroken wall surface from foot to level of second story sill was thus secured, a change of material occurring at that point to form the simple frieze that characterizes the earlier buildings. Even this was frequently omitted, as in the Francis apartments and many

other buildings, and the wall was let alone from base to cornice or eaves.

"Dress reform houses" they were called, I remember, by the charitably disposed. What others called them will hardly bear repetition.

As the wall surfaces were thus simplified and emphasized the matter of fenestration became exceedingly difficult and more than ever important, and often I used to gloat over the beautiful buildings I could build if only it were unnecessary to cut holes in them; but the holes were managed at first frankly as in the Winslow house and later as elementary constituents of the structure grouped in rhythmical fashion, so that all the light and air and prospect the most rabid client could wish would not be too much from an artistic standpoint; and of this achievement I am proud. The groups are managed, too, whenever required, so that overhanging eaves do not shade them, although the walls are still protected from the weather. Soon the poetry crushing characteristics of the guillotine window, which was then firmly rooted, became apparent, and single-handed I waged a determined battle for casements swinging out, although it was necessary to have special hardware made for them as there was none to be had this side of England. Clients would come ready to accept any innovation but "those swinging windows," and when told that they were in the nature of the proposition and that they must take them or leave the rest, they frequently employed "the other fellow" to give them something "near," with the "practical" windows dear to their hearts.

With the grammar so far established, came an expression pure and simple, even classic in atmosphere, using that much abused word in its best sense; implying, that is, a certain sweet reasonableness of form and outline naturally dignified.

I have observed that Nature usually perfects her forms; the individuality of the attribute is seldom sacrificed; that is, deformed or mutilated by cooperative parts. She rarely says a thing and tries to take it back at the same time. She would not sanction the "classic" proceeding of, say, establishing an "order," a colonnade, then building walls between the columns of the order reducing them to pilasters, thereafter cutting holes in the wall and pasting on cornices with more pilasters around them, with the result that every form is outraged, the whole an abominable mutilation, as is most of the architecture of the Renaissance wherein style corrodes style and all the forms are stultified.

In laying out the ground plans for even the more insignificant of these buildings, a simple axial law and order and the ordered spacing upon a system of certain structural units definitely established for each structure, in accord with its scheme of practical construction and aesthetic proportion, is practiced as an expedient to simplify the technical difficulties of execution, and, although the symmetry may not be obvious, always the balance is usually maintained. The plans are as a rule much more articulate than is the school product of the Beaux Arts.

The individuality of the various functions of the various features is more highly developed; all the forms are complete in themselves and frequently do duty at the same time from within and without as decorative attributes of the whole. This tendency to greater individuality of the parts emphasized by more and more complete articulation will be seen in the plans for Unity Church, the cottage for Elizabeth Stone at Glencoe, and the Avery Coonley house in process of construction at Riverside, Illinois. Moreover, these ground plans are merely the actual projection of a carefully considered whole. The "architecture" is not "thrown up" as an artistic exercise, a matter of elevation from a preconceived ground plan. The schemes are conceived in three dimensions as organic entities, let the picturesque perspective fall how it will. While a sense of the incidental perspectives the design will develop is always present, I have great faith that if the thing is rightly put together in true organic sense with proportions actually right the picturesque will take care of itself. No man ever built a building worthy the name of architecture who fashioned it in perspective sketch to his taste and then fudged the plan to suit. Such methods produce mere scene-painting. A perspective may be a proof but it is no nurture.

As to the mass values of the buildings the aesthetic principles outlined in proposition III will account in a measure for their character.

In the matter of decoration the tendency has been to indulge it less and less, in many cases merely providing certain architectural preparation for natural foliage or flowers, as it is managed in, say, the entrance to the Lawrence house at Springfield. This use of natural foliage and flowers for decoration is carried to quite an extent in all the designs and, although the buildings are complete without this efflorescence, they may be said to blossom with the season. What architectural decoration the buildings carry is not only conventionalized to the point where it is quiet and stays as a sure foil for the nature forms from which it is derived and with which it must intimately associate, but it is always of the surface, never on it.

The windows usually are provided with characteristic straight line patterns absolutely in the flat and usually severe. The nature of the glass is taken into account in these designs as is also the metal bar used in their construction, and most of them are treated as metal "grilles" with glass inserted forming a simple rhythmic arrangement of straight lines and squares made as cunning as possible so long as the result is quiet. The aim is that the designs shall make the best of the technical contrivances that produce them.

In the main the ornamentation is wrought in the warp and woof of the structure. It is constitutional in the best sense and is felt in the conception of the ground plan. To elucidate this element in composition would mean a long story and perhaps a tedious one, though to me it is the most fascinating phase of the work, involving the true poetry of conception.

The differentiation of a single, certain simple form characterizes the expression of one building. Quite a different form may serve for another, but from one basic idea all the formal elements of design are in each case derived and held well together in scale and character. The form chosen may flare outward, opening flower like to the sky, as in the Thomas house; another, droop to accentuate artistically the weight of the masses; another be noncommittal or abruptly emphatic, or its grammar may be deduced from some plant form that has appealed to me, as certain properties in line and form of the sumach were used in the Lawrence house at Springfield; but in every case the motif is adhered to throughout so that it is not too much to say that each building aesthetically is cut from one piece of goods and consistently hangs together with an integrity impossible otherwise.

In a fine art sense, these designs have grown as natural plants grow, the individuality of each is integral and as complete as skill, time, strength, and circumstances would permit.

The method in itself does not of necessity produce a beautiful building, but it does provide a framework as a basis which has an organic integrity, susceptible to the architect's imagination and at once opening to him Nature's wealth of artistic suggestion, ensuring him a guiding principle within which he can never be wholly false, out of tune, or lacking in rational motif. The subtleties, the shifting blending harmonies, the cadences, the nuances are a matter of his own nature, his own susceptibilities and faculties.

But self denial is imposed upon the architect to a far greater extent than upon any other member of the fine art family. The temptation to sweeten work, to make each detail in itself lovable and expressive is always great, but that the whole may be truly eloquent of its ultimate function restraint is imperative. To let individual elements arise and shine at the expense of final repose is, for the architect, a betrayal of trust for buildings are the background or framework for the human life within their walls and a foil for the nature efflorescence without. So architecture is the most complete of conventionalizations and of all the arts the most subjective except music.

Music may be for the architect ever and always a sympathetic friend whose counsels, precepts, and patterns even are available to him and from which he need not fear to draw. But the arts are today all cursed by literature; artists attempt to make literature even of music, usually of painting and sculpture and doubtless would of architecture also were the art not moribund; but whenever it is done the soul of the thing dies and we have not art but something far less for which the true artist can have neither affection nor respect.

Contrary to the usual supposition this manner of working out a theme is more flexible than any working out in a fixed, historic style can ever be, and the individuality of those concerned may receive more adequate treatment within legitimate limitations. This matter of individuality puzzles many; they suspect that the individuality of the owner and occupant of a building is sacrificed to that of the architect who imposes his own upon Jones, Brown, and Smith alike. An architect worthy of the name has an individuality, it is true; his work will and should reflect it, and his buildings will all bear a family resemblance one to another. The individuality of an owner is first manifest in his choice of his architect, the individual to whom he entrusts his characterization. He sympathizes with his work; its expression suits him, and this furnishes the common ground upon which client and architect may come together. Then, if the architect is what he ought to be, with his ready technique he conscientiously works for the client, idealizes his client's character and his client's tastes, and makes him feel that the building is his as it really is to such an extent that he can truly say that he would rather have his own house than any other he has ever seen. Is a portrait, say by Sargent, any less a revelation of the character of the subject because it bears his stamp and is easily recognized by anyone as a Sargent? Does one lose his individuality when it is interpreted sympathetically by one of his own race and time who can know him and his needs intimately and idealize them, or does he gain it only by having adopted or adapted to his condition a ready made historic style which is the fruit of a seedtime other than his, whatever that style may be?

The present industrial condition is constantly studied in the practical application of these architectural ideals and the treatment simplified and arranged to fit modern processes and to utilize to the best advantage the work of the machine. The furniture takes the clean cut, straight line forms that the machine can render far better than would be possible by hand. Certain facilities, too, of the machine, which it would be interesting to enlarge upon, are taken advantage of and the nature of the materials usually revealed in the process.

Nor is the atmosphere of the result in its completeness new and hard. In most of the interiors there will be found a quiet, a simple dignity that we imagine is only to be found in the "old" and it is due to the underlying organic harmony, to the each in all and the all in each throughout. This is the modern opportunity to make of a building, together with its equipment, appurtenances, and environment, an entity which shall constitute a complete work of art, and a work of art more valuable to society as a whole than has before existed because discordant conditions endured for centuries are smoothed away; everyday life here finds an expression germane to its daily existence; an idealization of the common need sure to be uplifting and helpful in the same sense that pure air to breathe is better than air poisoned with noxious gases.

An artist's limitations are his best friends. The machine is here to stay. It is the forerunner of the democracy that is our dearest hope. There is no more important work before the architect now than to use this normal tool of civilization to the best advantage instead of prostituting it as he has hitherto done in reproducing with murderous ubiq-

uity forms born of other times and other conditions and which it can only serve to destroy.

The exteriors of these structures will receive less ready recognition perhaps than the interiors, and because they are the result of a radically different conception as to what should constitute a building. We have formed a habit of mind concerning architecture to which the expression of most of these exteriors must be a shock, at first more or less disagreeable, and the more so as the habit of mind is more narrowly fixed by so called classic training. Simplicity is not in itself an end; it is a means to an end. Our aesthetics are dyspeptic from incontinent indulgence in "French-ite" pastry. We crave ornament for the sake of ornament; cover up our faults of design with ornamental sensualities that were a long time ago sensuous ornament. We will do well to distrust this unwholesome and unholy craving and look to the simple line; to the clean though living form and quiet color for a time, until the true significance of these things has dawned for us once more. The old structural forms which up to the present time, have spelled "architecture" are decayed. Their life went from them long ago and new conditions industrially, steel and concrete and terra cotta in particular, are prophesying a more plastic art wherein as the flesh is to our bones so will the covering be to the structure, but more truly and beautifully expressive than ever. But that is a long story. This reticence in the matter of ornamentation is characteristic of these structures and for at least two reasons: first, they are the expression of an idea that the ornamentation of a building should be constitutional, a matter of the nature of the structure beginning with the ground plan. In the buildings themselves, in the sense of the whole there is lacking neither richness nor incident but their qualities are secured not by applied decoration, they are found in the fashioning of the whole, in which color, too, plays as significant a part as it does in an old, Japanese woodblock print. Second: because as before stated, buildings perform their highest function in relation to human life within and the natural efflorescence without; and to develop and maintain the harmony of a true chord between them making of the building in this sense a sure foil for life, broad, simple surfaces and highly conventionalized forms are inevitable. These ideals take the buildings out of school and marry them to the ground; make them intimate expressions or revelations of the exteriors, individualize them regardless of preconceived notions of style. I have tried to make their grammar perfect in its way and to give their forms and proportions an integrity that will bear study, although few of them can be intelligently studied apart from their environment. So, what might be termed the democratic character of the exteriors is their first undefined offence the lack, wholly, of what the professional critic would deem architecture; in fact, most of the critic's architecture has been left out.

There is always a synthetic basis for the features of the various structures, and consequently a constantly accumulating residue of formulas, which becomes more and more useful; but I do not pretend to say that the perception or conception of them was not at first intuitive, or that those that lie yet beyond will not be grasped in the same intuitive way; but, after all, architecture is a scientific art, and the thinking basis will ever be for the architect his surety, the final court in which his imagination sifts his feelings.

The few draughtsmen so far associated with this work have been taken into the draughting room, in every case almost wholly unformed, many of them with no particular previous training and patiently nursed for years in the atmosphere of the work itself, until saturated by intimate association, at an impressionable age, with its motifs and phases, they have become helpful. To develop the sympathetic grasp of detail that is necessary before this point is reached has proved usually a matter of years, with little advantage on the side of the college trained understudy. These young people have found their way to me through natural sympathy with the work and have become loyal assistants. The members, so far, all told here and elsewhere, of our little university of fourteen years standing are: Marion Mahony, a capable assistant for eleven years; William Drummond, seven years; Francis Byrne, five years; Isabel Roberts, five years; George Willis, four years; Walter Griffin, four years; Andrew Willatzen, three years; Harry Robinson, two years; Charles E. White, Jr., one year; Erwin Barglebaugh and Robert Hardin, each one year; Albert McArthur, entering.

Others have been attracted by what seemed to them to be the novelty of the work, staying only long enough to acquire a smattering of form, then departing to sell a superficial proficiency elsewhere. Still others shortly develop a mastery of the subject, discovering that it is all just as they would have done it, anyway, and, chafing at the unkind fate that forestalled them in its practice, resolve to blaze a trail for themselves without further loss of time. It is urged against the more loyal that they are sacrificing their individuality to that which has dominated this work; but it is too soon to impeach a single understudy on this basis, for, although they will inevitably repeat for years the methods, forms, and habit of thought, even the mannerisms of the present work, if there is virtue in the principles behind it that virtue will stay with them through the preliminary stages of their own practice until their own individualities truly develop independently. I have noticed that those who have made the most fuss about their "individuality" in early stages, those who took themselves most seriously in that regard, were inevitably those who had least.

Many elements of Mr. Sullivan's personality in his art—what might be called his mannerisms—naturally enough clung to my work in the early years and may be readily traced by the casual observer; but for me one real proof of the virtue inherent in this work will lie in the fact that some of the young men and women who have given themselves up to me so faithfully these past years will some day contribute rounded individualities of their own and firms of their own devising to the new school.

This year, I assign to each a project that has been care-fully conceived in my own mind, which he accepts as a specific work. He follows its subsequent development through all its phases in drawing room and field, meeting with the client himself on occasion, gaining an all round development impossible otherwise, and insuring an enthusiasm and a grasp of detail decidedly to the best interest of the client. These privileges in the hands of selfishly ambitious or overconfident assistants would soon wreck such a system; but I can say that among my own boys it has already proved a moderate success, with every prospect of being continued as a settled policy in future.

Nevertheless, I believe that only when one individual forms the concept of the various projects and also determines the character of every detail in the sum total, even to the size and shape of the pieces of glass in the windows, the arrangement and profile of the most insignificant of the architectural members, will that unity be secured which is the soul of the individual work of art. This means that fewer buildings should be entrusted to one architect. His output will of necessity be relatively small—small, that is, as compared to the volume of work turned out in any one of fifty "successful offices" in America. I believe there is no middle course worth considering in the light of the best future of American architecture. With no more propriety can an architect leave the details touching the form of his concept to assistants, no matter how sympathetic and capable they may be, than can a painter entrust the painting in of the details of his picture to a pupil; for an architect who would do individual work must have a technique well developed and peculiar to himself, which, if he is fertile, is still growing with his growth. To keep everything "in place" requires constant care and study in matters that the old school practitioner would scorn to touch.

As for the future—the work shall grow more truly simple; more expressive with fewer lines, fewer forms; more articulate with less labor; more plastic; more fluent, although more coherent; more organic. It shall grow not only to fit more perfectly the methods and processes that are called upon to produce it, but shall further find whatever is lovely or of good repute in method or process, and idealize it with the cleanest, most virile stroke I can imagine. As understanding and appreciation of life matures and deepens, this work shall prophesy and idealize the character of the individual it is fashioned to serve more intimately, no matter how inexpensive the result must finally be. It shall become in its atmosphere as pure and elevating in its humble way as the trees and flowers are in their perfectly appointed way, for only so can architecture be worthy its high rank as a fine art, or the architect discharge the obligation he assumes to the public—imposed upon him by the nature of his own profession.

The Logic of the Plan

First Published: *Architectural Record*, January 1928

Plan! There is something elemental in the word itself. A pregnant plan has logic—is the logic of the building squarely stated. Unless it is the plan for a foolish fair.

A good plan is the beginning and the end, because every good plan is organic. That means that its development in all directions is inherent—inevitable.

Scientifically, artistically to foresee all is "to plan." There is more beauty in a fine ground plan than in almost any of its ultimate consequences.

In itself it will have the rhythms, masses, and proportions of a good decoration if it is the organic plan for an organic building with individual style—consistent with materials.

All is there seen—purpose, materials, method, character, style. The plan? The prophetic soul of the building-a building that can live only because of the prophecy that is the plan. But it is a map, a chart, a mere diagram, a mathematical projection before the fact, and, as we all have occasion to know, accessory to infinite crimes.

To judge the architect one need only look at his ground plan. He is master then and there, or never. Were all elevations of the genuine buildings of the world lost and the ground plans saved, each building would construct itself again. Because before the plan is a plan it is a concept in some creative mind. It is, after all, only a purposeful record of that dream, which saw the destined building living in its appointed place. A dream—but precise and practical, the record to be read by the like minded.

The original plan may be thrown away as the work proceeds—probably most of those for the most wonderful buildings in the world were, because the concept grows and matures during realization, if the mastermind is continually with the work. But that plan had first to be made. Ultimately it should be corrected and recorded.

But to throw the plans away is a luxury ill afforded by the organizations of our modern method. It has ruined owners and architects and enriched numberless contractors. Therefore, conceive the building in the imagination, not on paper but in the mind, thoroughly—before touching paper. Let it live there—gradually taking more definite form before committing it to the draughting board. When the thing lives for you-start to plan it with tools not before. To draw during conception or "sketch," as we say, experimenting with practical adjustments to scale, is well enough if the concept is clear enough to be firmly held. It is best to cultivate the imagination to construct and complete the building before working upon it with T square and triangle.

Working on it with triangle and T square should modify or extend or intensify or test the conception—complete the harmonious adjustment of its parts. But if the original concept is lost as the drawing proceeds, throw all away and begin afresh. To throw away a concept entirely to make way for a fresh one that is a faculty of the mind not

easily cultivated. Few have that capacity. It is perhaps a gift—but may be attained by practice. What I am trying to express is that the plan must start as a truly creative matter and mature as such. All is won or lost before anything more tangible begins.

The several factors most important in making the plans—after general purpose scheme or "project" are:

2nd—Materials
3rd—Building methods
4th—Scale
5th—Articulation
6th—Expression or Style

In the matter of scale, the human being is the logical norm because buildings are to be humanly inhabited and should be related to human proportions not only comfortably but agreeably. Human beings should look as well in the building or of it as flowers do.

People should belong to the building just as it should belong to them. This scale or unit of size of the various parts varies with the specific purpose of the building and the materials used to build it. The only sure way to hold all to scale is to adopt a unitsystem, unit lines crossing the paper both ways, spaced as predetermined, say 4'0" on centers—or 2'8" or whatever seems to yield the proper scale for the proposed purpose. Divisions in spacing are thus brought into a certain texture in the result; ordered scale in detail is sure to follow.

A certain *standardization* is established here at the beginning, like the warp in the oriental rug. It has other and economic values in construction. I have found this valuable in practice even in small houses. Experience is needed to fix upon the proper size of the unit for any particular building. Trained imagination is necessary to differentiate or syncopate or emphasize, to weave or play upon it consistently.

Scale is really proportion. Who can teach proportion? Without a sense of proportion, no one should attempt to build. This gift of sense must be the diploma Nature gave to the architect.

Let the architect cling, always, to the normal human figure for his scale and he cannot go so far wrong as Michelangelo did in St. Peter's in Rome. St. Peter's is invariably disappointing as a great building, for not until the eye deliberately catches a human figure for purpose of comparison does one realize that the building is vast. All the details are likewise huge and the sense of grandeur it might have had if the great masses were qualified by details kept to human scale—this effect of grandeur—is lost in the degradation of the human figure. A strange error for a sculptor to make.

The safest practice in proportion is not to attempt to allow for "perspective," stilting domes as he did, changing pitches of roofs as many do, and modifying natural lines and masses to meet certain views from certain vantage points as the Greeks are said to have done, but to make the constitution of the thing right in itself. Let the incidental perspectives fall when and how they will. Trust Nature to give proper values to a proper whole. The modifications she may make are better than any other. There is something radically wrong with a scheme that requires distortion to appear correct.

In the matter of materials. These also affect scale. The logical material under the circumstances is the most natural material for the purpose. It is usually the most beautiful—and it is obvious that sticks will not space the same as stones nor allow the same proportions as steel. Nor will the spacing adjustable to these be natural to made blocks or to slabs or to a plastic modeling of form.

Sticks of wood will have their own natural volume and spacing determined by standards of use and manufacture and the nature of both.

A wood plan is slender: light in texture, narrower spacing.

A stone or brick plan is heavy: black in masses, wider in spacing.

Combination of materials: lightness combined with massiveness.

A cast block building: such massing as is felt to be adequate to the sense of block and box and slab; more freedom in spacing.

The purely or physically plastic structure: center line of thin webbing with a flesh covering on either side; unit system may be abandoned.

Then there are the double wall constructions requiring great skill in spacing so that the interior shell will work simply with the outer shell. And there are as many others as there are combinations of all these.

But the more simple the materials used—the more the building tends toward a mono material building—the more nearly will "perfect style" reward an organic plan and ease of execution economize results. The more logical will the whole become.

A wood plan is seen in tile plan for the Coonley house at Riverside and in the plan for "D101 house."

A cast block and slab building: the plan for Unity Temple at Oak Park.

Brick plans: the plan for the D. D. Martin residence in Buffalo, and the Ullman house in Oak Park, Illinois.

A steel and glass plan for a skyscraper, concrete supports and floor slabs: this plan will be used later in this series to illustrate another article.

The purely "plastic" structure may be seen in the "Einstein Tower" by Mendelsohn and buildings by European Modernists.

A double wall construction, in this case of precast blocks, is seen in the Ennis house at Hollywood.

A thin concrete slab structure: the merchandise building in Los Angeles.

In the matter of building methods. These methods too are meantime shaping the plan. In the Coonley house—the 4'0" unit works with 16" centers as established in carpenter practice for the length of laths, the economical spacing of studs and nailing—bearings, standard lumber lengths.

In Unity Temple-the only limit was the mass of concrete that could withstand the violent changes of climate and remain related to human scale and easy construction. The box and blocks, however, determine the shape of every feature and every detail of the features, as it was all cast in "boxes."

So a unit suitable for timber construction was adopted as the false work in which its cast was made of lumber. Multiples of 16", syncopated, was the scale adopted.

In the Martin house, brick was used. Brick lends itself to articulation in plan and is an easy material to use architecturally. Bricks naturally make corners and the corners are easily used for play of light and shade. The Martin house is an organized brick pier building. It is when assembling groups of piers in rhythmical relation to the whole that brick comes out best according to its nature. A 7' 9" unit reduced by minor mullions to 3'9", was used, in the horizontal only. There are other views of brick as legitimate as this one, to be used according to the individual "taste" of the designer. The broken masses of textured walls, for instance.

In the steel and glass building there are no walls. The method yields best to suspended screens, shop fabricated. A mechanized fabric enters here to give the form and style that is Architecture. The structural supports and floor slabs in this case happen to be concrete. They could be protected steel as well. Planned on a 4' 0" unit, emphasis on alternate verticals. No emphasis on horizontals.

In the precast block building, the method of building wholly determines the form and style. This is a mono material structure planned on multiples of 16 inches square, both horizontal and vertical. No emphasis.

The slab building is an expression of another method. Cast slabs, set sidewise and lengthwise, and flatwise, making everything, as may be seen in the result planned on multiples of 7' 0".

Concerning articulation. The Ennis house will serve to illustrate the principle which, once grasped, is simple.

In the building, each separate portion of the building devoted to a special purpose asserts itself as an individual factor in the whole.

The dining room associated with terraces is one mass. The living room with bedroom attached, another mass standing at the center on a terrace of its own—the dominating feature of the group.

Mr. Ennis's bedroom, semidetached and used as a study or office, is another and terminal mass.

At the rear is the kitchen unit, a subordinate mass. All are connected by a gallery passing along the group at the rear. Finally the terrace wall ends in a detached mass to the rear of the lot-the garage and chauffeur's quarters.

A little study will show how each separate room makes its own characteristic contribution to the whole mass.

The completed whole crowns the end of a high ridge in Hollywood and is a precast slab block building woven together with steel.

These articulations are as obvious in the plan as in the perspective. The Coonley house is similarly articulate.

Articulate buildings of this type have their parallel in the music of Bach particularly, but in any of the true form masters in music.

It may be readily seen that in this particular direction lies infinite variety in expression. The sense of it is fundamental in any architectural release.

In the matter of expression and style.

As a matter of logic in the plan, it is easy to see there can be none except as the result of scale, materials, and building method. But with all that properly set, there is the important human equation at work in every move that is made. The architect weaves into it all his sense of the whole. He articulates—emphasizes what he loves.

No matter how technically faithful his logic may have been to his scale and materials and method—over and above all that, living in the atmosphere created by the orchestration of those matters, hovers the indefinable quality of style. Style emanating from the form, as seen by the man himself. And while it speaks to you of all those important matters, it leaves you imbued by dignity, grace, repose, gaiety, strength, severity, delicacy, and of rhythmical order, in a musical sense, as the master wills just as music does. Usually you hear music as you work. But not necessarily.

So every true building is of the quality of some man's soul, his sense of harmony and "fitness," which is another kind of harmony—more or less manifest in the fallible human process.

And his building will nobly stand, belonging to its site-breathing this message to the spirit quite naturally, so long as his work was well done or the course of human events does not inundate or human ignorance willfully destroy his building.

In the Nature of Materials: A Philosophy
First Published: *An Autobiography*, 1932

Our vast resources are yet new; new only because architecture as "rebirth" (perennial Renaissance) has, after five centuries of decline, culminated in the imitation of imitations, seen in our Mrs. Plasterbuilt, Mrs. Gablemore, and Miss Flat top American architecture. In general, and especially officially, our architecture is at long last completely significant of insignificance only. We do not longer have architecture. At least no buildings with integrity. We have only economic crimes in its name. No, our greatest buildings are not qualified as great art, my dear Mrs. Davies, although you do admire Washington.

If you will yet be patient for a little while—a scientist, Einstein, asked for three days to explain the far less pressing and practical matter of "Relativity"—we will take each of the five new resources in order, as with the five fingers of the hand. All are new integrities to be used if we will to make living easier and better today.

The first great integrity is a deeper, more intimate sense of reality in building than was ever pagan—that is to say, than was ever "Classic." More human than was any building ever realized in the Christian Middle Ages. This is true although the thought that may ennoble it now has been living in civilization for more than twenty centuries back. Later it was innate in the simplicities of Jesus as it was organic 500 years earlier in the natural philosophy, Tao (The Way), of the Chinese philosopher Lao-tse. But not only is the new architecture sound philosophy. It is poetry.

Said Ong Giao Ki, Chinese sage, "Poetry is the sound of the heart."

Well, like poetry, this sense of architecture is the sound of the "within." We might call that "within," the heart.

Architecture now becomes integral, the expression of a new old reality: the livable interior space of the room itself In integral architecture the *room-space itself must come through*. The room must be seen as architecture, or we have no architecture. We have no longer an outside as outside. We have no longer an outside and an inside as two separate things. Now the outside may come inside, and the inside may and does go outside. They are *of* each other. Form and function thus become one in design and execution if the nature of materials and method and purpose are all in unison.

This interior space concept, the first broad integrity, is the first great resource. It is also the true basis for general significance of form. Add to this for the sake of clarity that (although the general integration is implied in the first integrity) it is in the nature of any organic building to grow from its site, come out of the ground into the light—the ground itself held always as a component basic part of the building itself. And then we have primarily the new ideal of building as organic. A building dignified as a tree in the midst of nature.

This new ideal for architecture is, as well, an adequate ideal for our general culture. In any final result there can be no separation between our architecture and our culture. Nor any separation of either from our happiness. Nor any separation from our work.

Thus in this rise of organic integration you see the means to end the petty agglomerations miscalled civilization. By way of this old yet new and deeper sense of reality we may have a civilization. In this sense we now recognize and may declare by way of plan and building—the *natural*. Faith in the *natural* is the faith we now need to grow up on in this coming age of our culturally confused, backward twentieth century. But instead of "organic" we might well say "natural" building. Or we might say integral building.

So let us now consider the second of the five new resources: glass. This second resource is new and a "super material" only because it holds such amazing means in modern life for awakened sensibilities. It amounts to a new qualification of life in itself. If known in ancient times glass would then and there have abolished the ancient architecture we know, and completely. This super material GLASS as we now use it is a miracle. Air in air to keep air out or keep it in. Light itself in light, to diffuse or reflect, or refract light itself.

By means of glass, then, the first great integrity may find prime means of realization. Open reaches of the ground may enter as the building and the building interior may reach out and associate with these vistas of the ground. Ground and building will thus become more and more obvious as directly related to each other in openness and intimacy; not only as environment but also as a good pattern for the good life lived in the building. Realizing the benefits to human life of the far reaching implications and effects of the first great integrity, let us call it the interior space concept. This interior-space realization is possible and it is desirable in all the vast variety of characteristic buildings needed by civilized life in our complex age.

By means of glass something of the freedom of our arboreal ancestors living in their trees becomes a more likely precedent for freedom in twentieth-century life, than the cave.

Savage animals "holing in" for protection were more characteristic of life based upon the might of feudal times or based upon the so called "classical" in architecture, which were in turn based upon the labor of the chattel slave. In a free country, were we ourselves free by way of organic thought, buildings might come out into the light without more animal fear; come entirely away from the pagan ideals of form we dote upon as "Classic." Or what Freedom have we?

Perhaps more important than all beside, it is by way of glass that the sunlit space as a reality becomes the most useful servant of a higher order of the human spirit. It is first aid to the sense of cleanliness of form and idea when directly related to free living in air and sunlight. It is this that is coming in the new architecture. And with the integral character of extended vistas gained by marrying buildings with ground levels, or blending them with slopes and gardens; yes, it is in this new sense of earth as a great

human good that we will move forward in the building of our new homes and great public buildings.

I am certain we will desire the sun, spaciousness and integrity of means to ends more year by year as we become aware of the possibilities I have outlined. The more we desire the sun, the more we will desire the freedom of the good ground and the sooner we will learn to understand it. The more we value integrity, the more securely we will find and keep a worthwhile civilization to set against prevalent abuse and ruin.

Congestion will no longer encourage the "space makers for rent." The "space maker for rent" will himself be "for rent" or let us hope "vacant." Give him ten years.

These new space values are entering into our ideas of life. All are appropriate to the ideal that is our own, the ideal we call Democracy.

A NEW REALITY: GLASS

A resource to liberate this new sense of interior space as reality is this new qualification called glass: a supermaterial qualified to qualify us; qualify us not only to escape from the prettified cavern of our present domestic life as also from the cave of our past, but competent actually to awaken in us the desire for such far reaching simplicities of life as we may see in the clear countenance of nature. Good building must ever be seen as in the nature of good construction, but a higher development of this "seeing" will be construction seen as nature-pattern. *That* seeing, only, is inspired architecture.

This dawning sense of the *Within* as *reality* when it is clearly seen as *Nature* will by way of glass make the garden be the building as much as the building will be the garden: the sky as treasured a feature of daily indoor life as the ground itself.

You may see that walls are vanishing. The cave for human dwelling purposes is at last disappearing.

Walls themselves because of glass will become windows and windows as we used to know them as holes in walls will be seen no more. Ceilings will often become as window walls, too. The textile may soon be used as a beautiful overhead for space, the textile an attribute of genuine architecture instead of decoration by way of hangings and upholstery. The usual camouflage of the old order. Modern integral floor heating will follow integral lighting and standardized unitary sanitation. All this makes it reasonable and good economy to abolish building as either a hyper boxment or a super borough.

Haven't senseless elaboration and false mass become sufficiently insulting and oppressive to our intelligence as a people? And yet, senseless elaboration and false mass were tyrannical as "conspicuous waste" in all of our nineteenth century architecture either public or private! Wherever the American architect, as scholar, went he "succeeded" to that extent.

ANOTHER REALITY: CONTINUITY

But now, as third resource, the resource essential to modern architecture destined to cut down this outrageous mass waste and mass lying, is the principle of continuity. I have called it tenuity. Steel is its prophet and master. You must come with me for a moment into "engineering" so called. This is to be an unavoidable strain upon your kind attention. Because, unfortunately, gentle reader, you cannot understand architecture as *modern* unless you do come, and paradoxically, you can't come if you are too well educated as an engineer or as an architect either. So your common sense is needed more than your erudition.

However, to begin this argument for steel: classic architecture knew only the post as an *upright*. Call it a column. The classics knew only the beam as a *horizontal*. Call it a beam. The beam resting upon the upright, or column, was structure throughout, to them. Two things, you see, one thing set on top of another thing in various materials and put there in various ways. Ancient, and nineteenth century building science too, even building a la mode, consisted simply in reducing the various stresses of all materials and their uses to these two things: post and beam. Really, construction used to be just sticking up something in wood or stone and putting something else in wood or stone (maybe iron) on top of it: simple super imposition, you see? You should know that all "Classic" architecture was and still is some such form of direct super imposition. The arch is a little less so, but even that must be so "figured" by the structural engineer if you ask him to "figure" it.

Now the Greeks developed this simple act of super imposition pretty far by way of innate tasteful refinement. The Greeks were true estheticians. Roman builders too, when they forgot the Greeks and brought the beam over as a curve by way of the arch, did something somewhat new but with consequences still of the same sort. But observe, all architectural features made by such "Classic" agglomeration were killed for us by cold steel. And though millions of classic corpses yet encumber American ground unburied, they are ready now for burial.

Of course this primitive post and beam construction will always be valid, but both support and supported may now by means of inserted and welded steel strands or especially woven filaments of steel and modern concrete casting be plaited and united as one physical body: ceilings and walls made one with floors and reinforcing each other by making them continue into one another. This Continuity is made possible by the tenuity of steel.

So the new order wherever steel or plastics enter construction says: weld these two things, post and beam (wall and ceiling) together by means of steel strands buried and stressed within the mass material itself, the steel strands electric welded where steel meets steel within the mass. In other words the upright and horizontal may now be made to work together as one. A new world of form opens inevitably.

Where the beam leaves off and the post begins is no longer important nor need it be seen at all because it no longer actually is. Steel in tension enables the support to slide into the supported, or the supported to grow into the

support somewhat as a treebranch glides out of its tree trunk. Therefrom arises the new series of interior physical reactions I am calling "Continuity." As natural consequence the new esthetic or appearance we call *Plasticity* (and plasticity is peculiarly "modern") is no longer a mere appearance. Plasticity actually becomes the normal *countenance*, the *true esthetic* of genuine structural reality. These interwoven steel strands may so lie in so many directions in any extended member that the extensions may all be economical of material and though much lighter, be safer construction than ever before. There as in the branch of the tree you may see the cantilever. The cantilever is the simplest one of the important phases of this third new structural resource now demanding new significance. It has yet had little attention in architecture. It can do remarkable things to liberate space.

But plasticity was modest new countenance in our American architecture at least thirty five years ago in my own work, but then denied such simple means as welding and the mesh. It had already eliminated all the separate identities of post and beam in architecture. Steel in tension enters now by way of mesh and welding to arrive at actual, total plasticity if and when desired by the architect. And to prove the philosophy of organic architecture, form and function are one, it now enters architecture as the esthetic countenance of *physical reality*.

To further illustrate this magic simplifier we call "plasticity": see it as *flexibility* similar to that of your own hand. What makes your hand expressive? Flowing continuous line and continuous surfaces seen continually mobile of the articulate articulated structure of the hand as a whole. The line is seen as "hand" line. The varying planes seen as "hand" surface. Strip the hand to the separate structural identities of joined bones (post and beam) and plasticity as an expression of the hand would disappear. We would be then getting back to the joinings, breaks, jolts, and joints of ancient, or "Classic," architecture: thing to thing; feature to feature. But plasticity is the reverse of that ancient agglomeration and is the ideal means behind these simplified free new effects of straight line and flat plane.

I have just said that plasticity in this sense for thirty five years or more has been the recognized esthetic ideal for such simplification as was required by the machine to do organic work. And it is true of my own work.

As significant outline and expressive surface, this new esthetic of plasticity (physical continuity) is now a useful means to form the supreme physical body of an organic, or integral, American Architecture.

Of course, it is just as easy to cheat by simplicity as it is to cheat with "classical" structure. So, unluckily, here again is the "modernistic" architectural picturemaker's deadly facility for imitation at ease and again too happy with fresh opportunity to "fake effects." Probably another Renaissance is here imminent.

Architecture is now integral architecture only when Plasticity is a genuine expression of actual construction just as the articulate line and surface of the hand is articulate of the structure of the hand. Arriving at steel, I first used Continuity as actual stabilizing principle in concrete slabs, and in the concrete ferro block system I devised in Los Angeles.

In the form of the cantilever or as horizontal continuity this new economy by means of tenuity is what saved the Imperial Hotel from destruction, but it did not appear in the grammar of the building for various reasons, chiefly because the building was to look somewhat as though it belonged to Tokyo.

Later, in the new design for St. Mark's Tower, New York City, this new working principle economized material, labor, and liberated or liberalized space in a more developed sense. It gave to the structure the significant outlines of remarkable stability and instead of masonry mass significant outlines came out. The abstract pattern of the structure as a complete structural integrity of Form and Idea may be seen fused as in any tree but with nothing imitating a tree.

Continuity invariably realized remarkable economy of labor and building materials as well as space. Unfortunately there is yet little or no data to use as tabulation. Tests will have to be made continually for many years to make the record available to slide rule engineers.

In the ancient order there was little thought of economy of materials. The more massive the whole structure looked, the better it looked to the ancients. But seen in the light of these new economic interior forces conserved by the tensile strength of a sheet of plastic or any interweaving of strands of steel in this machine age, the old order was as sick with weight as the Buonarotti dome. Weak ... because there could be no co interrelation between the two elements of support and supported to reinforce each other as a whole under stress or elemental disturbance.

So this tremendous new resource of *tenuity*—a quality of steel—this quality of *pull* in a building (you may see it ushering in a new era in John Roebling's Brooklyn Bridge) was definitely lacking in all ancient architecture because steel had not been born into building.

The tenuous strand or slab as a common means of strength had yet to come. Here today this element of continuity may cut structural substance nearly in two. It may cut the one half in two again by elimination of needless features, such elimination being entirely due to the simplification I have been calling "plasticity."

It is by utilizing mass production in the factory in this connection that some idea of the remarkable new economics possible to modern architecture may be seen approaching those realized in any well built machine. If standardization can be humanized and made flexible in design and the economics brought to the home owner, the greatest service will be rendered to our modern way of life. It may be really born—this democracy, I mean.

Involved as a matter of design in this mass production, however, are the involute, all but involuntary reactions to which I have just referred: the ipso facto building code and the fact that the building engineer as now trained knows so little about them.

However, the engineer is learning to calculate by model making in some instances—notably Professor Beggs at Princeton.

The codes so far as I can see will have to die on the vine with the men who made them.

MATERIALS FOR THEIR OWN SAKE

As the first integrity and the two first new resources appeared out of the interior nature of the kind of building, called Architecture—so now, naturally, interior to the true nature of any good building, comes the fourth new resource. This is found by recognizing the nature of the materials used in construction. Just as many fascinating different properties as there are different materials that may be used to build a building will continually and naturally, qualify, modify and utterly change all architectural form whatsoever.

A stone building will no more *be* nor will it *look* like a steel building. A pottery, or terra cotta building, will not be nor should it look like a stone building. A wood building will look like none other, for it will glorify the stick. A steel and glass building could not possibly look like anything but itself. It will glorify steel and glass. And so on all the way down the long list of available riches in materials: Stone, Wood, Concrete, Metals, Glass, Textiles, Pulp and Plastics; riches so great to our hand today that no comparison with Ancient Architecture is at all sensible or anything but obstruction to our Modern Architecture.

In this particular, as you may see, architecture is going back to learn from the natural source of all natural things.

In order to get Organic Architecture born, intelligent architects will be forced to turn their backs on antique rubbish heaps with which Classic eclecticism has encumbered our new ground. So far as architecture has gone in my own thought it is first of all a character and quality of *mind* that may enter also into human conduct with social implications that might, at first, confound or astound you. But the only basis for any fear of them lies in the fact that they are all sanely and thoroughly *constructive*.

Instinctively all forms of pretense fear and hate reality. THE HYPOCRITE MUST ALWAYS HATE THE RADICAL.

This potent fourth new resource—the Nature of Materials—gets at the common center of every material in relation to the work it is required to do. This means that the architect must again begin at the very beginning. Proceeding according to Nature now he must sensibly go through with whatever material may be in hand for his purpose according to the methods and sensibilities of a man in this age. And when I say Nature, I mean inherent *structure* seen always by the architect as a matter of complete design. It is in itself, always, *nature-pattern*. It is this profound internal sense of materials that enters in as Architecture now. It is this, the fifth new resource, that must captivate and hold the mind of the modern architect to creative work. The fifth will give new life to his imagination if it has not been already killed at school.

And, inevitable implication! New machine age resources require that all buildings do *not* resemble each other. The new ideal does *not* require that all buildings be of steel, concrete or glass. Often that might be idiotic waste.

Nor do the resources even *imply* that mass is no longer a beautiful attribute of masonry materials when they are genuinely used. We are entitled to a vast variety of form in our complex age so long as the form be genuine—serves Architecture and Architecture serves life.

But in this land of ours, richest on earth of all in old and new materials, architects must exercise well-trained imagination to see in each material, either natural or compounded plastics, their own *inherent style*. All materials may be beautiful, their beauty much or entirely depending upon how well they are used by the Architect.

In our modern building we have the Stick. Stone. Steel. Pottery. Concrete. Glass. Yes, Pulp, too, as well as plastics. And since this dawning sense of the "within" is the new reality, these will all give the main *motif* for any real building made from them. The materials of which the building is built will go far to determine its appropriate mass, its outline and, especially, proportion. *Character* is criterion in the form of any and every building or industrial product we can call Architecture in the light of this new ideal of the new order.

THE NEW INTEGRITY

Strange! At this late date, it is modern architecture that wants life to learn to see life as life, because architecture must learn to see brick as brick, learn to see steel as steel, see glass as glass. So modern thought urges all of life to demand that a bank look like a bank (bad thought though a bank might become) and not depend upon false columns for credit. The new architecture urges all of life to demand that an office building look like an office building, even if it should resemble the cross section of a beehive. Life itself should sensibly insist in self defense that a hotel look and conduct itself like a hotel and not like some office building. Life should declare, too, that the railroad station look like a railroad station and not try so hard to look like an ancient temple or some monarchic palazzo. And while we are on this subject, why not a place for opera that would look something like a place for opera—if we must have opera, and not look so much like a gilded, crimsoned bagnio. Life declares that a filling station should stick to its work as a filling station: look the part becomingly. Why try to look like some Colonial diminutive or remain just a pump on the street. Although "just a pump" on the street is better than the Colonial imitation. The good Life itself demands that the school be as generously spaced and a thought-built good-time place for happy children: a building no more than one story high with some light overhead, the school building should regard the children as a garden in sun. Life itself demands of Modern Architecture that the house of a man who knows what home is should have his own home his own way if we have any man left in that con-

nection after F.H.A. is done trying to put them, all of them it can, into the case of a man who builds a home only to sell it. Our Government forces the home maker into the real estate business if he wants a home at all.

Well, after all, this line of thought was all new type common sense in architecture in Chicago only thirty years ago. It began to grow up in my own work as it is continuing to grow up more and more widely in the work of all the world. But, insulting as it may seem to say so, nor is it merely arrogant to say that the actual thinking in that connection is still a novelty, only a little less strange today than it was then, although the appearances do rapidly increase.

INTEGRAL ORNAMENT AT LAST!

At last, is this fifth resource, so old yet now demanding fresh significance. We have arrived at integral ornament— the nature pattern of actual construction. Here, confessed as the spiritual demand for true significance, comes this subjective element in modern architecture. An element so hard to understand that modern architects themselves seem to understand it least well of all and most of them have turned against it with such fury as is born only of impotence.

And it is true that this vast, intensely human significance is really no matter at all for any but the most imaginative mind not without some development in artistry and the *gift* of a sense of proportion. Certainly we must go higher in the realm of imagination when we presume to enter here, because we go into Poetry.

Now, very many write good prose who cannot write poetry at all. And although staccato specification is the present fashion, just as "functionalist" happens to be the present style in writing—poetic prose will never be undesirable. But who condones prosaic poetry? None. Not even those fatuously condemned to write it.

So, I say this fourth new resource and the fifth demand for new significance and integrity is ornament *integral to building as itself poetry*. Rash use of a dangerous word. The word "Poetry" is a dangerous word.

Heretofore, I have used the word "pattern" instead of the word ornament to avoid confusion or to escape the passing prejudice. But here now ornament is in its place. Ornament meaning not only *surface qualified by human imagination* but imagination giving *natural pattern* to structure. Perhaps this phrase says it all without further explanation. This resource—integral ornament—is new in the architecture of the world, at least insofar not only as imagination qualifying a surface—a valuable resource— but as a greater means than that: *imagination giving natural pattern to structure itself*. Here we have new significance, indeed! Long ago this significance was lost to the scholarly architect. A man of taste. He, too soon, became content with symbols.

Evidently then, this expression of structure as a pattern true to the nature of the materials out of which it was made, may be taken much further along than physical need alone would dictate? "If you have a loaf of bread break the loaf in two and give the half of it for some flowers of the Narcissus, for the bread feeds the body indeed but the flowers feed the soul."

Into these higher realms of imagination associated in the popular mind as sculpture and painting, buildings may be as fully taken by modern means today as they ever were by craftsmen of the antique order.

It is by this last and poetic resource that we may give greater structural entity and greater human significance to the whole building than could ever be done otherwise. This statement is heresy at this left wing moment, so—we ask, "taken how and when taken?" I confess you may well ask by whom? The answer is, taken by the true *poet*. And where is this Poet today? Time will answer.

Yet again in this connection let us remember Ong's Chinese observation, "Poetry is the sound of the heart." So, in the same uncommon sense integral ornament is the developed sense of the building as a whole, or the manifest *abstract pattern of structure itself*. Interpreted. Integral ornament is simply *structure pattern made visibly articulate* and seen in the building as it is seen articulate in the structure of the trees or a lily of the fields. It is the expression of inner rhythm of Form. Are we talking about Style? Pretty nearly. At any rate, we are talking about the qualities that make *essential architecture* as distinguished from any mere act of building whatsoever.

What I am here calling integral ornament is founded upon the same organic simplicities as Beethoven's Fifth Symphony, that amazing revolution in tumult and splendor of sound built on four tones based upon a rhythm a child could play on the piano with one finger. Supreme imagination reared the four repeated tones, simple rhythms, into a great symphonic poem that is probably the noblest thought built edifice in our world. And Architecture is like Music in this capacity for the symphony.

But concerning higher development of building to more completely express its life principle as significant and beautiful, let us say at once by way of warning: it is better to die by the wayside of left-wing Ornaphobia than it is to build any more merely ornamented buildings, as such; or to see right-wing architects die any more ignoble deaths of *Ornamentia*. All period and pseudo classic buildings whatever, and (although their authors do not seem to know it) most Protestant buildings, they call themselves internationalist, are really ornamental in definitely objectionable sense. A plain flat surface cut to shape for its own sake, however large or plain the shape, is, the moment it is sophisticatedly so cut, no less ornamental than egg and dart. All such buildings are objectionably "ornamental," because like any buildings of the old classical order both wholly ignore the *nature* of the *first* integrity. Both also ignore the four resources and both neglect the nature of machines at work on materials. Incidentally and as a matter of course both misjudge the nature of time, place and the modern life of man.

Here in this new leftish emulation as we now have it, is only the "istic," ignoring principle merely to get the "look" of the machine or something that looks "new." The province of the "ite."

In most so called "internationalist" or "modernistic" building therefore we have no true approach to organic architecture: we have again merely a new, superficial esthetic trading upon that architecture because such education as most of our architects possess qualifies them for only some kind of eclecticism past, passing, or to pass.

Nevertheless I say, if we can't have buildings with integrity we would better have more imitation machines for buildings until we can have truly sentient architecture. "The machine for living in" is sterile, but therefore it is safer, I believe, than the festering mass of ancient styles.

GREAT POWER

A far greater power than slavery, even the intellectual slavery as in the school of the Greeks, is back of these five demands for machine age significance and integrity. Stupendous and stupefying power. That power is the leverage of the machine itself. As now set up in all its powers the machine will confirm these new implicities and complicities in architecture at every point, but will destroy them soon if not checked by a new simplicity.

The proper use of these new resources demands that we use them all together with integrity for mankind if we are to realize the finer significances of life. The finer significance, prophesied if not realized by organic architecture. It is reasonable to believe that life in our country will be lived in full enjoyment of this new freedom of the extended horizontal line because the horizontal line now becomes the great architectural highway. The flat plane now becomes the regional field. And integral pattern becomes "the sound of the Usonian heart."

I see this extended horizontal line as the true earth line of human life, indicative of freedom. Always.

The broad expanded plane is the horizontal plane infinitely extended. In that lies such freedom, for man on this earth as he may call his.

This new sense of Architecture as integral pattern of that type and kind may awaken these United States to fresh beauty, and the Usonian horizon of the individual will be immeasurably extended by enlightened use of this great lever, the machine. But only if it gets into creative hands loyal to humanity.

What is needed most in architecture today is the very thing that is most needed in life—Integrity. Just as it is in a human being, so integrity is the deepest quality in a building; but it is a quality not much demanded of any building since very ancient times when it was natural. It is no longer the first demand for a human being either, because "Success" is now so immediately necessary. If you are a success, people will not want to "look the gift horse in the mouth." No. But then if "success" should happen today something precious has been lost from life.

Somebody has described a man of this period as one through the memory of whom you could too easily pass your hand. Had there been true *quality* in the man the hand could not so easily pass. That quality in the memory of him would probably have been "Integrity."

In speaking of integrity in architecture, I mean much the same thing that you would mean were you speaking of an individual. Integrity is not something to be put on and taken off like a garment. Integrity is a quality *within* and *of* the man himself. So it is in a building. It cannot be changed by any other person either nor by the exterior pressures of any outward circumstances; integrity cannot change except from within because it is that in you which *is you*— and due to which you will try to live your life (as you would build your building) in the best possible way. To build a man or building from within is always difficult to do because deeper is not so easy as shallow.

Naturally should you want to really live in a way and in a place which is true to this deeper thing in you, which you honor, the house you build to live in as a home should be (so far as it is possible to make it so) integral in every sense. Integral to site, to purpose, and to you. The house would then be a home in the best sense of that word. This we seem to have forgotten if ever we learned it. Houses have become a series of anonymous boxes that go into a row on row upon row of bigger boxes either merely negative or a mass nuisance. But now the house in this interior or deeper organic sense may come alive as organic architecture.

We are now trying to bring *integrity* into building. If we succeed, we will have done a great service to our moral nature—the psyche—of our democratic society. Integrity would become more natural. Stand up for *integrity* in your building and you stand for integrity not only in the life of those who did the building but socially a reciprocal relationship is inevitable. An irresponsible, flashy, pretentious or dishonest individual would never be happy in such a house as we now call organic because of this quality of integrity. The one who will live in it will be he who will grow with living in it. So it is the "job" of any true architect to envision and make this human relationship—so far as lies in his power—a reality.

Living within a house wherein everything is genuine and harmonious, a new sense of freedom gives one a new sense of life—as contrasted with the usual existence in the house indiscriminately planned and where Life is contained within a series of confining boxes, all put within the general box. Such life is bound to be inferior to life lived in this new integrity—the Usonian Home.

In designing the Usonian house, as I have said, I have always proportioned it to the human figure in point of scale; that is, to the scale of the human figure to occupy it. The old idea in most buildings was to make the human being feel rather insignificant—developing an inferiority complex in him if possible. The higher the ceilings were then the greater the building was. This empty grandeur was considered to be human luxury. Of course, great, high ceilings had a certain utility in those days, because of bad planning and awkward construction. (The volume of contained air was about all the air to be had without violence.)

The Usonian house, then, aims to be a *natural* performance, one that is integral to site; integral to environment; integral to the life of the inhabitants. A house integral with the nature of materials—wherein glass is used as glass, stone as stone, wood as wood—and all the elements of environment go into and throughout the house. Into this new integrity, once there, those who live in it will take root and grow. And most of all belonging by nature to the nature of its being.

Whether people are fully conscious of this or not, they actually derive countenance and sustenance from the "atmosphere" of the things they live in or with. They are rooted in them just as a plant is in the soil in which it is planted. For instance, we receive many letters from people who sing praises for what has happened to them as a consequence; telling us how their house has affected their lives. They now have a certain dignity and pride in their environment; they see it has a meaning or purpose which they share as a family or feel as individuals.

We all know the feeling we have when we are well dressed and like the consciousness that results from it. It affects our conduct and you should have the same feeling regarding the home you live in. It has a salutary effect morally, to put it on a lower plane than it deserves, but there are higher results above that sure one. If you feel yourself becomingly housed, know that you are living according to the higher demands of good society, and of your own conscience, then you are free from embarrassment and not poor in spirit but rich—in the right way. I have always believed in being careful about my clothes; getting well dressed because I could then forget all about them. That is what should happen to you with a good house that is a *home*. When you are conscious that the house is right and is honestly becoming to you, and feel you are living in it beautifully, you need no longer be concerned about it. It is no tax upon your conduct, nor a nag upon your self respect, because it is featuring you as you like to see yourself.

Notes

Abstract Essence

1 Frank Lloyd Wright, *An Autobiography* (New York: Horizon Press, 1932), 181.

2 Vincent Scully, introduction to *The Nature of Frank Lloyd Wright*, ed. Bolon, Nelson, Siedel, (Chicago: University of Chicago Press, 1988). Scully must also be credited as one of the only architectural historians to consistently call for investigations of "the complex question of the mind's making"; see "Frank Lloyd Wright and the Stuff of Dreams," *Perspecta* 16 (Cambridge: MIT Press, 1980): 9.

3 Martin Heidegger, "The Thinker as Poet," *Poetry Language Thought*, trans. A. Hofstadler (New York: Harper and Row, 1971), 5.

4 The best are Jonathan Lipman, *Frank Lloyd Wright and the Johnson Wax Buildings* (New York: Rizzoli, 1980); Jack Quinan, *Frank Lloyd Wright's Larkin Building* (Cambridge: MIT Press, 1987); Joseph Connors, *The Robie House of Frank Lloyd Wright* (Chicago: University of Chicago Press, 1984); Donald Hoffman, *Frank Lloyd Wright's Fallingwater* (New York: Dover, 1978), *Frank Lloyd Wright's Robie House* (New York: Dover, 1984), and *Frank Lloyd Wright's Dana House* (New York: Dover, 1996); Brian Carter, *Johnson Wax Administration Building and Research Tower* (London: Phaidon Press, 1998); Kathryn Smith, *Frank Lloyd Wright: Hollyhock House and Olive Hill* (New York: Rizzoli, 1992); James Steele, *Barnsdall House* (London: Phaidon Press, 1992); Paul Kruty, *Frank Lloyd Wright and Midway Gardens* (Chicago: University of Illinois Press, 1998); Joseph Siry, *Unity Temple* (Cambridge: Cambridge University Press, 1996); Robert McCarter, *Unity Temple* (London: Phaidon Press, 1997) and *Fallingwater* (London: Phaidon Press, 1994); and the astonishing Otto Antonia Graf, *Die Kunst des Quadrats: Zum Werk von Frank Lloyd Wright*, vols. I and II (Vienna: Verlag Bohlau, 1983) and *Erraumen: Zum Werk von Frank Lloyd Wright*, vols. III and IV (Vienna: Verlag Bohlau, 2002).

5 Ludwig Wittgenstein, *Culture and Value* (Chicago: University of Chicago Press, 1980), 22.

6 Frank Lloyd Wright, *A Testament* (New York: Horizon, 1957), 15.

7 The cataloging of all Wright's drawings, with duplicates placed in the Getty Foundation in Los Angeles, and the publication of selected drawings held in the Frank Lloyd Wright Archives, all have proved essential in this current endeavor, and Bruce Brooks Pfeiffer's leadership in this must be acknowledged, as it has literally changed the entire nature of Wright scholarship and study since these publications began to emerge in 1985; Bruce Brooks Pfeiffer and Yukio Futagawa, *Frank Lloyd Wright Mono-*

graph, vols. 1–8, *Frank Lloyd Wright Preliminary Studies*, vols. 9–11, and *Frank Lloyd Wright in His Renderings*, vol. 12 (Tokyo: ADA Edita, 1985–88). However, these publications represent only a fraction of Wright's drawings, and sales to private collectors in the 1980s of original drawings, undertaken by the Taliesin Fellowship in order to underwrite their private practice, the preservation of both Taliesins, and the non-self-supporting Frank Lloyd Wright School of Architecture, dispersed essential drawings, often documenting the early design sequence, making them permanently unavailable for future study. It is indeed a relief to be able to state, in this updated endnote, that these sales of drawings have been stopped, the drawings are now in the possession of the Frank Lloyd Wright Archives (under Pfeiffer's direction), the Taliesin Architects have recently disbanded, and both Taliesin East and West are overseen by the Frank Lloyd Wright Foundation, a preservation organization.

8 Wright, *A Testament*, 20.

9 This and all other quotes that follow by Froebel are from Friedrich Froebel, *Selected Writings* (New York: I. M. Lilley, 1898).

10 This and all other quotes by Emerson that follow are from Ralph Waldo Emerson, *Emerson: Essays and Lectures* (New York: Library of America, 1983).

11 Frank Lloyd Wright, *In the Cause of Architecture*, ed. F. Gutheim (New York: McGraw-Hill, 1975), 123.

12 Henry David Thoreau, *Walden and Other Writings*, ed. B. Atkinson (New York: The Modern Library, 1937).

13 Horatio Greenough, "Form and Function" (1852), reprinted in *Roots of Contemporary Architecture*, ed. Lewis Mumford (New York: Dover, 1972), 39.

14 Ibid., 38.

15 Ibid., 37.

16 Ibid., 33.

17 Louis Sullivan, *Kindergarten Chats and Other Writings* (New York: Dover, 1979), 177.

18 Ibid., 182–83.

19 Ibid., 179.

20 Ibid., 122.

21 Emerson, *Essays*, 240.

22 Frank Lloyd Wright, *An American Architecture* (New York: Horizon, 1955), 19.

23 Wright, *An Autobiography*, 153.

24 Wright, *In the Cause of Architecture*, 54.

25 Ibid., 53.

26 In this the best study is Kevin Nute, *Frank Lloyd Wright and Japan* (New York: Van Nostrand Reinhold, 1993); for a study focusing on Wright's study of Japanese woodblock prints, see Julia Meech, *Frank Lloyd Wright and the Art of Japan* (New York: Abrams, 2001).

27 Wright, *In the Cause of Architecture*, 230.

Academic Tradition
and the Individual Talent

1 Frank Lloyd Wright, *An Autobiography* (New York: Horizon Press, 1977), includes the following passages. "Books read together (with his Madison friend Robie Lamp): Hans Brinker, Ruskin's *Seven Lamps of Architecture*, a gift from Aunts Nell and Jane. Jules Verne's *Michael Strogoff*, *Hector Servadac*. Goethe's *Wilhelm Meister*. The *Arabian Nights* as always *Aladdin and his Lamp* and many tales" (53). "The hungry student read at this time, at home, Carlyle's *Sartor Resartus*, *Hero Worship*, *Past and Present*, the father's calf bound copy of Plutarch's *Lives*, Ruskin's *Fors Clavigera*, *Modern Painters*, *Stones of Venice* (gift of Aunts Nell and Jane), Morris's *Sigurd the Volsung*, and Shelley, Goethe's *Wilhelm Meister*, a little of William Blake, *Les Miserables*, Viollet-le-Duc's *Raisonne de l'architecture* (sic). But he doesn't know in the least what he read in the school course" (73). The former passage concerns high school years, the latter occurs in conjunction with his description of his time at the University of Wisconsin.

2 The present article is conceived as a sequel to Henry-Russell Hitchcock's classic but still too little-known "Frank Lloyd Wright and the 'Academic Tradition' of the Early Eighteen Nineties," *Journal of the Warburg and Courtauld Institutes* 7 (January–June 1944): 46–63. Hitchcock made little out of Wright's literal borrowings from precedent; one senses that, for all kinds of reasons, he chose to say less than he knew.

3 I would like to acknowledge many discussions with friends, students, and colleagues over the years. For this essay's purposes, Robert Twombly, historian, was enormously generous in lending his own literature search notes on the period. Andres Duany and Elizabeth Plater Zyberk, architects, have helped me with both their critical acumen and their boundless interest. Vincent Scully led me to the subject of Wright and his growing up, as well as to the practice of architecture. The enthusiasm that I and countless others have for architecture as humanist discipline was brought to fire by him, and no amount of thanks is enough.

4 For obscure reasons, some persist in giving Wright's birth year as 1869. Thomas S. Hines Jr., "Frank Lloyd Wright the Madison Years: Records Versus Recollections," *Journal of the Society of Architectural Historians* XXVI (December 1967): 227–33.

5 Robert C. Twombly, *Frank Lloyd Wright: His Life and His Architecture* (New York: John Wiley & Sons, 1979), 6–9.

6 Ibid., 10–11. Like so many events in

Wright's life, this became the seed germ of truth within a grander, mythicizing tale invented later; in this case, he claimed to have left college, in disgust at having the classical orders forced down his throat, a few months before being graduated.

7 Frank Lloyd Wright, *An Autobiography* (New York: Horizon, 1977), 48–49.

8 If the August 22, 1885, date of the letter from Wright to Uncle Jenkin given in *Frank Lloyd Wright: Letters to Clients* (Fresno: California State University, 1986) is a correct transcription, then it is possible that Wright may have been more than a contributor of decoration to a design by Silsbee. "I have forwarded to you today my preliminary sketches for 'Unity Chapel.' I have simply made them in pencil on a piece of old paper but the idea is my own and I have copied them from nothing." My own examination of the document indicates "1886" as a possible reading, in which case the sketches would have been for the Sioux City chapel published a few months later.

9 "Church and Parsonage: A Proposed Plan for All Souls, Chicago. Sermon by Jenkin Lloyd-Jones, May 17, 1885," *Unity* XV (June 20, 1885): 202.

10 Vincent J. Scully Jr. *The Shingle Style: Architectural Theory and Design from Richardson to the Origins of Wright* (New Haven and London: Yale University Press, 1955). Scully's illustrations draw heavily on Sheldon's *Artistic Country Seats*. Having first been made aware of that book's existence by Scully, I only later came to understand its importance to Wright.

11 Richard Lloyd-Jones died at eighty-six on December 6, 1885; George and Robert M. Crawford, eds. *Memoirs of Iowa County, Wisconsin* (Madison: Northwest Historical Association: 1913), 1, 261.

12 The drawing of the Helena Valley Chapel was printed in the *Fourth Annual Report of All Souls Church* (Chicago: January 6, 1887). Sixty-two years later, Wright was buried in the Chapel graveyard. His remains, sadly, have since been removed to Arizona.

13 Wilbert R. Hasbrouck, "The Earliest Work of Frank Lloyd Wright," *The Prairie School Review* XII, 4 (1970): 14–16.

14 Frank Lloyd Wright correspondence file for August 22, 1885–February 1, 1906.

15 Published May 29, 1888, according to James F. O'Gorman, "Henry Hobson Richardson and Frank Lloyd Wright," *Art Quarterly* XXXII (Autumn 1969): 292–315; date noted, 308. Even given other publications of the gate lodge, noted by O'Gorman earlier than this, the Wright design seems much more closely tied to the Richardson drawing than to photographs of the building, which emphasize the masonry texture. This may throw a little doubt into Wright's dating. Hitchcock doubts it for other reasons; *Journal of the Society of Architectural Historians* XIX, 3 (October 1960): 129–131. His review of Wright's *Drawings for a Living Architecture* remarks, concerning the elevation, "My present belief is that the drawing reproduced is of the early 1890s, not more than a year before 1890, certainly, and even more certainly not later than 1893" (129).

16 "Catalogue at Auction, Nov. 29, 1909, household effects of Louis Sullivan,"

Williams, Barker & Severn Co., Auctioneers. Collection of Burnham Library, Art Institute of Chicago. The Sheldon book is item 191 under "Architectural Books."

17 There is perhaps still another ghost in the Cooper House's academic machine. Wright's disciplining of McKim's plan could be regarded as done according to the example set by E. E. Viollet-le-Duc, one foreign architect Wright did profess to admire. Viollet's odd, anti-urban "Modern French Town Mansion" appears on 278 of the *Discourses on Architecture* (translation of the *Entretiens sur l'architecture* of 1863 and 1872, Boston: J.R. Osgood and Co., 1875 and 1881). The book was also in Sullivan's library; item 213 in the auction catalog cited in note 15.

18 Burnham's obituary of Atwood appeared in *Inland Architect and News Record*, January 1896, 56–57. "I was acquainted with much of his work," wrote Burnham, "and the opinion of Professor Ware and Mr. Price weighed strongly in his favor." See also Ann Lorenz Van Zanten "Atwood, Charles B." *in* Adolph K. Placzek ed. *Macmillan Encyclopedia of Architects* I (New York: Free Press, 1982), 114–115.

19 *Inland Architect and New Record*, July 1891, 73 and *Economist*, July 1891, where the cost of construction is noted. *Building* XI (September 7, 1889): 82, noted that "G. W. Maher, who has been practicing at 823 Insurance Exchange Building for several years, has taken as partner Mr. C. S. Corwin, who has been with Mr. J. L. Silsbee for a number of years." Regarding this partnership I must disagree with H. Allen Brooks in *The Prairie School* (New York: W.W. Norton & Co., 1976), 34 n25. The Corwin in question is more likely Wright's friend Cecil than Cecil's brother Charles, an artist, because the firm was an architecture firm and the announcement of the partnership implying a state of equal responsibility was in a building journal. Charles worked on a grand perspective for Wright's Cheltenham Beach project of 1895 and painted the "Aladdin" or "Fisherman and the Genie" mural in the new playroom of the Oak Park house the same year, but such work by no means indicates he was qualified as an architect. On a photograph of the mural in the Taliesin archives (Catalog 9309), which shows tubes of paint still on the mantel below the painting, is written "Charles Corwin the figures FLW Design Charles Corwin painter brother of Cecil Corwin."

20 For the plan to bring Mrs. Sullivan to Chicago, see Robert C. Twombly, *Louis Sullivan, His Life and Work* (New York: Viking, 1986), 205–07. The addresses located on the map are from *The Lakeside Annual Directory of the City of Chicago*, various years.

21 *Architectural Record* 3 (March 1892): 348.

22 *Inland Architect and News Record*, November 1891, 55.

23 *Inland Architect and News Record*, June 1892, 66.

24 Hitchcock, "Frank Lloyd Wright and the 'Academic Tradition,'" 60.

25 "House at Chelsea, Mass. for John F. Low, Esq.," Stevens & Cobb, Architects. *Architecture and Building* 12, 5 (February 1, 1890).

26 Wright, *An Autobiography*, 132–33.

27 *Wisconsin State Journal* (May 12, 1893).

"Several plans have been considered, and the committee decided to recommend those by Frank Wright, a former Madison boy, now a Chicago architect."

28 Ann Lorenz Van Zanten, "Atwood, Charles B."

29 *Catalogue of the Chicago Architectural Club Exhibition* (1894). Those who have known architects *en charrete* occasionally to lose the forest for the trees will be amused to count the number of columns to right and left of center in the drawing; there is no site condition enforcing the imbalance. The other five drawings Wright exhibited were from the hand of Ernest Albert, an artist, who on his own account showed drawings of Richardson's Warder House in Washington and of the "Gate and Lodge, Ames's Estate, Mass."

30 It can be argued that the two fundamental Greek models are the Parthenon and the Erechtheion. The former is more congenial to the academy, because it is symmetrical, self-contained, and its rules are teachable. Wright, however, was attracted by the latter, and it is not a stretch to say that the high classic Prairie Houses show him to be the last great Greek Revival architect.

31 Hitchcock, "Frank Lloyd Wright and the 'Academic Tradition,'" plate 12a.

32 The Whittier House is plate 3 in *A Monograph of the Works of McKim, Mead & White 1879–1915* (New York: Architectural Book Publishing, 1915). Leland Roth, *McKim Mead & White Architects* (New York: Harper & Row, 1983), 382 n58, notes a publication of it in March 1886; Van Rensselaer, "Recent Architecture," *Century* 31: 679–80.

33 Roth, *McKim Mead & White Architects*, 94–95 and 384 n.85. The Phoenix House was published in "Great American Architects," *Architectural Record* special issue on McKim, Mead & White (May 1895), though Roth notes it had been published previously, "the brick side walls were clearly the supporting members and the decorated spandrel panels between floors was just as clearly not" (95).

34 Frank Lloyd Wright, *Ausgeführte Bauten und Entwürfe von Frank Lloyd Wright* (Berlin: Wasmuth, 1910), plate 1.

35 Frank Lloyd Wright, "In the Cause of Architecture," *Architectural Record*, March 1908, 155–221; 156.

36 The author of the article was Wright's close friend Robert C. Spencer Jr., who likely had contact with the Boston magazine's staff dating from his time at MIT and his work at Shepley, Bullfinch & Coolidge, successor firm to H. H. Richardson. In other times and places Spencer's ties to Wright might have been seen as a conflict of critical interest. In fact, the illustration opening the article is a rendering by Spencer himself, a revision of an 1895 Wright scheme, an ancestor (and successor) of the Husser House designed initially for C. A. McAfee of Kenilworth (see the monogram in the lower-left-hand corner, an entanglement of R, C, S, and JR).The design has fascinating sets of variants, at least three in number, which are beyond the scope of this essay to discuss beyond two matters. The plan and drawing reproduced in volume 1 of the Wright monograph date not from 1895 but from 1900, judging from the address on them, 435 The Rookery,

Wright's 1900 office according to that year's *Exhibition Catalogue of the Chicago Architectural Club*. Much confusion in dating has resulted from a mass of new drawings of earlier projects (Wright, being Wright, always somehow tinkered), which seem to have been produced expressly to present in the Architectural Review and at the Architectural Club show. The 1895 project, of which no drawing seems to have survived, may have been based on Richardson's Stoughton House, Wright's well-worn source of inspiration that was also in George William Sheldon's *Artistic Country Seats* (New York: D. Appleton & Co., 1886). If so, it is another, even more direct, illustration of the changes in Wright's mind-set between 1895 and 1899. In 1895, house comes from house; by 1899, house (Husser) comes from monument (Winn Library), even though McAfee is the precursor of Husser. Richardson remains the source of Wright's inspiration, but his understanding has changed and deepened.

37 For a discussion of the *analytique*, 166ff. of Richard A. Moore, "Academic 'Dessin' Theory in France after the Reorganization of 1863," *Journal of the Society of Architectural Historians* XXXVI, 3 (October 1977): 145–74. An example of how it was treated in practice can be found in John F. Harbeson, *The Study of Architectural Design* (New York: Pencil Points Press, 1927); the first section is entitled "The 'Analytique' or Order Problem." An American student *analytique* from 1896, almost contemporary with Wright's, is reproduced in M. Katherine Lines, "Roman Composite Order," *The American Renaissance 1876–1917* (New York: Brooklyn Museum, 1979), 93.

38 Leon Batista Alberti, *The Ten Books of Architecture*, book VI, chapter 2. *De re aedificatoria*, written ca. 1451; reprint of 1755 Leoni English edition (New York, 1986).

39 MIT attendees, besides Sullivan, in Wright's vicinity included Robert C. Spencer Jr. (1886), Myron Hunt (1890–92), Marion Mahoney (graduated 1894), Dwight Heald Perkins (1885–88), Alfred Hoyt Granger (graduated 1887), and James Gamble Rogers (1891–92). Some of these are noted in Brooks in *The Prairie School*, others in Henry F. and Elsie Rathburn Withey, *Biographical Dictionary of American Architects (Deceased)* (Los Angeles, 1956).

40 Wright, "In the Cause of Architecture," 157.

41 David Van Zanten has written insightfully on the shifting importance given to different building types from the late eighteenth to the late nineteenth century. His contention is that before the French Revolution palaces were considered the supreme type; the "representation" of the ruler was the aimed-for end. Later, the interest in proper "representation" extended to other public and semipublic building types. David Van Zanten, *Designing Paris: The Architecture of Duban, Labrouste, Duc, and Vaudoyer* (Cambridge, 1987), 226ff.

42 Katherine Taylor pointed out this remarkable passage to me, and I am greatly in her debt. The anonymous review of Viollet-le-Duc's *Discourses on Architecture* is in *The Atlantic Monthly*, March 1876, 383–84.

43 This is not the place to examine the complex ways Wright used regular grids in his planning. Suffice it to say that the idea he employed a "tartan" or irregular grid is a misinterpretation and that a full study of the question is needed. Similarly, academic use of the Durand grid in the latter half of the nineteenth century is a matter of extreme importance long overdue for serious investigation. Durand's lectures, which advocated the grid for use by the military engineers under his tutelage, were published as *Pricis des Leçons d'Architecture Données a l'école Polytechnique* (Paris, 1802–05) and *Partie Graphique des Cours d'architecture Faits a l'école Royale Polytechnique depuis sa Reorganization* (Paris, 1821). But there are indications that the architecture students of the École des Beaux-Arts disdained the tool as simpleminded, and no Beaux-Arts or Beaux-Arts-influenced text that I have examined has made any mention of the regular grid. Guadet seems to advocate a regular rhythm of axes, and does so in close proximity to a recommendation to use graph paper in doing sketches; "Dessin par les axes," vol. I, 40–44, "Example de croquis a main levee sur papier quadrille," 53. Still, this is not the same thing as using a regular planning module. In England, however, the grid, directly derived from Durand, is advocated as late as 1888 in the ninth edition of Joseph Gwilt's *An Encyclopedia of Architecture: Historical, Theoretical, & Practical*, 935–42. In Germany, Leovon Klenze drew his 1854 Athenaum project for Munich on a grid, but then he was a pupil of Durand; see *Fünf Architecten des Klassizismus in Deutschland* (Dortmund, 1977), 199–200. It is possible, given the influence of the Polytechnique on the Beaux-Arts in the latter third of the nineteenth century, that grids were such a commonplace item that, like pencils, they needed no comment, but one would like to know for certain; on that influence see Moore, "Academic 'Dessin' Theory in France."

44 The titles of the articles seem chosen to emphasize the salient characteristics of each type: "home" and "town" bespeak a stable rootedness, while the "lots of room!" comes from the arrangement of long internal visual diagonals made possible by the spiral of spaces lapped at their corners.

45 *Architectural Record*, July 1905, 60–65.

46 Wright, *Exhibition Catalogue of the Chicago Architectural Club*, 156.

47 Kenneth Clark, *The Nude: A Study in Ideal Form* (Princeton: Princeton University Press, 1956), 293.

48 Richardson's office certainly thought this way, as is evidenced by publication of a collection à la Durand, albeit of perspectives. *American Architecture and Building News*, August 11, 1886, fig. 2.61.

49 James F. O'Gorman, *Henry Hobson Richardson and His Office: Selected Drawings* (Cambridge: Harvard University Press, 1974), 156.

50 Whether the Froebel system was so critical is a matter of some debate. From once being a commonplace, the assertion came to be commonly questioned but is now enjoying a revival. Of course, Froebelians contend that Wright's uniform grid came out of not academic practice but his kindergarten experi-

ence. For a discussion and bibliography, see Jeanne S. Rubin, "The Froebel Wright Kindergarten Connection, A New Perspective," *Journal of the Society of Architectural Historians* XLVIII, 1 (March 1989): 24–37, and Richard MacCormac's essay in this book.

51 Discovered by Charnpoiseau in fragments in 1863 and pieced back together, the Nike only gained its present critical prominence in 1863 when it was situated at the top of the Escalier Daru. See Anon., *The Louvre: 7 Faces of a Museum* (Paris: Éditions de la Réunion des Musées nationaux, 1987), 109. Wright would have been a young adult in 1883, at the time of attendant publicity.

Evolution of the Prarie House

1 Vincent J. Scully Jr., *The Shingle Style and the Stick Style* (New Haven: Yale University Press, 1971).

2 Henry-Rusell Hitchcock, *In the Nature of Materials* (New York: Duen, Sloan and Pearce, 1942), fig. 20.

3 Grant Carpenter Manson, *Frank Lloyd Wright to 1910: The First Golden Age* (New York: Van Nostrand Reinhold, 1958).

4 Hitchcock, *Nature of Materials*.

5 Grant Carpenter Manson, *Frank Lloyd Wright to 1910*.

6 Hitchcock, *Nature of Materials*.

7 Frank Lloyd Wright, "In the Cause of Architecture, I. The Logic of the Plan," *Architectural Record*, January 1928.

8 Hitchcock, *Nature of Materials*.

9 Robert C. Spencer, "The Work of Frank Lloyd Wright," *Architectural Review*, May 1900.

Chicago Frame

1 Louis H. Sullivan, *Autobiography of an Idea*, (New York, 1924), 314.

2 Montgomery Schuyler, "A Critique of the Works of Adler and Sullivan," *Architectural Record*, 1895. Reprinted in Schuyler, *American Architecture and Other Writings*, ed. William Jordy and Ralph Coe (Cambridge, 1961), 377–79.

3 Henry Russell Hitchcock, *In the Nature of Materials*, (New York: Duen, Sloan and Pearce, 1942), 68.

4 Quoted in Schuyler, "A Critique," 381.

5 Schuyler, "A Critique," 381.

6 Harriet Monroe, *John Root* (New York, 1968), 107.

7 Siegfried Giedion. *Space, Time and Architecture* (Cambridge, 1941), 215.

8 Sullivan, *Autobiography of an Idea*, 312–13.

9 Schuyler, "A Critique," 382.

10 Le Corbusier, *Towards a New Architecture* (London, 1927), 33.

Architectural Practice and Social Vision in Wright's Early Designs

For their helpful comments on earlier drafts of this essay, I would like to thank Thomas Bender, Joseph Connors, and Anthony Alofson.

1 Frank Lloyd Wright, "Chicago Culture," lecture to the Chicago Woman's Aid (1918). Wright Papers, Manuscript Division, Library of Congress. I have occasionally altered the spelling and punctuation of Wright's esoteric style or corrected typographical errors in his manuscripts.

2 Wright, "Chicago Culture."

3 Wright, "Chicago Culture."

4 Pertinent and interesting examples of this recent cultural history include Carl E. Schorske, *Fin de Siècle Vienna: Politics and Culture* (New York: Alfred A. Knopf, 1980); Neil Harris, *Humbug: The Art of P. T. Barnum* (Boston: Little, Brown, 1973); T. J. Jackson Lears, *No Place of Grace: Antimodernism and the Transformation of American Culture, 1880–1920* (New York: Pantheon, 1981); Elizabeth Kendall, *Where She Danced* (New York: Alfred A. Knopf, 1979); Peter Burke, *Popular Culture in Early Modern Europe* (New York: New York University Press, 1978); Carlo Ginzburg, *The Cheese and the Worms: The Cosmos of a Sixteenth Century Miller* (Baltimore: Johns Hopkins University Press, 1980); *Faire de l'histoire: nouveaux objets*, ed. Jacques Le Goff and Pierra Nora (Paris: Gallimard, 1974); Richard Hoggart, *The Uses of Literacy: Changing Patterns of English Mass Culture* (Fair Lawn, N.J.: Essential Books, 1957); and Steven L. Kaplan, ed., *Understanding Popular Culture: Europe from the Middle Ages to the Nineteenth Century* (Berlin and New York: Mouton, 1984). Important work is also being done by American scholars studying the social and political roles of popular and folk culture in early modern Europe, most notably Natalie Zemon Davis and Robert Darnton. For an interesting adaptation of these ideas to another American city, see William R. Taylor, "Toward the Launching of a Commercial Culture: New York City, 1880–1939," paper prepared for the Social Science Research Council, New York City Working Group, 1984.

5 Frank Lloyd Wright, *An Autobiography.* (New York: Horizon Press, 1977), 617.

6 On this aspect of Wright's early career, see H. Allen Brooks, "Steinway Hall, Architects and Dreams," *Journal of the Society of Architectural Historians* XXII (October 1963): 171–75. In Chicago, as in New York, Steinway Hall provided space for free concerts and other public cultural activities, in addition to commercial office space, as did the Fine Arts Building, where Wright also chose to set up an urban office.

7 Frank Lloyd Wright, "The Architect," paper read before the Second Annual Convention of the Architectural League of America. Auditorium Hotel, Chicago, June 1900. Reprinted in *The Brickbuilder* IX (June 1900): 124; and in *Construction News* X (June 16–23, 1900): 518. Also mentioned in Wright, "A Philosophy of Fine Art," lecture to the Chicago Chapter of the Architectural League of America, Chicago Art Institute (1900). Papers, Manuscript Division, Library of Congress.

8 Wright, *An Autobiography*, 166.

9 The relation of these themes to architectural design is treated in depth in Gwendolyn Wright, *Moralism and the Model Home: Domestic Architecture and Cultural Conflict in Chicago, 1873–1913* (Chicago: University of Chicago Press, 1980).

10 Frank Lloyd Wright, "The Modern Home as a Work of Art," lecture to the Chicago Woman's Club (1902). Wright Papers, Manuscript Division, Library of Congress. Also mentioned in Wright, "A Small House with 'Lots of Room in It,'" *Ladies' Home Journal* IIXX (July 1901): 15.

11 Frank Lloyd Wright. "In the Cause of Architecture," *Architectural Record*, March 1908, 158.

12 Frank Lloyd Wright, "This 'Ideal' Architect," lecture to the College Endowment Association, Evanston, Illinois (1901). Wright Papers, Manuscript Division, Library of Congress.

13 Frank Lloyd Wright, "The Modern Home as a Work of Art," lecture to the Chicago Woman's Club (1902). Wright Papers, Manuscript Division, Library of Congress.

14 Herbert Croly, "New York as the American Metropolis," *Architectural Record*, March 1903, 199.

15 Helen Campbell, *Household Economics: A Course of Lectures in the School of Economics of the University of Wisconsin* (New York: G. P. Putnam's Sons, 1896), 98–105. See also Helen Campbell. "Household Furnishings." *Architectural Record*, October–December 1896, 97–104.

16 In "Architecture of Ideas," *Architectural Record*, April 1904, 363, Herbert Croly praised the "new midwestern architects who are departing from tradition," especially Louis Sullivan and "a very able architect, who issued from Mr. Sullivan's office, Mr. Frank Wright." There is some discussion of Croly's attitudes in David W. Levy, *Herbert Croly of the New Republic* (Princeton: Princeton University Press, 1985), and of Wright in particular on pp. 90–92.

17 Robert C. Spencer Jr. "The Work of Frank Lloyd Wright." *Architectural Review*, June 1900, 61–72; reprinted (Park Forest, Illinois: Prairie School Press, 1964), 182.

18 Homer Hoyt, *One Hundred Years of Land Values in Chicago* (Chicago: University of Chicago Press, 1933), 215.

19 See G. Wright, *Moralism and the Modern Home*, and also Stephen J. Diner, *A City and Its Universities: Public Policy in Chicago, 1892–1919* (Chapel Hill: University of North Carolina Press, 1980), as well as the many writings by Professors Talbot, Breckinridge, and Zueblin.

20 Frank Lloyd Wright, "The American System of House Building," *Western Architect* IXV (September 1916): 99.

21 Wright, Frank Lloyd, *Ausgeführte Bauten und Entwürfe von Frank Lloyd Wright* (Berlin: Ernst Wasmuth, 1910); translated and reprinted as *Buildings, Plans and Designs* (New York: Horizon Press, 1963). Wright's introduction reprinted in Frank Lloyd Wright, *Frank Lloyd Wright: on Architecture* ed. F. Gutheim (New York: Gosset and Dunlap, 1941), 65, from which this and future page references are taken.

22 Scholarship on the progressives as cultural and political reformers is abundant. Two works that specifically attempt to bring together some of these individuals, including Wright, in order to examine their attitudes about cultural life are Robert M. Crunden, *Ministers of Reform: The Progressives' Achievement in American Civilization, 1889–1920* (New York: Basic Books, 1982); and John Higham, "The Reorientation of American Culture in the 1890's," in *Writing American History: Essays on Modern Scholarship* (Bloomington: Indiana University Press, 1970), 73–102.

23 Wright's schemes provided for a population of 1,032 families and 1,550 individuals at a minimum, living in detached houses, duplexes, fourplexes, row houses, and apartment buildings for families or single women or men.

24 Randolph Bourne, "Our Unplanned Cities," *New Republic* III (June 26, 1915): 202–03; reprinted in *The History of a Literary Radical and Other Papers by Randolph Bourne*, ed. Van Wyck Brooks (New York: S. A. Russell, 1956): 145.

25 Frank Lloyd Wright, *Frank Lloyd Wright: Drawings for a Living Architecture* (New York: Horizon Press, 1959): 197.

26 Frank Lloyd Wright, "Architecture, Architect and Client," lecture to the University Guild, Evanston, Illinois (1896). Excerpts in Wright Papers, Manuscript Division, Library of Congress, and in Wright, *On Architecture* (1941), 4–6.

27 Wright, "This Ideal Architect."

28 On the history of professionalization during this critical period, see, in particular, Thomas L. Haskell, ed., *The Authority of Experts* (Bloomington: Indiana University Press, 1984); Alexandra Oleson and John Voss, ed., *The Organization of Knowledge in Modern America, 1860–1920* (Baltimore: Johns Hopkins University Press, 1979); Thomas L. Haskell, *The Emergence of Professional Social Science: The American Social Science Association and the Nineteenth Century Crisis of Authority* (Urbana: University of Illinois Press, 1977); Mary O. Furner, *Advocacy and Objectivity: A Crisis in the Professionalization of American Social Science, 1865–1905* (Lexington: University Press of Kentucky, 1975); Magali Sarfatti Larson, *The Rise of Professionalism: A Sociological Analysis* (Berkeley: University of California Press, 1977); and Charles E. Rosenberg, *No Other Gods: On Science and American Social Thought* (Baltimore: Johns Hopkins University Press, 1976).

29 Frank Lloyd Wright, "A Philosophy of Fine Art," (variation of "This Ideal Architect") lecture to the Chicago Chapter of the Architectural League of America, Chicago Art Institute (1900). Papers, Manuscript Division, Library of Congress.

30 Wright, "The Architect" and "A Philosophy of Fine Art."

31 Frank Lloyd Wright, "Art in the Home," paper read before the Home Decorating and Furnishing Department of the Central Art Association's Third Annual Congress, Chicago (May 1898). Reprinted in *Arts forAmerica* VII (June 1898): 583.

32 Wright, "The Architect" and "A Philosophy of Fine Art."

33 Wright, "The Architect" and "A Philosophy of Fine Art" and "The 'Ideal' Architect."

34 T. W. Heyck. *The Transformation of Intellectual Life in Victorian England* (New York: St. Martin's Press, 1982), 190.

35 Wright, *An Autobiography*, 166.

36 Frank Lloyd Wright, "In the Cause of Architecture, Second Paper," *Architectural Record*, May 1914, 406.

37 "Successful Houses, III," *House Beautiful*, February 15, 1987, 64–69; Alfred H. Granger, "An Architect's Studio," *House Beautiful*, December 1899, 36–45; reprinted in Joy Wheeler Dow, *The Book of a Hundred Houses* (Chicago: Herbert S. Stone, 1902). (Stone was the publisher of *House*

Beautiful and an avid promoter of the Arts and Crafts aesthetic in Chicago.)

38 *National Builder*, October 1905, 29; 43; December 1906, 35; 55; April 1913, 80–83. Fred T. Hodgson, the editor, described the Fricke house as having "a massive look and is somewhat unique in style, but withal quite pleasing." Wright's "The Architect" appeared in the Chicago- and New York–based *Construction News* X (June 16–23, 1900): 518–19, 538–40.

39 Wright, "In the Cause of Architecture, Second Paper," 410.

40 Wright, "In the Cause of Architecture," 156.

41 Wright, "Art in the Home," 582, and Frank Lloyd Wright, "The Art and Craft of the Machine," (revised version of 1901 essay of the same name), paper read before the Chicago Chapter of the Daughters of the American Revolution (1904). Reprinted in *The New Industrialism* (Chicago: National League of Industrial Art, 1902), 107; 111.

42 Wright, "Chicago Culture."

43 Wright, "Art in the Home," 580.

44 Frank Lloyd Wright, "The Art and Craft of the Machine," paper read before the Chicago Arts and Crafts Society, Hull House (March 6, 1901) and the Western Society of Engineers (March 20, 1901). Reprinted in *Frank Lloyd Wright: Writings and Buildings*, ed. Edgar Kaufmann and Ben Raeburn (New York: Meridian Books, World Publishing Company, 1960), 68.

45 Wright, "The Modern Home as a Work of Art."

46 Wright, "The Architect," 125, and "A Home in a Prairie Town," 4.

47 Wright, "Art in the Home," 581.

48 Helen Campbell. "Chicago." *The Brickbuilder* VII (May 1908): 107.

49 Edward Bok, *The Americanization of Edward Bok* (New York: Charles Scribner's Sons, 1924), 240–43; G. Wright, *Moralism and the Model Home*, 136–40.

50 Wright, "Art in the Home," 584.

51 The City Club Bulletin listed early lectures by George Herbert Mead, Graham Taylor, Jens Jensen, Lawrence Veiller, Benjamin Marsh, Raymond Unwin, and Jacob Riis, among others. By 1910, however, George E. Hooker, speaking on the "Causes of Congestion in Chicago," balanced an appeal for regionalism with the statement: "City planning stands for that official application of intelligent design to city growth which . . . shall produce an efficient and at the same time pleasing physical condition" (my emphasis) (*Bulletin* 3 [June 29, 1910], 331).

52 Wright. "The American System of House Building," 122.

53 Wright, "Art in the Home," 583, and Wright, "This 'Ideal' Architect."

54 Wright, "This 'Ideal' Architect."

55 John Dewey. *My Pedagogic Creed* (Chicago: E. L. Kellogg & Co., 1897; reprinted in *John Dewey on Education*, ed. Reginald D. Archambault, 427–39. New York: Modern Library, 1964), 429.

56 Wright, "The Modern Home as a Work of Art."

57 Wright, "The Modern Home as a Work of Art."

58 Wright, "The Art and Craft of the Machine," 58, 73, and Wright, "This 'Ideal' Architect."

Schooling the Prairie School

Research for this essay was carried out in 1986 during a Visiting Senior Fellowship at

the Center for Advanced Study in the Visual Arts at the National Gallery of Art, Washington, DC. I wish to thank the staff of that institution for all their help and personal kindness. This paper parallels Otto Antonia Graf's monumental *Die Kunst des Quadrats: Zum Werk von Frank Lloyd Wright.*

1 See for example, H. P. Berlage's remarks on Wright's work in H. Allen Brooks, ed., *Writings on Wright* (Cambridge: MIT Press, 1981), 131–33.

2 Sigfried Giedion, *Space, Time and Architecture* (Cambridge: Harvard University Press, 1941), 413.

3 Frank Lloyd Wright himself mentions the anecdote in *An Autobiography* (1932; New York: Horizon Press, 1977), 34–36. It has been developed in some detail in Grant Manson, *Frank Lloyd Wright to 1910: The First Golden Age* (New York: Van Nostrand Reinhold, 1958); and Richard MacCormac, "The Anatomy of Wright's Aesthetic," in Brooks, *Writings on Wright*, 161–74, originally published in the *Architectural Review*, February 1968, 143–46.

4 Robert C. Spencer Jr., "The Work of Frank Lloyd Wright," *Architectural Review*, June 1900, 61–72; facsimile ed. (Park Forest, Illinois: Prairie School Press, 1964).

5 When Walter Burley Griffin from the studio won the competition to design Canberra, the capital city of Australia (see below), he described himself to the Australian authorities as a onetime partner of Wright's. They, on writing to Wright for confirmation of this, were informed by him that the studio had been organized cooperatively. He politely denied that Griffin had been a true partner.

6 Barry Byrne, "On Frank Lloyd Wright and his Atelier," *Journal of the American Institute of Architects* 39 (1963): 109–12.

7 Reproduced in Brooks, *Writings on Wright*, 83–92.

8 J. J. P. Oud, "The Influence of Frank Lloyd Wright on the Architecture of Europe," *Wendingen*, 1925, 85–86.

9 Frank Lloyd Wright, "The Third Dimension," *Wendingen*, 1925, 57.

10 Frank Lloyd Wright, *Genius and the Mobocracy* (New York: Duell, Sloan and Pearce, 1949), 55 and passim.

11 What follows is noted, but without great emphasis, in Sherman Paul, *Louis Sullivan: An Architect in American Thought* (Englewood Cliffs: Prentice-Hall, 1962); H. Allen Brooks, *The Prairie School: Frank Lloyd Wright and His Midwest Contemporaries* (Toronto: University of Toronto Press, 1972); and Narciso Menocal, *Architecture as Nature: The Transcendentalist Idea of Louis Sullivan* (Madison: University of Wisconsin Press, 1981).

12 On the history of the club, see Wilbert R. Hasbrouck, "The Early Years of the Chicago Architectural Club," *Chicago Architectural Club Journal* 1 (1981): 7–14; and John Zukowsky, "The Chicago Architectural Club, 1895–1940," *Chicago Architectural Club Journal* 2 (1982): 170–74.

13 See Arthur Huen's review of the exhibition in *Construction News*, March 18, 1900. It was also in 1900 that Robert C. Spencer Jr. published the first extensive article on Wright's work (see note 4 above).

14 The league published the *Architectural*

Annual, edited by Albert Kelsey, in 1900, 1901, 1906, and 1907.

15 Sullivan's message, the list of delegates, and the schedule of events were published in the *Inland Architect*, June 1899.

16 The addresses were published as "The Modern Phase of Architecture," *Inland Architect*, June 1899, 40; and "The Young Man in Architecture," *Inland Architect*, June 1900, 38–40.

17 Published in *Construction News*, June 16 and 23, 1900, 518–19, 538–40, and elsewhere.

18 *Construction News*, June 16 and 30, 1900, for example, published from among the papers delivered at the 1900 convention the Beaux-Arts ideas of A. B. Trowbridge as well as the Arts and Crafts proposals of Elmer Grey.

19 *Inland Architect*, June 1901, documented this meeting in detail.

20 See the Lorch papers preserved in the Bentley Historical Library at the University of Michigan. French very sadly gave Lorch notice in a touching letter dated May 11, 1901.

21 *Architectural Review*, April 1908, 69–74.

22 On the origin of the term, "Chicago school," see Brooks, *The Prairie School*. The designation of architectural systems—like "steel-cage construction"—as "Chicago" had been common since 1890 and was already applied to domestic design around 1900, but Tallmadge seems to have attached the label officially.

23 Sullivan described the building thus in a letter to Daniel Burnham of October 16, 1893: "*The thought we sought to express in the Transportation Building was this: An architectural exhibit.*
The thought subdivided itself as follows:
1. A natural, not historical, exhibit.
2. To be expressed by elementary masses carrying elaborate decoration.
3. All architectural masses and subdivisions to be bounded by straight lines or semicircles, or both in combination, to illustrate the possibilities of very simple elements when in effective combination."
(Quoted in full in William Jordy, "The Tall Buildings," *Louis Sullivan: The Function of Ornament* (New York: W. W. Norton, 1986), 106–08.

24 Norris Kelly Smith, *Frank Lloyd Wright: A Study in Architectural Content* (Englewood Cliffs: Prentice-Hall, 1966); 2d. rev. ed. (Watkins Glen: American Life Foundation and Study Institute, 1979). I find it hard to agree with most of the details of Smith's argument, but the basis—the assumption that Wright had social objectives—is unassailable and timely.

25 Neil Levine has kindly discussed his book manuscript in progress on this subject with me on many occasions. [2004: Now published as *The Architecture of Frank Lloyd Wright* (Princeton: Princeton University Press, 1996).] See Neil Levine, "Hollyhock House and the Romance of Southern California," *Art in America*, September 1983, 150–65; idem, "Frank Lloyd Wright's Diagonal Planning," in Helen Searing, ed., *In Search of Modern Architecture* (New York: Architectural History Foundation/MIT Press, 1982), 245–77.

26 Joseph Siry, "Carson Pirie Scott: Louis Sullivan and the Modern Department Store,"

manuscript kindly lent to the author and soon to be published by the University of Chicago Press. [2004: Now published as *Carson Pirie Scott: Louis Sullivan and the Chicago Department Store* (Chicago: University of Chicago Press, 1988).]

27 Barry Byrne, when he was still alive, thus described their functions in the office.

28 Alfred Granger, "An Architect's Studio," *House Beautiful*, 1899, 36–45.

Form and Philosophy
This essay was previously published in *Environment and Planning B 1*. This paper develops arguments first presented in the author's Master's thesis, "An investigation of space and form in the architecture of Frank Lloyd Wright," presented at University College, London, in 1965.

1 Robert C. Spencer Jr., "The Work of Frank Lloyd Wright," *Architectural Review*, May 1900, 61–72.

2 Peter Collins, *Changing Ideals in Modern Architecture* (London: Faber and Faber, 1965).

3 Grant Manson, "Wright in the Nursery. The influence of Froebel education on the work of Frank Lloyd Wright," *Architectural Review*, February 1953, 143–146.

4 M. K. Boelte and J. Drauss, *The Kindergarten Guide: An Illustrated Handbook Designed for the Self Instruction of Kindergartners, Mothers and Nurses* (New York: E. Steiger, 1877).

5 Frank Lloyd Wright, *The Future of Architecture* (New York: Horizon Press, 1953).

6 Frank Lloyd Wright, *A Testament* (New York: Horizon Press, 1957).

7 Rudolf Wittkower, *Architectural Principles in the Age of Humanism* (London: Tiranti, 1952).

8 Frank Lloyd Wright, "In the Cause of Architecture," *Architectural Record*, March 1908, 120–155.

9 Wright, *A Testament*.

10 Boelte and Drauss, *Kindergarten Guide*.

11 Frank Lloyd Wright, *The Natural House* (New York: Horizon Press, 1954).

12 Boelte and Drauss, *Kindergarten Guide*.

13 Wright, *Natural House*.

14 Boelte and Drauss, *Kindergarten Guide*.

15 Wright, "Cause of Architecture" (1908).

16 Frank Lloyd Wright, "In the Cause of Architecture," *Architectural Record*, February 1928, 145–151.

17 Wright, *A Testament*.

18 Frank Lloyd Wright, "Frank Lloyd Wright Talks on His Art," *New York Times Magazine*, October 4, 1953, 26–27, 47.

19 Rudolf Arnheim, *Art and Visual Perception* (London: Faber and Faber, 1956).

20 Dr. Ross Ashby suggested a biological explanation for this in "Art and communication theory," lecture given to the Institute of Contemporary Arts, April 7, 1960.

21 Colin Rowe and Robert Slutzky, "Transparency: Literal and Phenomenal," *Perspecta* 8 (1963): 45–54.

22 Georg Kepes, *Language of Vision* (Chicago: Paul Theobald, 1959).

23 Frank Lloyd Wright, untitled (a portfolio of recent work), *Architectural Record*, January 1950, 73–108.

24 Colin Rowe, "Chicago Frame," *Architectural Review*, November 1956, 285–289.)

25 Frank Lloyd Wright, *Genius and Mobocracy* (New York: Duell, Sloan and Pearce, 1949).

26 Grant Manson, "Sullivan and Wright: An Uneasy Union of Celts," *Architectural Review*, June 1955, 348–351. See also G. Manson, *Frank Lloyd Wright to 1910* (New York: Reinhold, 1958).

27 Wright, *Genius and Mobocracy*.

28 Louis H. Sullivan, *A System of Architectural Ornament* (Washington: The Press of the American Institute of Architects, 1924).

29 Collins, *Changing Ideals*.

30 Sullivan, *System of Ornament*. The possibility of describing inspiration in biological terms was realized in the eighteenth century and later developed by Goethe and Coleridge (Collins, *Changing Ideals*, 151).

31 Asa Gray, *School and Field Book of Botany* (New York: Ivison Blakeman Taylor, 1869).

32 Sullivan, *System of Ornament*.

33 Ibid.

34 Wright, *Genius and Mobocracy*.

35 Henry-Russell Hitchcock, "Frank Lloyd Wright and the Academic Tradition of the Early Eighteen Nineties," *Journal of the Warburg and Coutauld Institutes* 7, 1 and 2 (1944): 46–63.

36 Le Corbusier, *Vers une architecture* (Paris: Éditions Cres, 1923).

37 Manson, *Wright to 1910*.

38 Wright, *A Testament*.

39 Sullivan, *System of Ornament*.

40 Wright, "Cause of Architecture" (1908).

41 W. C. Behrendt, *Modern Building: Its Nature, Problems and Forms* (London: Martin Hopkinson, 1938).

42 Arnheim, *Art and Perception*.

43 Sullivan, *System of Ornament*.

44 Frank Lloyd Wright, *Ausgeführte Bauten und Entwürfe von Frank Lloyd Wright* (Berlin: Ernst Wasmuth, 1910). English edition, *Buildings, Plans, and Designs by Frank Lloyd Wright* (New York: Horizon Press, 1963).

45 Wright, "Cause of Architecture" (1908).

46 Wright, untitled (1951).

47 In spite of the fact that one cannot see all the corners of the cube from the front of the house and that, in any case, one of the corners is incomplete, it seems that, in such a situation, the visual information is sufficient for the observer to infer the completeness of the form. See M. D. Vernon, *The Psychology of Perception* (Harmondsworth: Penguin Books, 1962), 60, for a discussion of experiments that indicate this.

48 Frank Lloyd Wright, "Address to the Junior Chapter of the American Institute of Architects, New York City, 1952," *An American Architecture* (New York: Horizon Press, 1955).

Enspacement:
The Main Sequence from 4 to 6
1 Frank Lloyd Wright, *The Future of Architecture* (New York: Horizon Press, 1953), 147.

The Text-Tile Tectonic
1 "The Life-work of American Architect Frank Lloyd Wright," *Wendingen* (1925; reprint, New York: Horizon Press, 1965) 57.

2 Barry Berdoll, "Primordial Fires: Frank Lloyd Wright, Gottfried Semper and the Chicago School" (Paper delivered at Buell Center Symposium on Fallingwater, Columbia University, November 8, 1986), 4.

3 Roula Geraniotis, "Gottfried Semper and the Chicago School" (Paper delivered at Buell Center Symposium on the German influ-

ence on American architects, Columbia University, 1988), 5.

4 Donald Hoffmann, *The Architecture of John Wellborn Root* (Baltimore and London: Johns Hopkins University Press, 1973), 91. See also J.A. Chewing's entry on Root in *MacMillan Encyclopedia of Architecture*, vol.3, 606.

5 Geraniotis, "Gottfried Semper," 5.

6 Geraniotis, "Gottfried Semper," 11.

7 David Van Zanten, entry on Owen Jones in *MacMillan Encyclopedia of Architecture*, vol .2, 514.

8 Louis Sullivan, "Suggestions in Artistic Brickwork" 1910; reprinted *The Prairie School Review* 4, 1967, 24.

9 Frank Lloyd Wright, "In the Cause of Architecture IV," *Architectural Record*, October 1927; reprinted New York: McGraw-Hill, 1975, 146.

10 James F. O'Gorman, *The Architecture of Frank Furness* (Philadelphia: Philadelphia Museum of Art, 1973), 33, 37.

11 Narciso Menocal, *Architecture as Nature: The Transcendentalist Idea of Louis Sullivan* (Madison: University of Wisconsin Press, 1981), 7, 31.

12 Owen Jones, *The Grammar of Ornament* (1856; reprinted New York: Portland House 1987), 154.

13 Jones, *Grammar*, 5

14 Jones, *Grammar*, 95

15 Jones, *Grammar*, 156

16 Louis Sullivan, *A System of Architectural Ornament According with a Philosophy of Man's Power* (1924; reprinted New York: Eakins Press, 1966), text accompanying Plate 3.

17 Gottfried Semper, *The Four Elements of Architecture & Other Writings*, trans. Harry Mallgrave and Wolfgang Herrmann (New York: Cambridge University Press, 1989). See in particular the prolegomena to "Style in the Technical and Tectonic Arts" (1860), 196.

18 Rudolph Gelpke, "Art and Sacred Drugs in the Orient," *World Cultures and Modern Art* (Munich: Bruckman, 1972), 18-21. Gelpke argues after Georg Jacob and Henri Michaux that the culture of Islam has a mystical hallucinatory origin.

19 Claude Humbert, *Islamic Ornamental Design* (New York: Hastings House, 1980), 13–17.

20 Frank Lloyd Wright, *Frank Lloyd Wright: Writings and Buildings*, ed. Edgar Kaufman and Ben Raeburn (New York: Meridian Books, 1964), 58–60.

21 Wright, *Writings and Buildings*, 66.

22 Sigfried Giedions, *Space Time and Architecture* (Cambridge: HUP, 1967), 352–354. See also p.347 for an illustration of St. Mary's Church, Chicago of 1833, the first all balloon frame building.

23 Wright, "On Building Unity Temple," *Writings and Buildings*, 76.

24 Wright, *Writings and Buildings*, 225.

25 Ibid.

26 Wright, *Writings and Buildings*, 215–216.

27 Frank Lloyd Wright, *An American Architecture* (New York: Horizon Press, 1955), 218.

28 See the entire issue dedicated to the work of F.L. Wright, *Architectural Forum*, January 1938, 79.

29 John Sergeant, *Frank Lloyd Wright's Usonian Houses* (New York: Whitney Library of Design, 1976) 19.

Warp and Woof

This essay is an extended version of appendix I from the author's *Frank Lloyd Wright's Usonian Houses: The Case for Organic Architecture*. The author is indebted to Richard MacCormac and Madeleine Thatcher for the use of their drawings.

1   Grant Carpenter Manson, "Wright in the Nursery: The Influence of Froebel Education on the Work of Frank Lloyd Wright," *Architectural Review*, June 1953, 349–51.
2   Richard MacCormac, "The Anatomy of Wright's Aesthetic," *Architectural Review*, February 1968, 3–6.
3   Richard MacCormac, "Froebel's Kindergarten Gifts and the Early Work of Frank Lloyd Wright" *Environment and Planning B 1* (1974): 29–50.
4   Frank Lloyd Wright quoted in Edgar Kaufman and Ben Raeburn, eds., *Frank Lloyd Wright Writings and Buildings* (Cleveland: Meridian, 1960), 221–22.
5   E. Frank, "Organic Architecture, Organic Philosophy and Frank Lloyd Wright," unpublished paper, Avery Library, Columbia University, New York (1963): 27.
6   Frank Lloyd Wright in F. Gutheim, ed., *Frank Lloyd Wright: On Architecture* (New York: Duell, Sloan and Pearce, 1941), 38.
7   Frank Lloyd Wright in Edgar Kaufman, ed., *An American Architecture:* (New York: Horizon Press, 1955), 217.
8   Lao Tzu, *The Way of Life (Tao-Te-Ching)*, W. Bynner trans. (London: Lyrebird Press, 1944).
9   Kakuzo Okakura, *The Book of Tea* (1906; reprinted New York: Dover, 1964), 40.
10 Frank Lloyd Wright, *A Testament* (New York: Horizon Press, 1957), 306–307.

From the Prairie House to Fallingwater

1   For documentation of all Wright houses mentioned, see: Henry-Russell Hitchcock, *In the Nature of Materials* (New York: Duell, Sloan, and Pearce, 1942).
2   See, e.g., Sandra Honey, "Who and What Inspired Mies van der Rohe in Germany," *Architectural Design* 2/3 (1979): 99–102.
3   See, e.g., Lewis Mumford, *Roots of Contemporary American Architecture* (New York: Grove Press, 1959).
4   In pursuit of this thought I was later confirmed and encouraged by Vincent Scully, "Wright vs. the International Style," *Art News*, March 1954.
5   Auguste Choisy, *Histoire de l'architecture*. 2 vols. (Paris: Gauthier-Villars, 1899).
6   Title of Le Corbusier's book published by Reynal & Hitchcock, New York, 1947, and reprinted by The Institute of Contemporary Art, Boston, 1948.
7   John Berger, *The Moment of Cubism*, (London: Weidenfeld and Nicolson, 1969).

A Beat of the Rythmic Clock of Nature

This essay is a revised version of one I delivered at the symposium to honor Edgar Kaufmann Jr., on the fiftieth anniversary of the completion of Fallingwater (November 8, 1986). The symposium was sponsored by the Buell Center for the Study of American Architecture, Planning, and Preservation, Columbia University, and was organized under the direction of Robert A. M. Stern. I

remain grateful to Edgar Kaufmann Jr. for his encouragement and tireless enthusiasm during the preparation of this paper. For helpful information, I thank William Wesley Peters, Robert Sweeney, M. J. Hamilton, Tom Graham, Jack Quinan, Neil Levine, and Peter Becker. Research for this paper was conducted at the Frank Lloyd Wright Foundation, Scottsdale, Arizona, and Spring Green, Wisconsin. Bruce Brooks Pfeiffer and his staff, Indira Berendston, Oscar Muñoz, Penny Fowler, and Margo Stipe, provided guidance at the Taliesin Archives. I also consulted the Wright Collection at the Getty Center for the History of Art and the Humanities, and I must thank Nicholas Olsberg, Gene Waddell, Stephen Nonack, Pamela Kratochvil, and Brent Sverdloff.

1   Jenkin Lloyd-Jones, "The River of Life," *Jess: Bits of Wayside Gospel* (New York: MacMillan, 1899), 126. I am grateful to Tom Graham, who provided this and other excerpts from the sermons of his grandfather.
2   My interest in water and architecture was inspired by Charles W. Moore, whose writings and conversations have helped shape my understanding. His unique and brilliant Ph.D. dissertation, "Water and Architecture," completed at Princeton University, September 1957, has permanently altered my perception of water in an architectural setting. Before his death in 1993, Moore revised and condensed his dissertation, and it was published posthumously as *Water and Architecture* (New York: Abrams, 1994).
    My investigation of the role of water in Wright's architecture began with my research into the design evolution of Olive Hill, Wright's commission for Aline Barnsdall in Hollywood, California. For a discussion of how water was used in Wright's plans for Olive Hill, see my *Frank Lloyd Wright, Hollyhock House and Olive Hill: Buildings and Projects for Aline Barnsdall* (New York: Rizzoli International, 1992), especially 58–60, 66–71, and 94. At the symposium, "Frank Lloyd Wright: Beyond Conventional Boundaries," sponsored by the Society of Architectural Historians at the Museum of Modern Art, April 27, 1994, I delivered a paper, "Between Heaven and Earth: The Sacred Role of Water." The theme explored the dialectic between art and nature allegorized through the play of water in four projects and two master plans of the 1940s and '50s: Monona Terrace, Pittsburgh Point Park Civic Center, Baghdad Opera House, Florida Southern College, the Huntington Hartford Estate, and Marin County Civic Center.
3   On the chronology of Wright's trips to Japan between 1905 and 1922, see my "Frank Lloyd Wright and the Imperial Hotel: A Postscript," *Art Bulletin* 67 (June 1985), 296–310. For a detailed discussion of Wright's 1905 journey, see Masami Tanigawa, "Wright The Tourist" and "The Wrights' 1905 Itinerary" in *Frank Lloyd Wright's Fifty Views of Japan: The 1905 Photo Album*, ed. Melanie Birk (San Francisco: Frank Lloyd Wright Home and Studio Foundation and Pomegranate Artbooks, 1996), 15–19 and Margo Stipe, "Wright's First Trip to Japan," *Frank Lloyd Wright Quarterly* 6, (Spring 1995): 21–23.
4   Wright received advice from a friend, Shu-

gio Hiromichi, a Japanese government official. Shugio provided letters of introduction to members of the Japanese art community, who could give detailed information about what to see in Kyoto, including the "Horiuji temples." Shugio also notes that Wright had retained a native guide who accompanied him on his travels. Letter from Shugio Hiromichi, Tokyo, to Wright, Kyoto, March 18, 1905, Frank Lloyd Wright Archives.
5   Neither the Morse nor the Conder book are listed in Margaret Klinkow, *The Wright Family Library* (Oak Park: Frank Lloyd Wright Home and Studio Foundation, 1994); but, there is an entry for Josiah Conder, *The Floral Art of Japan* (Yokohama, Shanghai, Hong Kong, and Singapore: Kelly and Walsh Ltd., 1899). This is the revised second edition of *The Flowers of Japan and the Art of Floral Arrangement* (1893). For a detailed discussion of Wright and Morse, see Kevin Nute, *Frank Lloyd Wright and Japan* (New York: Van Nostrand Reinhold, 1993), 36–46.
6   Some of the waterfall images are hand-tinted and may be postcard views rather than photographs taken by Wright. Photographs #985–988, #990–999, Frank Lloyd Wright photo album, 1905, Frank Lloyd Wright Home and Studio Research Center, Oak Park, Illinois, Gift of David and Gladys Wright.
7   The 160-acre site of Horseshoe Inn was purchased September 17, 1906, by Willard H. Ashton. Warranty Deed #101585 filed October 6, 1906, Larimer County, Colorado. The land, which is called Horseshoe Park, is located today at the eastern end of Rocky Mountain National Park below Mount Chapin looking up Chapin Pass near Estes Park, Colorado. The name Horseshoe Park may have been derived from the winding curves of the Fall River, which resembled a horseshoe. In June 1908, Ashton, president and general manager of Horseshoe Ranch and Inn Company, announced that construction would begin in the summer and be complete by fall for a new hotel designed by Frank Lloyd Wright to replace the existing Horseshoe Inn. "Beautiful New Hotel for Horse Shoe Park," *The Mountaineer*, June 4, 1908, 1. For undocumented reasons, Ashton chose instead to build a more conventional structure, which incorporated the older building. The new hotel opened in the summer of 1909. In 1915, the United States federal government dedicated the surrounding area as a national park. Horseshoe Inn continued operation under new owners until 1931, when the National Park Service appropriated the property, the hotel burned to the ground, and the land returned to its natural state. Henry F. Pedersen Jr., *Those Castles of Wood: The Story of the Early Lodges of Rocky Mountain National Park and Pioneer Days of Estes Park, Colorado* (Estes Park, Colorado: Henry F. Pedersen Jr., 1993), 85–96.
8   For the best single source of information and analysis of Taliesin, see the collection of essays by Neil Levine, Scott Gartner, Anthony Alofsin and Narciso G. Menocal in *Wright Studies I, Taliesin, 1911–1914*, ed. Narciso G. Menocal (Carbondale and Edwardsville: Southern Illinois University Press, 1992). See also my *Frank Lloyd Wright's Taliesin and Taliesin West* (New York: Harry M. Abrams Inc, 1997); and Yukio Futagawa, ed., with

Bruce Brooks Pfeiffer, text, *Frank Lloyd Wright Selected Houses, 2: Taliesin* (Tokyo: A.D.A. Edita, 1990), and Walter Creese, *The Crowning of the American Landscape: Eight Great Spaces and Their Buildings* (Princeton: Princeton University Press, 1985), 141–278.

9 Wright's maternal ancestors, the Lloyd-Jones family, named the three eastern hills Byrn Mawr, Bryn Bach, and Bryn Canol. Maginel Wright Barney with Tom Burke, *The Valley of the God-Almighty Joneses* (New York: Appleton-Century, 1965), 56. The three western hills do not have any names that have come down in history; but they are distinguished by the buildings that Wright designed for them: the windmill, Romeo and Juliet (1897); the farm buildings, Midway Farm (1938); and Wright's studio-residence, Taliesin.

The Northwest Ordinance of 1787 ordered the measuring of new lands according to town and range. The surveying began in Wisconsin in the 1830s. Jack Holzhueter in conversation with M.J. Hamilton, November 1986; M.J. Hamilton to author, November 1986. The land was laid out in square sections of 160 acres. The Lloyd-Jones Valley is situated in Iowa County, Wyoming Township, range four east, section 30. Sections are typically further divided into quadrants for the purpose of land ownership. They are generally noted as the northwest quarter (NW 1/4), the northeast quarter (NE 1/4), the southwest quarter (SW 1/4), and the southeast quarter (SE 1/4). All evidence indicates that Wright's mother purchased the site in April 1911. Creese, 250; Alofsin illustrates the deed in *Wright Studies I*, 99. The parcel referred to consists of most, but not all, of the southern half of the northwest quarter of Section 30. I am grateful to M. J. Hamilton for the background to the Northwest Ordinance.

10 Wright, "Taliesin: The Chronicle of a House with a Heart," *Liberty* 6 (March 23, 1929): 21.

11 Wright built this dam and created the waterfall at the time he constructed Taliesin in 1911. Few photographs of the surrounding landscape from the period 1911–1914 are known to exist. Proof of the existence of the dam appears in "Wright Holding His Bungalow," *Baraboo Weekly News*, January 4, 1912. The newspaper article states that Wright was experimenting with a new type of construction "which will hold water by 'suspension' rather than 'compression.'" I am grateful to Robert L. Sweeney, who called this citation to my attention.

Evidence suggests that Wright was aware of a historical antecedent for the waterfall, which had been present in the valley during his youth. Wright's uncle John Lloyd-Jones, had operated a family grist mill alongside the stream in the late nineteenth century, where young Wright spent his summers working the farmland. Maginel Barney, 82–83; Creese, 245, illustration 2.

12 The history of the project has been chronicled and analyzed by Mark Reinberger, "The Sugarloaf Mountain Project and Frank Lloyd Wright's Vision of a New World," *Journal of the Society of Architectural Historians* 43 (March 1984): 38–52. Although Reinberger does not illustrate a topographical map of the site, there is no reference to an existing

waterway in his text, his photograph, or his diagram of the site.

13 The property proposed for development included the lower slopes of the western end of Emerald Bay including Fannette Island. "Milflores, Emerald Bay, Lake Tahoe," September 1923, a land survey, Frank Lloyd Wright Foundation, no file number. At the time Wright executed his plans, the land was owned by Jesse Armstrong, who along with her mother, Margaret Jane McKay Armstrong, vacationed in the buildings (a two-story hotel, seven cabins, and a kitchen) of the former "Emerald Bay Resort." Margaret Armstrong had renamed her vacation retreat "Milflores." Many years later in an oral history, Jesse Armstrong remembered Wright's visit to Emerald Bay concerning the real estate scheme for the property. She probably saw his drawings at some time because she remarked, "even though he had peculiar ideas of architecture, everyone didn't respond to them." Mrs. Walter Bush, interview with Jessie (*sic*) Armstrong, no date, ms., 70/130c, Bancroft Library, University of California, Berkeley. Mrs. Walter (Sally) Bush in telephone communication with author, August 23, 1991, stated that the interview was conducted ca. 1968–70.

The exact details of the business arrangement are still unclear. Wright appears to have considered buying the property himself. This fact is contained in a letter from the Armstrong's lawyer, Frank P. Derring, San Francisco, to Wright's lawyer, E. E. Prussing, Los Angeles, December 5, 1923, with reference to payment of a commission to "Mr. Pizzotti." In a letter from Prussing to Wright, December 17, 1923, in which he included Derring's letter, Prussing states, "Mr. MacMeekin has telephoned me recently and I have told him the situation." This reference may allude to a financial backer or partner. Copies of these letters are in the possession of the author. For a chronology of the land ownership of Emerald Bay, see Paul E. Nesbitt, *The History of Emerald Bay, Location of Emerald Bay State Park* (Sacramento: Department of Parks and Recreation, Resource Protection Division, 1989). Nesbitt notes that between 1905 and 1925, the north shore of Emerald Bay was a legal subdivision of eighty-one lots known as Emerald City. Nesbitt, 8–9.

14 For a description of Emerald Bay and Lake Tahoe, see George Wharton James, *The Lake of the Sky: Lake Tahoe in the High Sierras of California and Nevada* (Boston: L. C. Page and Company, 1915), especially 222–29; and Edward B. Scott, *The Saga of Lake Tahoe, II* (Lake Tahoe: Sierra-Tahoe Publishing, 1973), 372–73. Emerald Bay remains almost the same untouched wilderness that Wright observed in 1923. Various plans for development in the 1920s and '30s failed to materialize, and by the mid-1950s the State of California purchased the land for a state park. All of the natural features that appear in Wright's plan are recognizable today. I am grateful to Robert Sweeney, who shared details of his research on a trip we made to Lake Tahoe in August 1991.

15 For the best source of documentation on Doheny Ranch and Emerald Bay, Lake Tahoe, see Robert L. Sweeney, *Wright in*

Hollywood: Visions of a New Architecture (New York: Architectural Foundation, 1994), 10–19 and 102–07.

16 Timothy Doheny, grandson of Edward L. Doheny, provided information about water on Doheny Ranch. "The property had its own water. There were seven caves, all dug out by old prospector friends of my grandfather with pick and shovel. Spring caves were then dug out, and the water was pumped into reservoirs. Some of the reservoirs were fed by two spring fed caves; others by one. Beautiful water. We used to spend a lot of time in those caves. . . . There was all limestone flooring and pockets of what they called 'cave curls,' little lime balls. The whole floor was wavy limestone. This water was running on the limestone floor, and it would all run into a trap, and your pipeline would take it out to a reservoir. Beautiful springs, you can't believe, just beautiful water." Charles Lockwood and Peter V. Persic, *Greystone Historical Report* (submitted to the City Council, City of Beverly Hills, August 30, 1984).

17 The only other building in Wright's career where a waterfall emanates from a point on the major axis is Wolf Lake Amusement Park (1895) in Chicago. Although there were several schemes for Wolf Lake, the most interesting proposed a biaxial plan extending the building mass into the lake. The semicircular scheme was bisected by a central water chute that allowed boats and riders to moves down a slide into a chute basin.

18 The Hoopes Water Wheel Co., Springfield, Ohio, to Frank Lloyd Wright, Spring Green, Wisconsin, October 31, 1925, Frank Lloyd Wright Correspondence, Taliesin West, Scottsdale, Arizona.

19 Bruce Brooks Pfeiffer, ed., *Frank Lloyd Wright: Letters to Clients* (Fresno, California: Press at California State University, Fresno, 1986), 82.

20 An example of Wright's use of a decorative pictorial device in the Prairie Houses is the sumac leaf represented in the art glass windows of the Susan Lawrence Dana House (1900–02), Springfield, Illinois. Compare this with the palette of the walls of Taliesin, which imitate the color of the sand along the banks of the nearby Wisconsin River.

21 Moore, *Water and Architecture*, 204.

22 Wright repeats this same form at the Huntington Hartford House and the Hartford Play Resort (1947), Hollywood, California.

23 After 1936, Wright designed two other houses, which followed the composition of Fallingwater—the Gregor Affleck House (1941), Bloomfield Hills, Michigan, and the unbuilt John A. Gillin House (1950), Dallas, Texas. Both lack the power and conviction of his earlier experiments.

Frank Lloyd Wright's Diagonal Planning

I want to thank Robert McCarter for inviting me to contribute to this new edition and for suggesting that I republish the present essay. Little did he suspect the ironies involved, for the essay was originally written in 1980–81 with the intention of its being included in the double issue of *Oppositions* that ultimately became the basis for his first *Primer*. When, during the process of preparing the piece, I was informed, first, that a contribution from me was no longer desired and, second, that the issue had been canceled. I used it as my contribution to *In Search of Modern Architecture: A Tribute to Henry-Russell Hitchcock*, edited by Helen Searing (1982). It was the first article I published on Wright and shows many signs of that. It was written following a trip across the United States in 1976 to visit his buildings and represents an initial attempt to come to terms with the perceptual and intellectual experience of that trip. Based solely on the primary visual material of the buildings and existing secondary published works, it had none of the benefits of consultation of the architect's drawings and other papers in the Frank Lloyd Wright Archives.

Much of what I wrote in 1980–81 I would take issue with now, although I still fundamentally believe that the main argument is compelling and sound in its essentials. When faced with the question of whether to revise the text for the present publication in a draconian fashion, I decided not to do so and only to correct mistakes, change language and phrasings here and there, add some new information where it seemed absolutely necessary, and update the framing introduction and conclusion. The only entirely new addition is the two-paragraph section on the Death Valley project. This was something I knew at the time to be significant but had no way yet of understanding. The footnotes represented another problem entirely. Owing to the extraordinary development in Wright scholarship since 1981, the task of bringing them up to date would not only have been enormous; it would also have thrown the text itself into a rather unfavorable light. For that reason, I decided simply to eliminate completely irrelevant references and add just ones that I felt were crucial to aiding the reader.

As I wrote in the first footnote in the original publication of this essay, I also want to thank Bruce Brooks Pfeiffer, Director of Archives, The Frank Lloyd Wright Foundation, and Virginia Kazor, then Curator, Hollyhock House, for their help in the summer of 1976. I also remain extremely grateful to the many homeowners and building managers who allowed me to visit their Wright structures as well as to Harvard University, which helped support the trip with a grant from the Harvard Graduate Society Fund. That trip greatly benefited from the guide William Storrer had just published two years previously, *The Architecture of Frank Lloyd Wright: A Complete Catalog*. My greatest debt, however, goes to Vincent Scully, whose writings and lectures helped form my understanding of Wright. His influence is in evidence throughout this essay.

Much of the material in this essay was incorporated in my *Architecture of Frank Lloyd Wright*. Anyone interested in learning more about buildings and projects discussed here or about their relation to other aspects of Wright's career and thinking should refer to this larger study.

1   Bruce Brooks Pfeiffer and Yukio Futagawa, eds., *Frank Lloyd Wright*, 12 vols. (Tokyo: A.D.A. Edita, 1984–88): vols. 1–8, *Mono-graph*; vols. 9–11, *Preliminary Studies*; vol. 12, *In His Renderings*. Philip Johnson, "The Seven Crutches of Modern Architecture," *Perspecta* 3 (1955): 44.

2   Reyner Banham, "The Wilderness Years of Frank Lloyd Wright," *Journal of the Royal Institute of British Architects* 76 (December 1969): 512–19.

3   When this was written (1980–81), the things I found most useful in helping me form the concept of diagonal planning in Wright's work were: Vincent Scully, "Michelangelo's Fortification Drawings: A Study in the Reflex Diagonal," *Perspecta* 1 (1952): 38–45; Bernard Pyron, "Wright's Diamond Module Houses: His Development of Non-Rectilinear Interior Space," *Art Journal* 21 (Winter 1961–62): 92–96; B. Pyron, "Wright's Small Rectangular Houses: His Structures of the Forties and Fifties," *Art Journal* 23 (Fall 1963): 20–24; Edgar Kaufmann, Jr., "Centrality and Symmetry in Wright's Architecture," *Architect's Yearbook* 9 (1960): 120–31; John Sergeant, *Frank Lloyd Wright's Usonian Houses: The Case for Organic Architecture* (New York: Whitney Library of Design, Watson-Guptill Publications, 1976), esp. 183–87; and H. Allen Brooks, "Frank Lloyd Wright and the Destruction of the Box," *Journal of the Society of Architectural Historians* 38 (March 1979): 7–14.

4   John Lloyd Wright, *My Father Who Is on Earth* (New York: G. P. Putnam's Sons, 1946), 127. Wright himself never theorized his use of the diagonal, nor did he ever write much in a concerted way about it. The most extended discussion in print is in Frank Lloyd Wright, *An Organic Architecture: The Architecture of Democracy*, Sir George Watson Lectures of the Sulgrave Manor Board for 1939 (London: Lund Humphries, 1939), 3, 9–11.

5   Banham, "The Wilderness Years," was critical in pointing out the importance of this period in Wright's work.

6   In one of the first important reappraisals of Gothic architecture, Jacques-Germain Soufflot, in his "Mémoire sur l'architecture gothique," read to the Lyons Academy in 1741, stressed the significance of the diagonal in the creation of Gothic spatial effects (reprinted in Michael Petzet, *Soufflots Sainte-Geneviève und der Französische Kirchenbau des 18. Jahrhunderts* [Berlin: Walter de Gruyter and Co., 1961], 135–42).

7   See Vincent Scully, *The Shingle Style and the Stick Style: Architectural Theory from Downing to the Origins of Wright*, rev. ed. (New Haven: Yale University Press, 1971), esp. 71–164.

8   Eugène-Emmanuel Viollet-le-Duc, *Entretiens sur l'architecture*, 2 vols. (Paris: A. Morel, 1863, 1872), 2:283–90; English trans., Benjamin Bucknall, *Lectures on Architecture* (Boston: James R. Osgood, 1881). For the "butterfly plan," see Jill Franklin, "Edwardian Butterfly Houses," *Architectural Review*, April 1975, 220–25.

9   Vincent Scully noted the similarity between the Appleton House and Wright's Hanna House in *The Shingle Style*, 145.

10 On Wright's debt to the Beaux-Arts tradition, see Henry-Russell Hitchcock, "Frank Lloyd Wright and the 'Academic Tradition' of the Early Eighteen-Nineties," *Journal of the Warburg and Courtauld Institutes* 7 (January–June 1944): 46–63.

11 Some elements similar to the Studio House project may be seen in the Spencer Cottage, built at Lake Delavan, Wisconsin, in 1902.

12 Frank Lloyd Wright, *An Autobiography* (London, New York, and Toronto: Longmans, Green and Company, 1932), 171.

13 Frank Lloyd Wright, *An Autobiography*, new ed. (New York: Horizon Press, 1977), 191.

14 For the California and Arizona work of the 1920s, see Alofsin, *Lost Years*; and Robert L. Sweeney, *Wright in Hollywood: Visions of a New Architecture* (New York: Architectural History Foundation, 1994); and David G. De Long, ed., *Frank Lloyd Wright: Designs for an American Landscape, 1922–1932* (New York: Harry N. Abrams, in association with Canadian Center for Architecture, Library of Congress, and FLW Foundation, 1996).

15 This is noted, in Wright's hand, on one of the overall perspectives of the project.

16 The source of this idea is the fireplace in the living room of Hollyhock House, completed just prior to the Doheny project. See my "Landscape into Architecture: Frank Lloyd Wright's Hollyhock House and the Romance of Southern California," *AA Files: Annals of the Architectural Association School of Architecture* 3 (January 1983): 22–41; reprinted as "Hollyhock House and the Romance of Southern California," *Art in America*, September 1983, 150–65. Wright had previously set an indoor pool diagonally opposite the fireplace in the entrance hall of the Dana House in Springfield, Illinois (1902–04) and the Bogk House in Milwaukee, Wisconsin (1916–17) but never placed the hearth within the pool itself until the house built for Barnsdall in 1919–21.

17 As noted above, the description of the Death Valley project was not included in the original publication of this essay. It is based on a visit to the site and archival research done in 1983.

18 Wright, *Organic Architecture*, 3; and Frank Lloyd Wright, "Plasticity, Terminals, Third Dimension, Music and Architecture," lecture to the Taliesin Fellowship, August 27, 1952, Frank Lloyd Wright Foundation, Scottsdale, Arizona. Wright noted that the "reflex" allowed for a "perfect flexibility" and was "the natural easy attitude" for organizing buildings in relation to one another and to the landscape. Unlike the domineering rigidity of "the major-axis and the minor-axis of classic architecture," the diagonal implied a lack of resistance, a relaxation of the will that "yields to circumstances, to pressure" to produce "a plastic form." One of the first times he associated diagonality with "graceful reflexes" was in his discussion of Ocatilla and San-Marcos-in-the-Desert Hotel project (see below) in his *Autobiography* (1932 ed.), 303.

19 See now Kathryn Smith, *Frank Lloyd Wright, Hollyhock and Olive Hill: Buildings and Projects for Aline Barnsdall* (New York: Rizzoli International, 1992), 180–89.

20 On the plan reproduced in *Architectural Forum*, January 1938, 33, the square sand box is mislabeled as the pool.

21 The corner windows of the south-facing side of the Ennis House dining room are

contemporaneous; the only earlier example seems to be the canted, leaded windows of the playroom projecting from the nursery of Hollyhock House, apparently done by 1921. All Wright's earlier corners have a vertical mullion. No true corner window appears to have preceded it in Europe, the one in Rietveld's Schröder House in Utrecht (1924) having a vertical mullion that disappears only when the window is opened.

22 See Hans L. C. Jaffé, "The Diagonal Principle in the Works of Van Doesburg and Mondrian," *The Structurist* 9 (1969): 14–21; Donald McNamee, "Van Doesburg's Elementarism: New Translations of His Essays and Manifesto Originally Published in De Stijl," ibid., 22–29; and Theo van Doesburg, "Painting: From Composition to Counter-Composition," "Painting and Sculpture: About Counter-Composition and Counter-Sculpture. Elementarism (Fragment of a Manifesto)," trans. in H. L. C. Jaffé, *De Stijl* (New York: Harry N. Abrams, 1967), 201–17.

23 Van Doesburg, "Painting and Sculpture," 213–17. This was written between December 1925 and January 1927.

24 Frank Lloyd Wright, *An Autobiography*, new ed. (New York: Duell, Sloan and Pearce, 1943), 311.

25 Ibid., 314; and *Autobiography* (1977 ed.), 333, 339.

26 On Wright's debt to the International Style, see Vincent Scully, "Wright vs. the International Style," *Art News*, March 1954, 32–35, 64–66; and Edgar Kaufmann, Jr., "Frank Lloyd Wright's Years of Modernism, 1925–1935," *Journal of the Society of Architectural Historians* 25 (March 1965): 31–33; and my "Abstraction and Representation in Modern Architecture: The International Style and Frank Lloyd Wright," *AA Files: Annals of the Architectural Association School of Architecture* 11 (Spring 1986): 3–21.

27 I should like to thank Robert McCarter for reminding me of the relevance of the Taliesin expansion project in this sequence.

28 Frank Lloyd Wright, in *Architectural Forum*, January 1938, 83.

29 Curtis Besinger, "To Appreciate the Pleasures of this House," *House Beautiful*, January 1963, 101, 103 (special issue devoted to the Hanna House).

30 Wright, in *Architectural Forum* (January 1938), 36. Donald Hoffmann pointed out Wright's use of the 30/60-degree triangle in siting the house in *Frank Lloyd Wright's Fallingwater: The House and Its History* (New York: Dover Publications, 1978), 18.

31 Architectural Forum 68: 32–35.

32 Wright, in *Architectural Forum* (January 1938), 83.

33 Ibid., 68. It is now known that the Taliesin apprentice Cornelia Brierly played an instrumental role in the planning of the house and, in particular, the development of the hexagonal module.

34 In "Frank Lloyd Wright Designs a Honeycomb House," *Architectural Record*, July 1938, 60.

35 Wright, in *Architectural Forum* (January 1938), 68.

36 The semicircular second Jacobs House, designed in 1943–44 and built in Middleton, Wisconsin, in 1946–48, is a direct development of the idea of hinging and pivoting. The module of the house is a 6-degree sector of a circle whose center is the middle of the circular sunken garden. Vincent Scully, *Frank Lloyd Wright* (New York: George Braziller, 1960), 30, noted that "its arc partly encloses a deep earth hollow, and it sends its overhangs out to pick up the continuities of the prairie horizon."

37 Frank Lloyd Wright, in *Architectural Forum*, January 1948, 137.

38 Wright, *Autobiography* (1943 ed.), 453–54. In the 1977 edition, Wright changed the phrase to "as though it had stood there during creation" (480).

39 In the original publication of this essay, the description was misleading, based as it was on a single visit to the site following a typical tour that immediately takes one onto the prow terrace down the path running along its southwestern edge. My later understanding was much informed by Philip Johnson's exacting description in his remarkable "100 Years, Frank Lloyd Wright and Us," orig. pub. *Pacific Architect and Builder* (March 1957), reprinted in Johnson, Writings (New York: Oxford University Press, 1979), 193–98.

40 Wright, *Autobiography* (1943 ed.), 452.

41 Ibid., 453.

42 Ibid.

43 Cf. Colin Rowe and Robert Slutzky, "Transparency: Literal and Phenomenal," *Perspecta* 8 (1963): 45–54; repr. in C. Rowe, *The Mathematics of the Ideal Villa and Other Essays* (Cambridge and London: MIT Press, 1976), 159–83.

44 Wright, *Organic Architecture*, 3.

Consecrated Space

1 We exclude from this list only the Johnson Wax Research tower and the Price Tower. Wright's taproot schemes are clearly of another morphological type. The Price Tower in particular is related to the pinwheel Prairie House, which is anchored by a central chimney mass. The Hillside Home School, Taliesin, and Taliesin West are not urban buildings and consequently lie outside of this discussion. Wright, of course, built scores of other nonresidential, urban buildings, many of which do not conform to this *parti*, but this essay confines itself to his most important buildings. His 1947 Unitarian church in Shorewood Hills, Wisconsin is an intriguing variant on the parti. The building's major circulation spine skewers the main space, dividing it into the sanctuary and the foyer. This foyer is clearly demarked as a secondary space by a dome in the ceiling over it. Brevity precludes a complete analysis of the church in this essay. The author is also indebted to Robert McCarter for several ideas incorporated into the essay during the editing process.

2 Emphasis added.

3 Kenneth Frampton has written of Wright that, "where the urban environment was regarded as a fallen world, as an alienating occidental 'nowhere' beyond redemption, the American landscape was seen as an Edenic promise, as an oriental paradise garden that was still imbued with the unspoilt ethos of aboriginal man. It was as though Wright, Romantic Emersonian to the last, could never bring himself to accept the often provisional and ugly reality of the late nineteenth-century American city." Jonathan Lipman, *Frank Lloyd Wright and the Johnson Wax Buildings* (New York: Rizzoli International Publications 1986), xi.

4 David van Zanten, "Schooling the Prairie School: Wright's Early Style as a Communicable-System" in T*he Nature of Frank Lloyd Wright*, ed. Bolon et al. (Chicago: University of Chicago Press, 1988), 80–81.

5 The Abraham Lincoln Center, whose design was begun by Wright in 1897, was not built according to his plans.

6 Jack Quinan, *Frank Lloyd Wright's Larkin Building: Myth and Fact* (New York: Architectural History Foundation, 1987), 38.

7 Jack Quinan, "Transcendency in the Light Court of Frank Lloyd Wright's Larkin Administration Building," 1982. Unpublished essay. Most of the material in it was later incorporated into Quinan's *Frank Lloyd Wright's Larkin Building: Myth and Fact*. The author thanks Quinan for sharing this paper with him.

8 Quinan, *Larkin Building*, 108.

9 Letter published in H. Allen Brooks, ed., *Writings on Wright* (Cambridge: MIT Press, 1981), 91.

10 Frank Lloyd Wright, *An Autobiography*, 3rd ed. (New York: Horizon Press, 1977), 179. Emphasis added by author.

11 Ibid., 200. Emphasis added.

12 Ibid., 201.

13 Ibid., 205.

14 Ibid., 204–205.

15 Correspondence between representatives of the Imperial Hotel and Wright was initiated in 1912. According to Kathryn Smith, letters indicate that a preliminary design was completed in 1913 or 1914. Construction was completed in 1923.

16 H. Th. Wijdeveld, ed., *The Life-Work of the American Architect Frank Lloyd Wright* [Wendingen edition] (Santpoort, Holland: C. A. Mees, 1925), 106. Emphasis added.

17 Kenneth Frampton, *Modern Architecture: A Critical History* (New York: Oxford University Press, 1980), 62.

18 Frank Lloyd Wright, *Sixty Years of Living Architecture: The Work of Frank Lloyd Wright* (New York: Solomon R. Guggenheim Museum, 1953), 8–9.

19 As built, the Imperial Hotel finials were simplified considerably and no longer resembled strongly those on the Imperial Castle. The ridge-end finials were apparently removed entirely at a later date when the hotel was reroofed, and do not appear in late photos of it.

20 The author acknowledges Professor Ross Erdman of the University of Illinois, who made this observation in a conversation with him.

21 The company instituted profit sharing in 1917, and, in spite of a severe decline in business during the Great Depression, Herbert Johnson refused to lay off any employees.

22 Wright, *An Autobiography*, 498.

23 Herbert Johnson interviewed by Edward Wilder, 1940. Transcript in Johnson Wax Company archives.

24 "Guggenheim Museum in Progress," *Architectural Record*, May 1958, 185.

25 Herbert Muschamp, *Man About Town: Frank Lloyd Wright in New York City* (Cambridge MIT Press, 1983), 111.

26 The author acknowledges a student in Yale's architecture program circa 1983, whose name the author has been unable to determine, who pointed this out to him.

27 The exterior of this building bears a fascinating resemblance to Bruno Taut's Glass House of 1914.

28 The circle, having neither beginning nor end, symbolizes God. The Greek cross, of course, is derived from the crucifix.

29 Vincent Scully, *Frank Lloyd Wright* (New York: George Braziller, 1960), 31–32.

30 The author thanks Mr. Robert Weill, congregant of Beth Sholom Synagogue, for providing information on the synagogue.

31 The Imperial Hotel is the only one of the urban buildings that permits a view of any of its surrounding. However, this exception reinforces the rule, because Wright designed the massing of the building such that the only possible view out of the site from the public spaces is of the Imperial Palace grounds, and the Palace grounds were not profaned environment to Wright, as he made clear in an above quote (see note 17). Before designing the Johnson Wax Administration Building, Wright passionately attempted to persuade his clients to relocate that company to the countryside. One must assume that had Wright succeeded in this he would have designed a very different, more outwardly oriented building for Johnson.

32 Interviewed by the author for *Frank Lloyd Wright and the Johnson Wax Buildings*.

The Integrated Ideal

1 Horatio Greenough, "Form and Function" (1853), in *Roots of Contemporary American Architecture*, ed. Lewis Mumford (New York: Dover, 1972), 54.

2 Ralph Waldo Emerson, *Emerson: Essays and Lectures* (New York: Library of America, 1983), 394.

3 Johann Wolfgang von Goethe, *Italian Journey* (San Francisco: Northpoint Press, 1982), ix.

4 Ludwig Wittgenstein, *Culture and Value* (Chicago: University of Chicago Press, 1980), 24.

5 Ibid., 8.

6 Frank Lloyd Wright, *An American Architecture* (New York: Horizon Press, 1955), 33.

7 Edgar Tafel, *Apprentice to Genius* (New York: Dover, 1979), 3.

8 Frank Lloyd Wright, *In the Cause of Architecture* (New York: McGraw-Hill, 1975), 153.

9 Ibid.

10 A freehand sketch by Wright of such a floral arrangement in the Oak Park Studio is in the collection of the Avery Library, Columbia University, New York.

11 Frank Lloyd Wright, *An Autobiography* (New York: Horizon, 1932), 182.

12 Ibid.

13 Joseph Connors, *The Robie House of Frank Lloyd Wright* (Chicago: University of Chicago Press, 1984), 26.

14 Wright, *American Architecture*, 206.

15 Wright, *An Autobiography*, 173.

16 Wright, *In the Cause of Architecture*, 59.

17 Wright, *An Autobiography*, 61.

18 Frank Lloyd Wright, *The Natural House* (New York: Horizon, 1954), 181.

19 Wright, *In the Cause of Architecture*, 61.

20 Ibid., 56. Note that Wright published the statement that the plan was the solution and the elevation was the expression in 1908, almost twenty years before Le Corbusier published, as his own, a virtually identical statement on the relationship between plan and elevation.

21 Ibid., 153.

22 Wright, *American Architecture*, 44.

23 Henri Bergson, *Time and Free Will* (1888; reprinted, New York: Harper and Row, 1960), 112.

24 Emerson, *Essays*, 487.

25 Connors, *Robie House*, 44.

26 Wright, *In the Cause of Architecture*, 59.

27 Wright, *An Autobiography*, 34.

28 Louis Sullivan, *Kindergarten Chats and Other Writings* (New York: Dover, 1979), 192.

29 Wright, *An Autobiography*, 218.

30 Wright, *American Architecture*, 58.

31 Wright, *In the Cause of Architecture*, 58.

32 Ibid., 163.

33 Ibid., 156–59.

34 Wright, *American Architecture*, 194.

35 Connors, *Robie House*, 19.

36 Frank Lloyd Wright, *A Testament* (New York: Horizon, 1957), 220.

37 Tafel, *Apprentice*, 50.

38 Wright, *In the Cause of Architecture*, 154.

39 Ibid., 153.

40 Ibid., 58.

41 Frank Lloyd Wright, *The Japanese Print: An Interpretation* (1912; reprinted New York: Horizon, 1967), 12.

42 David van Zanten, "Schooling the Prairie School: Wright's Early Style as a Communicable System," in *The Nature of Frank Lloyd Wright*, ed. Bolon et al. (Chicago: University of Chicago Press, 1988), 71; also republished in this volume.

43 Wright, *American Architecture*, 80. Wright's source, Kakuzo's paraphrase of Lao Tzu, was from a book Wright was given in the 1920s; Okakura Kakuzo, *The Book of Tea* (1906; reprinted Tokyo: Tuttle, 1956), 45. Kakuzo quotes Lao Tzu as stating, "only in emptiness lay the truly essential. The reality of a room, for instance, was to be found in the vacant space enclosed by the roof and the walls, not in the roof and walls themselves. The usefulness of a water pitcher dwelt in the emptiness where water might be put, not in the form of the pitcher or the material of which it is made. Emptiness is all potent because all containing. In emptiness alone motion becomes possible."

44 Ibid., 208–210.

45 Ibid., 146.

46 Ibid., 75–85. This essay is noteworthy as the only instance where Wright employed diagrams to illustrate his point—normally he simply referred to his own built work.

47 This combination of views out, or prospect, and lack of views in, or refuge, has been identified by the landscape sociologist Jay Appleton as essential to the creation of a sense of place in the landscape; *The Experience of Landscape* (1975; reprinted, New York: John Wiley, 1996). Grant Hildebrand employed Appleton's concepts of prospect and refuge to analyze the residential designs of Wright in *The Wright Space* (Seattle: University of Washington Press, 1991).

48 Paul Valéry, "The Method of Leonardo" (1894), reprinted in *Paul Valery: An Anthology* (Princeton: Princeton University Press, 1965), 82.

49 Wright, *American Architecture*, 96, 196.

50 Frank Lloyd Wright, *The Future of Architecture* (1930; New York: Horizon, 1953), 162.

51 Friedrich Froebel, *Selected Writings* (New York: Lilley, 1898), 109.

52 Wright, *An Autobiography*, 175.

53 Wright, *American Architecture*, 84.

54 Connors, *Robie House*, 25.

55 Wright, *Japanese Print*, 12.

56 The pervasiveness of this phrase, which Wright first used in 1932, is evident in the title of Henry-Russell Hitchcock's book, the first comprehensive monograph on Wright, *In the Nature of Materials* (New York: Hawthorne, 1942).

57 Wright, *In the Cause of Architecture*, 208.

58 While Wright's associate Walter Burley Griffin applied for a patent for the concrete-block construction system in 1917, it was initially conceived by Wright in this 1906 project, while Griffin was still in Wright's employ.

59 Wright, *In the Cause of Architecture*, 155.

60 Wright, *An Autobiography*, 178, 372.

61 Wright, *American Architecture*, 28.

62 Ibid., 61.

63 Ibid., 67.

64 Wright, *In the Cause of Architecture*, 60.

65 Tafel, *Apprentice*, 165.

66 Wright, *American Architecture*, 61.

67 Ibid., 51.

68 Wright, quoted in N. K. Smith, *Frank Lloyd Wright: A Study in Architectural Content* (Watkins Glen: American Life, 1979), 180.

69 Juni-chiro Tanizaki, *In Praise of Shadows* (New Haven: Leete's Island Books, 1977), 38.

70 Emerson, *Essays*, 424.

71 Leonardo, quoted in Valery, *Anthology*, 36.

72 Wright, *In the Cause of Architecture*, 53.

73 Wright, *American Architecture*, 18.

74 Wright, *An Autobiography*, 181.

75 "We are living in the era of the disturbed plan," said Alex Wall in a 1988 Columbia University lecture. I hope that Wright's position relative to both "historicist" and "deconstructivist" postmodernism would by this point be evident to the reader.

76 Wright, *American Architecture*, 28–29.

77 F. Scott Fitzgerald wrote in *The Crack-Up* (1936): "The test of a first-rate intelligence is the ability to hold two opposed ideas in the mind at the same time, and still retain the ability to function"; vol. 3 of *The Bodley Head Scott Fitzgerald* (London: Bodley Head, 1963), 388. Contemporarily fashionable rhetoric, often making claims to being philosophy, rejects "dialectical" thought—the resolution of two opposed ideas. But this does not in the least effect the fact that resolving paradoxes through dialectical thought has admirably served the greatest architectural minds of our era (Wright, Le Corbusier, Aalto, and Kahn, among many others) and that, unlike current theoretical rhetoric, it is not merely a fashionable mode of thought but, rather, is a fundamental aspect of human nature.

78 Emerson, *Essays*, 287.

79 Wright, *American Architecture*, 239.

80 Ibid., 80. See also note 43 above for Wright's source in Lao Tzu and Okakura.

Illustration Credits

Thomas Ahule, *The Book of the Fair: Columbian Exhibition 1893*: 54b
Architecture 1 (1900): 60t
Architectural Forum (January 1938): 251b, 256b, 257, 260b
Architectural Review (June 1900): 41, 47
Architectural Record (1928): 303b
C.D. Arnold and H.D. Higinbotham, *Official Views of the World's Columbian Exposition*: 178t
Art Institute of Chicago: 290
Ausgefuhrte Bauten und Entwurfe von Frank Lloyd Wright: 9, 10, 16t, 70, 71t, 72t, 72c, 74t, 74c, 76l, 77tl, 78t, 82tr, 89, 90bl, 90br, 92tl, 92bl, 92r, 138, 180, 219t, 219bl, 220t, 220br, 238, 239tr, 239cr, 266r, 269, 270r, 271, 274b, 275t, 277l, 292, 294l, 296, 298br, 302r, 304b, 307t, 323b, 326b, 332, 334t
Ausgefuhrte Bauten und Entwurfe von Frank Lloyd Wright; re-arranged and annotated by author: 315
Morris Baptiste (drawings): 280tc, 280tr
John Beres (drawings): 91, 93
Robert Blatter (drawings) 18, 19, 320t
John Brandies: 186b, 198b
© Judith Bromley (photograph): 222t
Courtesy of the University at Buffalo, SUNY: 300t, 316t, 316b, 319, 323t
Albert Bush-Brown, *Louis Sullivan*: 176
Stuart Cohen, *Chicago Architects*: 34
C.W. Condit, *The Rise of the Skyscraper*: 88
Peter Cook (photographs): 7, 14, 31, 103, 181t, 187t, 199, 200, 205, 209, 213t, 215, 267l, 272, 279, 285, 287, 311t, 322, 329. 336, 337
The Dream City: 38t
© Frank Lloyd Wright Foundation: 28, 38b, 40r, 44–45, 87, 105, 107–109, 147–148, 179, 182t, 182c, 183t, 183c, 184t, 185, 189, 206t, 214, 223t, 225t, 225bl, 226, 227tl, 227b, 229l, 230t, 231, 231bl, 240, 242, 243, 245t, 246, 248–250, 251l, 252–253, 256t, 258–259, 260t, 268r, 276t, 282, 284r, 294r, 295, 298t, 300b, 301, 304t, 321, 330t, 331, 335
Frank Lloyd Wright Preservation Trust: 217
H[einrich] de Fries, *Frank Lloyd Wright: Aus dem Lebenswerke eines Architekten*: 245b
Henry Fuermann (photograph); Courtesy of the Domino's Pizza, Inc. Archives: 233
Otto Antonia Graf (drawings): 149bl, 150-69
Eulogio Guzman (drawings): 223c, 223b, 230b, 231br
Herve Hamon (drawing): 299
H. R. Hitchcock, *The Architecture of H .H. Richardson and His Times*: 27t, 48b
H. R. Hitchcock, *In the Nature of Materials*: 29l, 33t, 35, 66t, 76r, 77cr, 78l, 84t, 90tl, 182b, 183b, 236, 239br, 262, 291
Bernhard Hoesli (drawings): 206c, 206b, 207–208, 210, 212, 213b; 213br
John Howe Papers, Northwest Architectural Archives, University of Minnesota Libraries,

St. Paul: 221bl
Claude Hubert, *Islamic Ornamental Design*: 177
Inland Architect and New Record (September 1890): 26t
Inland Architect and New Record (August 1887): 26b
Inland Architect and New Record (June 1887): 27b
Jitendra Jain (drawing): 184b
Wenzel Jamnitzer, *Perspektiva corporum regularium*: 145b
Courtesy S. C. Johnson and Son, Inc: 278
Owen Jones, *The Grammar of Ornament*: 173t, 173b
Kacey Jurgens (drawing): 181r
From Donald Kalec, *The Home and Studio of Frank Lloyd Wright*: 55
Steven Klausner (drawings): 11, 289, 308b
Balthazar Korab (photographs): 13, 23, 30, 68t, 94, 265, 280b, 283l, 283br, 326t
Katrina Kuhl (drawings) 186t, 186c
Neil Levine, collection: 239tl, 263
Jonathon Lipman (drawings): 266l, 268l, 270l, 273r, 275r, 276b, 277r, 280tl, 281b, 238tr, 284l
Jonathon Lipman, collection: 281t
Richard MacCormac (drawings): 125, 128–131, 134–137, 139–143
Grant Carpenter Manson, *Frank Lloyd Wright to 1910: The First Golden Age*: 37t
Mark Maturo (drawings) 15, 16b
Robert McCarter (drawings) 12, 17, 42, 288r, 297, 298bl, 302l, 303t, 305–306, 307b, 308t, 308c, 310, 313–314, 317–318, 320b, 325, 333, 334bl
Robert McCarter (photograph) 20
Herb McLaughlin (photograph); Herb and Dorothy McLaughlin, Archives and Manuscripts, University Libraries, Arizona State University, Tempe: 261
A Monograph on the Works of McKim, Mead and White, 1879-1915: 40l
Hugh Morrison, *Louis Sullivan, Prophet of Modern Architecture*: 33b
The Museum of Modern Art, New York: 237
The Museum of Modern Art, New York; Katherine S. Dreier Bequest: 247t
Richard Nickel Archives, Chicago: 145t
Pennsylvania Academy of Fine Arts: 174
Patrick Pinnell (drawings): 32, 39, 51–52
Tim Street Porter (photographs): 171, 191, 194b, Private collection: 235
Mariana Griswold van Rensselaer, *Henry-Hobson Richardson and His Works*: 48t,
Paul Rocheleau (photographs): 54t, 57, 81, 187b, 188
William Rozner and Eulogio Guzman (drawing): 224br
Arlene Sanderson (photograph), Frank Lloyd Wright Home and Studio Foundation: 267r
R.M. Schindler Collection, Architectural Drawing Collection, University of California, Santa Barbara: 224t

Werner Seligmann (drawings): 60l, 61, 63–65, 66l, 67, 68l, 69, 72b, 73, 74b, 75, 77tr, 77br, 78, 82tl, 82br, 84b, 85
Gottfried Semper, *Der Stil in den technischen und tektonischen Kensten oder praktische Aesthetik*: 178c
Karen Sharp and Steven Klausner (drawing): 288l
George William Sheldon, *Artistic Country Seats*: 29r, 35c, 37b, 58t, 58l, 59t, 59r
Stedelijk Museum, Amsterdam: 247b
Samuel Stewart (photograph); courtesy of the Western Pennsylvania Conservancy: 228
Ezra Stoller © Esto (photograph): 255t
Roger Strauss III (photograph): 222b
Sullivan, *A System of Architectural Ornament According with a Philosophy of Man's Powers* (1924): 133, 149tl, 149tr, 175
Edgar Tafel (photo of Wright print), *Apprentice to Genius: Years with Frank Lloyd Wright*: 330b
Madeleine Thatcher (drawings): 193, 194t, 195–197, 198t, 201
United States Patent Office, Official Gazette, December 1897: 146
Flora Vara (drawings): 219br, 220bl, 224bl, 225br, 227tr, 229r
Wendingen (1925), "The Work of Frank Lloyd Wright": 273l, 274t, 275l, 275c, 311b, 335br
Western Architect, (January 1913): 221tr
Charles E. White (drawing): 71
G. E. Woodard, *Woodard's Country Homes*: 178b
Frank Lloyd Wright, *The Japanese Print: An Interpretation*: 312t
Frank Lloyd Wright, *The Natural House*: 255b

Author Biographies

Kenneth Frampton

Architect, professor, critic, historian, and author. Ware Professor of Architecture, Graduate School of Architecture, Planning and Preservation, Columbia University; Chairman of Architecture, 1986–89. Frampton has also taught at the Institute for Architecture and Urban Studies, Princeton University, the Royal College of Art in London, the University of Virginia, the ETH Zurich, the Berlage Institute in Amsterdam, and Accademia di Architettura in Mendrisio, Ticino, Switzerland. He is the author of numerous books, including *Labor, Work and Architecture: Collected Essays on Architecture and Design* (2002), *Technology, Place and Architecture: The Jerusalem Seminar in Architecture* (1998), *Studies in Tectonic Culture* (1995), *Modern Architecture: A Critical History* (1980), and monographs on a number of architects, including Le Corbusier, Tadao Ando, Pierre Chareau, Arata Isozaki, Richard Meier, Steven Holl, and Alvaro Siza. He served as technical editor of *Architectural Design* (London) and editor of *Oppositions* (New York). Among his awards are the ACSA Topaz Medallion, the AIA Honors Award for Criticism, and the UIA International Prize for Criticism. He has practiced in the offices of Douglas Stephens, London, and Richard Meier and Partners, New York.

Otto Antonia Graf

Architectural historian, professor, and author. Professor of Art History, Akademie der Bildenden Künste, Vienna; Director, Museum of the 20th Century, Vienna, 1964–70. Graf is the author of a four-volume study on Frank Lloyd Wright, *Die Kunst des Quadrats: Zum Werk von Frank Lloyd Wright I und II* (1983), *Erraumen: Zum Werk von Frank Lloyd Wright III und IV* (2002); and an eight-volume study on Otto Wagner, including *Otto Wagner 1 and 2, Das Werk des Architekten* (1985); *Otto Wagner 3, Die Einheit der Kunst* (1990); *Otto Wagner 4, Sicard und Van der Null* (1994); *Otto Wagner 5, Baukunst des Eros 1863–1888* (1997); *Otto Wagner 6, Baukunst des Eros 1889–1899* (1999); *Otto Wagner 7, Baukunst des Eros 1900–1918* (2000); *Otto Wagner, Buildings and Projects, 1–4, Tokyo* (1998); and *Otto Wagner, Beiheft, denkend zeichnen-zeichnend denken* (1999).

Bernhard Hoesli

Architect and professor. Hoesli was Principal of Bernhard Hoesli Architects, Zurich, and previously Hoesli and Aebli Architects, Zurich, 1960–70. He was Professor Emeritus of Architecture at the ETH (Swiss Federal Institute of Technology) in Zurich, where he was director of the first-year program from 1959 to 1981, chair of the Department of Architecture from 1968 to 1972, and director of the Institute of History and

Theory from 1976 to 1980. Hoesli worked in the office of Le Corbusier, during which time he studied painting with Fernand Léger. He also taught at Cornell University and at the University of Texas at Austin, where he was a founding member of the "Texas Rangers." He is the author of *Transparency* (1968, German; 1997, English; with Colin Rowe and Robert Slutzky). After his untimely death, Hoesli's writings and his teaching at the ETH were comprehensively documented in *Teaching Architecture: Bernhard Hoesli at the Department of Architecture at the ETH Zurich* (1989), and his collages were exhibited, "Bernhard Hoesli: Collages" (2001). Hoesli died in 1984.

Neil Levine

Architectural and art historian, professor, and author. Emmet Blakeney Gleason Professor of History of Art and Architecture, Harvard University, where he is past chair of the Department of History of Art and Architecture. He has taught at the University of London, where he held the Banister Fletcher Professorship, and at Cambridge University, where he held the Slade Professorship, among other academic appointments. He was a Fulbright Scholar and, most recently, a Guggenheim Fellow. He is the author of *The Architecture of Frank Lloyd Wright* (1996), as well as numerous scholarly essays on Wright, his first being the essay republished in this volume. He was the editor of *Vincent Scully: Modern Architecture and Other Essays* (2003), and is currently completing a book, *The Urbanism of Frank Lloyd Wright*. He is on the editorial board of the journal *Wright Studies*, is past vice-president for Preservation Services of the Frank Lloyd Wright Building Conservancy, and was adviser and extended interview subject for the Ken Burns film *Frank Lloyd Wright*.

Jonathan Lipman

Architect and author. Principal of Jonathan Lipman and Associates, Architects, Fairfield, Iowa; Lipman is the principal architect for Vedic City, Iowa. He previously practiced in Washington, DC. Lipman is the author of *Frank Lloyd Wright and the Johnson Wax Buildings* (1986) and author of the historic-structures reports, prepared for the National Trust for Historic Preservation, for Frank Lloyd Wright's Pope-Leighey House (1987), and Frank Lloyd Wright's Wingspread (1994). He was the curator for the exhibitions "Frank Lloyd Wright and the Johnson Wax Buildings, Creating a Corporate Cathedral" (Renwick Gallery of the Smithsonian Institution, 1986); "The Non-Residential Architecture of Frank Lloyd Wright" and "The Architecture of Frank Lloyd Wright" (National Museum of Modern Art, Kyoto, Japan, 1991); and "The Wright State: Frank Lloyd Wright and Wisconsin" (Milwaukee Art Museum, 1992).

He was the architectural consultant on the film *Uncommon Places: The Architecture of Frank Lloyd Wright*. He has served as a visiting scholar at the Cornell University School of Architecture, Art and Planning and as a consulting editor for *Oppositions* (where this book project first began).

Sir Richard MacCormac

Architect. Chairman of MacCormac Jamieson Prichard, Architects, London. MacCormac has taught at Cambridge University, the University of Halifax, Hull University, and the University of Edinburgh, and his involvement in education has led to a series of university commissions in London, Oxford, Bristol, Lancaster, and Cambridge. Numerous architectural works from MacCormac's distinguished practice have been widely published and awarded, and the firm itself has received the profession's highest honors. He has also published articles on urban design, housing, and architectural history, including his early study of Wright and Froebel, "The Anatomy of Wright's Aesthetic," originally published in *Architectural Review*. He is a Fellow of the Royal Society of Arts and a Royal Academician, and was President of the RIBA from 1991 to 1993, and for two terms a member of the Royal Fine Arts Commission. In 1994 he was awarded the CBE, and he was knighted in 2001.

Robert McCarter

Architect, professor, and author. Principal of D-Mc² Architecture, Gainesville, Florida, and Professor of Architecture at the University of Florida, where he was director of the School of Architecture from 1991 to 2001. McCarter has also taught at Columbia University and North Carolina State University and previously practiced architecture in New York and California. He is the author of *Louis I. Kahn* (2005), *William Morgan: Selected and Current Works* (2002), *Frank Lloyd Wright* (1997), *Unity Temple: Frank Lloyd Wright* (1997), and *Fallingwater: Frank Lloyd Wright* (1994), and he edited *Frank Lloyd Wright: A Primer on Architectural Principles* (1991), *Pamphlet Architecture 12, Building: Machines* (1987), and the first four issues of the journal *ABSTRACT* (1988–91). Forthcoming books include a study on Alvar Aalto and a biography of Frank Lloyd Wright. Among his awards are the Rotch Traveling Studio Award in 2003, with which he led a graduate studio to Finland, and a Graham Foundation grant in 1989 for the research on Frank Lloyd Wright that is here published.

Patrick Pinnell

Architect. Principal of Patrick Pinnell, Architecture and Town Planning, Higganum, Connecticut. He began practice in Washington, DC, where he was a principal in Cass and Pinnell, Architects, 1978–88. Since 1989 he has been based in the New Haven and Hartford, Connecticut, region. Pinnell was a Visiting Professor of Architecture, teaching theory and design, at Yale University, for a number of years, and he has also taught at the University of Illinois (Chicago), the University of Miami, the University of Maryland, and the Institute for Architecture and Urban Studies, where he was also director of the lecture program. Pinnell has lectured and published widely in this country, Europe, and Japan, and he is the author of *Yale: The Campus Guide* (1999). He was selected by the Architectural League of New York for their series Emerging Voices, and his work has received a variety of awards for architectural design and historic preservation, and his columns on architecture and urbanism for the *Hartford Courant* and *New Urban News* received an American Planning Association award in 2003.

Colin Rowe

Architectural historian, professor, and author. Rowe was Professor Emeritus of Architecture at Cornell University for forty years, where he directed the Graduate Urban Design program. He also taught at Cambridge University, the University of Texas at Austin, where he was a founding member of the "Texas Rangers," and the University of Maryland, and was a visiting professor at the University of Oregon and the University of Florida, among other institutions. He was the author of *Italian Architecture of the 16th Century* (2002, posthumous, with Leon Satkowski), *Transparency* (1997, with Robert Slutzky and Bernhard Hoesli), *As I Was Saying: Recollections and Miscellaneous Essays*, volumes I, II, and III (1996, edited by Alexander Caragonne), *The Architecture of Good Intentions* (1994), *Collage City* (1978, with Fred Koetter), and *The Mathematics of the Ideal Villa and Other Essays* (1976). Rowe received numerous awards for his theoretical and historical studies, including most notably the Gold Medal from the Royal Institute of British Architects in 1995. Rowe died in 1999.

Werner Seligmann

Architect and professor. He was principal of Werner Seligmann and Associates, Architects and Urban Designers, Syracuse New York, and Dean of the College of Architecture at Syracuse University for thirty years. He was a fellow in the American Academy in Rome and taught at Harvard University, Yale University, Cornell University, the ETH Zurich, and the University of Texas at Austin, where he was among the "Texas Rangers." He built extensively, including the Ithaca Center and Elm Street Housing, Ithaca, and he exhibited at the XVII Triennale in Milan. His architectural and urban design work was published and exhibited widely, including the major retrospective "25 Years of Work of Werner Seligmann and Associates," which toured the US in 1986. He was the editor of the book *Mario Campi, Franco Pessina Architects* (1987). Seligmann died in 1998.

John Sergeant

Architect, professor, and author. Professor Emeritus of Architecture, Department of Architecture, Cambridge University. He has also taught at the Bartlett University College, London, Liverpool University, and the University of Houston (Texas). He has practiced with Skidmore, Owings and Merrill Architects, San Francisco, among other firms. He is author of the classic and still-unsurpassed book *Frank Lloyd Wright's Usonian Houses: The Case for Organic Architecture* (1976). He has written a number of essays on the architecture of Frank Lloyd Wright, as well as on the work of Glenn Murcutt, Jorn Utzon, and Rafael Moneo. In his practice, he has built work in Northern England, London, and Cambridge. Sergeant has retired from teaching and now lives in Spain, where he has restored a medieval tower and is currently working on a Japanese Ryokan in Andorra.

Kathryn Smith

Architectural historian, professor, historic preservation consultant, and author. Former professor of architecture at the Southern California Institute of Architecture (SCI-Arc) in Santa Monica. She is the author of *Frank Lloyd Wright: Hollyhock House and Olive Hill, Buildings and Projects for Aline Barnsdall* (1992), *Frank Lloyd Wright's Taliesin and Taliesin West* (1997), and *Frank Lloyd Wright: America's Master Architect* (1998), as well as numerous scholarly essays on the work of Frank Lloyd Wright, including most recently "The Show to End All Shows: Frank Lloyd Wright and the Museum of Modern Art, 1940" (2005). Forthcoming books include *Wright on Exhibit, 1894–1959* and *Wright's Water Gardens*. She has been the Scholar in Residence at the Robie House (2003), recipient of the Wright Spirit Award in Professional category for the Frank Lloyd Wright Building Conservancy (2001), and received a Graham Foundation Fellowship (1991); she is also on the Advisory Committee to the Robie House Restoration Committee and Taliesin Preservation, Inc.

David Van Zanten

Architectural and art historian, professor, and author. Professor of Art History at Northwestern University, Chicago. He has also taught at McGill University and the University of Pennsylvania, and he was a Fulbright Scholar. He is the author of *Sullivan's City: The Meaning of Ornament for Louis Sullivan* (2000), *Designing Paris: The Architecture of Labrouste, Duc, and Vaudoyer* (1987), and *Building Paris: Architectural Institutions and the Transformation of the French Capital, 1830–1870* and is coauthor of *The Architecture of the Ecole des Beaux Arts* (1975) and *Louis Sullivan: The Function of Ornament* (1986).

Gwendolyn Wright

Architectural historian, professor, and author. Professor of Architecture, Graduate School of Architecture, Planning and Preservation, Columbia University. She is the author of *The Politics of Design in French Colonial Urbanism* (2000), *Moralism and the Model Home: Domestic Architecture and Cultural Conflict in Chicago, 1873–1913* (1981), and *Building the Dream: A Social History of Housing in America* (1981); she is editor of *Formation of National Collections of Art and Archaeology* (1996) and *The History of History in American Schools of Architecture, 1865–1975* (1996); forthcoming are book-length studies on twentieth century American housing and a cultural history of modern architecture in the US. She is one of four hosts of the PBS series *History Detectives*. She has received a number of prestigious fellowships, including ones from the Guggenheim Foundation, the Getty Center for the History of Art, the Ford Foundation, and the National Endowment for the Humanities.

Bibliography
on Frank Lloyd Wright

Book-Length Studies or Essay Collections

Aguar, Charles E. and Berdeana Aguar. *Wrightscapes: Frank Lloyd Wright's Landscape Designs* (New York: McGraw-Hill, 2002).

Alofsin, Anthony (ed.). *Frank Lloyd Wright: Europe and Beyond* (Berkeley: University of California Press, 1999).

Alofsin, Anthony. *Frank Lloyd Wright: The Lost Years, 1910–22* (Chicago: University Press of Chicago, 1993).

Alofsin, Anthony. *Frank Lloyd Wright: An Index to the Taliesin Correspondence* (5 vols.) (New York: Garland, 1998).

Bandes, Susan (ed.). *Affordable Dreams: The Goetsch-Winkler House and Frank Lloyd Wright* (East Lansing: Michigan State University Press, 1991).

Birk, Melanie (ed.). *Frank Lloyd Wright's Fifty Views of Japan* (San Francisco: Pomegranate, 1996).

Blake, Peter. *Frank Lloyd Wright: Architecture and Space* (Harmondsworth: Penguin, 1964).

Bolon, C., R. Nelson, and L. Seidel (eds.). *The Nature of Frank Lloyd Wright* (Chicago: University of Chicago Press, 1988).

Brooks, Allen (ed.). *Writings on Wright* (Cambridge: MIT Press, 1981).

Brooks, Allen. *The Prairie School: Frank Lloyd Wright and His Midwest Contemporaries* (New York: Norton, 1972).

Carter, Brian. *Johnson Wax Administration Building and Research Tower: Frank Lloyd Wright* (Architecture in Detail) (London: Phaidon Press, 1998).

Cleary, Richard. *Merchant Prince and Master Builder: Edgar J. Kaufmann and Frank Lloyd Wright* (Seattle: University of Washington Press, 1999).

Connors, Joseph. *The Robie House of Frank Lloyd Wright* (Chicago: University of Chicago Press, 1984).

De Long, David. *Auldbrass: Frank Lloyd Wright's Southern Plantation* (New York: Rizzoli, 2003).

De Long, David (ed.). *Frank Lloyd Wright: Designs for an American Landscape* (New York: Abrams, 1996).

De Long, David (ed.). *Frank Lloyd Wright and the Living City* (Milan: Skira, 1998).

Drexler, Arthur. *The Drawings of Frank Lloyd Wright* (New York: Horizon/Museum of Modern Art, 1962).

Dunham, Judith, and Scott Zimmerman. *Details of Frank Lloyd Wright: The California Work* (San Francisco: Chronicle, 1994).

Eaton, Leonard. *Two Chicago Architects and Their Clients* (Cambridge: MIT Press, 1969).

Etlin, Richard. *Frank Lloyd Wright and Le Corbusier* (Manchester: Manchester University Press, 1994).

Futagawa, Yokio, and Bruce Brooks Pfeiffer (eds.). *Frank Lloyd Wright Monograph* (Tokyo: ADA Edita):
Volume 1: *Monograph 1887–1901* (1986)
Volume 2: *Monograph 1902–1906* (1987)
Volume 3: *Monograph 1907–1913* (1987)
Volume 4: *Monograph 1914–1923* (1985)
Volume 5: *Monograph 1924–1936* (1985)
Volume 6: *Monograph 1937–1941* (1986)
Volume 7: *Monograph 1942–1950* (1988)
Volume 8: *Monograph 1951–1959* (1988)
Volume 9: *Preliminary Studies 1889–1916* (1985)
Volume 10: *Preliminary Studies 1917–1932* (1986)
Volume 11: *Preliminary Studies 1933–1959* (1987)
Volume 12: *In His Renderings 1887–1959* (1984)

Futagawa, Yokio, and Bruce Brooks Pfeiffer (eds.). *Frank Lloyd Wright: Selected Houses* (Tokyo: ADA Edita):
Volume 1: *Selected Houses* (1991)
Volume 2: *Selected Houses: Taliesin* (1990)
Volume 3: *Selected Houses: Taliesin West* (1989)
Volume 4: *Selected Houses: Fallingwater* (1990)
Volume 5: *Selected Houses* (1990)
Volume 6: *Selected Houses* (1991)
Volume 7: *Selected Houses* (1991)
Volume 8: *Selected Houses* (1991)

Futagawa, Yokio (ed.), and Paul Rudolph. *Frank Lloyd Wright: Kaufmann House, "Fallingwater"* (Tokyo: ADA Edita, 1970).

Futagawa, Yokio (ed.), and Arata Isozaki. *Frank Lloyd Wright: Johnson and Son Administration Building and Research Tower* (Tokyo: ADA Edita, 1970).

Futagawa, Yokio (ed.), and Bruce Brooks Pfeiffer. *Frank Lloyd Wright: Solomon Guggenheim Museum* (Tokyo: ADA Edita, 1975).

Futagawa, Yokio (ed.), and Masami Tanigawa. *Frank Lloyd Wright: Taliesin East and Taliesin West* (Tokyo: ADA Edita, 1975).

Futagawa, Yokio (ed.). *Global Interiors: Houses by Frank Lloyd Wright, Volume I and II* (Tokyo: ADA Edita, 1975, 1976).

Gebhard, David and Scott Zimmerman. *Romanza: The California Architecture of Frank Lloyd Wright* (San Francisco: Chronicle, 1988).

Gill, Brendan. *Many Masks: A Life of Frank Lloyd Wright* (New York: Putnam's, 1987).

Gossel, Peter (ed.). *Frank Lloyd Wright* (Cologne: Taschen, 1994).

Graf, Otto Antonia. *Erraumen: Zum Werk von Frank Lloyd Wright*, vols. III and IV (Vienna: Verlag Bohlau, 2002).

Graf, Otto Antonia. *Die Kunst des Quadrats: Zum Werk von Frank Lloyd Wright*, vols. I and II (Vienna: Verlag Bohlau, 1983).

Gurda, John. *New World Odyssey, Annunciation Greek Orthodox Church and Frank Lloyd Wright* (Milwaukee: Milwaukee Hellenic Community, 1986).

Hanks, David. *The Decorative Designs of Frank Lloyd Wright* (New York: Dutton, 1979).

Hanna, Paul and Jean. *Frank Lloyd Wright's Hanna House* (Carbondale: Southern Illinois University Press, 1981).

Heinz, Thomas. *The Vision of Frank Lloyd Wright* (Edison, NJ: Chartwell, 2000).

Heinz, Thomas. *Dana House* (London: Academy Editions, 1995).

Heinz, Thomas. *Frank Lloyd Wright: Interiors and Furniture* (London: Academy Editions, 1994).

Heinz, Thomas. *Frank Lloyd Wright* (New York: St. Martin's Press, 1992).

Hildebrandt, Grant. *The Wright Space: Pattern and Meaning in Frank Lloyd Wright's Houses* (Seattle: University of Washington Press, 1991).

Hitchcock, Henry-Russell. *In the Nature of Materials: 1887–1941, The Buildings of Frank Lloyd Wright* (New York: Duell, Sloan and Pierce, 1941).

Hoffmann, Donald. *Frank Lloyd Wright's House on Kentuck Knob* (Pittsburgh: University of Pittsburgh Press, 2000).

Hoffmann, Donald. *Frank Lloyd Wright, Louis Sullivan and the Skyscraper* (New York: Dover, 1998).

Hoffmann, Donald. *Frank Lloyd Wright's Dana House* (New York: Dover, 1996).

Hoffmann, Donald. *Understanding Frank Lloyd Wright's Architecture* (New York: Dover, 1995).

Hoffmann, Donald. *Frank Lloyd Wright's Fallingwater: The House and Its History* (New York: Dover, 1979, 1993).

Hoffmann, Donald. *Frank Lloyd Wright's Hollyhock House* (New York: Dover, 1992).

Hoffmann, Donald. *Frank Lloyd Wright: Architecture and Nature* (New York: Dover, 1986).

Hoffmann, Donald. *Frank Lloyd Wright's Robie House* (New York: Dover, 1984).

Hoppen, Donald. *The Seven Ages of Frank Lloyd Wright* (New York: Dover, 1998).

Izzo, Alberto and Camillo Gubitosi (eds.). *Frank Lloyd Wright: Drawings 1887–1959* (Firenze: Centro Di, 1981).

Jacobs, Herbert, and Katherine Jacobs. *Building with Frank Lloyd Wright* (San Francisco: Chronicle, 1978).

James, Cary. *The Imperial Hotel* (Vermont: Tuttle, 1968; New York: Dover, 1993).

Johnson, Donald Leslie. *Frank Lloyd Wright versus America: The 1930's* (Cambridge: MIT Press, 1990).

Kalec, David, and Thomas Heinz. *Frank Lloyd Wright Home and Studio, Oak Park, Illinois* (Oak Park: Frank Lloyd Wright Home and Studio Foundation, 1975).

Kaufmann Jr., Edgar. *Nine Commentaries on Frank Lloyd Wright* (Cambridge: MIT Press, 1989).

Kaufmann Jr., Edgar. *Fallingwater: A Frank Lloyd Wright Country House* (New York: Abbeville, 1986).

Kief-Niederwohrmeier, Heidi. *Frank Lloyd Wright und Europa* (Stuttgart: Karl Kramer, 1983).

Kruty, Paul. *Frank Lloyd Wright and Midway Gardens* (Urbana: University of Illinois Press, 1998).

Laseau, Paul, and James Tice. *Frank Lloyd Wright: Between Principle and Form* (New York: Van Nostrand Reinhold, 1992).

Levine, Neil. *The Architecture of Frank Lloyd Wright* (Princeton: Princeton University Press, 1996).

Lind, Karla. *Lost Wright* (New York: Simon and Schuster, 1996).

Lipman, Jonathan. *Frank Lloyd Wright and the Johnson Wax Buildings* (New York: Rizzoli, 1986).

Manson, Grant Carpenter. *Frank Lloyd Wright to 1910: The First Golden Age* (New York: Van Nostrand Reinhold, 1958).

McArthur, Shirley duFresne. *Frank Lloyd Wright: American System-Built Homes in Milwaukee* (Milwaukee: North Point Historical Society, 1983).

McCarter, Robert (ed.). *Frank Lloyd Wright: A Primer on Architectural Principles* (New York: Princeton Architectural Press, 1991).

McCarter, Robert. *Fallingwater: Frank Lloyd Wright* (Architecture in Detail) (London: Phaidon Press, 1994).

McCarter, Robert. *Unity Temple: Frank Lloyd Wright* (Architecture in Detail) (London: Phaidon Press, 1997).

McCarter, Robert. *Frank Lloyd Wright* (London: Phaidon Press, 1997).

Meech, Julia. *Frank Lloyd Wright and the Art of Japan* (New York: Abrams, 2001).

Meehan, Patrick. *Frank Lloyd Wright Remembered* (Washington, DC: National Trust for Historic Preservation, 1991).

Meehan, Patrick. *Truth against the World: Frank Lloyd Wright Speaks for an Organic Architecture* (New York: Wiley, 1987).

Meehan, Patrick. *Frank Lloyd Wright: A Research Guide to Archival Sources* (New York: Garland, 1983).

Menocal, Narcisco (ed.). *Fallingwater and Pittsburgh* (Wright Studies, volume 2) (Carbondale: Southern Illinois University Press, 2000).

Menocal, Narcisco (ed.). *Taliesin 1911–1914* (Wright Studies, volume 1) (Carbondale: Southern Illinois University Press, 1992).

Muchamp, Herbert. *Man about Town: Frank Lloyd Wright in New York City* (Cambridge: MIT Press, 1983).

Nute, Kevin. *Frank Lloyd Wright and Japan* (New York: Van Nostrand Reinhold, 1993).

Patterson, Terry. *Frank Lloyd Wright and the Nature of Materials* (New York: Van Nostrand Reinhold, 1994).

Peisch, Mark. *The Chicago School of Architecture: Early Followers of Sullivan and Wright* (New York: Random House, 1964).

Pfeiffer, Bruce Brooks, and Robert Wojtowicz. *Frank Lloyd Wright + Lewis Mumford: Thirty Years of Correspondence* (New York: Princeton Architectural Press, 2001).

Pfeiffer, Bruce Brooks. *Frank Lloyd Wright: The Masterworks* (New York: Rizzoli, 1993).

Pfeiffer, Bruce Brooks (ed.). *Frank Lloyd Wright: Drawings* (New York: Abrams, 1990).

Pfeiffer, Bruce Brooks (ed.). *Frank Lloyd Wright: Letters to Apprentices Frank Lloyd Wright: Letters to Architects Frank Lloyd Wright: Letters to Clients* (New York: Rizzoli, 1989).

Quinan, Jack. *Frank Lloyd Wright's Larkin Building: Myth and Fact* (Cambridge: MIT Press, 1987).

Quinan, Jack. *Frank Lloyd Wright's Martin House* (New York: Princeton Architectural Press, 2004).

Reisley, Roland. *Usonia, New York: Building a Community with Frank Lloyd Wright* (New York: Princeton Architectural Press, 2001).

Riley, Terrance (ed.). *Frank Lloyd Wright, Architect* (New York: Abrams/Museum of Modern Art, 1994).

Rosenbaum, Alvin. *Usonia: Frank Lloyd Wright's Design for America* (Washington, DC: National Trust for Historic Preservation, 1993).

Sanderson, Arlene. *Wright Sites: A Guide to Frank Lloyd Wright Public Places* (River Forest: Frank Lloyd Wright Building Conservancy, 1991; New York: Princeton Architectural Press, 1995).

Satler, Gail. *Frank Lloyd Wright's Living Space* (Dekalb: Northern Illinois University Press, 1999).

Scully, Vincent. *Frank Lloyd Wright* (New York: Braziller, 1960).

Secrest, Meryle. *Frank Lloyd Wright* (New York: Knopf, 1992).

Sergeant, John. *Frank Lloyd Wright's Usonian Houses* (New York: Whitney, 1976).

Siry, Joseph. *Unity Temple: Frank Lloyd Wright and Architecture for Liberal Religion* (Cambridge: Cambridge University Press, 1996).

Sloan, Julie. *Light Screens: The Complete Leaded-Glass Windows of Frank Lloyd Wright* (New York: Rizzoli, 2001).

Smith, Kathryn. *Frank Lloyd Wright: America's Master Architect* (New York: Abbeville, 1998).

Smith, Kathryn. *Frank Lloyd Wright's Taliesin and Taliesin West* (New York: Abrams, 1997).

Smith, Kathryn. *Frank Lloyd Wright: Hollyhock House and Olive Hill* (New York: Rizzoli, 1992).

Smith, Norris Kelly. *Frank Lloyd Wright, A Study in Architectural Content* (Englewood Cliffs, NJ: Prentice-Hall, 1979).

Steele, James. *Barnsdall House: Frank Lloyd Wright* (Architecture in Detail) (London: Phaidon Press, 1992).

Storrer, William Allin. *The Frank Lloyd Wright Companion* (Chicago: University of Chicago Press, 1993).

Storrer, William Allin. *The Architecture of Frank Lloyd Wright: A Complete Catalog* (Cambridge: MIT Press, 1974, rev. 1978).

Sweeney, Robert. *Wright in Hollywood: Visions of a New Architecture* (Cambridge: MIT Press, 1994).

Sweeney, Robert. *Frank Lloyd Wright: An Annotated Bibliography* (Los Angeles: Hennesey and Ingalls, 1978).

Tafel, Edgar. *Apprentice to Genius: Years with Frank Lloyd Wright* (New York: Dover, 1979, 1985).

Tafel, Edgar. *About Wright* (New York: Wiley, 1993).

Tanigawa, Masami. *Measured Drawings: Frank Lloyd Wright in Japan* (Tokyo: Graphic-sha, 1980).

Toker, Franklin. *Fallingwater Rising: Frank Lloyd Wright, E. J. Kaufmann, and America's Most Extraordinary House* (New York: Knopf, 2003).

Twombley, Robert. *Frank Lloyd Wright: An Interpretive Biography* (New York: Harper and Row, 1973).

Wright, Frank Lloyd. *Ausgeführte Bauten und Entwürfe von Frank Lloyd Wright* (Berlin: Wasmuth, 1910).

Wright, Frank Lloyd. *Frank Lloyd Wright, Ausgefuhrte Bauten* (Berlin: Wasmuth, 1911).

Wright, Frank Lloyd. *The Japanese Print: An Interpretation* (1912; New York: Horizon, 1967).

Wright, Frank Lloyd. *The Life-Work of Frank Lloyd Wright* (Amsterdam: Wendingen, 1925).

Wright, Frank Lloyd. *In the Cause of Architecture* (reprint of *Architectural Record* essays, 1908–1929), F. Gutheim (ed.) (New York: McGraw-Hill, 1975).

Wright, Frank Lloyd. *The Disappearing City* (New York: Payson, 1932).

Wright, Frank Lloyd. *An Autobiography* (New York: Duell, Sloan and Pierce, 1932, 1943).

Wright, Frank Lloyd. *Frank Lloyd Wright: On Architecture*, F. Gutheim (ed.) (New York: Grosset and Dunlap, 1941).

Wright, Frank Lloyd. *When Democracy Builds* (Chicago: University of Chicago Press, 1945).

Wright, Frank Lloyd. *Genius and the Mobocracy* (New York: Duell, Sloan and Pierce, 1949).

Wright, Frank Lloyd. *The Future of Architecture* (New York: Horizon, 1953).

Wright, Frank Lloyd. *Sixty Years of Living Architecture* (New York: Solomon R. Guggenheim Museum, 1953).

Wright, Frank Lloyd. *The Natural House* (New York: Horizon, 1954).

Wright, Frank Lloyd. *An American Architecture* (New York: Horizon, 1955).

Wright, Frank Lloyd. *A Testament* (New York: Bramhall House, 1957).

Wright, Frank Lloyd. *The Living City* (New York: Horizon, 1958).

Wright, Frank Lloyd. *Drawings for a Living Architecture* (New York: Horizon, 1959).

Wright, Frank Lloyd. *Frank Lloyd Wright: Writings and Buildings*, Edgar Kaufmann Jr. and Ben Raeburn (eds.) (New York: Horizon, 1960).

Wright, Frank Lloyd. *Frank Lloyd Wright: Collected Writings*, Bruce Brooks Pfeiffer (ed.) (New York: Rizzoli):
Volume 1: *Collected Writings 1894–1930* (1992)
Volume 2: *Collected Writings 1930–1932* (1992)
Volume 3: *Collected Writings 1932–1939* (1993)
Volume 4: *Collected Writings 1939–1949* (1994)
Volume 5: *Collected Writings 1949–1959* (1995)

Zevi, Bruno. *Frank Lloyd Wright* (Bologna: Zanichelli, 1979).

Zevi, Bruno and Edgar Kaufmann Jr. *La Casa sul Cascata di F. L. Wright: Frank Lloyd Wright's Fallingwater* (Milan: ET/AS Kompass, 1963).

Index

Italicized page numbers refer to illustrations.

Abbreviations:
FLW = Frank Lloyd Wright;
Mies = Mies van der Rohe;
MMW = McKim, Mead & White